THE ARCHAEOLOGY OF HOUSEHOLD

edited by

Marco Madella, Gabriella Kovács,
Brigitta Kulcsarne-Berzsenyi and Ivan Briz i Godino

OXBOW BOOKS
Oxford and Oakville

Published by
Oxbow Books, Oxford, UK

© Oxbow Books and the individual authors, 2013

ISBN 978-1-84217-517-0

Front cover: Traditional house in the agricultural village of Jandhala (Gujarat, India). By M. Madella

Back cover: (left): Traditional preparation of the archaeological camp kitchen during the field season for the excavation of Datrana (Gujarat, India). The floor is plastered with a mixture of clay and cow dung. By M. Madella. (right): Temporary camp of farmers in North Gujarat (Loteshwar, India). By M. Madella

This book is available direct from:

Oxbow Books, Oxford, UK
(Phone: 01865-241249; Fax: 01865-794449)

and

The David Brown Book Company
PO Box 511, Oakville, CT 06779, USA
(Phone: 860-945-9329; Fax: 860-945-9468)

or from our website

www.oxbowbooks.com

A CIP record for this book is available from the British Library

Library of Congress Cataloging-in-Publication Data

The archaeology of household / edited by Marco Madella, Gabriella Kovacs, Brigitta Kulcsarne-Berzsenyi and Ivan Briz i Godino.
    pages cm
  Includes bibliographical references.
  ISBN 978-1-84217-517-0
 1. Household archaeology--Case studies. 2. Material culture--Case studies. 3. Bronze Age. I. Madella, Marco. II. Kovacs, Gabriella. III. Kulcsarne-Berzsenyi, Brigitta. IV. Godino, Ivan Briz i.
  CC77.H68A74 2013
  930.1--dc23

2013022333

Printed and bound in Great Britain by
Short Run Press, Exeter

Contents

Contributors

Myrian Álvarez
Área de Antropología. Centro Austral de Investigaciones Científicas-CONICET. Argentina
Email: myrianalvarez@gmail.com

Juan Antonio Barceló
Departament de Prehistòria. Universitat Autònoma de Barcelona. Spain
Email: juanantonio.barcelo@uab.es

Ivan Briz i Godino
ICREA-CaSEs-Departament d'Arqueologia i Antropologia. IMF-CSIC. Spain./Ass. research. Departament of Archaeology. University of York. UK
Email: ibriz@imf.csic.es

Pedro V. Castro-Martínez
Departament de Prehistòria. Universitat Autònoma de Barcelona. Spain
Email: pedro.castro@uab.es

Ignacio Clemente Conte
Departament d'Arqueologia i Antropologia. IMF-CSIC. Spain
Email: ignacio@imf.csic.es

Gary Coupland
Department of Anthropology. University of Toronto. Canada
Email: coupland@chass.utoronto.ca

Thomas Doppler
Integrative Prähistorische und Naturwissenschaftliche Archäologie. Universität Basel. Switzerland
Email: thomas.doppler@unibas.ch

Nicolau Escanilla-Artigas
Departament de Prehistòria. Universitat Autònoma de Barcelona. Spain
Email: nicolau.escanilla@uab.cat

TRINIDAD ESCORIZA-MATEU
Departamento de Historia, Geografía e Historia del Arte. Universidad de Almería
Email: tescoriz@ual.es

JORDI ESTÉVEZ
Departament de Prehistòria. Universitat Autònoma de Barcelona. Spain
Email: jordi.estevez@uab.cat

ROSARIO GARCÍA HUERTA
Departamento de Historia. Universidad de Castilla-La Mancha. Spain
Email: rosario.garcia@uclm.es

GABRIELLA KOVÁCS
McBurney Laboratory. Department of Archaeology. University of Cambridge. UK.
"Matrica" Museum. Hungary
Email: antropologus@yahoo.com

KRISTIAN KRISTIANSEN
Institutionen för Historiska Studier. Göteborgs Universitet. Sweden
Email: k.kristiansen@archaeology.gu.se

NINA KÜNZLER WAGNER
Department of Pre- and Protohistory, University of Zurich. Switzerland
Email: nina.kuenzlerwagner@web.de

URS LEUZINGER
Amt für Archäologie des Kantons Thurgau. Switzerland
Email: urs.leuzinger@tg.ch

MARCO MADELLA
ICREA, CaSEs, Arqueologia i Antropologia (IMF-CSIC) and Universitat Pompeu
Fabra. Spain
Email: marco.madella@icrea.cat

ALFREDO MAXIMIANO
Instituto Internacional de Investigaciones Prehistóricas de Cantabria. Spain
Email: maximianoam@unican.es

FRANCESCO MENOTTI
Institute of Prehistory and Archaeological Science. Universität Basel. Switzerland
Email: francesco.menotti@unibas.ch

FRANCISCO JAVIER MORALES HERVÁS
Departamento de Historia. Universidad de Castilla-La Mancha. Spain
Email: Fco.Morales@uclm.es

CHRISTIAN MÜHLENBOCK
Medelhavsmuseet, Stockholm. Sweden
Email: christian.muhlenbock@medelhavsmuseet.se

JOAQUIM OLTRA-PUIGDOMÈNECH
Departament de Prehistòria. Universitat Autònoma de Barcelona. Spain
Email: joaquim.oltra@uab.cat

BRITTA POLLMANN
Integrative Prähistorische und Naturwissenschaftliche Archäologie. Universität Basel.
Switzerland
Email: britta.pollmann@unibas.ch

CHRISTOPHER PRESCOTT
Department of Archaeology, Conservation and History. University of Oslo. Norway
Email: christopher.prescott@iakh.uio.no

BRIGITTE RÖDER
Integrative Prähistorische und Naturwissenschaftliche Archäologie. Universität Basel.
Switzerland
Email: brigitte.roeder@unibas.ch

DAVID RODRÍGUEZ GONZÁLEZ
Departamento de Historia. Universidad de Castilla-La Mancha. Spain
Email: David.Rodriguez@uclm.es

DIANA SARKIS-FERNÁNDEZ
Departament de Prehistòria. Universitat Autònoma de Barcelona. Spain
Email: don-de-si-enlaproduccion@hotmail.com

MARIE LOUISE STIG SORENSEN
Department of Archaeology. University of Cambridge. UK
Email: mlss@cam.ac.uk

MAGDOLNA VICZE
"Matrica" Museum and Archaeological Park. Hungary
Email: info@matricamuzeum.hu

ASSUMPCIÓ VILA
Departament d'Arqueologia i Antropologia. IMF-CSIC. Spain
Email: avila@imf.csic.es

DÉBORA ZURRO
Departament d'Arqueologia i Antropologia. IMF-CSIC. Spain
Email: debora@imf.csic.es

1

The Archaeology of Household – an Introduction

Ivan Briz i Godino and Marco Madella

> 'Who built Thebes of the seven gates?
> In the books you will read the names of kings.
> Did the kings haul up the lumps of rock?'
> Bertoldt Brecht

The archaeology of household began its first steps in the late 1970s and early '80s as a "reaction" to historic-cultural (old) archaeology, which had a classificatory focus on tools to identify cultural identities, on both sides of the Atlantic. The new theoretical frame of processual archaeology nurtured the first steps of household archaeology with a move from grand theories of cultural change to the level where it was considered that social groups hinge directly with economic and ecological processes (Blanton 1994). Indeed, the processual archaeology approach relied more on anthropological theory (see Binford 1962) and the new multi-scale (from macro to micro) perspective in which attention was focused on the agents doing things and the relationship between these social entities (Ashmore 2002; Tringham 2001). Household archaeology became an archaeology at a small scale and the "living domain" was recognised as the unit where people's activities took place and, therefore, the fundamental element of human society (Ashmore and Wilk 1988, 1; Wilk and Rathje 1982). This strong anthropological and ethnographical element, also nourished by sociological research of works on domestic activities such as those by Bourdieu (1970 and 1977), brought in to being the need for recognising not only the agents but also their social roles within a specific social context (*e.g.* Conkey and Gero 1991).

With the incorporation of the archaeology of household into more ambitious theoretical frameworks, such as the Marxist models of power and social inequalities, this aspect of archaeology gained a more solid base. Feminist and gender anthropology, and social practice theories contributed most vitally to the theoretical framework (*e.g.* Bourdieu 1977; Moore 1988; but also see Rapoport 1990, 187). Indeed, they contributed to a move from historical archaeology models of power and labour control to models about construction and transformations of ideologies, identity, class, gender, *etc.*, where daily practice is considered to be the substantial set where negotiations of social agents take place. Often, there has been a direct identification of this daily practice with specific architectonical locations and the use of architectural remains (*e.g.* domestic architecture: Kent 1990; Blanton 1994) to describe household behaviour (Allison 1999). This assumption of an overlap between architectural space (physical units) and social behaviour (social units) is flawed and imposes a modern (specifically western) view of the world. A household can inhabit more than one structure (at any one time or at different times) or more households can share the same structure, and structures (in the sense of built environment) definitively do not always mark the boundaries of the household, with related household activities taking place inside and outside structures (*e.g.* Sulas and Madella 2012).

Household archaeology is somehow archaeology at a small scale rising from a criticism of macro-models of social change where the perspective of short-term changes and variability, as well as the "human level" of the past, is re-vindicated (Tringham 2001). Indeed, Wilk and Rathje (1982) saw it as a way of bridging the mid-level theory gap that was felt in the '80s and for analysing social change at a small scale in order to understand social evolutionary change. This small scale level in which household archaeology operates has been assumed to be the domestic space/unit, which became the fundamental category for analysis, taking inspiration from anthropology. Indeed, as archaeologists, we do not have households *per se* but the remains of household behaviour within a certain environment (which, we argue, could be built, architectural, or not). In certain cases, this "domestic" environment has been wrongly equated socially with 'family', as understood though our social construct of private relations and private spaces, familial relations and familial spaces (Stanish 1989; Hendon 1996; among others).

In post-processual theory, data and their meaning can be interpreted in many different ways, and indeed post-processualism epistemology recognises archaeology as an interpretative discipline counter to the search of true "facts" that characterised the processualist, hypothesis/deductive approach. Within the post-processualist mind frame, the built medium can be seen as a passive backdrop that reflects human actions (a container) but, moreover, as an active surrounding that inspires and is part of the symbolic sphere of social actions. This perspective has fuelled the inevitability of recovering a highly detailed archaeological record (also at micro-level in which micromorphology, microfossils and chemical characterisation of the sediments have been abundantly developed) for tracing human activities and their social constructs (*e.g.* Hodder 1999). Nowadays, this approach characterises also other theoretical perspectives and the archaeology at micro-scale is not only applied to household studies but more generally to the understanding of site formation processes and spatial variability of human activities as well as to understanding the life histories of people and places (*e.g.* Zurro *et al.* 2009; Weiner 2010; Briz *et al.* 2011; Lancelotti and Madella 2012; Madella and Lancelotti in press).

The chapters that form this book are partially the results of a conference and partially were specifically acquired for this publication. They are considerably wide in scope, geography and chronology because the main endeavour of the book was to collect examples of archaeological data generated through different theoretical methodological frames that can be useful in the understanding of social activities at small scale.

The first paper focuses on hunter-gatherers societies and a debate about the social dimension of space and its mathematical representation. The chapter by Barceló and Maximiano offers an interesting discussion about the mathematical constructs used for the identification of household activities and their spatial structure, and overall the use of formal models to explore the archaeological reality and social theories.

The following chapter by Briz *et al.* is centred on the analysis of household in hunter-fisher-gatherer societies from the Beagle Channel in Tierra del Fuego (South America). The studied sites, similarly to the ones from lacustrine contexts of Central Europe (see Doppler *et al.* and Menotti and Leuzinger), can offer a high-resolution clarification of the archaeological contexts through the highly organic shell-midden deposits characterising these settlements (Álvarez *et al.* 2011). Moreover, the ethnoarchaeological perspective applied to the Fuegian sites offers a methodological approach that uses micro-scale techniques and ethnographical information.

The processual standpoint and anthropological research have been part of the development of household archaeology and the fascinating chapter by Coupland offers a new perspective on complex hunter-gatherer societies of the western coast of North America: we feel confident that views about the absence of social complexity in hunter-gatherer societies must be reassessed after reading these pages about ideology and household activities.

The work by Estévez and Clemente returns to Tierra del Fuego and offers an insight on spatial activities in a Yámana social unit based on lithic and bone materials, and the variability of such activities in space and time during the several moments of occupation.

The following work by Castro *et al.* opens the vision to a global analysis of social complexity, its gendered subjects and the domestic groups in close relation to the origins of the state and social inequality in the Iberian Peninsula. These pages offer an insight into household archaeology from a Marxist and feminist theoretical point of view.

If shell-midden deposits can offer a high level of preservation, and therefore great possibilities for identifying household activities, lacustrine European Alpine archaeological sites are another example of this kind of deposit with a rich record. After a general introduction to household archaeology and its theoretical approach in Switzerland by Künzler-Wagner, the chapters by Doppler *et al.* on the Neolithic, and Menotti and Leuzinger on the Bronze Age demonstrate the importance of this type of site in the study of social change during prehistory. Doppler *et al.* explore the origins of lake-bound communities during the Neolithic, the concept of social landscape and a rethinking of the notion of household. Menotti and Leuzinger give us a remarkable historical revision of the role played by waterlogged circum-Alpine settlements (focusing on the Swiss area). These sites have a fine-scale resolution, also thanks to dendrochronology, that allows reconstruction of the chronology of the settlements at different scales, down to that of single house maintenance. This *fine-grained* archaeological evidence has great potential for reconstructing social meaning and detecting cultural change with a refined time control.

Privileged contexts investigated without effective techniques and methodological approaches, or linked together by a strong theoretical framework, cannot make important advances in archaeological research. The works of Stig Sørensen and Vicze (small find analysis) and Kovács (soil micromorphology) explore these conjunctions of methods and theory in the household archaeology of the Central European Bronze Age, establishing a clear discourse from the low scale data and analysis to general household interpretation.

The chapter by Prescott and Mühlenbock (Monte Polizzo, Sicily) offers an alternative perspective on the processes of accelerating social transformation and regional interaction taking place from *c.* 800 BC in the Mediterranean. Indeed, the authors argue that, although these changes were studied in terms of large-scale political and economic transformations, the impact of this historical situation can be studied valuably through the concepts of material culture and household to untangle this culturally complex and socially dynamic situation.

Finally, the last two chapters offer interesting works on long-term historical perspectives. Kristiansen focuses on cosmology, economy and long-term change in the Bronze Age of Northern Europe, the role cosmologies play in organising the physical landscape and the way this landscape is inhabited and used. The discourse is developed starting from a long-term perspective of the household to observe how changes at the micro-scale of life hinge with ecological settings. García Huerta *et al.* put forward a wide-ranging perspective on the architectural structures possibly inhabited by past households and their trajectory from prehistory (Iberian period) to the Middle Ages in the central Iberian Meseta (Spain).

There are considerable differences in time, geographic area and scope between the works presented in the chapters that make this book. It was not our intention to produce a comprehensive study of households in different societies and times but to focus on the possibilities that archaeology can bring to the study of the social constructs focusing on households. Therefore, this book does not pretend to enter the arena of the study of domestic behaviour as such but to explore an archaeology-led discussion on social and structural organisation at small-scale. The chapters can be some times in disagreement in their theoretical and methodological perspectives as part of this effort in "making it a discussion" and a starting point for reflection. Indeed, the chapters represent quite well the diversity of approaches of this fascinating topic in archaeology.

References

Allison, P. M. (1999) Introduction. In P. M. Allison (ed.) *The Archaeology of Household Activities*, 1–16. London and New York, Routledge.
Álvarez, M., Briz, I., Balbo, A. and Madella, M. (2011) Shell middens as archives of past environments, human dispersal and specialized resource management. *Quaternary International* 239(1–2), 1–7.

Ashmore, W. (2002) Decissions and dispositions: socializing spatial archaeology. *American Anthropologist* 104(4), 1172–1183.

Ashmore W. and Wilk, R. R. (1988) House and household in the Mesoamerican past: an introduction. In R. R. Wilk and W. Ashmore (eds) *Household and Community in the Mesoamerican Past*, 1–28. Albuquerque (NM), University of New Mexico Press.

Binford, L. (1962) Archaeology as anthropology. *American Antiquity* 28(29), 217–225.

Blanton, R. E. (1994) *Houses and Households: A Comparative Study, Interdisciplinary Contributions to Archaeology*. London and New York, Plenum Press.

Bourdieu, P. (1970) The Bereber house or the world reversed. *Social Science Information* 9(2), 151–170.

Bourdieu, P. (1977) *Outline of a Theory Practice*. Cambridge, Cambridge University Press.

Briz, I., Álvarez, M., Balbo, A., Zurro, D., Madella, M., Villagrán, X. and French, C. (2011) Towards high-resolution shell midden archaeology: experimental and ethno-archaeology in Tierra del Fuego (Argentina). *Quaternary International* 239(1–2), 125–134.

Conkey, M. and Gero, J. (1991) Tensions, pluralities and engendering archaeology: an introduction to women and prehistory. In J. Gero and M. Conkey (eds) *Engendering Archaeology: Women and Prehistory*, 3–30. Cambridge, Basil Blackwell.

Hendon, J. A. (1996) Archaeological approaches to the organization of domestic labor: household practice and domestic relations. *Annual Review of Anthropology* 25, 45–61.

Hodder, I. (1999) *The Archaeological Process: an Introduction*. London and New York, Wiley-Blackwell.

Kent, S. (ed.) (1990) *Domestic Architecture and the Use of Space: An Interdisciplinary Cross-cultural Study*. Cambridge, Cambridge University Press.

Lancelotti, C. and Madella, M. (2012) The "invisible" product: developing markers for identifying dung in archaeological contexts. *Journal of Archaeological Science*, 39(4), 953–963.

Madella, M. and Lancelotti, C. (in press) Taphonomy and phytoliths: A user manual. *Quaternary International*, http://dx.doi.org/10.1016/j.quaint.2011.09.008.

Moore H. L. (1988) *Feminism and Anthropology*. Minneapolis (MN), University of Minnesota Press.

Rapoport, A. (1990) *The Meaning of the Built Environment: A Nonverbal Communication Approach*. Tucson, University of Arizona.

Stanish, C. H. (1989) Household archaeology: testing models of zonal complementarity in the south central Andes. *American Anthropologist* 91(1), 7–24.

Sulas, F. and Madella, M. (2012) Archaeology at the micro-scale: micromorphology and phytoliths at a Swahili stonetown. *Journal of Archaeological and Anthropological Science*, DOI 10.1007/s12520-012-0090-7.

Tringham, R. (2001) Household archaeology. In N. J. Smelser and P. B. Baltes (eds) *International Encyclopedia of the Social & Behavioral Sciences*, 6925–6929. Amsterdam, Elsevier.

Weiner, S. (2010) *Microarchaeology: Beyond the Visible Archaeological Record*. Cambridge, Cambridge University Press.

Wilk, R. R. and Rathje W. L. (1982) Household archaeology. *American Behavioral Scientist* 25(6), 617–640.

Zurro, D., Madella, M., Briz, I. and Vila, A (2009) Variability of the phytolith record in fisher–hunter–gatherer sites: an example from the Yamana society (Beagle Channel, Tierra del Fuego, Argentina). *Quaternary International* 193(1–2), 184–191.

2

The Mathematics of Domestic Spaces

Juan A. Barceló and Alfredo Maximiano

Introduction

Space is one of the most difficult terms to define. This is the reason why there are so many definitions. The real problem is that archaeologists tend to apply this word to different referents:

- Space as a container of people and actions. Social action is produced *in* physical space, which exists independently of the social action. Here "physical space" refers to the surface of the ground where social action is (was) performed. Although it has usually been studied as a neutral container, it should be studied as the result of a myriad of processes performed *before* the social action. Furthermore, it is important to take into account that physical space has a dynamic nature because of the joint effects of "natural" or non-anthropic (bio-geologic) processes, and social actions. Although it seems static, it is constantly changing, because its formative mechanism is still acting, although we cannot observe it. As a dynamic entity, physical space plays a significant role in several interfacial phenomena, notably differentiating social action from bio-geologic formative processes. If physical space is the interface of social action, then we can define archaeological space as a sequence of finite states of a temporal trajectory, where an entity (ground surface) is modified successively. Between two successive modification states, we define observable spatiotemporal *discontinuities*. Natural and human processes modify physical space, and as a result we are able to distinguish its dynamics.
- Space as a socially produced thing and/or as a socially used instrument. Social action is shaped by the material and non-material things humans transform (and transformed) into products. Humans excavate pits, accumulate sediment, build walls, accumulate artefacts when producing garbage, define the social exclusivity of a place by defining property rights, *etc*. It is said that some of those products have a *spatial* nature, especially in relation to their size and mobility. A house, a pit, a hearth, a village, a political border, would be relevant examples. As such, we can say that "space" is socially produced, because it is the result of human work *in* physical space, which modifies the original characteristics of such physical space.
- Space as a relational structure. Space is one of the few fundamental quantities

in science, meaning that it cannot be defined via other quantities because there is nothing more fundamental known at present. Thus, similar to the definition of other fundamental quantities (like time and mass), space is defined via measurement. There are two possibilities:

Metric space is a mathematical structure where a set and the distance between elements of the set are defined. The metric space which most closely corresponds to our intuitive understanding of space is the 3-coordinate Euclidean space: from a particular point in space, the basic directions in which we can move are up/down, left/right, and forward/backward. Movement in any other direction can be expressed in terms of just these three. Moving down is the same as moving up a negative amount. Moving diagonally upward and forward is just as the name of the direction implies; *i.e.*, moving in a linear combination of up and forward. Time is often referred to as the "fourth coordinate". It is, in essence, one way to measure physical change. It is perceived differently from the three spatial dimensions in that there is only one of it, and that movement seems to occur at a fixed rate and in one direction. In other words, every member of the abstract geometric object we are calling "space" can be located by means of some "measures" of any kind. In this way is then possible to envision the possibility of three-, four-, five- or *n*-dimensional manifolds or spaces – all of whose points could be located by three, four, five, or *n* coordinates (Minkowskian spaces).

Topologic space. In this case, the definition of the set does not specify that its points are to be located by means of numeric coordinates with metric properties. It also does not specify how to measure the distance between them. It merely specifies how the points can be shown to relate to one another in terms of neighbourhoods. The notion of a neighbourhood describes the relationship between one of a space's points to a sub-collection of its points; it describes the state of one point in a topological space being near – infinitely near, in fact – to a sub-collection of its points, without the measurement of any distances whatsoever. The definition of one particular topological space differs from the definition of another in terms of which points, and which sub-collections of points, or "neighbourhoods", are specified.

The concept of space as an abstract geometric manifold transforms and broadens the mathematical meaning of the term space. Mathematicians use the concept of "space" to define a variety of unified collections of geometric and non-geometric objects (such as points, lines, spheres, or functions), together with a means by which the objects could be shown to relate to one another (such as a means for measuring the distance or "neighbourhood" between them). Through a process of abstraction, they thus began to classify such spaces into their respective types according to which relations were specified as binding together their component parts. The constructing of abstract spaces – which entails using the concepts and methods of geometry – is highly advantageous to archaeologists for the solving of diverse problems concerning social relationships.

Geometric ideas, however abstract, retain their intuitive appeal, sometimes allowing complexities to be grasped at once, without the need for long calculations.

Consequently, a proper definition of "domestic space" should go beyond of what we perceive or produce. It is, in essence, an abstract, imaginary, mathematical object. We consider then that "space" should be a property of interacting entities, as it was suggested by Leibniz in 17th century. The assumption is that "social space" is a unified set of physical objects and social agents, together with a means by which they could be shown to relate to one another (such as a means for establishing the complex and dialectic causal relationships among them). On the other hand, "time" is some function of modifications occurring among all them. Whereas a household is something we actually can "see" (at the archaeological site), domestic space cannot be "seen" in the normal sense of the word, because it has not got a unique referent, but it is an analytic relational concept to be measured and calculated.

Consequently, the title of this paper has all the sense. We understand "mathematics" as the study of computable order. In the mathematical study of the archaeology of domestic spaces we should deal with *events* and not with so called "spatial" objects: houses, activity areas, occupation floors, hearths. In our framework, an event is an expression of the fact that some social activity has taken place somewhere, and that as a consequence that location has some feature f. We also assume that this location is in a state s and that the features defining state s of that location are changing or not. "Location" should be understood in its spatial signification. We understand by it, a characteristic of a concrete event that defines how the quality of the event has changed from state 0_1 to state 0_2 at two different places E_1 and E_2, and at two different moments of time T_1 and T_2. The fact that a broken sherd of an animal bone of specific species s, with shape x been found at a location z, and the fact that a lithic tool with texture t is the most abundant at a neighbour location, are "events", because some social action or actions have been performed at this spatial and temporal location (event), with the purpose of producing a subsistence good, of maintaining some conditional properties of that place, or with the intention of materially fixing some reproductive behaviour.

The archaeological problem

The problem is that we cannot see in the present a series of actions performed in the past. In archaeology we do not have any personal witnesses of what happened. We do not have descriptions of past facts, or explanations of motivations, intentions nor goals. Even in the case of corpses found in burials, we do not have the "actors" and "actresses" of past activities; they are, in some sense, "products" or material consequences of what others did with them. What we only have is some material evidence of the outcomes of social activities performed in the past. Under these circumstances, how can we infer the causes of a social activity having been performed here and not elsewhere? How can we even infer the presence of such an event?

There is usually an enormous number of collections of material effects of a past event that are individually sufficient (given the right theoretical assumptions) to infer the social action's occurrence "there" and "then": the presence of a house means that someone built it, other people lived there for some time, and abandoned it after that. The trick is finding such material clues of past action, in terms of the perceived modifications caused by the same action, and preserved until today. In other words, we are looking for "a smoking gun": "a trace(s) that unambiguously discriminates one hypothesis from among a set of currently available hypotheses as providing "the best explanation" of the traces thus far observed" (Cleland 2002, 481). Instead of inferring test implications from a target hypothesis and performing a series of experiments, we should focus our attention on formulating mutually exclusive hypotheses about social action in the past and searching for evidentiary traces in the present to discriminate among them. In this way archaeologists are in the position of criminal investigators. Just as there are many different possibilities for catching a criminal, so there are many different possibilities for establishing what caused the perceptual properties of material effects of past labour operations. Like criminal investigators, we collect evidence, consider different suspects, and follow up leads. Unlike stereotypical criminal investigations, however, a smoking gun for an archaeological hypothesis merely picks one hypothesis as providing the best explanation currently available; it does not supply direct confirming evidence for a hypothesis independently of its rivals.

Any one of a large set of contemporaneous, disjoint combinations of traces is sufficient to conclude that the event occurred. We don't need to "perceive" every sherd of pottery or bone, or stone in order to infer that people lived here and did something. A surprisingly small number of appropriately dispersed fragments will do. The over determination of causes by their effects makes it difficult to fake past events by engineering the appropriate traces since there will typically be many other traces indicating fakery. This is not to deny that traces may be so small, far flung, or complicated that no human being nor intelligent machine could ever decode them.

For instance, we can rely on the most visible of all material consequences of social action: the modification of the ground surface where the action took place. Such modifications have different formal properties, among them: their "form" and their "frequency". We measure "form", when we refer to the interfacial boundaries of the perceived modification. A wall, a pit, a trench, an occupation floor can be represented in terms of the visual discontinuity they generate (a difference in colour, texture and/or composition). We consider the "frequency" aspect of the archaeological feature when we describe it as an "accumulation" of some material items on the ground surface where the action took place, or as the "intensity" of the action. Of course, those properties are parallel ways of analysing archaeological reality. That means, that any archaeological feature can be studied in terms of its interfacial boundary, or in terms of some quantitative or intensity measure.

The frequencies of archaeological features can be sampled and measured in terms of real, numerical values. In contrast, the form of the same features is an observable quality of the archaeological space that have a finite number of possible descriptive values, and uniform value within a single finite, irregular volume. Characteristic values are associated with discrete archaeological areas with distinct boundaries (a wall, an occupation floor, a pit, *etc*).

A probabilistic interpretation of social activity at the household scale

The original spatial location of the past social action is not known and it cannot be observed. It should be "inferred" on the basis of the observed relationships between the actual locations of its material evidences. We have to be able to infer the motivations and goals of social action on the basis of the perceived material transformations considered to be the consequence of such motivations and goals.

In this paper we will try to solve the archaeological problem by studying the accumulative evidences of social action – frequencies – (Barceló 2002; Maximiano 2005). Our approach for understanding form and interfacial boundaries evidences has been published elsewhere (Barceló 2000; 2005; Barceló *et al.* 2003; 2005; Vicente 2005).

Archaeologists traditionally have drawn their inferences about past behaviour from dense, spatially discrete aggregations of artefacts, bones, features, and debris. We have traditionally assumed that the main agent responsible for creating such aggregates was "only" human behaviour. Even though nowadays most archaeologists are aware of natural disturbance process and the complexities of archaeological formation, archaeological assemblages are still usually viewed as a "deposit" or aggregate of items, which are part of single depositional events (Mameli *et al.* 2002). Consequently, we usually speak of human behaviour being fossilised in archaeological "accumulations" or deposits. Our approach is based on the idea that the frequency of every archaeological variable is associated with a location and an extent (point, line, area, surface, volume), which in turn are defined by implicit data geometry.

We can assume that the probability that a social action occurs at a specific location should be related someway to the frequency of its material effects (the archaeological record) at nearby locations. Therefore, when the frequency of the archaeological feature at some locations increases, the probability that the social action was performed in its neighbourhood will converge towards the relative frequency at adjacent locations. Then, assuming that a measure of spatial density is a function of the probability an action was performed at that point, we will say that the area where spatial density values are more continuous is the most likely place where a social action was performed.

This can be easily computed by estimating the spatial probability density function associated to each location. If we know the relationship between the social action and its archaeological descriptor, the density probability function for the location of archaeological artefacts can be a good estimator for the spatial variability of the social action. Given a sample of known locations, what we need to calculate is then the density function. Locations are defined usually bi-dimensionally, Cartesian co-ordinates x and y, we can calculate an interpolated surface representing the form of a probability density distribution for two continuous random variables. This case can be generalised also to the multidimensional case (Chilès and Delfiner 1999; Mallet 2002; Wackernagel 2003; Remy 2004).

Such an interpolated surface is, in fact, a probabilistic map for the spatiality of social actions. It is a grid map that uses probability estimation of the behaviour state of each cell in a spatial lattice. In such a map near things appear to be more related than distant things (Tobler's law). For instance the synchronicity of social actions states that, all else being equal, activities that occur at the same time will tend to increase the joint frequency of their effects. In the same sense, all else being equal, elements that are located within the interfacial boundary defined by some previous spatiotemporal gradient be spatially related, configuring a "common region" (Palmer 1999).

Spatial processes are the mathematical models producing the probabilistic map as their realisation. To infer the cause (social action performed at the household level) from the effect (the frequency of material evidences measured at some finite set of locations), we have to rebuild the real frequency that was generated in the past by the social action. This theory forms the underpinnings of geostatistics. Geostatistics applies the theories of stochastic processes and statistical inference to spatial locations. It is a set of statistical methods used to describe spatial relationships among sample data and to apply this analysis to the prediction of spatial and temporal phenomena (Bailey and Gattrell 1995; Fotheringham *et al.* 2000; Haining 2003; Lloyd and Atkinson 2004).

Formally, a spatial archaeological data structure may be thought of as consisting of a set of locations (s_1, s_2, etc) in a defined "study region", R, at which the material consequences of some social action performed in the past (archaeological event) have been recorded. The use of the vector, s_i, referring to the location of the i_{th} observed event, is simply a shorthand way of identifying the "x" coordinate, s_{i1}, and the "y" coordinate, s_{i2}, of an event.

We use scalar fields to represent this geometric structure (Fig. 2.1).

5	2	0	0	0	6	0	0	0	0	1	1	0	0	0	0
10	2	0	0	1	3	0	0	0	0	3	2	0	0	0	0
21	21	5	0	0	6	1	0	0	0	0	0	0	0	0	1
26	11	6	2	2	27	3	0	1	0	11	11	5	0	1	4
7	22	10	2	8	15	1	0	9	19	6	0	3	6	10	13
31	21	12	4	22	13	0	2	13	14	1	0	5	2	5	0
74	33	46	23	28	14	4	5	10	29	6	5	14	10	4	2
0	14	15	22	9	13	2	9	7	0	3	4	33	13	0	0

Figure 2.1. An example of scalar field. Data: bird bone remains from the Túnel VII archaeological site (Tierra del Fuego, Argentina). Chronology: 19th Century.

A scalar value is a single component that can assume one of a range of values. A "scalar field" is a name we give to a function which takes in points in a two or three dimensional space (R^2 or R^3) and outputs real numbers. The scalar field is a concept spawn from the natural and physical sciences since they often deal with a region of an abstract space with a function attached to it. For example, the function that gives the temperature of any point in the room you are sitting is a scalar field. In an archaeological case, the function that gives the quantity of rabbit bones at any location of the site is a scalar field. A scalar field is a mathematical space, because it is a collection of scalar values together with a means by which those values are shown to be related to one another by defining a distance measure. "Distance" is defined as the difference between the values of any property at two (or more) spatial/temporal locations (Gattrell 1983).

Archaeological scalar field have the following four-dimensional generic format:

$$W_i (x, y, z, t)$$

The first 3 dimensions are spatial: rows, columns, and levels (or latitude, longitude, and height). The 4th dimension is time. Each w_i corresponds to a dependent variable, and can be used for quantitative variables (the frequency of bones, lithics, pottery, etc; but also sediment hardness, porosity; degree of consolidation, density, porosity, cohesion, strength, and elasticity). Then we consider a series of different w_i values at a position in the array defined by time and the three standard spatial coordinates. The archaeological definition of a household is then specified by a multidimensional array of points instead of a set of delimited objects (walls, floors, pits, stones, etc). The underlying mathematical definition of such a model is a set of scalar fields that defines the frequency properties of every location p in four-dimensional space.

The spatial process which generated the observed spatial frequencies can be understood as composed by a deterministic component (spatial "trend") and a stochastic variation. In the easiest case – not always the most usual with real data – we have:

$$Z = ax^2 + \beta y^2 + \delta xy + \varphi x + \varrho y + f$$
Spatial trend   Stochastic variation

The model is simply a mathematical representation of a polynomial surface showing the trend in the data and some uncertainty associated with the spatial process responsible for the properties of that particular surface. The spatial trend represents what we know about the process that formed the observed frequencies, that is, the social origin of the spatial process. Note that we need to know the polynomial parameters of the trend (a, β, δ, φ, ϱ) to describe it conveniently. The nature of f in this case is randomly unique for each observation of z. In fact, the model represents f as the identity matrix – each f at a particular z is independent of any other f (we might say the frequencies observed at different locations are independent).

If we do not have previous information about how z might have been formed, then estimates of these parameters must be generated from our actual observations of archaeological frequencies. Many surface interpolation algorithms are available, and most of them allow us to distinguish the stochastic component from the spatial trend as a residual of the interpolated surface.

Nevertheless, most of the times, it is fast impossible to give a single equation to characterise the spatial process. We should take into account that the spatial trend contains both the process that generated the original frequencies *prima facie*, and all post-depositional process that altered the original values. That means that we can never hope fully to characterise the process but we can investigate some properties that represent important aspects of what generated observed frequencies of archaeological features. In those cases, many aspects of spatial trends may be characterised in terms of the so-called "first-order" and "second-order" properties of the spatial distribution. Very informally, the first-order properties describe the way in which the expected frequency of material consequences of the social action varies across space, while second-order properties describe the covariance (or correlation) between frequencies at different regions in space. In seeking to understand "pattern" in observed spatial data, it is important to appreciate that this might arise either from region-wide "trends" (first-order variation) or from correlation structures (second-order variation), or from a mixture of both. In the first order case, frequencies of archaeological features vary from location to location due to changes in the underlying properties of the local environment. Example: frequencies of archaeological artefacts may be influenced by variations in terrain. In the second order case: frequencies of archaeological data vary from location to location due to local interaction effects between observations. Example: material consequences of social action tend to happen in areas where the social action has been performed. We should assume a second order pattern in the data is due to some process that varies spatially. That means that patterns arise due to variations in social actions performed at discrete locations.

More formally, first-order properties are described in terms of the "intensity", $\lambda(s)$, of the process, which is the mean number of events per unit area at the point s (Diggle 1983). This is defined as the mathematical limit (Fig. 2.2).

Where ds is a small region around the point s, $E()$ is the expectation operator and ds is the area of this region. $Y(ds)$ refers to the number of events in this small region.

We can use the average intensity in a scalar field to measure the likelihood of observing

$$\lambda(s) = \lim_{ds \,\to\, 0} \left\{ \frac{E(Y(ds))}{ds} \right\}$$

Figure 2.2.

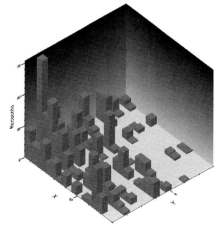

Figure 2.3. Histogram of intensity values. The data is the same as in Figure 2.1.

$$\hat{\lambda}_\tau(s) = \sum_{i-1}^{n} \frac{1}{\tau^2} \, k\left(\frac{s-s_i}{\tau}\right)$$

Figure 2.4.

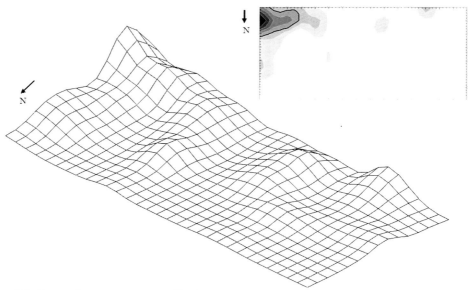

Figure 2.5. First order representation of bird remains variation at the Túnel VII archaeological site (interpolation using Delaunay Triangulation, Software: Rockworks 2004, Rockware Inc.).

the localised value of the material effect of some social event at a randomly-chosen location in the studied area. It can be computed from the histogram of intensity values in the data array (Fig. 2.3).

A number of other variation parameters and functions may also be calculated, based on the amplitude density function. Estimating the intensity of a spatial point pattern is similar to estimating a bivariate probability density. Formally, if s represents a vector location anywhere in R and $s_{1, ...}$, s_n are the vector locations of the n observed events, then the intensity, $\lambda(s)$, at s is estimated as shown in Figure 2.4.

Here, $k()$ represents a weighting function, which for convenience, is expressed in standardised form (that is, centred at the origin and having a total volume of 1 under the curve). This is the standard "kernel density estimation" (Bailey and Gattrell 1995; Barceló 2002; Baxter and Beardah 1997; Beardah and Baxter 2000) (Fig. 2.5).

The question that now arises is whether the observed intensities display any systematic spatial pattern or departure from randomness either in the direction of "clustering" or "regularity". More interesting questions include:

- Is observed clustering due mainly to natural background variation in the population from which intensities arise?
- Over what spatial scale does any clustering occur?
- Are "clusters" merely a result of some obvious *a priori* heterogeneity in the region studied?
- Are they associated with proximity to other specific features of interest, such as the location of some other social action or possible point sources of important resources?
- Are frequencies that aggregate in space also clustered in time?

All these sorts of questions serve to take us beyond the simple detection of non-randomness. Discriminating between random, clustered and regular patterns of observed frequencies of archaeological features is a fundamental concern, because it will help us to understand the nature of the causal processes (social actions) involved. The actual evidence of the presence of a social action should be statistically different from the random location of its material evidences through different spatial and temporal locations.

The second-order properties of a spatial point process, or spatial dependence, involve the relationship between numbers of events in pairs of sub regions within *R*. That is to say, that the description of such processes should be based on the analysis of the relationship between the difference in the frequency of concrete archaeological features observed at spatially adjacent points and the Euclidean distance (in the spatial case) or the Minkowskian distance (in the multidimensional spatiotemporal case) separating the observations. This is again formally defined in terms of a limit, the "second-order intensity" of the process (Fig. 2.6) with similar notation to that described above (Fig. 2.7).

Among the most important second-order properties to characterise a spatial process are "autocorrelation, stationarity and isotropy".

Spatial autocorrelation represents the lack of randomness of values of a variable due to spatial structuring. For positive spatial autocorrelation, locations near each other tend to have similar values; for negative spatial autocorrelation, locations near each other tend to have very different values. When spatial autocorrelation is zero, the frequencies of the material consequences of a single action appear to be randomly distributed.

Put another way, a social action is spatially auto-correlated if the frequency of its material consequences at a distinct location is associated with the value of the same kind of material evidences at neighbouring points. If a single action generated the spatial pattern of frequency values of archaeological materials we are observing, then at lesser distances the differences should be statistically dependent on each other in frequency, and at greater distances the differences should be statistically independent. In that case, the probability that the social action took place at one location would be equal to its probability value at any other location.

There are many different ways to measure the degree of spatial autocorrelation: Geary's *C*, Moran's *I*, *K*, *D*, *H*, and the "semivariogram", which is the plot of the variance of

$$\gamma(s_i, s_j) = \lim_{ds_i, ds_j \to 0} \left\{ \frac{E(Y(ds_i)Y(ds_j))}{ds_i ds_j} \right\}$$

Figure 2.6.

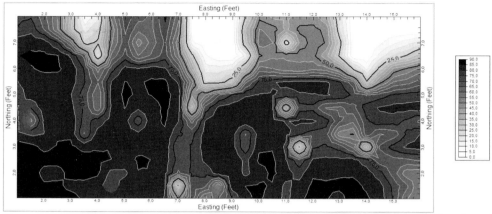

Figure 2.7. Second order representation of bird remains variation at the Túnel VII archaeological site using first derivatives. (Software: Rockworks 2004, Rockware Inc.). Compared with Figure 2.3, North is inversed.

the concentration values relative to the distance between data points (Diggle 1983; Cressie 1993; Bailey and Gattrell 1995; Houlding 2000; Fotheringham *et al.* 2000; Haining 2003; Lloyd and Atkinson 2004).

Simply put, spatial autocorrelation is a measure of the tendency for a random error to be similar to its neighbours, and it should exhibit what has been called second order stationarity. In the mathematical sciences, a "stationary process" is a stochastic process in which the probability density function of some random variable X does not change over time or position. As a result, parameters such as the mean and variance also do not change over time or position. In our case, we say that a spatial process is "stationary" if the intensity is constant over R, so that $\lambda(s) = \lambda$ and, in addition, $\gamma(s_i, s_j) = \gamma (s_i - s_j) = \gamma (d)$. The latter implies that the second-order intensity depends only on the vector difference, d (direction and distance), between s_i and s_j and not on their absolute locations. The process is further said to be "isotropic" if such dependence is a function only of the length, d, of this vector and not its orientation. Henceforth, we use the term "stationary" without qualification to mean stationary and isotropic.

As we suggested before, the area where spatial density values are more continuous (stationary) is the most likely place where a social action was performed. The material consequences of social action performed at a household scale will appear then as discontinuities in the spatial variation of frequency values of an archaeological feature. Clearly there is a relationship between the places in an abstract scalar field (measurement space) where the frequency of social effects show a change in value, and the places of physical space where the material effects of social activities differ.

The key idea is that effective discontinuities in the spatial probabilities of a social action often coincide with important limits in causal process having modified physical space. Domestic space, as any other kind of socially modified physical space, will be made real when interfacial discontinuities between successive events can be detected. Its study is then a matter of reporting at what spatial locations a change in the observable frequency of some archaeological feature leads to a change in the probability of its causing action or process. Discontinuity detection is essentially the operation of detecting significant local changes among spatially sampled values of some physical properties. Hoffman and Richards (1984) have proposed that a good rule of thumb is to divide the data array into components at "maximal concavities", which mathematically speaking, are the local minima of curvature. Formally, such a discontinuity in the spatial probabilities of the social action is defined as an observable edge in the first derivative of the mathematical function that describes the archaeological frequencies over space. This task can be approached by calculating the "spatial gradient" in the data array – that is, the direction of maximum rate of change of the perceived size of the dependent values, and a scalar measurement of this rate (Sonka *et al.* 1994; Palmer 1999). This spatial gradient describes the modification of the density and the size of archaeologically measured values and so regularity patterns in spatial variation can be determined. It is calculated by finding the position of maximum slope in its intensity function (a graph of the value of the dependent variable as a function of space). Thus, the intensity profile of spatial frequencies can be graphed as a curve in which the x axis is the spatial dimension and the y axis corresponds to the dependent variable (for instance, the quantity of some archaeological material at each sampled location).

Likewise, the directivity of such a probability gradient (or "aspect" of the scalar field) is simply the polar angle described by the two orthogonal partial derivatives.

Further improvements in the description of the probabilities for a social action given the frequency of its supposed material evidences can be given using the second order derivatives. This amounts to measure the convexity and curvature of the probability surface, for instance. However, much more theoretical work is needed to use these measures to understand the nature of spatial relationships generated by the material consequences of social action.

The dynamics of social activity at household level

In the preceding pages, we have described the spatiality of social action in terms of a deterministic process plus a stochastic component. This is a correct assumption only when analysing each social action or process in an isolated way. But social action fast never occurred without influence from other people, from natural processes, or from the physical environment itself. After all, "space" should be defined as a property of sets, collections or collectives.

The general idea around the dynamics of domestic spaces is that an action can generate the reproduction of similar actions around it, or it can prevent any other similar action in the same vicinity. Consequently, in real conditions, spatial processes are not deterministic, but dialectical. People interact, influence others, reinforce some actions, interfere with others and even sometimes prevent the action of other people. All those actions are "causes" for the spatiality of other actions. Some of the actions performed in the vicinity of the location increase the chances of one type of action and decrease the chances of others. Furthermore, we can even say that certain social actions are more probable at some locations than others "because" of the performance of a previous action at that place. This approach relies on a prior hypothesis of spatial smoothness, which considers that social actions are intentional, and therefore are performed in an intrinsically better or worse spatial/temporal location for some purpose because of their position relative to some other location for another action or a reproduction of the same action (Barceló and Pallarés 1998; Barceló 2002).

What is lacking in our account is a description of the dynamics of social action both in spatial "and" temporal terms. That is to say, temporality influences spatiality of social acts, and in a dialectical way, the spatial variation of actions influences the temporal sequence (reproduction) of the same actions. The task is then to look for changes in the spatial gradients of some archaeological frequencies, which appear to be *causally* linked to changes in the gradients of other frequencies at the same (or neighbouring) location at a successive time step.

We have to prove that what happens (or *happened*) in one location is the cause of what happens (or *will* happen) in neighbouring locations (Barceló 2002).

Formally speaking, solving this research problem involves the measurement of:

- How the spatial distribution of an action has an influence over the spatial distribution of (an)other action(s);
- How the temporal displacement of an action has an influence over the spatial distribution of (an)other action(s);
- How the temporal displacement of an action has an influence over the temporal displacement of (an)other action(s);
- How the spatial distribution of an action has an influence over the temporal displacement of (an) other action(s).

For this purpose, the concept of *attraction* can be used as a very appropriate analogy for studying how social agents, the products of their work and the physical environment in which behaviour took place are related, as it is the analogy of the gravitation law for studying spatial interaction (Haynes and Fotheringham 1984; Nijkamp and Reggiani 1992).

For instance, traditional conceptions defend the axiom that *environment* determines *the placement of a household*. That is, that domestic action is a consequence of

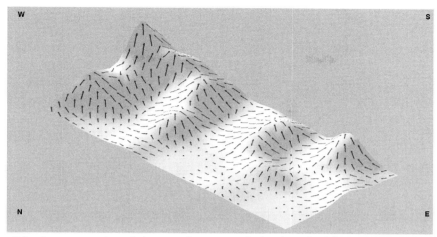

Figure 2.8. A representation of the spatial process, which relates bird bone remains at the Túnel VII site. This probability map is a superposition of a gradient and a directional model, with arrows at each grid node pointing uphill according to steepness of gradient that is the spatial points where attraction has its highest intensity. Oriented as Figure 2.3.

environmental features or the spatiality of resources. This is a too simple generalisation, because social actions are not *adapted* to the environment, but labour (hunting, fishing, and gathering) *attracts* the probabilities of situating residential actions (settlement) at that place. A household is just the place where social agents perform labour. The spatial and temporal location of labour increases the chances of settlement in the vicinity of that place, and decreases the chances of other social actions (see examples in: Barceló *et al.* 2002a; 2002b).

What we are really studying are archaeological events as *places of attraction*. Each identified spatial gradient constitutes a localised event in space and time, be it an individual, a collective action, or a series of actions, and develops together with its environment as a complex network of dialectical relationships at multiple levels, conditioning the performance of the action and successive actions performed in the neighbourhood. On the one side, it materialises a complex field of attraction, radiation, repulsion, and cooperation around this activity, producing the necessary energy for the functioning and even the existence of the social system. It is easy to see that under those circumstances, a deterministic model is an oversimplification of the spatial process.

We can use spatiotemporal gradients of the frequency of social effects to define the limits and intensity of an attraction field, which represents how the action has modified physical space around it. As we have seen previously, the spatial process (activities at the household) spaces can be represented in terms of probability surfaces interpolated at the locations of where the effects of the spatial process have been quantified (in the spatio-temporal case, the process is represented by a hyper-volume: see Barceló and Vicente 2004) (Fig. 2.8).

When such a basin is smooth, uniform and wide, all the locations have the same probability, and consequently the same causal contribution; that is, all potential locations have the same potential to induce changes around them (energy). When all the points have the same energy, we call an equipotential surface. The opposite pattern the response surface associated with actions which have strong spatial influence. Domestic space is generally not equipotential, because surface energy varies from location to location, producing the appearance of "topography" where flat locations have less intense effects (higher energy) than peaks. That is, if the representation of the attraction peak is deep and narrow, the action was concentrated.

Knowing that spatiotemporal variation is a function of the probability an action was performed at that place and at that time, we should consider that where the more activities be concentrated, the higher the probability of being such a location an *attraction* peak for other activities functionally related. The higher the frequency *and* diversity of archaeological elements, the more concentrated in physical space was the social action.

A remaining question is how the locational differences among the effects of cause *C* have determined or conditioned the differences among the effects of cause *B*. This property has also been called *locational inertia*: it is a time-lag effect that activities experience in the adjustment to new spatial influences (Wheeler *et al.* 1998). In other words, changes in the probability of a social action at some location and at some distance of the place of another action should determine changes in the probability value of the spatial variability of material effects (archaeological record), not only of the same action, but also of other actions performed at the same place at different times. The spatiotemporal variability of such an "influence" is what we call the dynamics of the socially configured relational space.

Conclusions

The archaeology of domestic spaces should be understood as the analysis of the *material consequences* of a series of social actions performed at a household level. We have based our approach on the assumption that *social space* is a unified set of physical objects and social agents, together with a means by which they could be shown to relate to one another. We have suggested that causal influence is what relates all components of social activity, and such causal influence can be discovered analysing the relationship between frequency variations and distance between spatiotemporal locations.

We suggest studying changes in the spatial gradients of some archaeological frequencies, which appear to be *correlated* to changes in the gradients of other frequencies at the same (or neighbouring) location. In such a way what happens (or *happened*) in one location can be causally related to what happens (or *will* happen) in neighbouring locations. Consequently, some locations in physical space can be considered as *spatiotemporal attractors*, conditioning the performance of the action and successive actions performed in the neighbourhood. Social activity is not an unconstrained flow of behaviours, but each social act appears influenced by other social actions and natural events, both *simultaneously* and also *after* the original one.

Domestic space is then a way to refer to relationships (the appearance of order, regularity and patterning) among household activities. It can be regarded as a complex relational framework in which a specific subset of social actions (human labour related to subsistence, maintenance and reproduction) and natural processes (the anthropic and non-anthropic formation and deformation of physical space) interacting with various agents of modification in what appears to be a statistical way. When there is some regularity in the location and distances of the material consequences of social activities performed at a household level, we say that there is a certain degree of *dependence* between different elements of the social activity. Whereas a household is something we should "see", domestic space cannot be "seen" but it is an analytic relational concept to be measured and calculated.

We should take into account that the key element in our analysis should be the study of what *social activity* is, and not just *where archaeological artefacts are.*

Acknowledgements

This research has been made possible through the collaboration with the Department of Archaeology and Anthropology at the Institució Milà i Fontanals (CSIC). Funding for the research has been provided by the Spanish Ministry of Science (Project HAR 2009-12258).

References

Bailey, T. and Gattrell, A. C. (1995) *Interactive Spatial Data Analysis.* Harlow, Prentice Hall.

Barceló, J. A. (2005) Multidimensional spatial analysis in archaeology, beyond the GIS paradigm. In T. Uno (ed.) *Reading the Historical Spatial Information in the World, Studies for Human Cultures and Civilizations Based on Geographic Information System*, 75–98. Kyoto, International Institute for Japanese Studies.

Barceló, J. A. (2002) Archaeological thinking: between space and time. *Archeologia e Calcolatori* 13, 237–256.

Barceló, J. A. (2000) Visualizing what might be. An introduction to virtual reality in archaeology. In J. A. Barceló, M. Forte and D. Sanders (eds) *Virtual Reality in Archaeology*, 9–36. Oxford, Archaeopress, British Archaeological Report S843.

Barceló, J. A., Maximiano, A. and Vicente, O. (2006) La multidimensionalidad del espacio arqueológico, teoría, matemáticas, visualización. In I. Grau (ed.) *La Aplicación de los SIG en la Arqueología del Paisaje*, 29–40. Alacant, Servicio de publicaciones de la Universidad de Alicante.

Barceló, J. A. and Vicente, O. (2004) Some problems in archaeological excavation 3D modelling. In Magistrat der Stadt Wien (ed.) *Enter the Past, The E-way into the Four Dimensions of Culture Heritage*, 400–405. Oxford, Archaeopress, British Archaeological Report S1227.

Barceló, J. A., de Castro, O., Travet, D. and Vicente, O. (2003) A 3D model of an archaeological excavation. In M. Doerr and A. Sarris (eds) *The Digital Heritage of Archaeology, Computer Applications and Quantitative Methods in Archaeology*, 85–90. Athens, Hellenic Ministry of Culture, Archive of Monuments and Publications.

Barceló, J. A., Piana, E. and Martinioni, D. (2002a) Archaeological spatial Modelling; a case study from Beagle Channel (Argentina). In G. Burenhult (ed.) *Archaeological Informatics: Pushing the Envelope*, 351–360. Oxford, Archaeopress, British Archaeological Report S1016.

Barceló, J. A., Pelfer, G. and Mandolesi, A. (2002b) The origins of the city, from social theory to archaeological description. *Archeologia e Calcolatori* 13, 41–64.

Barceló, J. A. and Pallarés, M. (1998) Beyond GIS; the archaeological study of social spaces. *Archeologia e Calcolatori* 9, 47–80.

Baxter, M. and Beardah, C. C. (1997) Some archaeological applications of Kernel Density Estimates. *Journal of Archaeological Science* 24, 347–354.

Beardah, C. C. and Baxter, M. (2000) Three-dimensional data display using Kernel Density Estimates. In J. A. Barceló, I. Briz and A. Vila (eds) *New Techniques for Old Times, Computer Applications and Quantitative Methods in Archaeology*, 163–169. Oxford, Archaeopress, British Archaeological Report S757.

Chilès, J. P. and Delfiner, P. (1999) *Geostatistics: Modelling Spatial Uncertainty*. London, Wiley Interscience.

Cleland, C. E. (2002) Methodological and epistemic differences between historical science and experimental science. *Philosophy of Science* 69, 474–496.

Cressie, N. C. (1993) *Statistics for Spatial Data*. London, Wiley Interscience.

Diggle, P. J. (1983) *Spatial Analysis of Spatial Point Patterns*. London, Arnold.

Fotheringham, A. S., Brunsdon, C. and Charlton, M. E. (2000) *Quantitative Geography: Perspectives on Spatial Data Analysis*. Beverly Hills, Sage Publications.

Gattrell, A. C. (1983) *Distance and Space: A Geographical Perspective*. Oxford, Oxford University Press.

Haining, R. (2003) *Spatial Data Analysis in the Social and Environmental Sciences*. Cambridge, Cambridge University Press.

Haynes, K. E. and Fotheringham, S. E. (1984) *Gravity and Spatial Interaction Models*. Beverly Hills, Sage Publications.

Hoffman, D. D. and Richards, W. A. (1984) Parts of recognition, special issue: visual cognition. *Cognition* 18(1–3), 65–96.

Houlding, S. W. (2000) *Practical Geostatistics: Modelling and Spatial Analysis*. Berlin, Springer-Verlag.

Lloyd, C. D. and Atkinson, P. M. (2004) Archaeology and Geostatistics. *Journal of Archaeological Science* 31(2), 151–165.

Mallet, J. L. (2002) *Geomodeling*. Oxford, Oxford University Press.

Mameli, L., Barceló, J. A. and Estévez, J. (2002) The statistics of archaeological deformation process, a zooarchaeological experiment. In G. Burenhult (ed.), *Archaeological Informatics: Pushing the Envelope*, 1–17. Oxford, Archaeopress, British Archaeological Report S1016.

Maximiano, A. (2005) *Métodos Geocomputacionales aplicados al análisis espacial en Arqueología*. Unpublished MA thesis, Universitat Autónoma de Barcelona.

Nijkamp, P. and Reggiani, A. (1992) *Interaction, Evolution, and Chaos in Space*. Berlin, Springer.

Palmer, S. (1999) *Vision Science, Photons to Phenomelogy*. Cambridge, The MIT Press.

Remy, N. (2004) *The Stanford Geostatistical Modelling Software (S-GeMS), Geostatistical Earth Modeling Software: User's Manual*. www.sgems.sourceforge.net

Sonka, M., Hlavac, V. and Boyle, R. (1994) *Image Processing, Analysis and Machine Vision*. London, Chapman and Hall.

Vicente, O. (2005) *La Aplicación de las nuevas tecnologías de visión computacional en el registro y modelización de yacimientos arqueológicos*. Unpublished MA thesis, Universitat Autónoma de Barcelona.

Wackernagel, H. (2003) *Multivariate Geostatistics*. Berlin, Springer.

Wheeler, J. O., Muller, P. O., Thrall, G. I. and Fik, T. J. (1998) *Economic Geography*. London, John Wiley Publications.

3

The Integrity of Social Space:
Hunters-Gatherers at the End of the World

Ivan Briz i Godino, Débora Zurro,
Myrian Álvarez and Assumpció Vila

What is household archaeology?

Since the beginning of archaeology as a discipline, the prevalently western archaeological research (consistent with its historical-cultural basis) considered "cultures" or "civilisations" as analytical units that could be analysed as a whole. The processual approach, on the other hand, introduced more detailed methodologies centered at a site-level scale and taking into account its internal and external relationships (Wilk and Rathje 1982).

The development and spread of this line of research during the 1970s and 1980s (Robin 2003) highlighted the need to establish diverse observational scales in archaeological research, as well as the need to identify different analytical units that could guide both fieldwork and analysis, as well as the interpretation of past societies (Flannery 1976, quoted by Ashmore 2002). Once different social units – considered socially relevant – were established the next step was to identify and limit the spatial correlation. These principles set the basis for the development of a specific archaeology of the household space during the following decade (Ashmore 2002).

"Household archaeology" was then generated as an attempt by functionalist archaeology (paradoxically, later post-processual archaeology followed this same trend) to analyse and evaluate those traits considered basic to human existence, in the sense that they were related to the everyday life.

This line of research addressed three basic objectives:

- First, to demonstrate the existence of a specific area of analysis (with its own physical and spatial correlation) that was separated from research concerning economic dynamics at the "macro" level (Bawden 1982; Hagstrum 2001).
- Secondly, to offer a focal role to architectural or spatial elements which were not substantial, (either in dimensions or in their possible functionality), but that constituted a significant material record for the group to be studied (for a historical review of this kind of research see Ashmore 2002; Blanton 1993; Hendon 1996; Spencer-Wood 1999).

- • Thirdly, to go beyond the assumption of a general "human" population without social differences between sexes (for references of research aiming "household archaeology" and women work, see Bowser and Paton 2004, William-Shuker 2005).

As in the case of other archaeological approaches developed from the 1980s, many of their elements, even if they were not made explicit, were originated from a socially committed scientific stance (Bourdieu 1977), and especially feminist theory and praxis (Conkey and Gero 1997). The starting point of these studies was the "domestic group" (Wilk and Rathje 1982), which had been taken from anthropology focused on particular cases (historical and current), in order to find material and spatial correlates according to that preconceived unit. Thus, the archaeological remains generated by this "minimal social unit" as the result of particular production and/or reproduction activities, were selected *a priori*. Within this theoretical framework the object of study was delimited on the basis of different criteria:

a. The existence of features related to the specific sphere of activities involved in the upkeep of kin-related groups ("familiar" consumption) that, in our current socio-historical context, have been included within and named as "the domestic";

b. The existence of a limited and restricted physical space: the "dwelling", which was defined as the specific space where the familiar unit develops its everyday life (including activities related to the individual, such as food preparation and consumption, resting, taking care of the ones in need, *etc.*). In this sense, the dwelling provides the material boundaries to the activities carried out by the domestic unit (Bermann and Estévez Castillo 1995). In spite of the common identification of the "domestic" with the house, authors such as Wilk and Rathje assumed that household spaces are not only the dwellings themselves but also the outer spaces (Hendon 1996, 48).

   Consequently, different criteria relative to spaces, activities and social agents (in this case, women) were superimposed without discrimination. According to these principles "household archaeology" included any research that fulfils one, two or all of these overlapping parameters.

Thus this approach aimed to articulate productions and social practices that were developed by autonomous familiar units in their own specific spaces, independently from the common practices and places used for the interaction with the rest of the individuals forming the wider social group (that is, the "public" sphere). This concept has been also criticised within the theoretical approach of "household archaeology" (Hendon 1996; Bowser and Patton 2004). Because of this ambiguity, many authors highlighted the methodological and theoretical problems concerning this concept (Stanish 1989) and even pointed out the need to widen the scope of this inquiry (Hendon 1996, 46–47).

   In order to overcome the inadequacies of the methodological tools to account for this issue, contemporary societies became again the focus of analysis. The need to include questions that had been relegated to the study of socio-political relationships, led anthropology and sociology to the development of analytical units to deal with activities that take place in the so-called "private" spaces. Within this framework the concept of gender was assumed as a heuristic tool for making interpretations instead of a "sexed" articulation of the social agents (Hendon 1996). Not surprisingly, the need to deal with particular practices and productions, basically linked to women lives, was initially proposed by structuralist historical materialism approaches (Bourdieu 1977).

Even though this perspective provided the grounds for including women as social agents that had been denied by androcentric approaches, it enclosed a restricted and atomised view of household phenomena to the extent that it failed to tie women activities with the domestic sphere. A paradox was raised since this proposal gave support to the ideas that it originally wanted to counteract (Bourdieu 1977). This problem has also been pointed out by researchers who analysed the development of "household" tasks in "non-household" spaces in our present day society (Spencer-Wood 1999).

From our concern, the direct and uncritical application of anthropological categories to the archaeological record avoided an adequate analysis and a deep comprehension of this topic. As Hendon suggested (1996) one of the main problems of the traditional proposal is the *a priori* association of production/consumption processes with particular spaces or what is more important, with specific social agents, without taking into account the variability of social forms. As a consequence household archaeology practice entailed a tautology in the recognition of its analytical unit: a "house" was defined as a place where a family develops the daily activities and a "family" grouped together people who inhabits in the same house. The assimilation of the existing implicit social concept in the initial analytical category prevented to clearly draw up the material correlates from which household phenomena could be identified and assessed at an archaeological level. In this sense, this approach did not provide independent operative units to recognise the materiality of the practices developed in the space of habitat. Which are the distinct spatial features or which are the material markers of the "domestic" places, remained unknown under this framework; hence it is difficult to appraise the relevance of distinguishing these places from the rest of social space embedded in human practices.

For that reason, the most productive lines in household archaeology have been focused on those case studies with a reduced social distance regarding our present society. Contrary in hunter-gatherer archaeology the applications have been scarce despite the activities developed by these groups are closely related to the practices analised by household aproaches.

Household archaeology and hunter-gatherer societies

The possibility to develop a household archaeology in hunter-gatherer research shows a series of difficulties, especially from a methodological point of view, which partially arises from the formation processes of the archaeological record. The aforementioned criteria traditionally used (see above) for addressing this issue from the pioneering work of Wilk and Rathje onwards, remain problematic or ambiguous for several reasons:

1.   In hunter-gatherer archaeology to identify a "house" or the limits of a dwelling unit constitutes a difficult methodological task (Hoffman 1999) due to the mobility patterns developed by these societies as well as to the nature of the habitat that they produced (Smith 2003), frequently constructed with perishable materials (Cribb 1991). In addition, the assumption that the site can fully represent the activities of a hunter-gatherer group has been largely questioned. The production and social reproduction processes of these societies could never have been exclusively circumscribed to a site-level scale; conversely their analysis demands a global scale of analysis, at least at semi-regional level (Binford 1983). Many researchers have demonstrated how the space daily used in production-consumption processes can vary enormously, and that part of this space can be set far from the habitation units. For example, in subarctic Dene populations activities related to deer hunting and processing take place far from dwelling units (Brumbach and Jarvenpa 1997, 418) In this sense, Winter's proposal (1976) about *cluster household* (Winter 1976 quoted by Bogucki and Grygiel 1981), is a valuable heuristic tool to tackle this topic independently from spatial boundaries centered in the dwelling unit. Robin (2003) also considers the household space in a broader sense.

2.   From an archaeological point of view, to establish the limits of open-air campsites as well as their internal relationships implies an added difficulty that has to be solved by means of specific excavation and sampling techniques. It is necessary to recognise short-term occupations and their stratigraphic relationships (for examples the researches carried out by Estévez and Vila (2000) or Orquera and Piana (1992 in hunter-gatherer contexts). In the case of shelter and caves, it has been generally uncritical assumed that the household physical space included the internal and external limits of the site. Some scholar proposed hypothesis about the presence of dwellings inside the caves (Lumley 1969; Leroi-Gourhan and Brézillion 1972; Ontañón 2002; Villa 2004). The need to evaluate the immediate space where the shelter is, as well as the differentiated appropriation of the inner space of the shelter, is an essential element for a proper analysis of this type of deposits.

3.   The identification of the social agents who carry out the different household activities (and, more specifically, the possibility to sex these processes) as well as the possibility of sexing the activities, by objective means and without preconceptions is a difficult task. Indeed, most of the associations have been made on the basis of *a priori* or present assumptions, or with the use of ethnographic analogies of doubtful exactitude (Wobst 1978; Gvozdover 2000; Sanahuja 2002).

4.   As it has already been mentioned, most hunter-gatherer activities and working processes are narrowly related to basic maintenance of individual life and, in

consequence, social life; these processes have been the field of research of "household archaeology". From our perspective, it is very difficult to consider as operative tools those categories that hinder the possibility to explore the specificity of dwelling units in relation to the entire social space. So, we believe that we cannot limit ourselves to a qualitative concept of these activities. We consider that "how" these activities are developed (also incorporating the spatial analysis) is the most operative way in this kind of archaeological contexts (Briz 2004).

Within household archaeology, several approaches have been focused on the identification of activity areas and on the internal structure of space. Following this, functional interpretations were carried out on the basis of implicit ethnographic analogies (for a critique, see Wünsch 1991). These approaches are framed within the French Paleoethnographic School, with special relevance of works carried out in the sites of Pincevent, as well as Verberie, Marsagny and Etiolles (Leroi-Gourhan and Brézillion 1966; Schmider 1984; Olive 1988; Rigaud and Simek 1991, just to cite a few). These studies start from what they call the habitat, understood as the "habitation unit and its pertinent articulated structures" (Leroi-Gourhan and Brézillion 1972, 326). The basic difference with respect to previous examples lies in the final goals: this line of research aimed to understand the internal spatial patterning (Wünsch 1991, for a review).

An archaeology for the analysis of hunter-gatherer societies

One of the challenges of archaeology is to work with appropriate scales to deal with social agents and practices, in order to understand and to define the dynamics of social processes (Dobres and Hoffman 1994; Allison 1999 among others). In this sense, the possibility of detecting at micro scale level, changes and continuities in production and consumption strategies as well as in their spatial organisation is an essential step to analyse hunter-gatherer societies. We consider that the most interesting approach should avoid any kind of *a priori* limitations. We should focus on the analysis of working processes as the key element of daily life of different social agents. At the same time, this analysis articulates the space firstly at social level and secondly at archaeological level.

Following these principles, our analysis is addressed to social relationships developed over time and space by hunter-gatherer societies (men, women, boys and girls). Contrary to the traditional assumption that usually considers the minimum social or familiar unit as the reference point to draw up this kind of studies, we argue that to define what a minimum social unit is, implies a problem *per se* that necessarily relies on our substantive theory as well as on our methodological framework (Lumbreras 1984a and 1984b).

From our perspective, the space is not considered a limit or a container of a social activity or even an independent variable. In contrast, it constitutes an inherent dimension in the development of social practices; these practices and relationships must be elucidated from the analysis of archaeological materials. Applying this approach to the archaeological record implies the improvement of different research lines that make possible not only the identification of production and consumption processes, but also their organisation and spatial articulation. Productive processes can vary enormously in hunter-gatherer societies by their nature, scale, frequency, and also in the specific way they are organised (Shott 1989). Consequently, it is necessary to generate the precise methodological tools that would make possible to identify its diversity, taking into account the formation processes of the archaeological record.

In our proposal, there are three essential lines of research. First, it is crucial to evaluate and adjust analytical scales in order to examine the archaeological evidence. In this sense, we think that a critical ethnoarchaeological analysis (*sensu* Estévez and Vila 1996a; Briz 2010a) of the ethnographical and ethnological sources constitutes an interesting methodological tool for proposing hypothesis about productive processes dynamics, their social organisation and their spatial-temporal articulation. Secondly, it is necessary to develop fieldwork methods to generate an adequate archaeological record in order to contrast these hypothesis. To accomplish this purpose, it is critical to carry out extensive excavations to obtain a high-resolution record according to our inquiry. Thirdly, and closely related with this previous point, it is necessary to work with multiple and interrelated lines of evidence. This implies not only the improvement of new techniques (by means of the adaptation of existing techniques from other disciplines, for instance), but also the development of analytical methods that encourage transdisciplinary research and reflect the relational character of the materials under study.

Hunters-gatherers of the Beagle Channel: a proposal for its study

The analysis of littoral groups from the northern coast of the Beagle Channel (Tierra del Fuego – Argentina) is extremely interesting not only for the study of diverse spheres of production and their spatial organisation, but also to test the methodological tools to deal with hunter-gatherer archaeology. The powerful and wide research trajectory that has been developed in this area offers the possibility of constructing a critical approach. The works that have been carried out systematically since 1975 generated not only a general panorama of the human occupation dynamics in the area but also the development of a fieldwork method to elucidate the formation processes of the archaeological record (Orquera and Piana 1992; 1999a). Since the 1980s, cooperative projects between Argentinean and Spanish research groups have focused their analysis on the contact period between local hunter-gatherer societies and European populations (Piana *et al.* 1992; Vila *et al.* 1997; 2007). One of the aims of this work was to discuss the theoretical-methodological basis of the Old World Palaeolithic and Mesolithic archaeology and to evaluate archaeological methods against the ethnographical and the archaeological data from an ethnoarchaeological perspective (Estévez and Vila 1996a; Vila and Piana 1993).

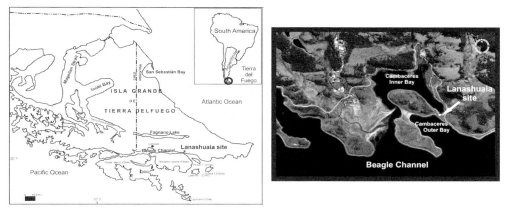

Figure 3.1. Map of Tierra del Fuego.

The etnographic record of the Beagle Channel region

The Europeans arrived from the mid-16th century and left an extensive ethnographic record of Beagle Channel societies (Orquera and Piana 1999b). The most important contributions during the contact period were the reports of the *Mission Scientifique du Cap Horn*, established in the area in 1883 on the occasion of the celebration of the International Polar Year, and the ethnohistorical compilation of the Austrian ethnologist M. Gusinde (1986).

The critical and ethnoarchaeological analysis of ethnographic sources is an interesting methodological perspective to generate hypothesis about the dynamics of productive processes and their social organisation in space and time. Moreover, this critical review provides the possibility to evaluate and tune the analytical categories to better approach the archaeological record. Consequently, it is a useful tool to improve our methods and our inferences about past societies.

According to the archaeological data, the northern coast of the Beagle Channel (Fig. 3.1) was inhabited by hunter-gatherers whose mode of life was addressed towards exploitation of marine coastal resources (Orquera and Piana 1999a). In historical times, these societies were called *Yamana* or *Yaghan* and their social collapse and disappearance took place at the beginning of the 20th century as a result of the incorporation of the Fuegian territory to the capitalist-industrial world (Orquera and Piana 1999b). During the second half of the 19th century the Anglican mission of Ushuaia was founded and the first systematic ethnographical studies of the region were started (Gusinde 1986).

The archaeological and ethnographical information suggests that they had a high mobility pattern, covering short distances, and a cyclic land use. They moved along the Fuegian Channel using canoes. Subsistence was based mainly on open sea hunting of pinniped mammals. They also captured guanacos, sea birds and fish. Mussels were gathered in large quantities and cetaceans were consumed when stranded (Orquera 1999; Orquera and Piana 1997; 1999a). Although pinnipeds were the main sources

Figure 3.2. Picture of the shell-midden stratigraphy from the Lanashuaia II site.

of fat and proteins, the Beagle Channel societies developed a complex dynamics of coastal resource exploitation and management (Juan-Muns 1994; Estévez and Martínez 1998; Orquera 1999; Estévez *et al.* 2001; Zangrando 2003; Mameli and Estévez 2005).

Nearly all known archaeological sites recorded in the Beagle Channel region are shell-middens composed of superimposed faunal residues, lithic artefacts, soil layers, coarse sand and charcoal remains. They are mainly located on the seashore and over 500 settlements of this type have been recorded, only in present-day Argentinean territory. These sites are normally isolated domes or annular structures. Thin shell lenses and occupational floors without the characteristic shell-midden units have also been identified (Orquera and Piana 1992; 1999a; Briz *et al.* 2009). Archaeological research carried out in this region led to the development of an excavation and recording method to better understand the shell-midden formation process. Differences in the matrix composition of the archaeological units as well as small stratigraphic discontinuities have been detected. Consequently, it has been possible to recognise very short episodes of midden deposition. As a result, a fine-scaled record of the past the societies activities was achieved.

According to the analysis of the formation process, the settlements had been used during short periods of time on a quite repetitive basis (Orquera and Piana 1992) (Fig. 3.2). In this sense, the annular shell-middens are interpreted as the results of the accumulation of food discards around the perimeters of huts that were placed in the same spot during different occupational events. Radiocarbon dating confirms this suggestion: several sites reveal successive short-term occupations over 6000 years while others show shorter sequences of just few hundred years (Orquera and Piana 1999; Orquera *et al.* 2011). In addition, the faunal record made clear that the sites have been reoccupied several times in different seasons and the occupations cover more than a full year in each case (Orquera and Piana 1999a; Estévez and Vila 2006; Briz *et al.* 2009). Besides, these studies demonstrated that the shell-middens had very rapid rates of sedimentation that contributed to the rapid burial and preservation of the archaeological remains (Orquera and Piana 1992; 1999a). The presence of high quantities of shells made of calcium carbonate also decreased the acidity of the soil providing better preservation settings for the organic artefacts. In turn, this provided the possibility to use independent lines of research such as use-wear analysis, residues analysis, faunal studies, *etc.* (Fig. 3.2; Briz *et al.* 2011).

The visual and written sources about the dwelling units are very extensive. The ethnographic documents showed that the *Yamana* had two types of houses: dome-like and conical ones. Both were built with trunks and branches and then covered with grasses and rushes, hides, moss and bark (Gusinde 1937, 367). Generally the huts were placed near the coast (Bove 1883; Hyades 1884, 557; Hyades and Deniker 1891, 343; Martial 1888, 188; Gusinde 1937, 352–365) and they were only occupied for a few days. Following Gusinde (1937, 355–371) the only occasions when the *Yamana* stayed in the same place for longer periods of time, were during the initiation ceremonies or when there was the presence of a stranded whale.

Hearths were located in the centre of the house and daily objects were placed inside the dwelling unit without any specific spatial order (Gusinde 1937, 408–409). The residues of daily activities were burnt or discarded all around the hut. These descriptions have been effectively contrasted in different archaeological works (Estévez and Vila 1996b; 2006; Orquera and Piana 1992; 1999a; Piana *et al.* 2000; Briz *et al.* 2011). Concerning the spatial localisation of technical activities, it is possible to infer that some tasks were performed inside while others took place outside the huts:

- *Outside the hut*: hide working (Gusinde 1937, 398–399), canoes manufacturing (Gusinde 1937, 428; Hyades and Deniker 1891, 351; Snow 1857, 338) and the initial stages of butchering (Gusinde 1937, 410 and 649) took place;
- *Inside*: the *Yamana* performed the activities that did not require extended spaces such as the manufacture of weapons and tools (Hyades 1884, 567; 1885, 549; Hyades and Deniker 1891, 220 and 367).

Very few activities were carried out in a particular period of the year. It is usually recorded that the canoes were made during the months of spring and summer (Bridges 1873, 90; 1897; Gusinde 1937, 427 and 440; Lothrop 1928, 143; Martial 1888, 203). During this period the bark is more flexible to work for building the canoe body. In contrast, guanaco hunting would have been concentrated in wintertime (Bove 1883, 98; Despard 1859, 52; Fitz-Roy 1839, 186–187; Gusinde 1937, 517; Hyades and Deniker 1891, 356; Martial 1888, 195) and fishing would have been a more frequent activity during the summer and autumn months.

In relation to instruments use-lives, Gusinde says that *Yamana* people did not "take care of" their everyday objects (Gusinde 1937, 408–409, 491 and 494). Hyades (1885, 520) mentioned the presence of abandoned baskets in the empty huts. On the other hand, it seems that *Yamana* paid specially attention to metal tools and shell knives underwent maintenance (Gusinde 1937, 476; Lothrop 1928, 140). Instruments maintenance has also been detected for basketry, as seen in *Yamana* materials deposited in European museums (J. Estévez, comm. pers.). According to the ethnographic sources, the intentional and systematic destruction or discarding of goods occurred exclusively when somebody died. Despard (1854, 259) stated that all the belongings of a dead person were thrown away into the sea; Bridges also observed this behavior but he also said that sometimes the belongings were burnt or were given to the people who had collaborated with the dead's family in his/her cremation (Bridges 1866, 206; 1897).

The *Yamana* were not an egalitarian society. Direct and indirect analysis of the sources offered an interesting standpoint of their social organisation (Barceló *et al.* 1994). The system discriminates women: at a level of production of goods, their contribution is similar to men, although the time investment in labour processes is lower. But the social importance of women productive activities was undervalued and the consumption of these products was also different (Vila and Ruiz 2001).

The analysis of the written sources provides following some clues concerning the nature of the formation processes of the archaeological record:

- The activities of transformation and discarding of resources were concentrated in the area next to the dwelling units or inside;
- The huts are the production-consumption and discard units organised around a central hearth but without any internal spatial organisation;
- According to the *Yamana* settlements patterns, it is possible to identify activity areas clustered around the houses and associated with combustion areas, which would tend to overlap because of the redundant occupation of the huts, constituting spatial management tendencies at an archaeological level.
- The most significant differences are in relation to indoor and outdoor activities. Differences in the frequency of labor processes would be identified among the areas of the settlement.

Consequently, to start to tackle the organisation of productive spaces it is necessary to relate the different depositional units. However, this information cannot completely direct our interpretations and it should only represent our preliminary hypothesis.

An archaeological example: the site of *Lanashuaia*

Fieldwork carried out during the southern summer of 2005 in the site *Lanashuaia* was addressed at obtaining a better understanding of the social space. According to our approach, we developed a methodological strategy aimed:

- To recognise meaningful spatial variability in a hunter-gatherer site.
- To identify possible different patterns in the materials and their distribution in the outside and inside areas.
- To develop a an excavation method and sampling techniques in order to identify,

evaluate and understand possible differences in the outside and inside record of a hunter-gatherer dwelling unit.

Our final objective is not reduced to the identification of spatial areas that can be more or less specialised in relation to their use. We intended to understand the dynamics that have generated that space envisioned as an evidence of the social relations that were implemented.

As we have seen, the activities that are systematically identified with "household" phenomena are closely related to hunter-gatherer archaeology. Nevertheless, the traditional approaches to this topic revealed inadequacies for its application to these particular contexts. The assumption of the existence of a physically limited space for daily life activities constitutes a weak argument to the extent that all human practices are developed in the social space as a whole: the dwelling unit is just a specialised area inside a general social space.

Two spatial categories are traditionally identified for this kind of analysis in hunter-gatherer societies: the inside and the outside area of the habitation unit. In the case of *Lanashuaia* (2005 fieldwork), we want to propose an alternative for a global comprehension of social space as a result of human practices. The possibility to discriminate between interior or exterior activities is only an aspect that deserves consideration; but it is not a condition for understanding how this space is created (see as a very good example: Smith 2003). The objective is not to find the differences between inside and outside but to understand, in the case that differences exist, the variability of productive activities performed during the occupation of the site that would not be identified in case of excavating only the inside of the hut. In this sense, a research strategy addressed only to the interior of the huts would produce a great bias in the archaeological data.

Following this line of reasoning, the perimetral area of the shell midden was excavated, assuming its potential link with housing unit that has to be proved on the basis of stratigraphic correlations and archaeological materials (that is, considering the artifacts not as part of a type-assemblage, but through the identification of significant association relationships, applying refitting techniques *etc.*).

Consequently, we decided to apply this framework in an archaeological site that had been partially studied: *Lanashuaia*. The integration of the results of this fieldwork season to the information that had previously obtained offered an excellent opportunity to test this proposal. The site had been excavated during two fieldwork episodes in 1994–1995 and 1995–1996 covering an area of 70 m^2.

Lanashuaia is a "shell-midden" characteristic of *Yamana* archaeological record. It is located on the isthmus that separates the inner and the outer Bay of Cambaceres (54°52,75´ South and 67°16,49´ longitude West) (Fig. 3.3), with a 19th century chronology (Piana *et al.* 2000; Vila *et al.* 1997). It is an annular structure rising above a central space as a result of production and consumption activities around its perimeter. The site is located on the inner Bay of Cambaceres beach and takes part

Figure 3.3. Image of the inner part of Cambaceres Bay, taken from the istmus where the site is.

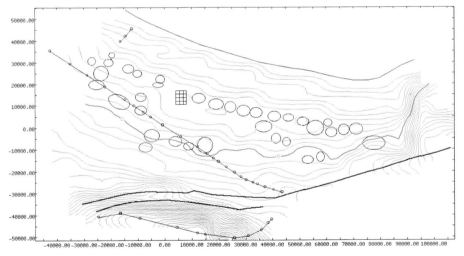

Figure 3.4. Topography of Lanashuaia area. See Fig. 3.5 for the grid corresponding to the fieldwork developed in 1995 and 96 (by J. Estévez).

of outstanding alignment of different shell-middens above the beach storm line that has been interpreted as indicative of a phenomenon of social aggregation due to the exploitation of a stranded whale (Piana *et al.* 2000) (Fig. 3.4).

The 2005 excavation was carried out in a small area of the remaining shell-midden,

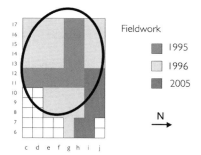

Figure 3.5. Grid of the site Lanashuaia with the different phases of the excavation. The oval corresponds to the approximate form of the shell-midden ring around the hut.

as well as the area close to the trench excavated in 1996 (Fig. 3.5) which had clear linking with activities carried out during the occupations of the site.

Qualifying space: some examples

The objectives of this project made it necessary to reassess our approach to archaeological materiality. As we have already said, we needed to generate an appropriate archaeological record for the identification of different working and consumption processes carried out in the site. To accomplish this aim the dynamic relationships between materials considered as outcomes of labour processes had to be traced. In consequence, from this relational perspective, the criteria of recurrence and association were of paramount importance at the level of spatial analysis as well as in relation to results coming from different techniques of analysis that must be methodologically articulated.

Specific sedimentary samplings were carried out. These were addressed at phytolith analysis (to understand possible consumption of plant resources), fatty acid analysis and organic matter analysis in order to identify possible remains of organic materials that can be the result of consumption processes. With regard to the evaluation of plant resource management by *Yamana* society, we needed to dissociate its consumption as food from its global use as goods (Piqué 1999; Zurro 2006). Following this, our archaeological interpretation would be closer to its ancient real social value. According to ethnographical sources, the use of these resources was important for *Yamana* society for many different purposes (Gusinde 1937).

Until now, phytolith analysis has only been carried out in Tierra del Fuego in shell-midden soils but not in shell-midden levels (Zurro and Madella 2004). The results from these analyses showed the viability of this application in this kind of contexts. Consequently, during the fieldwork in *Lanashuaia*, specific sampling was introduced to carry out phytolith analysis, in shell-midden levels as well as in sediments (humus and shell-midden soils). On the other hand, fatty acids analysis developed in this and other areas demonstrates its own capacity (Lozano *et al.* 1995) to answer archaeological questions. Secondly, we considered the need to establish dialectics relationship of archaeological materials, in the sense specified by Lumbreras:

> "If archaeology is the study of the material remains of social activity, then by definition, the unit must be any association that reveals directly the result of the social activity that generated it" (Lumbreras 1984a, 3).

Therefore, the analysis of the lithic materials (as well as the bone industry) had a special importance not only for the study of raw material procurement strategies or manufacture techniques, but because stone tools were embedded in nearly all the production processes developed by hunter-gatherer societies. They constitute the dynamic elements that allow linking of the spatial analysis with technological practices by means of residue and sediment analysis (control samples). Thus the labour processes, which include perishable materials, can be unveiled as well as working areas related to resource processing. The lithic analysis, under this economic and relational perspective, takes use-wear analysis as a critical method (Vila 1977; Álvarez 2003; Briz *et al.* 2005), combined with the study of the form-function dynamics (Briz 2004; 2010b). From this perspective tool production-consumption strategies could be identified (Briz 2004). This analysis of lithic tools, rejections and residues (Briz *et al.* 2005) is developed taking into account the rest of the analysis. The implementation of a "multidirectional" research line (including vegetal and other organic residues) has been one of the main interests in our research. By means of residue analysis we would like to establish the transitivity (Castro *et al.* in this volume) between archaeological materials; we aim to show the relational economic dynamics and at the same time to obtain a record that enhances the visibility of social activities. Although residue analysis is not a consolidated technique yet, during last years has been increased (Jahren *et al.* 1997; Barton *et al.* 1998; Kealhofer *et al.* 1999; Wadley *et al.* 2004). In order to improve its potential, it is necessary to carry out experimental programs for assessing its reliability.

The Beagle Channel region offers the chance to undertake a directed research. In the outer areas of the shell-midden appeared significant lithic concentrations. In these areas – where the materials are embedded in humic layers – we have implemented specific sampling strategies. It is interesting to remark that there have not been great environmental changes during the last 6000 years (Orquera and Piana 199a). This allows us to create reference collections with broad chronological validity.

Lithic artefacts from these layers (a total of 42) were selected in order to be treated for the extraction of possible residues from their edges. The selection of pieces was based, mainly on the general dimensions of the artefacts in order to make possible the extraction of the residues. For each piece we collected control sedimentary samples coming from close to where the piece was found as well as from the sediment directly in contact with a particular edge (as it was a blind test, the edge selection was carried out randomly). Residue analysis should be based on the association and recurrence between the type of residue found and the characteristics of the lithic artefact: raw material, form-function relationships and, finally, the technological process related to the manufacture. However, this is not a reliable method if we are unable to distinguish if the residue found in the piece corresponded to remains of the processed material or to a contamination (due to natural taphonomical processes or to anthropic contamination produced during the excavation or in the laboratory). It is not only the initial treatment of the pieces when they are recovered that is extremely important, but also the analysis of the sediment where the piece was placed. This last procedure is crucial to elucidate the source of the residues: if they were present in both the sediment and the lithic tool a post-depositional origin is the most plausible explanation. Apart from the sediments collected from every piece, another control sample was taken from a different portion of the site.) The recurrences of particular types of data associations as well as the spatial disposition of the materials are, in this sense, key elements to take into consideration.

This line of research should also increase our usual explanatory capacities in different fields. In hunter-gatherer sites, generally those areas without archaeological remains often appear as non-productive spaces. In *Lanashuaia* we undertook specific sedimentary sampling programmes for these areas with the aim of verifying the existence of productive activities, evidence of which might have disappeared at macroscopic level. For example, according to the ethnographic information, many raw materials used by *Yamana* people do not leave remains, such as basketry produced using perishable plants.

Conclusions: results outline and methodological reflections

The ongoing analysis of *Lanashuaia* materials has yielded some methodological reflections. First, we have confirmed interesting differences between the shell-midden and humic areas (Fig. 3.6). Each is situated around a central depression that is interpreted

Figure 3.6. Picture detail taken during the 2005 fieldwork, with limiting humic and shell-midden areas.

Figure 3.7. Picture of the humic area showing lithics, faunal remains and pebbles.

as the place where the hut was set (Estévez and Vila 2004; Briz *et al.* 2009). There was a different spatial distribution between different areas. In these humus units we found the following features (Fig. 3.7):

Lithic scatters
- lithic working areas identified by the presence of microflakes and knapping remains;
- assemblages of burned pebbles;
- big rocks.

Shell-middens
In contrast, in the shell-midden area, we found (Fig. 3.8):
- lower presence of lithics (with total absence of pebbles or big stones);
- faunal remains including whale and fish bones;
- bone tools (few awls and a harpoon base), as well as shell beads
- significant amounts of charcoal that always located in the inner side of the shell-midden.

Although it is necessary to carry out statistical analysis in order to test the significance of this pattern, it is clear that distribution of faunal and lithic remains shows differences depending on the location (Table 3.1).

Figure 3.8. Picture of the shell midden area showing some ictiofaunal remains from Lanashuaia II.

	Humus areas	Shell-midden areas
Faunal Record	9 $5\,m^2$	191 $7\,m^2$
Lithics	414 $9\,m^2$	190 $7\,m^2$

Table 3.1. Exploratory distribution of the materials between the humic and shell-midden areas.

From a methodological perspective

From the perspective of hunter-gatherer archaeology, we can go beyond the household approach. As we have already mentioned at the beginning, the research has to overcome traditional models to deal with an archaeological record for the study of social dynamics. The specificity of "household" space, discussed according to the criteria explained in the first part of this paper, is not operative for hunter-gatherer contexts as well as for any other kind of social organisation. The spaces for life maintenance of the "minimal social unit" are not the same in all societies and the activities are not developed separately, "privately" from the production and management of the whole social space. At the same time, the "communal" or "public" spaces are not generated independently from these social units and their manifestations.

We consider that the most profitable approach for this kind of research is the recognition of the global social space with its implications for understanding the physical environment where a society develops its existence, in the social and historical sense, on the basis of production and consumption processes. Once these activities are spatially articulated, we are able to obtain an appropriate image of the social space and then to begin the study of relationships. The space and activities generally considered as "household" are on the basis of social organisation and they are key elements to be evaluated in any social analysis. In this sense, they have to be included in the global analysis about the production and management of social space.

We are conscious about the advantages of tackling this issue on high-resolution shell-midden deposits that also afford a good preservation of archaeological materials. These specific conditions provide a profitable scenario to apply the analytical methods that we are carrying out in *Lanashuaia*. For that reason, we have proposed the articulation of different lines of research addressed at obtaining valuable information about labour organisation at different spatio-temporal scales. The final goal is to achieve high-resolution interpretations of the past.

Acknowledgments
We would like to thank Dr X. Terradas and Dr J. Estévez for their valuable comments during the preparation of this manuscript. We wanted to thank the Goodall family, especially to Dr. Natalie Goodall and the staff of Acatushun Museum, for their collaboration.

Fieldwork was developed within the project *The integrity of social space: ethnoarchaeology of sites from the Beagle Channel (Tierra del Fuego)*, funded by the Spanish Ministry of Culture in 2005.

This paper is produced in the frame of the following funding research projects: The Wenner-Green Foundation for Anthropological Research (Project: "Social aggregation: a Yámana Society's short term episode to Analyse Social Interaction"); *Ministerio de Ciencia e Innovación*, Spain (Project: "*Marcadores Arqueológicos de Relaciones Sociales: etnoarqueología de cazadores-recolectores en el Canal Beagle*"-HAR2009-06996) and *Consejo Nacional de Investigaciones Científicas y Técnicas, Argentina* (Project: "*Procesos de agregación social entre las sociedades cazadoras-recolectoras del canal Beagle: nuevas metodologías de análisis*"-PIP 0706).

References
Allison, P. M. (1999) *The Archaeology of Household Activities*. London and New York, Routledge.
Álvarez, M. (2003) *Organización Tecnológica en el Canal Beagle, El caso de Túnel I (Tierra del Fuego, Argentina)*. Unpublished PhD thesis, Universidad de Buenos Aires.
Ashmore, W. (2002) Decissions and dispositions: socializing spatial archaeology. *American Anthropologist* 104(4), 1172–1183
Barceló, J. A., Vila, A. and Argelés, T. (1994) KIPA: A computer program to analize the social position of women in hunter-gatherer societies. In I. Johnson (ed.) *Methods in the Mountains*, 165–172. Sydney, Sydney University, Archaeological Methods Series 2.
Barton, H., Torrence, R. and Fullagar, R. (1998) Clues to stone tool function re-examined: comparing starch grain frequencies on used and unused obsidian artefacts. *Journal of Archaeological Science* 25(12), 1231–1238.

Bawden, G. (1982) Community organization reflected by the household: a study of Pre-Columbian social dynamics. *Journal of Field Archaeology* 9(2), 165–181.

Bermann, M. and Estévez Castillo, J. (1995) Domestic artifact assemblage and ritual activities in the Bolivian Formative. *Journal of Field Archaeology* 22(4), 389–398.

Binford, L. R. (1983) *In Pursuit of the Past, Decoding the Archaeological Record*. London, Thames and Hudson.

Blanton, R. E. (1993) *Houses and Households, A Comparative Study*. New York, Plenum Press, Interdisciplinary Constribution to Archaeology.

Bogucki, P. I. and Grygiel, R. (1981) The household cluster at Brezsc Kujawski 3: small-site methodology in the Polish Lowlands. *World Archaeology* 13(1), 59–72.

Bourdieu, P. (1977) *Outline of a Theory Practice*. Cambridge, Cambridge University Press.

Bove, G. (1883) *Patagonia, Terra del Fuoco, Mari Australi (Rapporto del Tenente Giacomo Bove, capo della Spedizione, al Comitato Centrale per le Esplorazioni Antartiche), Parte I*. Genova.

Bowser, B. B. and Patton, J. Q. (2004) Domestic spaces as public places: an ethnoarchaeological case study of houses, gender, and politics in the Ecuadorian Amazon. *Journal of Archaeological Method and Theory* 11(2), 157–181.

Bridges, T. (1866) Moeurs et Cotumes des Fueguiens. *Bulletins de la Societe d'anthropologie* VII(1884), 169–183.

Bridges, T. (1873) Letters and pieces form its personal diary. *South American Missionary Magazine* I–XXIV.

Bridges, T. (1897) *An Account of Tierra del Fuego (Fireland) its Natives and their Languages*, Unpublished Ms.

Briz, I (2004) *Dinàmiques Econòmiques de Producció-consum en el Registre Lític Caçador-recol·lector de l'Extrem sud Amèrica, La Societat Yàmana*. Barcelona, Universitat Autònoma de Barcelona, PhD thesis, http://www.tdx.cat/handle/10803/5503

Briz, I. (2010a) Etnoarcheologia: che cosa, come, verso dove? *Quaderni di Thule. Rivista d'Americanistica* IX, 549–559.

Briz, I. (2010b) Dinámicas producción-consumo en conjuntos líticos: el análisis de los conjunto líticos de la sociedad Yámana. *Magallania* 38(2), 159–181.

Briz, I., Álvarez, M., Balbo, A., Zurro, D., Madella, M., Villagrán, X., French, C. (2011) Towards high-resolution shell midden archaeology: experimental and ethnoarchaeology in Tierra del Fuego (Argentina). *Quaternary International* 239(1–7), 125–134.

Briz, I., Clemente, I., Pijoan, J., Terradas, X. and Vila, A. (2005) Stone tools in ethnoarchaeological contexts: theoretical-methodological inferences. In X. Terradas, *Lithic Toolkits in Ethnoarchaeological Contexts*, 1–7. Oxford, Archaeopress, British Archaeological Reports S1370.

Briz, I., Estévez, J. and Vila, A. (2009) Analizando la variabilidad del registro arqueológico en sociedades cazadoras-recolectoras desde la etnoarqueología. *Arqueología Iberoamericana* 1, 5–16.

Brumbach, H. J. and Jarvenpa, R. (1997) Ethnoarchaeology of subsistence space and gender: a Subarctic Dene case. *American Antiquity* 62(3), 414–436.

Conkey, M. W. and Gero, J. M. (1997) Programme to practice: gender and feminism in archaeology. *Annual Review of Anthropology* 26, 411–437.

Cribb, R. (1991) *Nomads in Archaeology*. Cambridge, Cambridge University Press.

Cunningham, J. J. (2003) Transcending the 'Obnoxious Spectator': a case for processual pluralism in ethnoarchaeology. *Journal of Anthropological Archaeology* 22(4), 389–410.

David, N. and Kramer, C. (2001) *Ethnoarchaeology in Action*. Cambridge, Cambridge University Press.

Despard, P. (1854 and 1859) Letters and fragments from his personal diary. *The Voice of Pity for South America* IV a VIII (1857–1861).

Dobres, M. A. and Hoffman, C. (1994) Social agency and the dynamics of prehistoric technology. *Journal of Archaeological Method and Theory* 1(3), 211–258.

Estévez, J. and Vila, A. (1996a) Etnoarqueología: el Nombre de la Cosa. In Estévez and Vila (eds) 1996b, 17–23.

Estévez, J. and Vila, A. (eds) (1996b) *Encuentros en los Conchales Fueguinos*. Barcelona-Madrid, UAB-CSIC, Treballs d'Etnoarqueologia, 1.

Estévez, J. and Vila, A. (2000) Estratigrafías en Contexto. *KREI Círculo de Estratigrafía Analítica* 5, 29–61.

Estévez, J. and Vila, A. (2004) Stone and Bones, Together at Last: the Reocupations of a Yamana hut in Tierra del Fuego, Argentina. *Communication presented at the 69th Annual Meeting of the Society for American Archaeology*. Montreal, Canada.

Estévez, J. and Vila, A. (2006) Variability in the lithic and faunal record through 10 reoccupations of a XIX century Yamana hut. *Journal of Anthropological Archaeology* 25, 408–423.

Estévez, J. and Martínez, J. (1998) Archaeozoological researches at the Beagle Channel, Argentina. *Anthropozoologica* 26, 237–246.

Estévez, J., Piana, E., Schiavini, A. and Juan-Muns, N. (2001) Archaeological analysis of shell middens in the Beagle Channel, Tierra del Fuego Island. *International Journal of Osteoarchaeology* 11(1–2), 24–33.

Fitz-Roy, R. (1839) *Proceedings of the First Expedition (1826–1830) Under the Command of Captain P. Parker King, (R.N.), F.R.S. Narrative of the Surveying Voyages of His Majesty's Ships Adventure and Beagle between the Years 1826–1836 (vols I and II)*. London, Henry Colburn.

Gusinde, M. (1986 [1937]) *Los Indios de Tierra del Fuego*. Buenos Aires, Centro Argentino de Etnología Americana, Consejo Nacional de Investigaciones Científicas y Técnicas, II.

Gvozdover, M. D. (2000) Comments to Soffer, O., Adovasio, J.M. and Hyland, D.C., The 'Venus' Figurines: Textiles, Basketry, Gender, and Status in the Upper Paleolithic. *Current Anthropology* 41(4), 511–537.

Hagstrum, M. (2001) Household production in Chaco Canyon Society. *American Antiquity* 66(1), 47–55.

Hendon, J. A. (1996) Archaeological approaches to the organization of domestic labor: household Practice and domestic relations. *Annual Review of Anthropology* 25, 45–61.

Hoffman, B. W. (1999) Agayadan Village: household archaeology on Unimak Island, Alaska. *Journal of Field Archaeology* 26(2), 147–161.

Hyades, P. D. (1885) Une année au Cap Horn. *Le Tour du Monde* XLIX, 385–416.

Hyades, P. D. (1884) Notes hygiéniques et médicales sur les Fuégiens de l'Archipel du Cap Horn. *Revue d'Hygiéne et de Police Sanitaire* 6(7), 550–590.

Hyades, P. D. and Deniker, J. (1891) Antropologie et ethnographie. *Mission Scientifique du Cap Horn (1882–1883)*. Paris, VII, Gautier et fils.

Jahren, A. H., Toth, N., Schick, K., Clark, J. D. and Amundson, R. G. (1997) Determining stone tool use: chemical and morphological analyses of residues on experimentally manufactured stone tools. *Journal of Archaeological Science* 24(3), 245–250.

Juan-Muns, N. (1994) Fishing strategies in the Beagle Channel, Tierra del Fuego, Argentina: an ethnoarchaeological approach. *Archaeo-Ichtiological Studies OFFA* 51, 313–316.

Kealhofer, L., Torrence, R. and Fullagar, R. (1999) Integrating phytoliths within use-wear/residue studies of stone tools. *Journal of Archaeological Science* 26(5), 527–546.

Kramer, C. (1982) Ethnographic households and archaeological interpretation: a case from Iranian Kurdistan. *American Behavioral Scientist* 25(6), 663–675.

Leroi-Gourhan, A. and Brézillion, M. (1966) L'habitation magdalénienne n° 1 de Pincevent près Montereau (Seine-et-Marne). *Gallia Préhistoire* IX, 263–385.

Leroi-Gourhan, A. and Brézillion, M. (1972) L'habitation Magdalénienne n°1 de Pincevent, près Montereau (Seine-et-Mame). *Gallia Préhistoire* 9, 264–385.

Lothrop, S. (1928) *The Indians of Tierra del Fuego*. New York, Museum of the American Indians-Heye Foundation.

Lozano, J. M., Simó, R., Grimalt, J. O. and Estévez, J. (1995) Indicadores Químicos de Combustión en un Hogar del Paleolítico Medio del Yacimiento de Mediona I (Alt Penedès, Barcelona). *Trabajos de Prehistoria* 52(2), 67–77.

Lumbreras, L. G. (1984a) La Unidad Arqueológica Socialmente Significativa (I). *Gaceta andina* 10, 3.

Lumbreras, L. G. (1984b) La Unidad Arqueológica Socialmente Significativa (II). *Gaceta andina* 11, 3.

Lumley, H. (1969) Une Cabane Acheuléenne dans la Grotte du Lazaret. *Mèmoires de la Société Préhistorique Française* 7.

Mameli, L. and Estévez, J. (2005) *Etnoarqueología de Aves: el Ejemplo del Extremo Sur Americano*. Madrid, CSIC, Treballs d'Etnoarqueologia 5.

Martial, L. F. (1888) Histoire du Voyage. Mission Scientifique du Cap Horn (1882–1883). Paris, Gautier et fils.

Middleton, W. D. (2004) Identifying chemical activity residues on prehistoric house floors: a methodology and rationale for multi-elemental characterization of a mild acid extract of anthropogenic sediments. *Archaeometry* 46(1), 47–65.

Olive, M. (1988) *Une Habitation Magdalénienne d'Etiolles: l'unité P15*. Bourdeaux, SPF, Mémoires de la Société Préhistorique Française 20.

Ontañón, R. (2003) Sols et structures d'habitat du Paléolithique Supérieur, nouvelles données depuis les Cantabres: la Galerie Inférieure de La Garma (Cantabrie, Espagne). *L'Anthropologie* 107(3), 333–363.

Orquera, L. A. (1999) El Consumo de Moluscos por los Canoeros del Extremo sur, *Relaciones* 24, 307–327.

Orquera, L. A., Legoupil, D. and Piana, E. L. (2011) Littoral adaptation at the southern end of South America. *Quaternary International* 239(1–2), 61–69.

Orquera, L. A. and Piana, E. L. (1992) Un Paso Hacia la Resolución del Palimpsesto. In L. A. Borrero and J. L. Lanata (eds) *Análisis espacial en la arqueología Patagónica*, 21–52. Buenos Aires, Búsqueda de Ayllu SRL.

Orquera, L. A. and Piana, E. L. (1997) El Sitio Shamakush I (Tierra del Fuego, República Argentina). *Relaciones de la Sociedad Argentina de Antropología* XXI, 215–265.

Orquera, L. A. and Piana, E. L. (1999a) *Arqueología de la Región del Canal Beagle (Tierra del Fuego, República Argentina)*. Buenos Aires, Sociedad Argentina de Antropología.

Orquera, L. A. and Piana, E. L. (1999b) *La Vida Material y Social de los Yámana*. Buenos Aires, Eudeba-Instituto Fueguino de Investigaciones Científicas-IFIC.

Piana, E. L., Vila, A., Orquera, L. A. and Estévez, J. (1992) Chronicles of Ona-Ashaga: archaeology in the Beagle Channel. *Antiquity* 66(252), 771–783.

Piana, E. L., Estévez, J. and Vila, A. (2000) Lanashuaia: un sitio de canoeros del siglo pasado en la costa norte del canal Beagle. In J. Gómez (ed.) *Desde el Pais de los Gigantes, Perspectivas Arqueológicas en Patagonia, Actas de Cuartas Jornadas de Arqueología de la Patagonia,* II, 455–469. Río Gallegos, Universidad Nacional de la Patagonia Austral.

Piqué, R. (1999) *Producción y uso del combustible vegetal: una evaluación arqueológica*. Barcelona, UAB-CSIC, Treballs d'Etnoarqueologia 3.

Rigaud, J. P. and Simek, J. (1991) Intepreting spatial patterns at the Grotte XV, a multiple-method approach. In E. Kroll and T. Price (eds) *The Interpretation of Archaeological Spatial Patterning*, 199–220. New York, Plenum Press.

Robin, C. (2003) New directions in Classic Maya household archaeology. *Journal of Archaeological Research* 11(4), 307–356.

Sanahuja Yll, M. E. (2002) *Cuerpos sexuados, objetos y prehistoria*. Madrid, Ediciones Cátedra.

Schmider, B. (1984) Les habitations Magdaléniennes de Marsangy (Vallée de l'Yonne). In H. Berke, J. Hahn and C. J. Kind (eds) *Jungpaläolithische Siedlungsstrukturen in Europa*, 169–179. Tübingen, Verlag Archaeologica Venatoria, Institut für Urgeschichte der Universität Tübingen, Kolloquium, 8–14, Urgeschichte Materialhefte 6.

Shott, M. 1989. On tool-class use lives and the formation of archaeological assemblages. *American Antiquity*. 54(1), 9–30.

Smith, C. S. (2003) Hunter-gatherer mobility, storage, and houses in a marginal environment: an example from the mid-Holocene of Wyoming. *Journal of Anthropological Archaeology* 22, 162–189.

Snow, W. P. (1857) *A Two Year's Cruise off Tierra del Fuego, the Falkland Islands, Patagonia and in the River Plate (a Narrative of Life in the Southern Seas)*. London, Longman.

Spencer-Wood, S. M. (1999) The world their household: changing meanings of the domestic sphere in the nineteenth century. In P. M. Allison (ed.) *The Archaeology of Household Activities*, 162–189. London and New York, Routledge.

Stanish, C. H. (1989) Household archaeology: testing models of zonal complementarity in the south central Andes. *American Anthropologist* 91(1), 7–24.

Vila, A. (1977) Analyse fonctionnelle et analyse morphotechnique. *Dialektiké, Cahiers de Typologie Analytique 1977*, 54–58.

Vila, A. and Piana, E. (1993) Arguments per a una Etnoarqueologia. *Revista d'Etnologia de Catalunya* 3, 151–154.

Vila, A. and Ruiz del Olmo, G. (2001) Información Etnológica y Análisis de la Reproducción Social, El Caso Yamana. *Revista Española de Antropología Americana* 31, 275–291.

Vila, A., Mameli, L., Terradas, X., Estévez, J., Moreno, F., Verdún, E., Briz, I., Zurro, D., Clemente, I. and Barceló, J. A. (2007) Investigaciones etnoarqueológicas en Tierra del Fuego (1986–2006): reflexiones para la Arqueología Prehistórica Europea. *Trabajos de Prehistoria*, 64(2), 37–54.

Vila, A., Piana, E., Estévez, J. and Orquera, L. (1997) *Marine Reosurces at the Beagle Channel Prior to the Industrial Exploitation: an Archaeological Evaluation, UE Project: CI1*CT93-0015*. Ms.

Villa, P. (2004) Taphonomy and stratigraphy in European prehistory. *Before Farming* 1, 1–20.

Wadley, L., Lombard, M. and Williamson, B. (2004) The first residue analysis blind tests: results and lessons learnt. *Journal of Archaeological Science* 31(11), 1491–1501.

Whitridge, P. (2002) Social and ritual determinants of whale bone transport at a classic Thule winter site in the Canadian Arctic. *International Journal of Osteoarchaeology* 12, 65–75.

Wilk, R. R. and Rathje, W. L. (1982) Archaeology of household: building a prehistory of domestic life. *Special Issue of American Behavioral Scientist* 25(6), 617–639.

William-Shuker, K. L. (2005) *Cayuga Iroquois Households and Gender Relations During the Contact Period: An Investigation Of The Rogers Farm Site, 1660s–1680s*. Unpublished PhD thesis, University of Pittsburgh.

Wobst, H. M. (1978) The archaeo-ethnology of hunter-gatherers, or the tyranny of the ethnographic record in archaeology. *American Antiquity* 43, 303–309.

Wünsch, G. (1991) La organización del espacio interno de los asentamientos de Comunidades Cazadoras-Recolectoras: revisión crítica y alternativas. *Xama* 4–5, 161–218.

Zangrando, A. (2003) *Ictioarqueología del Canal Beagle. Explotación de peces y su implicación en la subsistencia humana*. Buenos Aires, Sociedad Argentina de Antropología.

Zurro, D. (2006) El análisis de fitolitos y su papel en el estudio del consumo de recursos vegetales en la Prehistoria. *Trabajos de Prehistoria* 63(2), 35–54.

Zurro, D. and Madella, M. (2004) A methodological approach for the study of phytoliths in hunter-gatherer sites: an example from a Yamana site (Tierra del Fuego, Argentina). *Communication Presented at the 5th International Conference on Phytolith Research, RAS*. Moscow.

4

Household Archaeology of Complex Hunter-Gatherers on the North-west Coast of North America

Gary Coupland

Introduction: complex hunter-gatherers of the North-west Coast

The study of complex hunter-gatherers has become a major topic in anthropological archaeology in recent years because of the theoretical challenge these societies pose to traditional evolutionary models that link the rise of complex societies to the advent of agriculture. It is now clear that complex hunter-gatherers were not just a rare anomaly of human history, found only on the North-west Coast in the last few centuries before European contact, but may, in fact, have existed at various times and places throughout the world since the late Pleistocene. The North-west Coast of North America, that long, narrow strip of rugged Pacific coastline from south-eastern Alaska to northern California (Fig. 4.1), provides classic examples of complex hunter-gatherers. At the time of European contact in the late 18th century, these societies fished, hunted and gathered with a focus on marine resources, produced and owned resource surpluses, practiced large-scale storage, had high population densities, lived in permanent villages of large, corporate households, and recognized pronounced social inequality. They kept slaves (Donald 1997; Ames 2001), made war (Ferguson 1984; Maschner 1997), and engaged the services of highly skilled craft specialists (Ames 1995). In short, for many scholars around the world North-west Coast societies epitomise complex hunter-gatherers.

Ethnographers have been writing of cultural complexity and social inequality on the North-west Coast since at least the time of Franz Boas, over a century ago. But North-west Coast archaeologists have begun to approach the topic only recently. Why is this so? I think a key reason is that we have lacked an analytical framework appropriate to the study of complex hunter-gatherers. Mortuary studies have been used to identify social differentiation, but if we wish to go beyond merely identifying complexity in the hunter-gatherer archaeological record, we need an approach that will allow us to investigate the practice of inequality and how it is reproduced on a daily basis. Such an approach is to be found in "household archaeology".

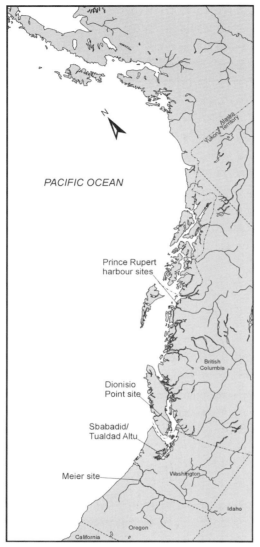

Figure 4.1. Northwest Coast of North America, showing sites and localities mentioned in the text.

Household archaeology and the North-west Coast

For many archaeologists, the starting point of household archaeology was the seminal volume edited by Richard Wilk and William Rathje (1982), but archaeologists (*e.g.* Willey 1956; Trigger 1967) have been thinking about and looking at domestic spaces occupied by small groups for a much longer time. From a North-west Coast perspective, the study of complexity must focus on the household because the household was the primary social and economic unit of society. Inequality on the North-west Coast began, and was reproduced, in the household.

From a comparative perspective, household can be a fluctuating and complex concept (Bender 1967; Yanigasako 1979; Wilk 1983; Hendon 1996), varying in meaning and function among and within societies. However, some common threads exist. Households tend to be small in relation to other social units, and relatively stable in terms of membership. In many small-scale societies household stability is fundamental to corporate identity. The household is also the primary unit of socialisation in most societies, the nexus between the individual and larger social structures. The household is the "daily", and it is primarily through the daily activities, routines and interactions of the household that the generative schemes and arbitrary rules and provisions of a culture, which may include hierarchy and social inequality, are inculcated and reproduced (Bourdieu 1977; Blanton 1994). In the study of complex societies, household archaeology provides an important counterpoint to the study of palaces, temples and tombs. Here, the household becomes the locus of adjustment, and perhaps resistance, to higher state authority.

Wilk and Rathje's treatment of the household has been appealing to archaeologists because of the emphasis placed on household function. Wilk and Rathje urged researchers to study households in terms of what they do (an approach well suited to archaeology) rather than who they are (an approach that inevitably leads to difficulty). From the perspective of function or activities, households produce and consume; they distribute and transmit (goods, rights, roles, property, *etc*); and they reproduce, both biologically and socially.

Much household archaeology to date, and certainly most North-west Coast household archaeology, has concentrated on the first of Wilk and Rathje's functions, production and consumption (see Ames 1995; 2006). To the extent that we can identify individual household living spaces (usually in the form of the dwelling or the dwelling cluster), and to the extent that we can distinguish primary household deposits from secondary refuse deposits (Schiffer 1976; 1987), we can usually say something useful about what households produced and consumed. The evidence is in the faunal and botanical remains, and in the artefacts and features related to various aspects of production.

Some studies stop right there – in this house they fished, in that house they hunted. But most studies try to go beyond mere description of what households produced to an understanding of the organisation of household production. For example, on the North-west Coast, Jim Chatters (1989) looked at the organisation of production within a large, multi-family house in the Puget Sound region near Seattle, Washington, dated to the early period of European contact (Fig. 4.1). The site is known as Sbabadid. The house was 27 m long by 9 m wide. At one end of the house Chatters found mainly marine hunting gear, including bone bipoints, thought to be parts of composite harpoons. At the other end he found mainly terrestrial hunting gear, including arrow points. He interpreted this spatial distribution as evidence of economic specialisation within the household, with spatially discrete production areas. Specialisation is generally consistent with a model of complexity and inequality involving centralised redistribution of resources. In a related study, this one of a 1600 year old house feature at Tualdad Altu in Puget Sound, Chatters (1989) found strikingly similar distributions of hunting artefacts and faunal remains to those of the Sbabadid house. He concluded that intra-household economic differentiation was a long term, stable feature of hunter-gatherer adaptation during the late prehistoric period on this part of the coast.

In another North-west Coast example, Colin Grier (2001, 2006) has looked at the spatial distribution of artefacts within houses (especially House 2) at Dionisio Point, a Marpole culture site in the Gulf Islands of south-western British Columbia (Fig. 4.1). House 2 was 20 m long and 10 m wide. Its occupation may have been slightly older than Tualdad Altu, about 2000 BP. Grier found most artefacts related to manufacturing and processing on one side of House 2, and most artefacts related to status and wealth (including shell beads and labrets) on the other side of the house. He distinguished the two sides of the house in terms of "producers" and "consumers" and argued that the organisation of production within this house revealed social relations of inequality.

Some household archaeologists are looking at issues of reproduction and socialisation within households (Blanton 1994; Pauketat and Alt 2005). How does the household go about rearing and training its members? How are cultural values communicated to the members of the household? What is the role of the house, itself, in this communication? It may seem at first glance that there is little archaeologists can do with these issues – and indeed, there is not much that North-west Coast archaeologists have done with these issues (but see Marshall 1989; 2000; 2006). But household archaeologists working in other areas have begun to examine these questions, and one archaeologist who is leading the way in this area of research is Richard Blanton (1994; 1995).

Houses and non-verbal communication

Blanton is interested in households and he is equally interested in the houses that contain them. He leans heavily on the work of non-archaeologists like Pierre Bourdieu (1977), Amos Rapoport (1969; 1982), Suzanne Blier (1987) and others who argue that the house, perhaps the most universal form of the built environment, does not just passively reflect social action, but actively shapes the perceptions and behaviours of others. In this agency-centred approach, the house itself becomes a critical unit of study because the built environment has an active role to play in the construction of society and culture. Investigation is focused on the size and shape of houses, their architecture, their decoration, and their internal divisions. These variables are thought to have a constitutive effect on meanings and perceptions, especially for those living within the house (Sanders 1990; Pauketat and Alt 2005).

So, one important and fairly obvious question is, "what can North-west Coast houses, or the archaeological remains of these houses, tell us about their occupants?" Blanton (1994) argues that houses communicate the status and identity of the household in two ways, "indexically" and "canonically".

Drawing on theories of consumption and consumer choice developed by Mary Douglas and Baron Isherwood (1979) and Grant McCracken (1988), Blanton presents indexical communication as a form of "marking". Households announce their social status, or at least make a claim to a certain level of status, through the house; through the size of the house, through the quality of its building materials, through the way the house was built, and through the elaboration and decoration applied to the house, especially to the front of the house. Through these media, houses "mark" the status of their occupants.

Indexical communication applies to the here and now. Statuses can change, sometimes very quickly, and in the indexical mode information is communicated about the "current" status of the household through the medium of the house. The indexical message is aimed at outsiders, not at members of the household. Thus, an imposing addition to the house or a fancy facade conveys to outsiders the message that this household is doing well; they have come into wealth and they are not afraid to display it. The overt display of wealth and high social status is critical because open, egalitarian societies typically invoke strong sanctions against such displays. Only in closed, hierarchical systems are marking services of this kind accepted as appropriate behaviour (Wilk 1983).

Houses are a particularly effective medium for expressing wealth, social identity, and power relations for several reasons. First, as message senders, houses create no ambiguity as to subject. As containers of people, houses are perfect signifiers of their occupants. Thus, the message issuing from the house can only be about those who live in it.

Second, house messages typically reach a large audience. As highly visible, enduring features of the cultural landscape, houses are capable of communicating information about their occupants to a large group of outsiders, and, because of the relative longevity of houses, the message is communicated for long periods of time, generations or more.

Third, because house forms can be modified through structural changes, or even completely rebuilt, the content of the message communicated by the house to outsiders can change. A renovation or new house is also a statement of the house owner's power. Anyone wishing to build a large, impressive house must have the power to mobilise a large labour force, often including unskilled workers and skilled specialists. No single task on the North-west Coast required greater mobilisation of labour and resources than house building. Ken Ames (1996) estimates that the late prehistoric Meier house on the southern North-west Coast, near Portland Oregon, required as much as 75,000 board feet (*c.* 23,000 m) of lumber, an amount that could be used to build up to seven single family houses today. Those providing construction labour for North-west Coast house building expected to be feasted and rewarded by the owner for their work. In the construction of large chiefly houses, each stage of the work was celebrated by a feast, necessitating great outlay of wealth by the owner and his family.

With respect to canonical communication, Blanton draws on Bourdieu (1973, 1977), who argues "inhabited space – and above all the house – is the principle locus for the objectification of the generative schemes" (Bourdieu 1977, 89). This is the concept of *habitus*, of daily practice and routines, and in this context the house stands as a physical metaphor of social relations and divisions based on arbitrary categories such as gender, age and rank. In the canonical mode, the house provides a material frame of reference that structures daily activities and interactions within the household, as well as less frequent formal household rituals. As Blanton (1994, 11) states, canonical messages: "communicated through the medium of the house pertain to the perduring features of social relations obtaining among the household members". It is the house, above all else, in which people live and in which their daily lives unfold. So, it is only natural that the social order and the spatial order of the house should be congruent.

Whereas indexical communication is aimed at outsiders, canonical communication is aimed within, at members of the household. Canonical messages are intended to reinforce, justify, and naturalise existing social relations within the household. Where indexical messages are often overt and blatant, canonical messages may be more subtle and nuanced. But, through the medium of the house, both types of messages are continuously sent. Blanton argues that the exterior of the house, and in particular the front façade, are critical to indexical communication because the first impression outsiders gain of the house is usually from the front exterior. But, indexical messages may continue to be sent from inside the house, indeed, from any public area of the house to which visitors might be invited. Canonical communication, according to Blanton, comes mainly from the interior of the house, from the most private regions of the house that visitors are rarely allowed to see. Canonical messages are sacred propositions, meant to be lived but not meant to be widely discussed.

How useful is Blanton's model for household archaeology on the North-west Coast? I think this model, with some modifications, has considerable utility for societies like those of the North-west Coast. After all, Levi-Strauss (1982) had North-west Coast societies in mind when he wrote of House Societies. I will look first at the record of houses and households on the North-west Coast at the time of European contact in the late 18th century. I will focus on the part of the coast I know best, the northern coast, traditional homeland of the Haida, Tsimshian, and Tlingit. Then I will turn to the archaeological evidence we have unearthed on the northern coast near the modern city of Prince Rupert, British Columbia.

Northwest coast houses and indexical communication

As indexical communication, North-west Coast houses of the early contact period could be grand affairs, requiring a huge capital expense and considerable architectural expertise (MacDonald 1983; Suttles 1991). Consider the steps involved in building a house. First, the wood had to be acquired – western red cedar over most of the coast, spruce in the far north – and this was often done at a considerable distance from the building site. The huge posts, beams, and timbers had to be transported over land (no easy task) and water (much easier). Entire tree trunks, cut to length, were used for the vertical house posts and for the horizontal roof beams they supported. The front and back gables of northern houses were enormous boards, often over 6 in (15 cm) thick, cut and adzed to a rectangular shape. In some northern houses, mortises in the gables received the roof beams (gables could support up to six roof beams) and mortises in the corner posts received the gables. In other houses the roof beams were supported by interior house posts and the gables were slotted into corner posts, such that the roof of the structure and the walls were completely independent of each other. Once the frame of the walls and roof was up, the planking and roof covering of the house could proceed. The corner posts were connected by grooved wall sills on all four sides. The grooves faced up to receive the vertical wall planks. Ethnohistoric descriptions of north coast chiefs' houses inform us that the wall planks were often custom fitted and could not be used on other structures (Barbeau 1950). Another style of house had horizontal wall planks. In these houses the wall planks were fitted together, one on top of the other, by tongue and groove joints. The roofing was usually in the form of

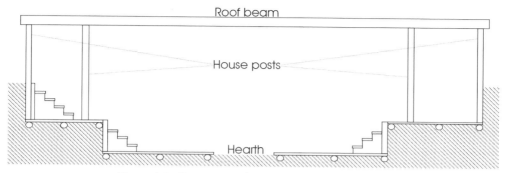

Figure 4.2. Cross-sectional view of a north coast da-ak.

large cedar shingles or planks, overlaid to allow for runoff. A ventilator was often built over the hearth to allow smoke to escape, and the more skilfully built ones could be tilted in different directions depending on the direction of the wind. As I mentioned earlier, Ames (1996) estimates that the house at the Meier site required 75,000 board feet (*c*. 23,000 m) of lumber, not to mention the skill and labour of many builders. Quite simply, building a big house on the North-west Coast was a daunting and hugely expensive proposition (Trieu Gahr 2006). The houses of some high ranking chiefs had dug out floors. Among the Tsimshian such houses were called *da-aks*, among the Haida, *da's* (Fig. 4.2). These houses were entered at ground level, or a few steps above ground level for ease of access in winter. Inside, at entrance level, was an upper platform or tier that ran around the inside perimeter of the house. This was often private space, partitioned for families of the household, and used as a sleeping platform. This platform enclosed a square or rectangular dug out pit, the *da-ak* that served as the main activity area of the household (Emmons 1991, 67). In the centre of the pit, or more commonly just forward of the centre of the pit, was the hearth. Some houses had more than one platform level surrounding the central pit. Two levels were not unheard of, and one Tsimshian house had many, according to its name, "Ten Levels Down" (Miller 1997, 46).

One of the largest houses ever built on the North-west Coast was the appropriately named "Monster House" (*Nie:wons*) of the Haida Chief Wiah at Massett on the Queen Charlotte Islands (Blackman 1972; MacDonald 1983). Wiah's house (Fig. 4.3) was probably built in the early 1840s. According to local histories, 2000 people contributed to its construction, all contracted and appropriately compensated by Wiah. The house had two levels around a central pit (Fig. 4.4), which according to Marius Barbeau (1950), was dug in a single day by the entire population of the village of Massett. It is said that the high beach ridge behind the village was formed by the earth removed from Monster House's central pit. As indexical communication, Monster House sent a clear message of affluence.

The houses of high ranking North-west Coast chiefs could be elaborately decorated too, especially in the north. Interior house posts and exterior memorial poles (the famous

Figure 4.3. Monster House, exterior view of house front.

Figure 4.4. Monster House, interior view showing central hearth (bottom left) and Chief Wiah's sleeping chamber (top right).

Figure 4.5. The rain screen in Whale House, Klukwan, south-eastern Alaska, circa 1895.

"totem poles") were carved with crests and other images representing the history and property of the household. The ends of roof beams extending beyond the front gable were sometimes carved, and in dug out houses the face boards or risers on platforms were often carved or painted. Occasionally, images were painted on house fronts. All this artistic work (and it included masks, bent wood boxes and other paraphernalia) was of the highest quality. Some wealthy households had a trained carver in residence. Ken Ames (1995) refers to such craftsmen as embedded specialists. They were attached specialists, probably not completely full time, but it is likely that the bulk of their labour was to produce wood carvings for their House chief. Most houses in need of a carver contracted out. In the 1830s, a wealthy *Chilkat Tlingit* chief from Klukwan apparently hired a renowned Tsimshian carver to produce the dance screen that hung inside his house (Fig. 4.5; Emmons 1991, 62). In short, house decorations, be they carvings or paintings, called for the work of highly trained specialists, and only the wealthiest households could afford them.

It seems relatively straight forward to see North-west Coast house decoration as indexical communication. Free-standing memorial poles and painted house fronts were exterior embellishments to the front of the house, and were therefore highly visible to outsiders. The poles, in particular, were essentially a visual history in crest images of the achievements of the House. Inside the house visitors could not help but notice the massive carved house posts, or the dance screens, or the carved face boards on platforms, or that the house was a *da-ak* (that it had a dug out floor). All of these visual cues would have communicated wealth and status to outsiders.

Location of the house in the village is another form of indexical communication seen on the North-west Coast (although the indexicality of house location might not have been as immediately obvious as house size or decoration; more a "symbol" than an "index"). Wiah's house was built in the centre of a long row of houses at Massett. This was the appropriate location for the house of the highest ranking chief in the village. House rank descended to either side of the central house. The houses at either end of the village were lowest ranked, or were the houses of commoners.

House size, construction material, extent and quality of decoration, and location in the village all communicated wealth, status, and power on the North-west Coast. But why would the household wish to send these messages? After all, social status on the North-west Coast, especially on the northern coast, was dependent on one's rank, and rank, although not immutable, was not easily changed. Certainly, building a big, fancy house, in and of itself, would not produce a change in rank. Change in rank could only be affected through potlatching. But a successful potlatch required a great outlay of wealth, and this in turn called for a huge investment of labour – a huge investment of household labour. And this is where an impressive house, as a medium of indexical communication, might be important, because the message of affluence sent to outsiders by such a structure could be a powerful way of attracting new labour into the house. The message is, essentially, "we are wealthy, we are affluent, come and live here, and you will do well".

A similar argument has been made by some North-west Coast scholars about the *potlatch*, itself. While most see the *potlatch* as ceremonial exchange intended to distribute resources to people, some have suggested that the *potlatch* might also have functioned to distribute people to resources (Adams 1973; Ames 1979). By making a public display of wealth, ready to be given away, the potlatch host announces his affluence. Again the message is, "live with us, and you will do well".

To whom was such a message directed on the North-west Coast? Certainly, not to everybody. North-west Coast societies have been described as "class-divided" (Donald 1985), and there were three major divisions. In the largest group were the people who inherited names or titles, including chiefs. Among the Tsimshian, these people were known as "*smikyet*", which roughly translates, "real people". Titles were owned by the household and inherited by household members. "Real people" rarely left their households; they would have to give up their title to do so. The lowest class of North-west Coast society was slaves. They were disenfranchised people, who were owned, usually by house chiefs, and they were treated as property. Slaves could be given away, but they were not free to leave their owner's house of their own volition. This left the intermediate class, between title-holders and slaves, the commoners. Commoners held no title; therefore they had no status. But they were free to take their labour wherever they could make the best lives for themselves. I believe that indexical messages of household affluence and wealth were mainly aimed at this the group, the commoners (and perhaps to "real people" who held very low ranked titles). They were the one group for whom chiefs could compete to add to their household labour. Commoners probably accounted for 15–20% of local populations on the North-west Coast.

North-west coast houses and canonical communication

Blanton (1994) sees house decoration, especially house front decoration, mainly as indexical communication. I think this applies to the painted house fronts (which were not common) and memorial poles (which were more common) of the North-west Coast. But house decoration on the North-west Coast was not only intended as indexical communication; there was a strong canonical element, as well. The crests and other images carved and painted on poles, house fronts, interior house posts, dance screens, platform risers, and so on, were more than just a display of affluence aimed at outsiders. They were also a constant reminder to the members of the household of the importance of hierarchy and rank. Through this elaborate decoration, and indeed through the size of the house and its location in the village, the North-west Coast house was the physical manifestation of a social structure that emphasised prestige, privilege and prerogative. Such houses were not just displaying a history of achievements in indexical fashion. They were also tangible statements about the importance of having history, of being a "real person".

Here is where I think Blanton's model could be modified to better fit the North-west Coast context. Virtually all of the indexical elements suggested by Blanton to mark status also worked in the canonical mode. Likewise, the interiors of North-west Coast houses were generally large, open spaces, the one possible exception being the back-centre space – the chief's space – which was sometimes screened off. Otherwise, these were communal houses; there were no deep, private recesses (or very few). Once inside the house, there was very little that a visitor could not see. Here, the distinctions between "outside and inside" and between "public and private" begin to break down. On the North-west Coast, the indexical "is" the canonical, and vice versa – all features of the house worked simultaneously in both modes.

The interior space of North-west Coast houses was organised in such a way as to inculcate and reinforce principles of hierarchy and rank (Fig. 4.6). In his recent book on the Tsimshian of the north coast of British Columbia, Jay Miller (1997, 46–47) states:

> "Ranks were graded from front to back and from centre to sides [of the house] ... Slaves and low-class people slept near the door ... Commoners had spaces or cubicles along the sides. Important families were located along the back, protected and prominently in view. The family of the man (sometimes the woman) holding the foremost name, and thereby the "owner" of the house, lived in the back centre."

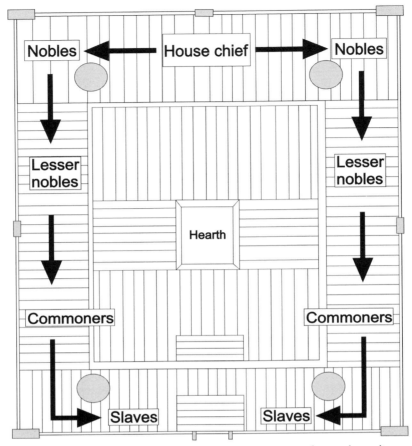

Figure 4.6. House floor plan, showing family sleeping areas arranged in a descending gradient of rank from the back-centre of the house to the front of the house.

In the Monster House at Massett, Chief Wiah had a private sleeping chamber in the back centre of the house (Blackman 1972). In Whale House at Kluckwan, the famous dance screen known as the Rain Screen was suspended between the two rear house posts, creating a partitioned space for the House Chief, for the ancestors of the House, and for the treasured heirlooms and other artwork that belonged to the House (Emmons 1991, 63). This back-centre area was simultaneously the area of highest status or rank within the house and the area of the house most symbolically charged with meaning, the ritual focal point of the house.

The arrangement of sleeping areas and family spaces within the house, from chief's quarters in the back-centre to slaves' area by the front entrance was a perfect spatial expression of household social relations, a "living floor plan" of social structure. I see this as a strong canonical message about the importance of hierarchy and rank to the members of the household. At the same time, it could also be an indexical message of household wealth and power. Archaeologically, this descending gradient of rank has been tested on the North-west Coast (although not very often). Steven Acheson (1998), for example, test-pitted late prehistoric and early historic house features in Gwaii Hanaas, southern Queen Charlotte Islands, and found that status-related items such as shell beads came predominantly from the back areas of the houses.

But, in addition to reinforcing principles of hierarchy and rank, North-west Coast houses also communicated another, equally important element of social structure, and that is communalism or corporate identity. As previously noted, North-west Coast house interiors were large, open spaces with sleeping areas around the edges, but few or no permanent interior partitions. Even the Rain Screen in Whale House could be quickly and easily set up and taken down. The central hearth area of North-west Coast houses was open space with unrestricted access to all household members (except perhaps during feasts). The physical openness of these houses must have reinforced the idea that, despite differences in rank, no member of the household was completely separate from any other. This is the essential paradox of "intermediate" societies, like those of the North-west Coast – the delicate balancing act between hierarchy and centralisation on the one hand and communalism and incorporation on the other. A seeming contradiction, and yet North-west Coast houses were ingeniously built to accommodate and reinforce both principles (Coupland *et al.* 2009).

Archaeological evidence from the Prince Rupert area

Over the past 16 years, we have been pursuing a programme of research in household archaeology in the area known as Prince Rupert harbour on the northern North-west Coast. Prince Rupert harbour covers an area of less than 25 km², but it is archaeologically rich, with over 100 recorded sites, at least 20 of which are village sites with rectangular house depression features. We have conducted excavations at five of these village sites, and we have excavated 10 house depression features (Fig. 4.7). In the remainder of this paper, I will present results from two excavated house features, House O at the McNichol Creek site, and House J at the Tremayne Bay site. Archaeological evidence suggests that both houses were "active" in terms of indexical and canonical communication of wealth and high social status.

McNichol Creek site, House O: indexical communication
The McNichol Creek site was the focus of our research from 1990 to 2000 (Coupland 1996; 2006; Coupland *et al.* 1993; 2003). The site is typical in layout of many village sites in Prince Rupert harbour (Fig. 4.8). It is located in a small bay, protected from high winds and storms. The site is fronted by a gravel beach. Above the high tide line are 15 house depression features arranged in two rows. The houses are rectangular in

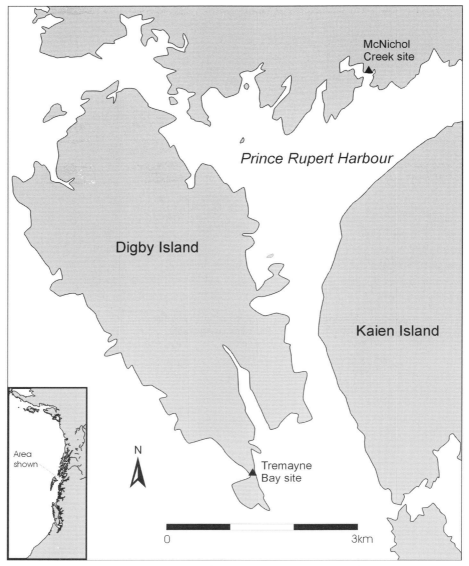

Figure 4.7. Prince Rupert harbour, showing sites mentioned in the text.

shape, with long axes oriented toward the beach. The back of the site is defined by a deep, crescent-shaped shell midden, apparently the refuse midden for the village. The site has been dated by 17 radiocarbon age estimates which range from 3000–800 BP (Coupland *et al.* 2003, 154). Over half of these dates cluster in the range between 1900 BP and 1400 BP, which we believe is the main period of village occupation at the site.

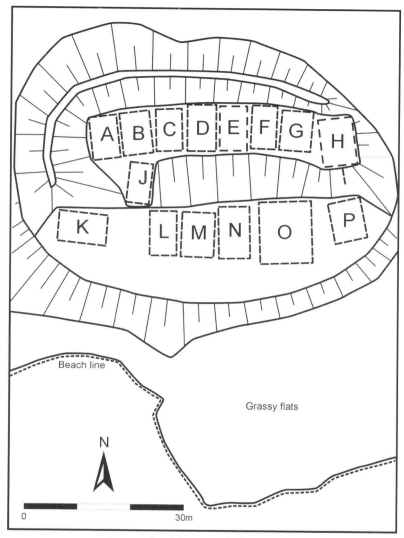

Figure 4.8. The McNichol Creek site.

Figure 4.9. "Box and dot" graph of house floor areas at the McNichol Creek, showing interquartile range (box) and median (vertical line within box).

House O is located in the front row of house depression features at McNichol Creek. Three radiocarbon assays date the occupation of this house to around 1650 BP. House O is distinguished from the other house features at the site in several ways that we think are related to the indexical communication of wealth and status. In short, we believe that House O was a chief's house.

The most obvious line of evidence of wealth and status in House O was its size. With an estimated floor area of 104 m², House O was significantly larger than all other houses at McNichol Creek (Fig. 4.9). The other 14 house features at the site range in area from about 50–75 m². House O is clearly an outlier in terms of size, and this must have made an immediate visual impression on visitors to the village. We see the size of House O as a clear indexical message of affluence.

Another way in which House O may have communicated its status to outsiders was through its location in the village. House O is located in the front row of house depressions at McNichol Creek, and although it is not in the centre of the front row, it is located at the confluence of the two main access routes into the site. One route leads up from the beach. The other leads into the site from the mouth of McNichol Creek (for which the site is named) on the east side of the site. Both routes bring the visitor directly to the front of House O (Coupland 2006). In this sense, House O was "front and centre" in the village, the appropriate location for a North-west Coast chief's house.

The materials used to build House O provide a third line of evidence of wealth and high status. Although nothing remains of the wooden structure of the house, there is evidence for the use of special materials to prepare the floor. A unique feature of House O is a thin clay surface that covers most of the central and rear portions of the house floor. It is not clear whether this clay surface was the actual floor of House O or the base on which wooden floor boards were laid. In any event, the special preparation of the floor of House O would have required additional construction labour and would have been highly visible to outsiders invited in to the house. We see this as another example of the indexical communication of status by House O.

It is also notable that the clay floor in House O was only found in the back of the house, the high status area. This special floor may have simultaneously operated in the canonical mode to reinforce the principle of social rank and hierarchy within the household.

Tremayne Bay site, House J: canonical communication

The Tremayne Bay site is located in Prince Rupert harbour about 5km south of the McNichol Creek site. Tremayne Bay has 24 house depression features. Most of the houses are arranged in four rows, but some appear to have been haphazardly placed (Fig. 4.10). The layout of houses in the village appears to have been constrained by the fact that the site is located on a narrow isthmus at the south end of an island. House J is located at the west end of a row of three house features, roughly in the middle of the site.

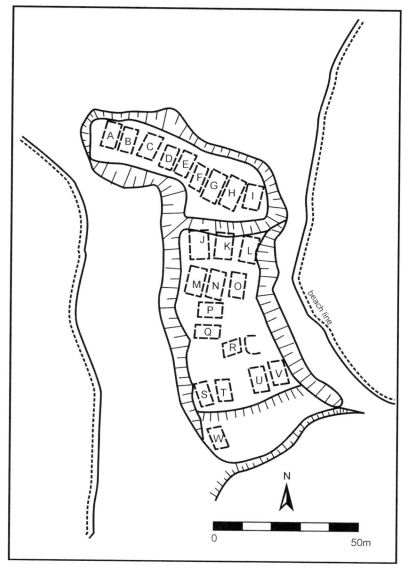

Figure 4.10. The Tremayne Bay site.

The Tremayne Bay site has been dated by eight radiocarbon age estimates, four of which date House J. According to these assays, the village at the Tremayne Bay site, including House J, was occupied about 2200–1900 BP.

House J was excavated in 2002. We focused our excavations on three areas of the house, the east and west sides and the back of the house. Of interest here are the results of excavation in the back area of the house. A pit feature, roughly circular in shape,

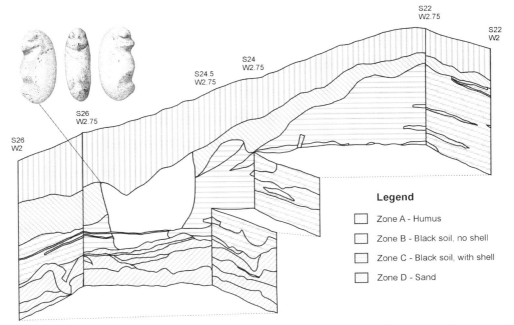

Figure 4.11. Profile of the back area of House J, Tremayne Bay site, showing pit feature and zoomorphic stone effigy recovered from near the surface of the pit.

about 1.0 m in diameter, and about 0.8 m deep was found in the back centre area of the house. A 4 m long shovel trench, dug from the refuse midden behind House J into the back area of the house, sectioned the pit and provides the profile shown in Fig. 4.11. As the figure shows, the pit cuts through house floor deposit (and surrounding shell midden), indicating that it was dug during the late or terminal occupation of the house.

Further excavation of the pit yielded several, scattered elements of human bone, including three vertebrae, a scapula, and a sacrum. These elements all came from the upper portion of the pit fill, near the surface. The pit, itself, did not contain a complete, articulated human burial. There were no human remains in the bottom of the pit that was sectioned by the shovel trench.

No artefacts or other faunal remains were recovered from directly within the pit, but we did find a pecked and ground zoomorphic stone effigy lying on the surface of the south edge of the pit. This smooth, polished, black stone weighs 1.8 kg and is 19 cm long. It is finished in low relief, with facial features – eyes, nose or beak, mouth – clearly visible. Pecking and polishing have also produced the outline of folded limbs on the body of the figure. Large, finished, and unbroken, this piece is beautifully made and highly stylised. It may represent a seal (baby seal?; Fig. 4.11).

How do we interpret this association of traits – pit, scattered human remains, and stone effigy figure – from the back of House J? I believe this association of traits is the result of a ritual performance conducted in the back area of House J at or near the time of abandonment of the house. The pit may have been dug originally to contain a human burial, but the human remains appear to have been removed from the pit. The scattered elements at the surface of the pit were probably left there during the removal process. To mark the removal of these human remains from the burial pit, the stone effigy was placed beside the surface of the pit.

The precise meaning of this ritual performance can only be guessed. But it is significant that the location of the ritual was in the back-centre of House J, the high status area of the house. Blanton (1995) has argued that the performance of ritual in the context of daily household routines – what he calls "ritualization of the habitus" – is strongly correlated to household inequality. "It is precisely in ritual and habitus that an order of household inequality is made to appear powerful and holy" (Blanton 1995, 113). Performance of household rituals, and the designation of ritual spaces within the house, sanctify and legitimise household hierarchies. Thus, through the performance of ritual, House J became a medium for the canonical communication of hierarchy.

Summary and conclusion

Household archaeology has emerged as an important approach to understanding past social and economic process on the North-west Coast of North America, as a series of recent volumes have shown (*e.g.* Matson *et al.* 2003; Sobel *et al.* 2006). North-west Coast households, organised at the time of European contact in the late 18th century as large, extended family or multifamily corporate groups, were the fundamental units of production and consumption. North-west Coast societies were not organised as complex chiefdoms into regional polities. Even villages were not true political units. The largest stable socio-political unit on the North-west Coast was the household. Thus, a research focus on the household is critical to any study of socio-political evolution on the North-west Coast. Recognising this, several North-west Coast scholars are currently developing research programmes in household archaeology with the household as the main unit of analysis.

Fewer scholars are focusing on the North-west Coast house as the main unit of analysis. I hope the current paper has shown that such a focus has potential. North-west Coast houses of the early historic period, and their prehistoric counterparts dating back over 3000 years, were often massive structures that in many cases have left substantial archaeological traces. The symbolic importance of these structures to the people that built them has been demonstrated on several occasions (Levi-Strauss 1982; MacDonald 1983; Marshall 1989; 2000). Using Blanton's (1994) model of non-verbal communication by the built environment, I have shown that North-west Coast houses communicated wealth, social status and power both indexically and canonically.

Indexically, the houses of high status North-west Coast chiefs were typically much larger than other, low status houses. The Monster House at Masset provides an excellent historic example of the importance of house size, and House O at the McNichol Creek site in Prince Rupert harbour shows that large houses have marked high status on the north coast for at least 1600 years. Painted house fronts and memorial poles, and the "front and centre" location of chiefs' houses in villages were also indexical symbols of high status.

Canonically, family sleeping areas within houses were arranged according to status or rank, providing a continuous visual cue to household members of the importance of hierarchy. In addition, sanctification of household inequalities through the ritualisation of domestic space is evident in House J at the Tremayne Bay site in Prince Rupert harbour. This dates the use of houses to canonically communicate hierarchy on the north coast to at least 2000 BP.

Finally, several elements of North-west Coast houses could operate simultaneously in the indexical and canonical modes. During feasts, potlatches and other rituals, guests were invited into houses where very little was blocked from view by walls or partitions. On these occasions, carved and painted house posts, platform risers and dance screens, which on a daily basis operated canonically to legitimise inequalities within the household, functioned indexically to communicate wealth and status to visitors. In a similar manner, painted house fronts and totem poles were highly visual markers of wealth and status to non-household members and, at the same time, canonical symbols to the household of the importance of hierarchy.

Research on the non-verbal communication of North-west Coast houses has just begun. I have tried to show in this paper some fruitful lines of inquiry on this subject. I expect future research to expand greatly on this theme because North-west Coast houses have much to say.

References

Acheson, S. (1998) *In the of the Ya'ats'xaatgay ('Iron People'): a Study of Changing Settlement Strategies Among the Kunghit Haida*. Oxford, Archaeopress, British Archaeological Report S711.

Adams, J. (1973) *The Gitksan Potlatch: Population Flux, Resource Ownership and Reciprocity*. Toronto, Holt, Rinehart and Winston.

Ames, K. (2006) Thinking about household archaeology on the North-west Coast. In Sobel *et al.* (eds) (2006), 16–36.

Ames, K. (2001) Slaves, chiefs and labour on the northern North-west Coast. *World Archaeology* 33, 1–17.

Ames, K. (1996) Life in the Big House: household labor and dwelling size on the North-west Coast. In G. Coupland and E. Banning (eds) *People Who Lived in Big Houses: Archaeological Perspectives on Large Domestic Structures*, 131–150. Madison (WI), Prehistory Press, Monographs in World Prehistory, 27.

Ames, K. (1995) Chiefly power and production on the North-west Coast. In D. Price and G. Feinman (eds) *Foundations of Social Inequality*, 155–181. New York, Plenum.

Ames, K. (1979) Stable and resilient systems along the Skeena River: the Gitksan/Carrier boundary. In R. Inglis and G. MacDonald (eds) *Skeena River Prehistory. Archaeological Survey of Canada*, 219–243. Ottawa, National Museum of Man, Mercury Series 87.

Barbeau, M. (1950) *Totem Poles*. Ottawa, National Museums of Canada, Bulletin 19.

Bender, D. (1967) A refinement of the concept of household: families, co-residence and domestic functions. *American Anthropologist* 69, 493–504.

Blackman, M. (1972) Nei:w)ns, the "Monster House" of Chief Wi:ha: an exercise in ethnohistorical, archaeological and ethnological reasoning. *Syesis* 5, 211–215.

Blanton, R. (1995) The cultural foundations of inequality in households. In D. Price and G. Feinman (eds) *Foundations of Social Inequality*, 105–127. New York, Plenum.

Blanton, R. (1994) *Houses and Households: a Comparative Study*. New York, Plenum.

Blier, S. (1987) *The Anatomy of Architecture: Ontology and Metaphor in Batammaliba Architectural Expression*. Cambridge, Cambridge University Press.

Bourdieu, P. (1977) *Outline of a Theory of Practice*. Cambridge, Cambridge University Press.

Bourdieu, P. (1973) The Berber House. In M. Douglas (ed.) *Rules and Meanings*, 98–110. Hammondsworth (UK), Penguin.

Chatters, J. (1989) The antiquity of economic differentiation within households in the Puget Sound region, North-west Coast. In S. MacEachern, D. Archer and R. Garvin (eds), *Households and Communities*, 168–178. Calgary, University of Calgary Archaeological Association.

Coupland, G., Clark, T. and Palmer, A. (2009) Heirachy, communalism and the spatial order of Northwest Coast plank houses: a comparative study. *American Antiquity* 74: 77–106.

Coupland, G. (2006) A Chief's House speaks: communicating power on the Northern North-west Coast. In Sobel *et al.* (eds) (2006), 80–96.

Coupland, G. (1996) This Old House: cultural complexity and household stability on the northern North-west Coast of North America. In J. Arnold (ed.) *Emergent Complexity: the Evolution of Intermediate Societies*, 59–73. Ann Arbor, International Monographs in Prehistory, Archaeological Series 9.

Coupland, G., Colten, R. and Case, R. (2003) Preliminary analysis of socioeconomic organization at the McNichol Creek Site, British Columbia. In R. Matson, G. Coupland and Q. Mackie (eds) *Emerging from the Mist: Studies in North-west Coast Culture History*, 152–169. Vancouver, UBC Press.

Coupland, G., Bissel, G. and King, S. (1993) Prehistoric subsistence and seasonality at Prince Rupert Harbour: evidence from the McNichol Creek Site. *Canadian Journal of Archaeology* 17, 59–73.

Donald, L. (1997) *Aboriginal Slavery on the North-west Coast of North America*. Berkeley, University of California Press.

Donald, L. (1985) On the possibility of social class in societies based on extractive subsistence. In M. Thompson, M. García and F. Kense (eds) *Status, Structure and Stratification: Current Archaeological Reconstructions*, 237–244. Calgary, University of Calgary Archaeological Association.

Douglas, M. and Isherwood, B. (1979) *The World of Goods: Towards an Anthropology of Consumption*. New York, WW Norton.

Emmons, G. (1991) *The Tlingit Indians* (edited with additions by F. de Laguna). Seattle, University of Washington Press-New York, American Museum of Natural History.

Ferguson, R. (1984) A Reexamination of the causes of North-west Coast warfare. In R. Ferguson (ed.) *Warfare, Culture and Environment*, 267–328. New York, Academic Press.

Grier, C. (2006) Temporality in North-west Coast households. In Sobel *et al.* (eds) (2006), 97–119.

Grier, C. (2001) *The Social Economy of a Prehistoric North-west Coast Plankhouse*. Unpublished PhD thesis, Arizona State University.

Hendon, J. (1996) Archaeological approaches to the organization of domestic labor: household practices and domestic relations. *Annual Review of Anthropology* 25, 45–61.

Levi-Strauss, C. (1982) *The Way of the Masks*. Seattle, University of Washington Press.

MacDonald, G. (1983) *Haida Monumental Art*. Vancouver, UBC Press.

Marshall, Y. (2006) Houses and domestication on the North-west Coast. In Sobel *et al.* (eds) (2006), 37–56.

Marshall, Y. (2000) Transformations of Nuu-chah-nulth houses. In R. Joyce and S. Gillespie (eds) *Beyond Kinship*, 73–102. Philadelphia, University of Pennsylvania Press.

Marshall, Y. (1989) The house in North-west Coast, Nuu-chah-nulth society: the material structure of political action. In S. MacEachern, D. Archer and R. Garvin (eds) *Households and Communities*, 15–21. Calgary, University of Calgary Archaeological Association.

Maschner, H. (1997) The evolution of North-west Coast warfare. In D. Martin and D. Frayer (eds) *Troubled Times: Violence and Warfare in the Past*, 267–302. New York, Gordon and Breach.

Matson, R., Coupland, G. and Mackie, Q. (2003) *Emerging from the Mist: Studies in North-west Coast Culture History*. Vancouver, UBC Press.

McCracken, G. (1988) *Culture and Consumption: New Approaches to the Symbolic Character of Consumer Goods and Activities*. Bloomington, Indiana University Press.

Miller, J. (1997) *Tsimshian Culture: a Light Through the Ages*. Lincoln, University of Nebraska Press.

Pauketat, T. and Alt, S. (2005) Agency in a postmold? Physicality and the archaeology of culture-making. *Journal of Archaeological Method and Theory* 12, 213–236.

Rapoport, A. (1982) *The Meaning of the Built Environment: a Nonverbal Communication Approach*. Beverly Hills, Sage.

Rapoport, A. (1969) *House Form and Culture*. Englewood Cliffs, Prentice Hall.

Sanders, D. (1990) Behavioral conventions and archaeology: methods for the analysis of ancient architecture. In S. Kent (ed.) *Domestic Architecture and the Use of Space*, 43–72. Cambridge, Cambridge University Press.

Schiffer, M. (1987) *Formation Processes of the Archaeological Record*. Alberquerque, University of New Mexico Press.

Schiffer, M. (1976) *Behavioral Archaeology*. New York, Academic Press.

Sobel, E., Trieu Gahr, A. and Ames, K. (eds) (2006) *Household Archaeology on the North-west Coast*. Ann Arbor, International Monographs in Prehistory, Archaeological Series 16.

Suttles, W. (1991) The shed-roof house. In R. Wright (ed.) *A Time of Gathering: Native Heritage in Washington State*, 212–222. Seattle, Burke Museum

Trieu Gahr, A. (2006) Architects to ancestors: the life cycle of plankhouses. In Sobel *et al.* (eds) (2006), 57–79.

Trigger, B. (1967) Settlement archaeology – its goals and promise. *American Antiquity* 32, 149–161.

Wilk, R. (1983) Little house in the jungle: the causes of variation in house size among modern Maya. *Journal of Anthropological Archaeology* 2, 99–116.

Domestic Space: Analysis of the Activities of a Hunter-Gatherer Social Unit at the Southern End of the American Continent

Jordi Estévez Escalera and Ignacio Clemente Conte

Introduction

From the middle of the 1980s we have carried out a series of ethnoarchaeological research projects on the northern coast of the Beagle Channel –Tierra del Fuego – Argentina (Fig. 5.1). This area was inhabited by groups of hunters-fishers-gatherers from approximately 6500 BP until the first half of the 20th century. These groups, named after the first contacts with Europeans as Yaghanes or Yamanas, were observed moving with canoes along the Fuegian channels. The information written by travelers,

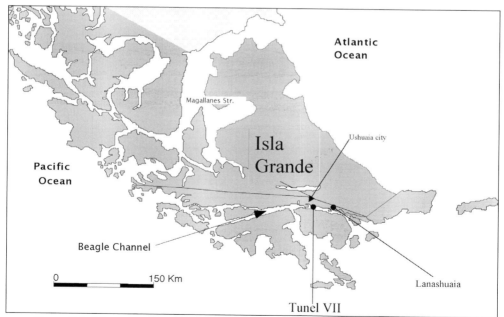

Figure 5.1. Map of Tierra del Fuego showing the location of the sites cited in the text.

missionaries and ethnographers about these Fuegian groups is extensive. Luís A. Orquera and Ernesto L. Piana (1999) compiled these sources, which describe the variability of the products manufactured and consumed by the Yamana. The Austrian missionary Patter Gusinde, who visited the area in the 1920s, described the beliefs, ceremonies and rituals, as well as other aspects of Yamana social life (Gusinde 1937). Large collections of ethnographic material held in European and American museums allowed us to study the items from an archaeological perspective (Estevez and Vila 2006). These conditions, as well as minor paleoenvironmental change, make this area a perfect subject to carry out ethnoarchaeological studies.

We define Ethnoarchaeology as a method to test analytical procedures, not simply as a system to provide analogy by observing living people. These data are used to test the methodology of excavation and archaeological analyses. Conclusions are evaluated through comparison with archived written and graphic sources. Ethnographic sources provide indirect information since they are biased from the perspective of the European observer; however, they illustrate all that we know about the organisation of Yamana people for production and their mechanisms for social reproduction. The next step is to look for the analytical methods, which use only archaeological (direct) sources, necessary to achieve a similar level of understanding about social organisation. We can, in this way, evaluate and calibrate the methods and apply them to prehistoric situations. (Vila and Wünsch 1990; Vila and Piana 1993; Vila 1998; Vila and Estévez 1999). In addition to the archaeological excavations, we also carried out complementary programs of experimental replications, taphonomical observations and experiments, and sampling tests. These were used to increase the understanding of the archaeological evidence as well as to evaluate the credibility of the ethnographic information.

The huts

The specific interest of this paper is the archaeological analysis of a daily domestic living space of Yamana. Domestic life of the Yamana is described and depicted in ethnographic records and in a film. These groups constructed simple huts to provide shelter from climate conditions. Each hut lodged a social reproductive unit. The described huts generally had a hemispherical shape, but in some cases they were conical. They were approximately 3.5 m in diameter and were constructed with sticks and branches, then finished or waterproofed by covering them partly with grasses and hides of sea lions (Fig. 5.2).

There was a central hearth and some times other secondary small hearths or embers inside to better distribute the heat. The garbage of consumption was discarded to the periphery of the hut. Generally the entrance faced towards the sea. Daily activities including the production and consumption of goods were carried out both inside and outside of the hut.

During our work in Tierra del Fuego we excavated a ritual hut that had also been

Figure 5.2. Picture of a Yamana hut from the end of the 19th century.

described by the missionary Gusinde. This allowed us to evaluate the differences between habitual and special constructions (Vila 2004).

Túnel VII

The site Túnel VII is placed on the banks of the northern coast of the Beagle Channel, 54° 49' 15" of southern latitude and 68° 09' 20" of western longitude, in a little cove a dozen of kilometres to the east of the city of Ushuaia. It is a shell midden deposit site, and like other shell middens presents a very good preservation of archaeological evidence. The dendrochronological information places these occupations between the end of the 18th and the end of the 19th century (Piana and Orquera 1996), already after the contact with Europeans.

We first excavated an area of 72 m², focusing later on an area of 32 m² in which the centre and the periphery of an occupation unit was located. The centre of the occupation was a circle of 3.5 m with a large hearth in the middle (Fig. 5.3). It was surrounded with accumulations of food waste (mainly the shells of mussels and other mollusks) and residues relating to varied processes of work and consumption. This pattern of residue accumulation creates the typical ring aspect observed in the shell-middens of this area.

The excavation methods employed have allowed us to dissect the palimpsest and to differentiate 274 stratigraphic units that correspond to punctual episodes of garbage deposition (Orquera 1996; Orquera and Piana 1996). It was therefore possible to establish a detailed sequence of the dynamics of occupation. With micro-stratigraphic analyses (Estévez and Vila 2000) we could identify a superposition of hearths, separated by thin layers of sediment, which correspond to short periods of abandonment (Fig. 5.4). The hearths were only slightly displaced from one occupation to the next. We could also isolate the marks of small postholes, marking an almost circular perimeter.

Figure 5.3. Excavation of the site Tunel VII remarking the periphery line of the hut and the location of the central fireplace.

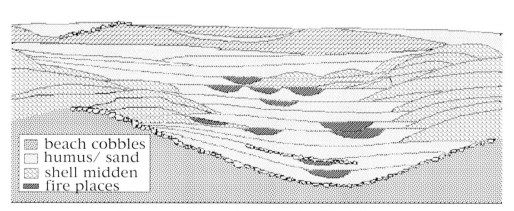

Figure 5.4. Scheme of the stratigraphy of Tunel VII site.

This has allowed us to verify the existence of at least ten discontinuous occupation episodes in which a hut centred on this space was constructed repeatedly (Fig. 5.5). Around these huts people also fulfilled other activities of production and consumption that left garbage and other remains evacuated from the inside of the hut deposited in this surrounding area.

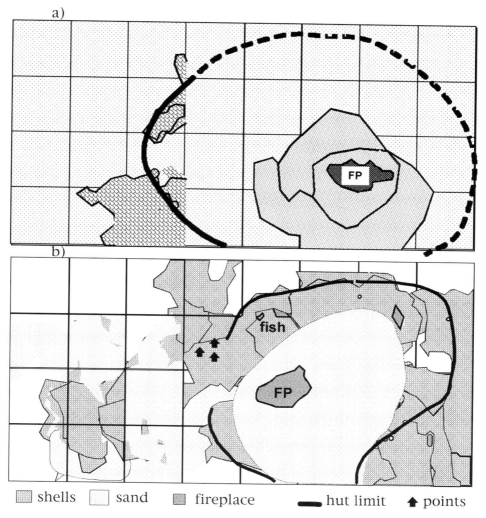

Figure 5.5 a) Schematic plan of the first occupation, and b) for the eighth occupation episodes of Tunel VII.

The generation of the evidence

People established the first occupation on the very little cobble beach. They probably slightly dug out the surface, making more regular a round narrow concavity by pushing some pebbles in a very rough way. They placed a hearth in the centre of the concavity. Later they occupied the same concavity where it had accumulated a light layer of humus and sand. The margins of the concavity increased in height due to residue deposition, largely due to the high volume of the consumed molluscs (Fig. 5.4).

The layer of humus that accumulated, especially in the centre of the concavity during periods of abandonment, allows us to establish the interruptions and to attribute most of the units of deposit to individual occupation episodes. Of course the continuity of the sequence of occupations and the sedimentary dynamics (biodisturbance and slides of the mollusc heaps) does not allow us to completely discount a certain mixture of materials from different occupations. An extensive task of lithic and bone reassemblage and rejoining has been undertaken in an attempt to evaluate the range of sediment movements.

The generated record has allowed us a qualitative approach to the dynamics and variability of the different occupations, the seasonal nature and the predominant activities in each of them (Estévez and Vila 2006b). The first two occupations are difficult to distinguish since it is only possible to identify the discontinuity between them in the centre of the concavity. The first occupation corresponds to the first settlement, when the hut was constructed on the beach. The second unit would be related with the second moment of occupation after a temporary abandonment of the hut, as is observed in the stratigraphy (Estévez and Vila 2000). Both occupations likely occurred in spring. The first occupation shows little bone artefacts; relatively few sea lion remains, but contains cetacean and some guanaco bones, and a strange consumption of austral parakeet (Mameli and Estévez 2004). The second occupation involved more stone knapping, bone working, sea lion consumption and working cetacean bones. People deposited consumed shells in midden on the south-west side of the hut.

The later occupations happened at different seasons. From the fourth occupation people began to accumulate rubbish on the eastern side of the hut, and the centre of the hut became clearly narrowed and encircled by the shell-midden amounts. During the fifth occupation (in winter) the entrance was oriented to the west and secondary fireplaces were situated in this direction, close to the entrance. During the next occupation the fireplace was again in the centre. A secondary hearth was placed on the outside of the structure, while the opening was directed again to the south, facing the sea. The next was a short winter occupation. The following two were summer occupations spaced more closely together in time. The occupations were linked with high levels of fish consumption and were almost only identifiable by a slight displacement of the central fireplaces. The last was for a short period during summer with lithic tools for animal processing and low but varied animal consumption. After this the centre of the concavity was no longer occupied as the central place for the huts, but covered by remains coming from other neighboring areas.

During all the occupations other huts occupied the beach alternatively or simultaneously. This can make it difficult to establish whether the remains accumulated on the very periphery of the excavated area relate to the activities within our hut or by another hut situated west of ours.

The residues of consumption were deposited by dropping and by simply sweeping towards the periphery of the living area. We assume that residues of small size (little secondary knapping flakes and minor pieces of bones, such as phalanges, chips of bone working) would be the best marker for places of production; although we believe that in the less well-swept outside areas, garbage or amortised tools would be dropped down at the end of the work.

Residues of food consumption include the remains of molluscs and other marine invertebrates, birds, marine mammals and guanacos (Estévez and Martinez 1997; Estévez *et al.* 2001). There are also bone residues from the production (masses of origin, residues and chips) and discard of instruments (harpoons, wedges, spatulas or smoothers, retouchers) and necklace beads. Finally there are lots of residues from the production and the consumption of lithic tools.

Ethnohistorical information about Yamana lithic tool use present contradictions with the archaeological information recovered (Mameli *et al.* 2005). Many ethnohistoric sources assessed that the Yamana were unable to work stone and therefore they had to acquire the arrows and other lithic weapon by exchange with the Ona, their neighbors from the north of the Isla Grande de Tierra del Fuego (Terradas *et al.* 1999). The large quantity of lithic remains recovered, Tierra del Fuego for instance in Túnel VII (22, 323), shows the opposite, since they demonstrate a good skill in this activity.

Igneous rocks such as rhyolite and cinerite, belonging to Lemaire´s geologic formation (Caminos 1980), were the most used for the manufacture of lithic tools (Clemente 1997; Terradas 1999; Clemente and Terradas 1993). Raw material could be gathered as boulders or cobbles along the beaches and on the moraine deposits remaining today along the northern coast of the Beagle Channel. The relative frequencies in the rocks (rhyolite and cinerite) gathered in Túnel VII is similar to the quantities represented in these secondary deposits. Nevertheless, it seems that after the stones were brought to the settlement people preferred to use cinerite rather than rhyolite for certain activities (Clemente and Terradas 1993). This can be explained by several factors. One is that people can obtain sharper knife-edges by flaking cinerite, a finer grained mineral that does not blunt so easily as rhyolite. The blocks of rhyolite usually present more internal fissures and are therefore more difficult to manage by flaking. As a result, rhyolite flaking produces a greater quantity of residues. The bifacial reduction of stone by narrow (pressure) retouch to manufacture products such as arrow points and daggers also produces a lot of residue.

The analyses of lithic technology recovered from Túnel VII and a contemporaneous site, Lanashuaia, allows us to distinguish two different processes related to lithic production (Pie and Vila 1990). On one hand there is bifacial reduction of cores, which is "stadial flaking" (Gyria 1997), for producing bifacial scrapers and the tips of larger weapons. This flaking technique generates numerous chips and/or residues. We also noted the accidental fracture of bifacial by-products (normally discarded and not used as instruments) in different stages of manufacture. This occurs especially at the more delicate moments of making stems and fins on the arrow and dagger points (Clemente 1997). This system of flaking uses a hard hammerstone for the first stadiums of flaking, and a retoucher – made of guanaco's metapodia – to continue the flaking by pressure to get the stems and fins. Another documented type of flaking is direct percussion to get flakes that could be used immediately, or slightly retouched (to shape them into scrapers). These fast produced flakes also could be transformed to arrow tips by pressure retouch.

Spatial analysis of the evidence and its spatial structure: the distribution of residues.

We have considered the lithic and bone remains to carry out this spatial distribution analysis. The recovery methodology applied during the excavation has been very important to our aim. The residues were recovered by thin units of deposit and by a grid of half square meters. Almost all of the objects (lithic remains and bone over 2 cm) were localised and recorded by its centimetre position in the grid.

This record allows us to analyse with accuracy the position of every object in space relative to synchronic and diachronic relations. Likewise, it is possible to analyse recurrences in the management of space and to establish a general pattern of spatial arrangement strategies (Wünsch 1996).

First we want to establish a comparative analysis between the first occupation and the full palimpsest. This is based on the distribution of consumption goods and residues, which show differences in the comparative patterns. This demonstrates how the compilation of the variable activities undertaken through the whole occupation varies from the information provided by a single occupation moment.

We visually study the distribution of the different items by half square metres. To analyse this distribution we will highlight two levels of concentrations in the squares: first those with a number of items higher than the average, and second those with quantities greater than one standard deviation above the average.

We present the results of the distribution of lithic remains from Túnel VII for the whole sample of occupations as well as those from the first occupation episode. Thus, we try to observe if the distribution of the whole palimpsest reflects, at some level, the same distribution patterns that are observed at the first moment of occupation of the Yamana hut.

In this heuristic essay, to demonstrate difference in discard patterns we visually analyse the distributions of the general categories of residues mentioned above. Other synthetic categories that may better represent concrete processes of work are not generated or addressed. Bone residues are distinguished by categories of birds, sea lions (fragments of the axial skeleton, extremities and flippers) and cetacean (major and minor fragments), as well as elements produced during the manufacture and discard of instruments and other bone objects.

For the lithic instruments usage, we are not going to enumerate the actions and worked materials involved since these have already been the aim of other papers (see Clemente 1996; 1997; 2005). We think that for our purpose, and according to the subject of this volume, it turns out to be more interesting to see if spatially specific distributions exist for different production activities carried out in the unit studied.

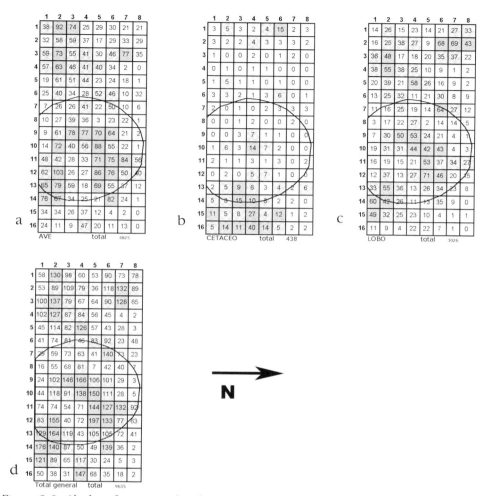

Figure 5.6. *Absolute frequencies distribution of the whole sample of faunal remains categories produced during 10 occupations. a) Total bird bones, b) total cetaceous bones, c) total sea lion bones, d) total bone remains.*

We believe that if this is the case, then the functional analysis turns out again to be fundamental to characterise the domestic space of hunter-gatherer societies.

Spatial distribution analysis

Faunal remains from the complete sample of nine occupation episodes concentrate on the NW of the interior of the huts (Fig. 5.6). There is also a concentration in the south-eastern limit of the same hut and two more concentrations outside of the hut

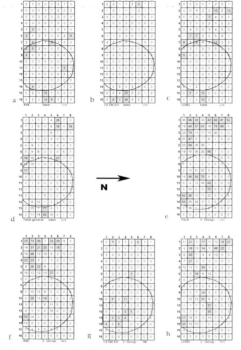

to the south-west and north-west. This later concentration could originate from residues of neighboring huts. Finally, there is an accumulation concentrated towards the west on the outside limits of the hut. Birds and sea lions are the categories that contribute to the accumulation inside the hut. Bird remains also greatly contribute to the accumulation in the south-west, whereas sea lion is a large contributor to the north-west concentration. Finally cetacean bones and lesser birds are the remains that accumulated on the outside of the hut to the east.

Comparing this situation with that of the first episode of occupation we verify that notable differences do exist: during the first episode most of the fauna concentrates on the external periphery of the hut and on a large spot to west and north-west. Birds were recovered in large quantities in the south-west, with another strong concentration in east. Sea lion remains are spread over the whole external western area and on a secondary spot in the east. Finally, the cetacean concentrates outside of the hut on the east. It is after the second phase of occupation when bone refuse begins to accumulate inside the space of the hut. This produces the accumulation

Figure 5.7. Absolute frequencies distribution of the sample of faunal remains categories produced during the first occupations. a) bird bones in basal level, b) cetaceous bones in basal level, c) sea lion bones in basal level, d) total bone remains in basal level, e) total bone remains in second occupation, f) bird bones in second occupation, g) cetaceous bones in second occupation, h) sea lion bones in second occupation.

that characterises the whole picture of the palimpsest, which is the main accumulation of bone refuse inside of the huts. In the second phase of occupation there are a few noticeable accumulations in the west of the excavated area. These correspond to accumulations of refuse that developed in part from an adjacent hut. It is also remarkable that in this phase of the accumulation, cetacean remains no longer concentrate in the east (Fig. 5.7).

The residues from the manufacture of bone objects (for the most part chips from cutting cetacean bones were found inside in the south-east and in a smaller deposit in the western periphery of the huts. The necklace beads were basically left inside the structure.

As we can observe in Figure 5.8a, the most significant concentrations of the lithic remains are in three discrete areas of the excavated surface. The largest extension corresponds to the space occupied by the hut; however, considering the number of remains the most important concentration is located to the north-west of the excavation. Greater importance may be found there considering that the concentration may continue towards the west (over the unexcavated area). The third concentration, although less important in extension and by number of items, is located between the previous two concentrations outside of the hut to the west. Figure 5.8b reflects the fragments and chips (FST and LST) smaller than 2 cm that are residues generated from lithic production. Other lithic residues are located in the same areas, which might indicate that these are the places where people manufactured lithic instruments. Figure 5.8c shows the location of the hammerstones and anvils. That they are located mainly inside the hut and within its immediate periphery indicate that they were used in flaking close to the areas of lithic production or that these were very controlled instruments ready for use as soon as needed.

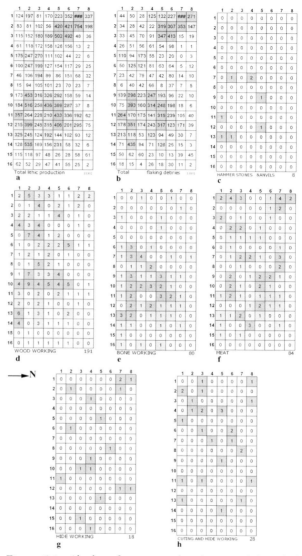

Figure 5.8. Absolute frequencies distribution of the whole sample of lithic products during 10 occupations.

Figures 5.8d–8h show the lithic tools used to work different materials. Wood is one of the most commonly worked materials (Fig. 5.8d) using lithic tools. This work was done mainly in the exterior of the hut, although some woodworking was also carried out inside the structure. It will be interesting, in future works, to consider the size of the tools used and the actions realised. This would verify if there was some selection of tool characteristics according to the activities undertaken in a specific location. Nevertheless, bone working concentrates in the area related to the interior of the hut (Fig. 5.8e), whereas the tools for butchering (dismembering and filleting) are scattered over almost the whole excavated area, with major concentrations in the west part of the grid (especially the butchering of sea lions) and in the hut interior (meat cutting related to consumption and cooking). The next two figures (Figs 5.8g and 8h) show the distribution of the instruments that have worked skin: hide scrapers (Fig. 5.8g) or skin knifes (Fig. 5.8h). Knifes involved in the mentioned skin cutting are mostly distributed outside of the hut. They may also be related to activities such as butchering and skinning the animals before the dismembering them into smaller pieces. Skinning and dismembering was also done inside the hut, although with less intensity. This may be related to the fact that the skins of small mammals and some birds, such as cormorants, penguins, etc. were used by the Yamana to manufacture certain products (loincloths, belts or hair bands) that could be produced inside of the hut. Two concentrations of bird bones occur there. Tools, which demonstrate the transverse movements for scrapping leather, are distributed over the whole area, inside as well as outside of the hut. Anyway, it is logical to assume that the skins of the large animals should be cleaned and scraped outside of the hut since the central interior hearth would create a space problem for such activities. We must also remember that, according to ethnographic information and corroborated by the analysis of ethnographic materials (Mansur 1983; Mansur and Clemente in press), Yamana people also worked skin, using knives and scrapers made of *Aulacomya* shells.

To compare the global picture of the palimpsest formed by the ten occupation episodes described above, we have considered separately the lithic remains related to the first activities developed in the place (shown in Fig. 5.9a–9e) and the activities realised during a second occupation episode after a temporary abandonment (Fig. 5.9f–9i). In the first occupation people carried out stone flaking preferably in the central and eastern sector of the excavated grid (Fig. 5.9a). The instruments for woodworking lie, for the most part, to the exterior of the hut, in the central and western part of the grid (Fig. 5.9b). Perhaps these activities might be related to the building of the hut. Whereas the set of instruments related to soft cutting (animal matter, that is butchering) were found mainly in the exterior (western sector) (Fig. 5.9d). The tools for working hard materials (bone) concentrate inside or in the close surroundings of the hut (see Fig. 5.9c). Although some examples were found inside the hut, instruments related to skin working (Fig. 5.9e) were mainly recovered in the exterior towards the western sector. This also coincides with a butchering activity area.

On the other hand, if we observe the distributions of the second moment of occupation (Fig. 5.9f–9i) it is apparent that, similar to the analysis of the complete Tunnel VII sample, there are already two definite flaking areas, one inside and one other outside of the hut (Fig. 5.9f). The cores and hammerstones used for lithic production are located inside of the hut. We can also observe two areas for woodworking, one inside

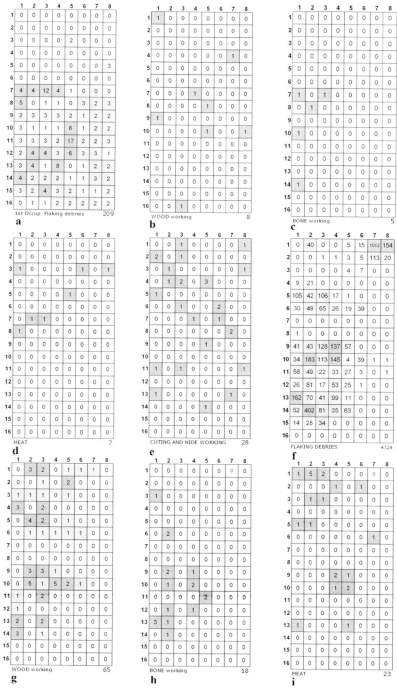

Figure 5.9. Absolute frequencies distribution of the sample of lithic products during the first and second occupations.

the hut and other one in the sector south-west of the grid (Fig. 5.9g). This is the same case for tools used in butchering activities where two separate areas are apparent (Fig. 5.9i). Tools for working bone are mainly located inside the hut (Fig. 5.9h).

As presented earlier, the location of lithic tools in Túnel VII show a spatial distribution of production activities that reflects a social strategy for organising space. Despite the maintenance activities resulting from cleaning and sweeping this domestic space, the same tool types and therefore the activities are found to recur in the same places. This is found both at the general level of the palimpsest, and in the particular case of the first two occupations. In addition to the general manufacture of lithic tools, the interior of the hut was also used for woodworking, processing meat products as well as for working bone to obtain other goods (like harpoons, wedges, necklace beads). It is interesting to note that the hammerstones were kept inside the hut. This was a way to have them always under control, ready to be used when needed. The activities developed outside the hut are certain butchering activities and skinning, as well as woodworking (in the SW sector).

Discussion and Conclusions

The documented activities in Túnel VII are: the arrangement of space, production of goods (which means by-products, products and rejects), consumption of products and especially the management of production waste.

We have tried to analyse spatial arrangement and densities of consumed products by categories resulting from use/wear and technological analysis on lithic and bone residues, as well as from the analysis of faunal resources exploitation.

General trends of the spatial arrangement strategies in Túnel VII show the differences between the inside and outside of the hut. Inside the hut a main fireplace was placed in the centre of a reasonably cleaned, slightly concave surface. Some larger materials are tossed and swept to the periphery of these areas including shells of consumed molluscs. A circle of shell-midden and other waste accumulates around this area, raising a crown that surrounds the centre of this occupied area. Other discarded remains and secondary fireplaces inside the hut can be interpreted as working areas that are close to sitting or sleeping areas. Nevertheless throughout the occupations, the quantity of small remains deposited in the inside of the hut is diffused through maintenance sweeping. As a result, the complete palimpsest shows a significant concentration of remains inside of the hut. Birds were consumed and deposited in concentrated spots, especially in the interior. Outside, there is evidence of working areas and locations with cetacean bone residues. Sea lion (especially the larger individuals) was butchered outside and was consumed both inside and outside of the hut. These remains were unevenly distributed and sometimes shared with other huts.

In addition, we can also conclude that lithic production develops in two clearly differentiated areas: inside the hut and in the exterior towards the most western sector

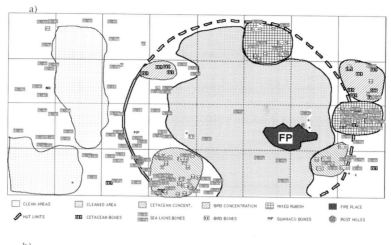

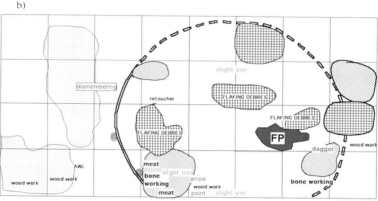

Figure 5.10. a) Map of faunal remains and concentrations. b) Map of the distribution of residues concentrations and used tools in Tunel VII first occupation.

of the excavation. In the exterior people obtained flakes and fragments that could have been used for activities documented in these external areas, especially woodworking and sea lion butchering. Likely due to the more comfortable conditions, the interior of the hut was used for more laborious activities, such as the finishing of bifacial points. The presence of a retoucher inside the hut during the first occupation may support this hypothesis. Although it may also be due to the item being a valued good that, similar to hammerstones, people would want to have under close control to prevent loss, and to have it available when needed.

This general image can be compared with the one that is obtained for the single occupations, similar to this first occupation on which we have centered. Plotting the different types of waste and isolating the visualised accumulations (Fig. 5. 10) allow us to understand how the deposition of residues occurred.

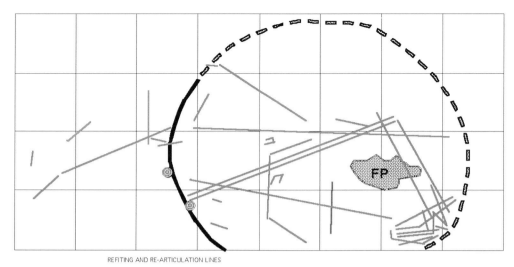

REFITING AND RE-ARTICULATION LINES

Figure 5.11. Map of the refitting and rearticulation lines in the material deposited during the first occupation of Túnel VII.

We argue that instruments of work will not always be located in the place where they were used. This results from the activities of cleaning and maintenance of the domestic space displacing and redepositing the items in other places. Nevertheless, the task of deciphering the stratigraphy of Túnel VII (Estévez and Vila 2000), together with the reassembly and the rejoins of skeletons, allow us to assess the general dynamics of deposit. Actually the lines that join pieces, which match or articulate together, show us a dynamic that does not exceed the limits of the build structure (Fig. 5.11). There are lines that cross from east to west in the interior of the hut, others join points in the exterior deposit, and finally we have a set of connections in the deposit of waste that existed in the south-east limit of the structure. These correspond with an area of accumulation of swept garbage of the consumption of birds.

Inside the hut it is possible to identify aggregates of bird remains both to the right and left of the hut entrance, and a third close to the central hearth. A reasonably clean area exists in the centre of the hut and around the hearth. In the periphery, at the rear part of the interior of the hut another accumulation occurs with mixed remains of sea lion and birds. More to the left at the rear there is a small accumulation of cetacean bone chips. It is possible to identify an area with mixed and heterogeneous waste in the periphery to the East of the hut. This includes the remains of birds, cetacean, guanaco and big pieces of consumed of sea lion. More to the north but completely in the exterior to the hut we found an accumulation with cetacean remains of different sizes.

The remains of sea lion are found over the whole western periphery outside of the hut. Nevertheless two areas stay reasonably clean inside this dispersion of remains. In one of them there were flakes that served for cutting and sawing wood along with a bone awl that could also be used in this type of work (to perforate and to sew pieces of wood or bark, for example). Residues of sea lion surround the other clean area and there is a non-curated tool (a simple flake) that served for butchering animals. The rest of the lithic tools are concentrated inside the hut, and we can correlate them to works that were fulfilled there: maintenance tasks of the instruments, retouching for final shaping of tools (a used retoucher and three concentration areas of flaking residues), as well as rejected or unfinished elements from manufacture or broken, amortised elements (fragments of arrow points and dagger points).

As we have commented earlier, in the second moment of occupation the remains of birds spread over the whole western part of the interior of the hut and the area occupied by the remains of sea lion is also extended towards the hut's interior, whereas other spots of little cetacean remains are found inside the hut.

After these analyses we can assess that certain, but not all of the general tendencies observed in the general distribution of all the products recur in the analysis of the first occupation, which by principle could be the most affected by taphonomic factors and by the proper human activities that followed later on the same place.

The distribution of all the remains in a sample of different recurrent occupations (a palimpsest) compared with the analysis of the different occupation levels in a deposit (like that in Túnel VII), where it is possible to identify and separate short moments of occupation and deposit, make it possible to identify if there are tendencies and recurrences in the deposit of the tools and remains. These correlations are the result of strategies relating to the organisation of space for certain activities. The recurrence of this organisation of the deposit and of the re-localisation of remains indicates the strength of the rules in the management of the space. The strategies appear to be less determined by processes related to subsistence and environmental constraints; rather, the use of space is more dependent on the variables of social organisation, which inform us about the social relationships.

To obtain our final goal we have to continue with the analysis of all the distributions and individual reassemblies, but also must look for synthetic categories that are more representative of the real social value of the produced and consumed goods. This has to consider other variables like the raw material used and different utility indices. Other information can come from the horizontal distribution of other categories, such as those derived from the soil micromorphology, fat and phytolith analysis of sediments, as well as from the ethnographic, experimental and taphonomical approaches. We will continue this analysis for all the occupations of Túnel VII. Then we will be able to compare them with the occupations of other sites of the Tierra del Fuego hunter-gatherer groups that we are presently being analysed.

Acknowledgments
This work has been funded by a research fund of the Spanish Research Agency of the Ministry for Science and Technology through the project *"Determinación de las causas*

de la variabilidad del registro arqueológico en sociedades cazadoras-recolectoras a través de un ejemplo etnoarqueológico" (BHA 2002-04109).

The translation was revised by Ryan Brady of California State University, Sacramento.

References

Caminos, R. (1989) Cordillera Fueguina. *Segundo Simposio de Geografía Regional Argentina* 2, 1463–1501.

Clemente Conte, I. (2005) The manufacture and use of leather consumption goods by the Yamana of Tunel VII, Northern coast of Beagle Channel (Argentina): an ethnographic evaluation and its archaeological comparision. In X. Terradas (ed.) *Lithic Toolkits in Ethnoarchaeological Contexts. (Proceedings of the XIVth UISPP Congress)*, 41–45. Oxford, Archaeopress, British Archaeological Report S1370.

Clemente Conte, I. (1997) *Los instrumentos líticos de Túnel VII: una aproximación etnoarqueológica.* Madrid, UAB-CSIC, Treballs d'Etnoarqueologia, 2.

Clemente Conte, I (1996) *Instrumentos de trabajo lithic de los yámanas (canoeros-nómadas de la Tierra del Fuego): una perspectiva desde el análisis funcional.* Unpublished PhD. Thesis, Universitat Autònoma de Barcelona.

Clemente Conte, I. and Terradas, X. (1993) Matières premières et fonctions: l'exemple de l'outillage lithique des yamana (Terre de Feu). In P. C. Anderson, S. Beyries, M. Otte and H. Plisson (eds) *Traces et fonction: le gestes retrouvés*, 513–521. Liège, CNRS, ERAUL 50 (II).

Estévez, J. and Martínez, J (1997) Archaeozoological researches at the Beagle Channel, Argentina. *Anthropozoologica* 25–26, 237–246.

Estévez, J., Piana, E., Schiavini, A. and Juan-Muns, J. (2001) Archaeological analysis of shell midden in the Beagle Channel, Tierra del Fuego Island. *International Journal of Osteoarchaeology* 11, 24–33.

Estévez, J. and Vila, A. (2000) Estratigrafías en contexto. *KREI* 5, 29–61.

Estévez, J. and Vila, A. (2006) Variability in the lithic and faunal record through ten reoccupations of a XIX century Yamana hut. *Journal of Anthropological Archaeology* 25, 408–423.

Gyria, E. Y. (1997) *Tejnologuicheskii Analisz kamennij industrii. Metodika mikro-makroanalisz devnij orudii truda.* Sant Petersburg, Rosiiskaia Akademia Nauk. Institut Istorii Materialnoi Kulturi.

Gusinde, M. (1937) *Die Feuerlandindianer. 2 Band. Die Yamana.* Mödling bei Wien, Verlag der Internat, Zeitschrift Anthropos.

Mameli, L. and Estévez, J. (2004) *Etnoarqueozoología de aves: el ejemplo del extremo sur americano.* Treballs d'Etnoarqueologia 5. Madrid, CSIC.

Mameli, L., Estévez, J. and Piana, E. L. (2005) Deep impact: stones in bones. Some though about the ethno-archaeology contrast. A view from Tierra del Fuego. In X. Terradas (ed.) *Stone Tools in Ethnoarchaeological Contexts (Proceedings of the XIVth UISPP Congress)*, 9–18. Oxford, Archaeopress, British Archaeological Report S1370.

Mansur, M. E. (1983) *Traces d'utilisation et technologie lithique: exemples de la Patagonie.* Unpublished PhD. Thesis, Université de Bourdeaux I.

Mansur, M. E. and Clemente, I. (in press) ¿Tecnologías invisibles? Confección, uso y conservación de instrumentos de valva en Tierra del Fuego. In *Actas del XIV Congreso Nacional de Arqueología Argentina.* Rosario.

Orquera, L. A. (1996) Túnel VII: la estratigrafía. In J. Estévez and A. Vila (eds) *Encuentros en los conchales fueguinos*, 83–103. Madrid-Barcelona, CSIC-UAB, Treballs d'Etnoarqueologia 1.

Orquera, L. A. and Piana, E. L. (1999) *La vida material y social de los Yámana*. Buenos Aires, Instituto Fueguino de Investigaciones Científicas-Eudeba.

Orquera, L. A. and Piana, E. L. (1996). Túnel VII: la excavación. In J. Estévez and A. Vila (eds) *Encuentros en los conchales fueguinos*, 47–82. Madrid-Barcelona, CSIC-UAB, Treballs d'Etnoarqueologia 1.

Pié, J. and Vila, A. (1992) Relaciones entre objetivos y métodos en el estudio de la industria lítica. In R. Mora, X. Terradas, A. Parpal, and C. Plana (eds) *Tecnología y cadenas operativas líticas*, 271–278. Barcelona, Universitat Autònoma de Barcelona, Treballs d'Arqueologia 1.

Terradas, X. (2001) *La gestión de los recursos minerales en las sociedades cazadoras-recolectoras*. Madrid, CSIC, Treballs d'Etnoarqueologia 4.

Terradas, X. (1997) Lithic raw material procurement strategies of the Yamana people (Tierra del Fuego, Argentina). In R. Schild and Z. Sulgostowska (eds) *Man and Flint*, 123–126. Warszawa, Institute of Archaeology and Ethnology-Polish Academy of Sciences.

6

Domestic Units, Definition and Multiform Archaeological Appearance. Economy and Politics in Unlike Domestic Prehistoric Groups of the Western Mediterranean

Pedro V. Castro-Martínez, Nicolau Escanilla-Artigas, Trinidad Escoriza-Mateu, Joaquim Oltra-Puigdomènech and Diana Sarkis-Fernández

Economy and politics in domestic units

The production of social life

Production is a global reality for social reproduction, but its becoming tangible is multiple, varying through time, history and space. The various spheres of production that we can define cannot be understood in isolation, since all are part of the same reality. Differentiating between the aforementioned spheres provides the reflexive and analytic bases of social reality (past and present). In underlining the existence of all the dimensions of social production (and not only the production of objects, which is the one that has almost exclusively been considered), we would like to reveal the hidden multiple dimensions of the work of women and men. And it is important to first establish the bases for the production of social life, because households, as domestic spaces, have often been spaces where many realities of social reproduction have been hidden.

Social materiality is made up of men, women and the objects they produced through labour. Through their work, men and women are the creators of social life. Relationships between women, men and objects are social practices, social life (Castro *et al.* 1996; 2002). Their existence is made possible by production, through the work that socialises material things (Castro *et al.* 1998; 2002; 2003a). Since production is social and consumption is individual (Marx 1857–58, 5–34), productive labour (and production politics) also exists in access to social production. Distribution will only exist in production conditions, because production is the sphere of creation of material conditions. This leads us to understand social production as being the result of the relationship between work and consumption-use.

All society (re)produces itself by means of basic production, the production of objects and the production of maintenance (Castro *et al.* 1998). This supposes that the production of bodies (basic) generates future social subjects (women and men), and that the production of objects generates products for social and individual use-consumption, and also that the production for maintenance of subjects and objects is also necessary for the existence of social life (Castro *et al.* 2002; 2003a).

Basic production is the biological production of sexual individuals, exclusively the work of women. This production can only be increased by overworking women, not by the division of labour or the improvement of means of labour, although these can help to control it. The production of objects provides food or other end products and tools and other transitive objects. The production for maintenance of objects increases the labour value of objects without changing their value of use, given that this incorporates more work, without changing their original use. Finally, social subjects' maintenance work provides the necessary care and attention to guarantee the life and conditions for socialisation of women and men, particularly in the early phases of infancy, or in situations of risk due to illness, accident or age, although it also contributes to offering added value to the vital reality of individuals.

Labour, consumption and social life
Social relationships between agents (women and men) and objects are established through work or consumption-use (enjoyment or suffering). Social practices always imply the labour of social subjects and/or use-consumption of social products (Castro *et al.* 1996; 2002; 2003b).

Any activity that implies the investment of time and energy in the execution of some activity for a social end (relational) is labour. Therefore, labour can be related to economic practices (production of subjects and objects) or to political-ideological practices. In any case, labour is oriented towards the (re)production of society, maintaining or seeking to transform it. Labour (the work of women and men) is the agent that acts on the matter (basic matter) with the use, when necessary, of certain means of labour (tools and infrastructures). The most direct results are social products (objects and subjects), obtained in their initial production or the result of their maintenance. At the same time, all production generates a certain amount of refusals, materiality that did not exist prior to the labour processes that generated it, its sub-products. The presence, abundance or absence of sub-products indicates the different productive processes, along with their intensity and the management of sub-products generated.

Work gives social life to objects. If we put work and the other factors of the labour processes (basic matter, means of labour) on the same level, we lose the perspective that is the work of men and women (social subjects), the only productive agent. Assuming the symmetry of these factors is an idealisation that could lead us to value Capital as a productive agent, or to believe that the land already contains the product, making it possible to legitimatise the benefits of capitalists or the income of landowners (Castro *et al.* 2002; 2003b).

A first group of products are end objects. End products are the objectives of social production, and are produced for individual consumption or social benefit. These objects can be consumed, when they are destroyed through the use for which they were produced; a clear example is food. But end products can also be enjoyed (a house) or suffered (a burka) in an individual and/or collective way. In such a case, the benefit or suffering does not imply the disappearance of the object. Like labour, activities involving the consumption-social use of end products can generate sub-products, and may need means of consumption.

Products can also be medial objects if they are the basic matter or means of work, when the objective of their production is for them to be incorporated into new labour processes, whether in the obtaining of subjects (basic production) or of objects, or in the maintenance tasks of the same. In this group we find products destined for destruction during work (for example fuels), as well as by tools and fixed structures (infrastructures).

Therefore, products are:

a. Social subjects (women and men). Productive agents, generates social materiality by means of work.
b. Basic Matter of new productive processes (work processes)
c. Means of labour used in economic practices, in work processes (tools or infrastructures).
d. End objects destined for individual consumption – use by social subjects (food, medicines, clothes, etc).
e. End objects used in political-ideological practices, aimed at management, reproduction or transformation of social life (singular objects).

Labour division, exploitation and reciprocity

Social production generates the objective conditions for relationships between subjects and social objects and for the reality of work and consumption (of participation in work processes or in access to benefits of social materiality). The first division of labour is implied in basic production, in the sexual biological reproduction of our species, since only women can assume the work of gestation and childbirth ("labour" in English). From here, an increase in the amplitude and complexity of social production can involve the mechanisms of distribution of work. No division of labour is the direct evidence or demonstration of asymmetry. The division of labour will be implemented socially, by the need for an increase in the productivity (greater product volume or less investment of work) or by the politics of labour load distribution.

The division of labour lays the bases for social relations, since it limits the environment of participation of various collectives in production, and because social subjects are socially recognised on the basis of their participation in specific tasks. Nevertheless, the distribution of work does not in itself involve the existence of situations of exploitation between collectives. Only when appropriation (property) is imposed and leads to the asymmetry of access to products, are situations of exploitation established among collectives. And then, the division of labour is consolidated as a mechanism for reproducing relationships of exploitation. We cannot accept that the distribution of work involves social asymmetry and exploitation, since, given the sexual nature of our species and the specialisation of the work involved in basic production, the consequence would be to accept the natural principle of exploitation among sexes. Neither can we assume that technological (craft or medical) specialisation involve asymmetric benefits, because then we would only be able to eliminate exploitation, abandoning all professionalisation of tasks.

To approach the existing relationship between division of labour and exploitation, we must avoid the confusion between specialisation and asymmetric distribution of work. Specialisation can take place in conditions of symmetry in the quantity of work carried out and in the quantity of social benefits obtained. However, asymmetry in work implies that there are collectives that appropriate the work performed by others, *i.e.* relationships of exploitation are established.

Exploitation lies in the individual appropriation of social product (appropriated surplus). Relationships of exploitation are established when a collective has the social mechanisms to guarantee a material benefit that is not in harmony with the volume of work performed, with the consequence that material benefit proceeds from the work of another collective. That asymmetry between collectives, in terms of work performed and material benefit, can be summarised in different ways (Castro *et al.* 2003b). Different forms of exploitation may be accompanied by mechanisms of domination and alienation, in order for the symmetry or asymmetry of social relationships to have a direct expression in political and ideological forms. Patriarchy and the state are political-ideological forms of the exploitation of men over women or of the extended exploitation of a social group over extensive collectives.

In comparison to situations of exploitation, societies with symmetrical social relationships are those based on reciprocity and in the inexistence of coercive control over part of a group. Symmetry does not imply equality between the different parts of society, but rather a balance between the subjects that they are made up of. Reciprocity demands the inexistence of relationships based on the imposition of hegemonic power and is only possible when there are compensations between subjects.

A historical and/or archaeological priority of every investigation is to differentiate between situations of reciprocity and situations of exploitation. In reciprocal social relationships there is no existence of exploitation and subjects participate in a similar way (based on their differences) in economic and/or political-ideological work. This reciprocity is not based on an equitable distribution of social benefits, but on a suitable compensation linked to the subjects' needs (and not on the relationship between needs and work, since there may be subjects that do not work but need to consume).

A highly adequate environment for the study of reciprocity or exploitation relationships, and their characteristics, is that of domestic groups. From here, we will tackle the questions relating to its definition and expression, and to how we can perform a social analysis that integrates the proposals formulated up to now.

Domestic groups, archaeology and the fallacy of the universality of the family
Archaeological studies of domestic groups are scarce, in part due to the difficulties for or disinterest in obtaining material evidence. On this topic, archaeological interpretations respond to socio-centric notions, presupposing universals or using selected and not archaeologically contrasted ethnographic analogies. The consequence is the abuse of a certain idea of the universal family. For this reason, we must start by clearly delimiting the concepts to be utilised.

This is not as simple as it might seem. In the first definitions of the 19th century, the family was presented as "a basic social unit comprising people linked by marital and descent ties, with a common residence" (González 1993, 322). Later, Levi-Strauss defined it as a:

> "… social group that possesses, at least, the three following characteristics: 1) Have its origin in marriage. 2) Is formed by the husband, the wife and children born from marriage, although it is conceivable that other kin find their place near the nuclear group. 3) The members of the family are united by a) legal ties; b) religious, economic or other types of rights and obligations c) a precise network of sexual rights and prohibitions, plus a variable and diversified quantity of psychological feelings such as love, affection, respect, fear, etc." (Lévi-Strauss 1956, 17).

These two examples clearly show how the "official" concept of family has been significantly transformed in anthropology. In fact, it has changed so much that given the incapacity to find a definition that fits the known cases, some authors have preferred to stop using it and prefer to talk of a *procreative nucleus* and *domestic groups*, coming to the conclusion that the family would correspond to the most generalised form of *procreative nucleus* (San Román *et al.* 2003, 3). Assuming this proposal, its use as an analytic term should be restricted to the designation of a specific category of *procreative nucleus*, which unites residence, economy and biological reproduction. The family, as a social category, is more variable over space and time. Therefore, the defence of the universality of a specific form of family, related to the links in terms of relationships and political affinity, and representative of a whole community, should be considered an absurdity that must be overcome.

Since the family norm in Christian ideologies has been the model of the nuclear family (monogamous, independent), this model is frequently projected in a universal way. Evidently, it is an essentialist position, lacking of all kinds of scientific evidence, but that we often find even in projections to the early development of the human species.

Nevertheless, it appears essential that the family notion be defined before it can be studied in archaeological cases. Thus *family*: (a) Does not have a valid, universal form for the totality of societies, and (b) in a specific social formation there does not necessarily have to be a single family model, but there can be several coexisting forms. However, we will be able to observe the existence of a predominant social normality, especially when it is destined to control situations of reproduction and patriarchal exploitation, as the control of women finds a highly adequate framework in terms of family norms.

We understand the family to be one of the expressions of parental politics, in certain historical situations. An expression of economic and political-ideological practices, that is neither univocal nor generalisable, but that is extensively represented. We would agree that the concept of the family relates to a group of people linked by marriage (whatever form this might take), engaged in the procreation and care of children, and with a common residence, the domestic unit (Castro *et al.* 2003a, 94).

Other social expressions can configure domestic groups, on the basis of the politics of kinship or another type of politics, and can also involve a common residence (the domestic unit) and/or be linked to the procreation and care of children. But we prefer to define these as other types of groups (for example, matricentric groups, single parent groups or communes, by referring to known models). Therefore, we rule out the universality of the family, as opposed to the idea that has recently been imposed, even in its legal form, considering "family" to be all domestic groups or as all affiliate (of sons and daughters) groups. We would only speak of the family when the basis of the politics of affiliation to children is marriage with a common residence, with the consequent situation of exogamy, in whatever form that may be (heterosexual or not; monogamous or not). As for the affiliation of children, we consider them to be inserted into a family when they are assigned to a marital unit, by consanguinity or by adoption.

Defining the family as a group with affiliation to children, based on marriage, and ruling out other expressions of affiliation as being families, we can study past societies, above all on the basis of archaeological studies, without the ballast of a universal idea of the family. If we prejudge the universality of the family, "familism" values will easily be projected, associated to the *bourgeoisie* family. And we can quickly fall into the trap of identifying all domestic groups or all groups with affiliation to children with a universal idea of marriage, forgetting and avoiding other possibilities of affiliation or of configuring the procreative or domestic group. It would therefore be fundamental to seek mechanisms to establish the bases of domestic groups or groups with affiliation to children, especially in archaeology. Besides, patriarchal politics are mainly aimed at the constitution of family groups by heterosexual marriage, assigning women to men by means of family links (daughters and wives). Therefore, one of the main objectives of identifying domestic forms or affiliation links where that marital attachment does not exist, especially in prehistoric studies, is avoiding any naturalisation of female dependence and detecting alternative situations to those of dominant patriarchal norms, extensively known through available historiographic sources and through ethnographic descriptions of recent societies.

Domestic units, domestic groups and family

The social places of common residence of a domestic group are domestic units. In archaeological cases, we can identify domestic units on the basis of archaeological materiality. Domestic units are those structural units where a recurrence of activities is found (Castro *et al.* 1996; 2002; 2003a). Therefore, identification of domestic units is relatively simple, because they tend to be presented by recurrence. This recurrence can be found both in the architectural configuration and in the confluence of a series of specific activities. A recurrence that is generally produced in a series of specific activities and in the way these are produced and organised in space. Obviously, it is not possible to establish *a priori* a list of activities that can be found, since each social formation has its own specific expression.

Relationships between social groups and social spaces are structural relationships (people only have access to those spaces they are allowed access to, unless social rules are broken), and we can link domestic groups to domestic units. Therefore, domestic units are associated with groups based on consanguinity, affinity and/or other political norms, whether families or not.

Domestic groups have a fundamental social objective, the production of social subjects, and specifically their maintenance. Domestic groups are basically of reduced size, facilitating practices of cares and socialisation. That turns out to be more efficient, due to the relationship of proximity that is established within these types of groups. The maintenance of children is, undoubtedly, a priority, due to the special characteristics of the human species, in which children's autonomy develops slowly. Nevertheless, care of subjects of advanced age, the sick and injured, and, in general, any man or woman finds their central place in domestic practices. The production of social subjects is closely related in all social formations with domestic groups. Consequently, we can suggest that we will find one or other form of domestic group in every human society.

Obviously, in domestic units there are also activities linked to the production of objects (obtaining them, manufacturing them, maintaining them), and above all consuming/using/enjoying production (by direct relationship with the maintenance of social subjects). Among these activities, the ones, that are recurrent in all domestic groups, are those that we will be able to consider constituent of domestic practices in a society. On the other hand, not every activity that is to be found in a domestic space will be part of domestic practices. If it is not recurrent, it will have to be linked to the extra-domestic sphere, since the extra-domestic activities of social subjects residing in a domestic space can include the presence of certain elements. Their singular presence is relevant to the aims of any kind of sociological explanation.

Another question to be considered in the definition of domestic groups is that they should not be confused with kinship groups, defined by the politics of kinship. The aggregates of relatives are defined in terms of classification systems, which politically institutionalise a series of units, a series of links and categories, determining, at the same time, guidelines of proximity-distance and of affiliation, normally linked to a family order of different degrees (for example, lineages, brothers-sisters, grandfathers-grandmothers, cousins, uncles-aunts, *etc*). The attachment of individuals, or specifically of men and women, to these classifications involves certain rights (of membership, of birth, of inheritance of certain properties) or certain relationship norms (for example, politics of definition of exogamy and, consequently, marriage politics). This all forms part of the political institutions of a society, although, undoubtedly, also productive work groups, evidently including the politics of basic production (of procreation).

Additionally, we cannot establish any equivalence between a domestic group (residence group connected with a domestic unit), and a group maintaining social subjects. Therefore, we can find forms of organising the maintenance practices of individuals (care of children, elderly, sick or, in general to the members of a specific group) that involve several domestic units. In such cases, the subjects' maintenance tasks will be governed by certain policies, based on family duties or those of other types of kinship unit, to circles of proximity (for example, cooperation between neighbours) or even on other political reasons (social aid for individuals with determined rights to citizenship, according to certain "welfare state" policies).

Evidently, the networks of social relationships and policies that determine the associated practices to the production of the maintenance of individuals, as occurs with other fields of economics, politics or ideology, transcend specific social spaces. Social places suppose the existence of certain social groups (for example, domestic groups in domestic units, or individuals recruited for certain purposes in barracks or monasteries). But political-ideological and economic networks define groups that act in spheres that affect different social places (and, of course, also different places of settlement). In archaeology, we can register the physical evidence of social places (physically structured by social work, as buildings or as some other type of physical conditioning), and we can link those social places with spatial social groups. But we should also study the social forms that configure practices that interrelate with different social places, in order to find out about social life in a specific social formation.

Finally, archaeological studies should not overlook the existence of domestic groups that occupy more than one domestic unit, in a temporary or seasonal way. That is to say, we can find displacements during certain annual periods; when a single domestic group is associated to two or more domestic units. The problems of semi-permanent and nomadic settlements are well documented in prehistoric studies. Of course, we can obtain seasonal indicators (for example, botanical species associated to certain months), in order to define the occupation rank of domestic units.

Everyday life versus domestic life

The idea and reality of everyday life is often explicitly identified with domestic life. This supposition specifically affects women. It is assumed that domestic space is a field in which women are enclosed and become refuges. We should also be able to find statements that generally identify, beyond the female collective, daily spaces with domestic spaces. But in that imaginary equation, daily routines are associated to private life, a concept that will be examined in a later section.

It has frequently been concluded that women's daily life is found in the domestic space. In that prison-refuge women develop routine tasks, connected with housework and care for the family. That idea obviously responds to a reality that we are able to track in recent historic situations. It greatly affects the wives and daughters of the bourgeoisie and the related social sectors of the middle urban class in recent centuries. There is an ideology and certain practices that convert wives and daughters into prisoners-refugees of domestic places, where their central role will be the creation (procreation) and care of the family. Perhaps, we are able to track similar situations among the dominant classes in other historic situations. We can find confinement-refuge in the harems of polygamous aristocracies in some Asian or African countries, in the treatment of the wives of Judeo-Christian-Islamic patriarchs, in the Greek *oikos* or the Roman *domus*, where wives of the civil elite were confined, or in the internment of medieval noble women in palaces, castles and convents. But that historic concept is only coherent with the slanted image of a history of hegemonic groups in present capitalism, which has its roots in those antecedents. But this is a fragmentary perspective, since it only affects specific social sectors, women of the patriarchal dominant classes, whose central function is to provide heirs to their husbands and to transmit their genealogies.

We cannot accept the equation of female daily life = domestic space as a generalisation, not even in the historic situations mentioned. In recent centuries, rural and working urban women have taken part in extra-domestic work as much as, or even more intensely than, their husbands, parents and children. The "Industrial Revolution" at the beginning of modern-day capitalism was based on the organisation of factories and assembly plants, where female work had and still has a scarcely recognised prominence. The same can be said for the women of tributary communities, servants of Judeo-Christian-Muslim patriarchs, slaves in Greece or Rome, or peasantry that maintained the European medieval nobility. Consequently, the reduction of female daily life to the domestic sphere is a present-day vision; one that is evidently bourgeoisie and that whenever directed to other historic periods only views the conditions of women with family links in the dominant classes.

Therefore, we must avoid ambiguity in the conceptualisation of daily life. A clear definition must be established. We consider daily life to be the place where the times of social subjects recur. Daily life is the time when social practices are repetitively experienced, when activities are reiterated at standardised times, in accordance with cycles, calendars or clocks. It is the time for the economic and/or political-ideological recurrence of the practices of social subjects. Each man, and each woman, participates in a recurrent way, and probably in a routine way, in different activities, whether in domestic environments and/or extra-domestic environments. We would be wrong to confuse recurrence in space, in the social place of domestic life, with recurrence in time. In the present, daily recurrence affects domestic environments, working environments and the environments of the consumption of goods. Customs, habits, undoubtedly the most conservative norms, are imposed in the routine experiences of social subjects. A social formation, a historic situation, has a characteristic material description of the configuration of the daily life of the collective that forms it. Criticism of daily life has already been made, since it is in that recurrent reality of men and women where we find the form of the prominent social and historical changes (Debord 1961; Lefebvre 1962; Trotsky 2005 [1923]). Daily life is the concretion of material conditions and political-ideological impositions on social subjects; its continuity or transformation appears more relevant than persistence-change in other institutional or technical environments.

In archaeology, before tackling the reality of daily life in a specific situation social subjects need to be situated in the places where they act. In order to do this, we should avoid universal and ahistorical essentialisms, which identify *a priori* certain subjects and certain spaces, just as we have seen with the domestic = daily life equation. There is no "natural" place for the daily life of any social subject.

Privacy of domestic spaces and its misunderstandings

In certain social formulations, domestic units are assimilated with private spaces. Private and public are opposed, an opposition that is the equivalent to that between domestic and extra-domestic. But we believe that this assimilation results from two misunderstandings: locating the space of freedom of the individual in a domestic space and maintaining the old patriarchal notion of domestic space as a place of "patrimony" (inheritance) and "matrimony" (marriage).

In the first misunderstanding, the idea of privacy is identified with intimacy. Each individual has his own space (property). Private property (appropriation) justifies an omnipotent legalised right. Private property, as a supreme value of individual liberty, would be expressed in the space itself, the private space, recognised in the domestic unit. At present, privatisation is centred on the individual. The individualisation of women and men, as subjects-consumers, privatises the individual. Nevertheless, this notion of private-intimate-own is only ideological, for it reinforces the self-recognition of individuals as independent entities, as subjects of a liberty that is only permitted in private and in the market. However, political-ideological constraints infiltrate with efficacy into domestic units. Domestic places are spaces for religion, for moral norms or for the mass media; they justify the regulation of extra-domestic institutions, aimed at the socialisation of children, and are the bulwarks of duties of kinship and, evidently, cover ways of organising domestic labour (by agreement, by consensus, by slavery).

In opposition, "public" spaces are identified with those places where the ideology of the free individual-consumer believes they find bonds with privacy-intimacy. Because of this, the ideological notion of "public" spaces applies to all those common extra-domestic spaces, even if they are private property. The equivalence between extra-domestic and "public" leads us to identify all those places of specialised work as "public", where tasks are submitted to the capitalist market (factories, stores, offices). Perhaps that is why in recent years the "public" space par excellence (as opposed to "private" – domestic) has become the Mall, the Shopping Centre, paradoxically a private-appropriate space, the property of multinationals and franchises. The notion of "non-place" (Augé 1992), relating to spaces of anonymity, lacking an identity reference, relational norms or historic meanings, has recently replaced the idea of "public", faced with the banalisation and commercialisation of "leisure". Nevertheless, whatever the sense might be behind "private-public" opposition, we find actualism, typical of spaces produced by capitalism, that avoids the true private ownership of social places and which we would find hard to apply to social formations where capital is not dominant.

In the second misunderstanding, the notion of privacy, linked to domestic space, recalls the sense of patriarchal private ownership. That is the ideological, political and economic appropriation that the patriarchy (the patriarch) performs on his house and family, in the Roman sense of the term: the patriarch's ownership his "patrimony", "matrimony", "offspring" and servants. In this perspective, there is no doubting the identification between privacy and the patriarchal ownership. And here, the domestic place is opposed to "public", since it is a space outside the *Res Publica*, where external laws do not rule, but rather the law of the father. Ideology and Law have accepted that patriarchal power, exercised over the wife or wives, sons and daughters and servants, is similar to that which the owner has over any private property, absolute power. Only recently the privacy of domestic spaces has been questioned, in that the state has been involved in behaviours "in intimacy" as a result of patriarchal use of violence against women and children.

In dealing with these misunderstandings, we believe it is pertinent to conclude that domestic units should not be assimilated to private spaces in a mechanical, presentist and/or patriarchal way. If seeking places that are privately appropriated, we will be able to find them inside and outside of domestic units. And as for domestic units, the recognition of domestic groups as collectives gives them a community nature, although we can find the politics of servants or patriarchy in them. If the idea of "public" is linked to accessibility for all the members of a community, we should make sure that this really is so before utilising the term as an adjective. In conclusion, we prefer to avoid the use of the duality "private *versus* public" until we know the nature of the control-exploitation or symmetry-reciprocity relationships in each social space.

The Son Ferragut Horizon, the Alfa Building and his context (8th–6th centuries BC)

A primary case, that illustrates the study of prehistoric domestic units in western Mediterranean communities, is the analysis of the Alpha Building. This is a completed analysis, so we can offer the evidence and resultant hypothesis.

The study of the Alpha Building of Puig Morter in Son Ferragut (Sineu, Mallorca, Balearic Islands, Spain) has concluded that this was a housing model that had not previously been considered as such in the *Recent Prehistory* of Mallorca. The analysis of the material remains from this archaeological site and from other contemporaneous contexts have led to the definition of a historical period that we have called the *Son Ferragut Horizon*, for which we aim to examine the social relationships that existed at the time (Castro *et al.* 2003a).

In the settlement of Puig Morter, two other constructions of similar characteristics and size to the Alpha Building have been identified (the Beta and Kappa Buildings) as well as a *Talaiot* with a square plan (Gamma). All these buildings seem to have constituted the urban complex of the community that built and used the Alpha Building. Furthermore, there are various sections of a walled enclosure, with a watchtower at the

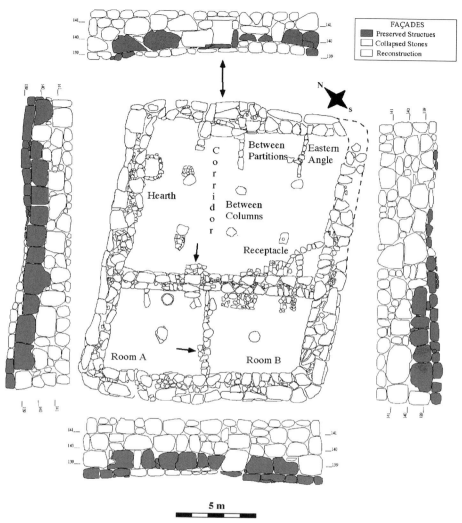

Figure 6.1. Alfa Building, Puig Morter, Son Ferragut (from Castro et al. 2003a).

highest sector (Phi Building), and other remains of structures that were not necessarily synchronic with the Alpha Building.

The Alpha Building (Fig. 6.1) was constructed with double-faced stonewalls with rubble infill. The outer bond features orthostats in a horizontal row on a footing. The plan is shaped like a parallelogram with an area of 296 m². It constitutes an architectural unit, formed by a series of structured spaces, in which two groupings can be distinguished, separated by a partition wall. The first corresponds to a portico-courtyard, and the second to two interior rooms, A and B. The courtyard is delimited by six wooden columns on stone bases and was surrounded by a series of covered spaces, separated either by the columns or by partition (small stone walls), protruding from the perimeter wall. These areas are as follows: The Hearth Space, the Corridor, the Area Between the Partitions, the Area in the Eastern Angle, the Area Between the Columns and the Receptacle Area. The two interior rooms, divided by a small stonewall, probably had a flat roof held up by three polylithic columns. The building was accessed from outside via a doorway with a monolithic threshold, and three steps that lead down to the courtyard. From the courtyard, Room A was entered through another doorway with a downward staircase. A door in the separating wall connects Rooms A and B.

Six radiocarbon analyses of the Alpha Building, and the synchronisation of the results with data from other sites enabled us to locate the Son Ferragut Horizon in the interval between 750/700 and 525/475 cal BC. During this phase, there are clear indications of the coexistence of a number of different communities with living units of markedly different architectural characteristics. Freestanding units like the Alpha Building from Puig Morter coexisted with smaller-sized interconnected housing, and *Talaiots*, like those in settlements such as the nearby Son Fornés. This type of domestic unit is the best known in Mallorcan settlements, and configures aggregates that incorporate tower-like buildings (*Talaiots*). However, the Alpha Building model, freestanding and with a courtyard, is not unknown, since Room 10 in Ses Païsses (Artà) corresponds to a domestic unit of similar characteristics.

The Alpha Building is the only one to have been excavated in the settlement of Puig Morter, and a comparison had to be made with the only contemporary settlement with a high quality archaeological record, the nucleus of Son Fornés (Gasull *et al.* 1984a; 1984b). The aim of the comparison was to make an exact establishment of whether we are dealing with a domestic unit with recurrent social practices (the criterion for the identification of domestic units). By comparing the activities detected here with those in the housing units in the settlement of Son Fornés we can confirm that the Alpha Building was a domestic unit. A series of recurrences can be indicated which support the identification of these social spaces as domestic units: butchering of sheep and goats; culinary preparation of sheep, goats and cattle; grinding of cereals; processing of dairy products; cooking of foods; supply and storage of water; supply of fuel; cleaning; storage for everyday and long term use; pottery manufacture; consumption of sheep, goats and cattle; and, finally, sleeping. Nevertheless, the differences in the sizes of the domestic units suggests that the Alpha Building, at almost 300 m², must have housed a domestic group of more than three times the size of the domestic groups in Son Fornés. In this sense, we have used a range of criteria to estimate the size of the Alpha Building group, which seems to have been around 20 to 26 individuals, while in the houses in Son Fornés there were six to nine. These differences between domestic groups in two contemporary communities, only 10 km apart, imply a certain social and political heterogeneity, through which we are now beginning to get an idea of Mallorcan prehistory.

Social activities and the domestic character of the Alpha Building

The analysis of the social materiality of the Alpha Building in Puig Morter enabled us to detect the different activities that took place in this living unit, to locate them in the different parts of the building, and to establish the networks of social practices within the framework of the domestic group that occupied this social space. Firstly, the very construction of the Alpha Building implied a high volume of productive activity, similar to that involved in the building of the largest tower-formed buildings known in Mallorca, *Talaiot 1* from Son Fornés.

The domestic group's livestock production was limited to sheep and goats, bred for meat and dairy products. These were slaughtered, butchered and cooked in the Hearth Area, and spaces around the Corridor. It can be concluded that beef, as well as limited quantities of pork, arrived readily prepared for cooking and eating. The final processing took place in the Hearth Area and the Corridor. The high level of fragmentation of the bone remains indicates an intensive reduction of the portions of meat cooked, judging by the dense concentration of splinters in the Hearth Area.

The existence of *Triticum aestivum* starch on a slab in the Area between the Partitions indicates the availability of cereals. These were used for baking flat bread at a low heat and on slabs, which were taken to the place of consumption, where they have been found. Furthermore, the presence in the Hearth Area of a flint sickle tooth with marks of usage can be related to the maintenance of sickles used for cereal harvesting. Study of the macrolithic equipment suggests that a millstone from the Hearth Area and a mortar from the Receptacle Area could have been related to the making of flour.

Ceramic production in the Alpha Building was mainly domestic. This is suggested by indirect evidence of the presence of raw materials: the bringing of cave clays to the building can be deduced from the presence of stalactites. Two tendencies have been detected in the pottery production in the Alpha Building, implying the existence of two differentiated techniques in the elaboration and firing of vessels. The general indication is that the standardisation of the products was limited, as they are highly heterogeneous in their morphological variety, as well as in their technical characteristics, which suggests the inexistence of any overwhelming specialisation of the work, which is typical of domestic production.

On the basis of the study of faunal remains, three principal areas of alimentary consumption have been identified, two of sheep and goats and the third of cattle. The Hearth Area and the Area Between the Partitions constitute the spaces for everyday consumption of sheep and goat meat. This situation implies the existence of two groups within the domestic unit, who met regularly for meals. The first ate in the Hearth Area, the space where the majority of the productive activities were concentrated, implying that this group included those people who worked in those activities. In contrast, the second group met in the Area Between the Partitions, in which there are no indications of work activities, and where the only elements that were not associated with alimentary consumption are singular objects (not associated with household production tasks), implying that this group was separated from the production registered in the portico-courtyard of the Alpha Building.

The communal consumption of beef took place in the central part of the courtyard, around the Area Between the Columns. The whole domestic group probably met to eat beef. Room B, the most interior space of the Alpha Building only presents remains of sporadic food consumption. It can therefore be suggested that this was a specialised sleeping area. The same can be said of Room A, where there were also storage vessels. It is important to highlight the identification of two stone slingshot balls, one of which was in the Area Between the Partitions, which indicate the existence of specialised war weaponry. Furthermore, other singular objects were found in this area, a fragment of copper rod, and a hemispherical bowl with perforations along the rim and a shell pendent. It must be stressed that these objects were found in an area where no work processes took place and where, apparently, only consumption occurred.

In terms of alimentary consumption equipment, we have evidence of three stone slabs found, respectively, in the Area Between the Partitions, the Receptacle Area and Room B. Phytholith analyses performed on them indicate, as has already been noted, the presence of *Triticum aestivum* starch resulting from flour processing. We can also relate the presence of pottery containers to production practices. These could have been used as tableware (cups, dishes and pots) in the Hearth Area, Between the Partitions and next to the Receptacle Area.

In conclusion, there is evidence of a clear dichotomy between spaces with regard to the functions of the activities carried out, and the places where consumption occurred. It is clear that the Hearth Area and the Corridor are very similar, being the places where the majority of the working activities were carried out. The Receptacle Area and Room A also appear to have been related, due to the storage activities that characterised them. At the other extreme of the social use of the space, there is a clear relationship between Room B and the Area Between the Partitions, due to their exceptional status as places separated from any type of work involving the production of objects. Foodstuffs were consumed in these places, and specific items were concentrated, as well as being a place where individuals slept.

Domestic groups, reciprocity and exploitation

The archaeological record from the *Son Ferragut Horizon* shows the coexistence of different organisational forms of domestic groups of differing sizes. Although the documentation of different activities has been extended, we are not in a position to close the debate about the nature of the social relationships within and between the different Mallorcan communities at this phase. Nevertheless, we feel that various hypotheses can be considered. These hypotheses all match the available empirical evidence, taking domestic groups into account, as well as communities and internal social relations, and make it possible to consider the conditions for the reproduction of social life.

Hypothesis a: Monogamous family communities

This hypothesis presupposes an extended family that is monogamous and dependent, in households like Son Ferragut, in which three generations lived together, with an average of four children per marriage, in accordance with a ratio that fits the estimates of a nuclear family unit in a household like Son Fornés. The sexuation of the workforce in an extended family based on monogamous marriage provides a sexual composition comparable to that of an independent monogamous family, in such a way that the presence of a man and a woman in each matrimonial union gives rise to a similar situation to that of a nuclear family with sexual division of labour. Both share the same concept of socialisation and labour, which facilitates exogamy between groups. But differences between communities with extended families and those of nuclear families have implications on the potential for organising the workforce, which is larger in extended families. In this situation, the division of the domestic group detected in the Alpha Building can be explained in terms of division by sex, with women and children linked to labour and consumption in the Hearth Area, and men associated with the Area Between the Partitions, war and activities carried out outside the dwelling area. If the work done by males did not compensate for the labour carried out in the domestic space, this would be a situation of internal exploitation within the domestic groups, to the benefit of the male collectives.

Hypothesis b: Polygynous domestic groups

According to this hypothesis, the domestic unit in the Alpha Building involved a family made up of a man and at least three or four women with their children. The existence of independent polygynous families establishes labour conditions that benefited men. The demands of polygamy itself imply that the men did not all have access to several women, such that, unless there were very high male mortality rates for some reason, conditions were established whereby some men, through marriage, benefited from female labour to a greater extent than others, who were stuck in a situation of monogamy. This could be the case for domestic units like Son Fornés, where records do not suggest the existence of any polygynous situation, given the small size of the domestic cells. Only if the head of the family lived outside of the domestic unit could a similar situation to that of Son Ferragut be explained. In the internal context of the Alpha Building, the two groups identified would result from a sexual division of labour, consumption and sleeping, with specific areas for men (father and sons), separated from the productive labour within the living unit (Fig. 6.2).

Hypothesis c: Family servitude

The Alpha Building could also represent a domestic unit made up of an independent monogamous family unit and the individuals serving them. According to this hypothesis, the division of labour, consumption and rest in the differentiated spaces could be explained on the basis of the configuration of social classes. The components

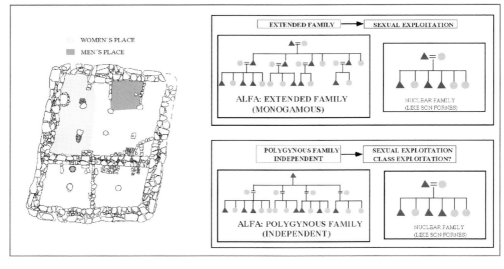

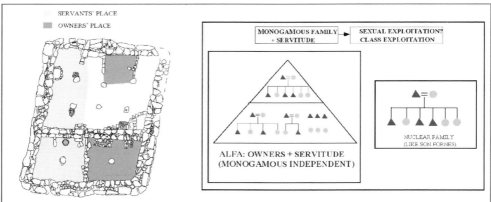

Figure 6.2. Social hypotheses for domestic group in Alfa Building (from Castro et al 2003a).

of a property-owning family would occupy the Partitions Area and Room B, while the dependent men and women would live in the Hearth Area and in Room A. The resulting social panorama would imply that in the *Son Ferragut Horizon* there was a dominant social class which lived in communities such as Puig Morter, and which might have taken on, for their own advantage, the labour of dependent sectors, settled in other communities, such as Son Fornés. This social model does not exclude, but rather reinforces, the probable exploitation of women.

As we have suggested in each of the three possible compositions of the domestic group that lived in the Alpha Building, the explanation that daily consumption managed by the domestic group itself was fragmented implies that the group itself is also fragmented. That is to say that there was a situation of social division within the group itself, which could imply a level of social exploitation. This segmentation of the domestic group could imply two situations: (a) Men and women from the Alpha Building assembled to eat and work in different spaces. If the domestic group was formed by 16–20 individuals, the male sector would have been made up of four–six individuals, with their space in the Area Between the Partitions, and the rest would have been made up of women and children of different ages, who would have worked and eaten in the Hearth Area; or (b) the family owners of the Alpha Building and dependent individuals would have occupied the differentiated spaces at daily meal times. The first group would have been located in the Partitions Area, while the second would have resided in the usual workspaces. This second group of dependent subjects could have been made up of relatives without property rights, servants or slaves.

In both hypotheses the consumption of beef would have represented a regrouping of the whole domestic unit, in the framework of certain practices, which would have ideologically reinforced the domestic group as unit. If we could prove the first hypothesis, in which men and women ate together, we could suggest the existence of social distance between the female and young collective and men, who benefited from the productive labour performed by women and children, with no form of material compensation. However, if we suppose that the men carried out tasks outside the Alpha Building and were perhaps involved in warlike activities and political management, we would need to consider the existence of relative exploitation (more hours of work by one sector than the other). This is difficult to determine accurately, especially as we have no information regarding asymmetries of consumption. Only in the case of the independent polygynous family it is possible to confirm sexual exploitation due to the inherent political composition of polygamy, and also of class, given that a marriage with several wives responds to a social ideal, which only a few men in the group can achieve. If we could prove the second possibility, this would imply class exploitation by a monogamous family that owns the Alpha Building of servants who work for them, and social classes on the intercommunity level.

A fourth hypothesis, referring to the occupation of the Alpha Building by a matricentric group, was proposed in previous publications (Castro *et al.* 2003). Nevertheless, the revision of the production conditions now enables us to rule out this hypothesis. Therefore, we can argue that the heterogeneousness of the tendencies of pottery production, verified by the ceramic products, as well as the evidence that this work was performed in the domestic group, leads us to suggest that external contributions to the group were made by certain men and/or women, probably through marriage. The learning of different techniques in other domestic groups would explain such technological changeability, but would be incompatible with matricentric units, where there was no exogamy or marriage.

South-east Iberia in Millares Horizons (*c.* 3200–2300 cal BC)

The second case study is based on the gathering of available evidence of a certain historic situation, the *Millares Horizons*. We offer the hypothesis made possible by the information available, in this case from bibliography, since we have not yet performed a first hand analysis of domestic archaeological contexts (Castro *et al.* 1998; Castro and Escoriza 2004). The reality here is a frequent one in Mediterranean archaeological research. The extensive documentation of detailed chronological stratigraphic registers that was so common to excavation methodologies and practices for a long time, and the generalisation and monopoly of preventive excavations (the result of extensive and intensive building speculation) that were never published. This situation has produced an almost total misrecognition of the internal organisation of architectonic spaces, especially with reference to Domestic Units. The case of *Millares Horizons* is no exception in this general panorama, and is in fact something of a paradigm of this. Despite the large number of excavations, references for the internal distribution of the materials and of the structural descriptions of these spaces are highly scarce, almost inexistent (exceptionally we can use the distributions of products and sub-products from Los Millares "Fortín 1": Molina *et al.* 1986; Ramos *et al.* 1991).

Nevertheless, with the evidence we do have, we can search the recurrences that enable us to identify and analyse the domestic units in the *Millares Horizons*, so as to attempt to build sociological hypotheses about the organisation of the domestic groups. Based on the long list of known settlements of the *Millares Horizons*, since the excavations of Siret at the end of the 19th century (Leisner and Leisner 1943), we have detected a series of guidelines that signify the starting point for our proposals.

Before revisiting the structural characteristics of the buildings, we can make a brief review of the elements that make it possible to visualise social activities in the settlements, which enable us to identify the domestic groups on the basis of their recurrence and their relation to the production of social life (Castro *et al.* 1998; Castro and Escoriza 2004). Sadly, this review is very brief. We can only indicate the presence of hearths, probably used for lighting, cooking and/or heating in buildings whose recurrent architecture may suggest that they were domestic units. Something absolutely unique is the location of storage pits in these spaces, although these are highly frequent in open settlements, and in exterior spaces. Perhaps some cases, in which conservation was possible, where baskets of esparto have been documented, and also some ceramic vessels with toasted cereal, respond to practices of domestic storage, but for now there is a lack of precision in terms of their recurrence in all units. Continuing with work on processing cereals, another important activity known to exist in possible domestic units was grinding, and here it is noted that stone-mills were found individually, inside the curve plant buildings, next to the hearths, in Los Millares, which may constitute a recurrent activity in domestic practices. Therefore, for now, only three activities (cooking, storage and grinding) could be proposed as recurrent social practices in the domestic groups of the *Millares Horizons*. Other economic activities (flint work, pottery,

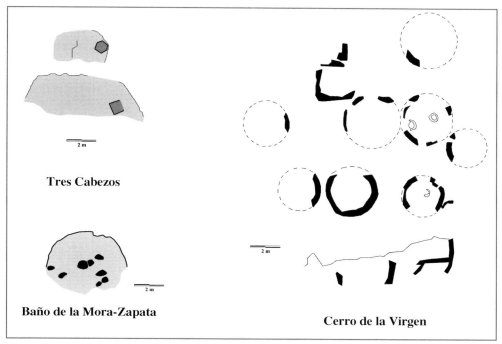

Figure 6.3. Freestanding Buildings. "Pit huts" and oval stonewalled buildings. South East Iberia (from Castro and Escoriza 2004).

work with bones, weaving, metallurgy), although mentioned in association to units of a possible domestic nature, seem to represent exceptional activities, and not activities in the sphere of domestic practices.

An analysis of the architectural characteristics starts with emphasising the differences between the construction of architectonic structures, between fortified villages and open villages, so as to identify recurrences that make it possible to recognise domestic units. On the one hand, fortified villages tend to represent long-time occupations, with different phases implying changes in the architectonic structures. At the same time, it is not unusual for these settlements to appear, during early occupation, without fortifications and ramparts, although they could have defensive ditches. Meanwhile, open villages appear to have been occupied for less time and have a different architectonic technology to fortified ones.

We can indicate three types of architectural units, which offer a repetition of models and forms, and that suggest that they were domestic units (Castro and Escoriza 2004). First, there are buildings with curved walls, which present some variability with regard to the construction techniques used in the walls (stone, mud bricks). Second, we have "pit huts", semi-excavated units on the ground with walls made of perishable materials, mainly located on open sites and pertaining to the first phase of settlements that would be fortified later (Fig. 6.3). Finally, there are buildings with adjoining rooms with dividing walls, made of stone, and having angular forms. The first two models of possible domestic units are freestanding buildings without compartmentalisation, while the third model implies a different organisation in terms of the politics of the domestic groups and the organisation of the space, given that they were compartmentalised units. The bibliography pays little attention to this latter model, despite its special architectural nature.

Partial conclusions can be made. There was major heterogeneity in the construction methods employed in the different settlements. The same variability is found in the spatial distribution of architectonic units. There are also diachronic transformations in the building techniques of the same settlement, such as the settlement of Los Millares (Arribas *et al.* 1987; Molina and Cámara 2005) or Terrera Ventura (Gusi and Olaria 1991). This evidence suggests the existence of synchronic unlike domestic groups, or modifications in the conception of domestic units over time

The "pit hut" type of possible domestic unit can be described as having hut floors, which were partially dug into the ground. There are some documented cases of depths of more than one metre, which meant the need for ramps or stairways. These huts were located in open settlements where storage pits were also found. In order to identify and separate these from storage pits, they should measure about 3 m, since these are considered to be the minimum dimensions for habitable space. The roof of these structures was a cover made of plant materials that were held up by wooden posts. Post-holes are another way of distinguishing "pit huts" from storage pits. There is certain variability in the dimensions of "pit huts", about 4–5 m (La Torreta de Elda, Campico de Lébor, El Capitán, Baño de la Mora) (Val Caturla 1948; Ayala 1985; Jover *et al.* 2000–01; Siret 2001; Castro and Escoriza, 2004). We can normally find "pit huts" at the early stages of occupation of fortified settlements, before the construction of ramparts. But coexistence with other models is suggested by chronometric dates.

Buildings with curved walls are present in almost all settlements (Fig. 6.4). They were constructed using stone base-board, with vegetal frames covered with clay, such as, for example, Los Millares (Arribas *et al.* 1987; Ramos 2004; Molina and Camara 2005), Almizaraque (Delibes *et al.* 1986) and Cabezo del Plomo (Muñoz 1986), or with mud bricks in Cerro de la Virgen (Kalb 1969; Schüle 1986). In some cases, these buildings seem to only have walls of clay, propped up by wooden posts (Terrera Ventura I, Almizaraque) (Gusi and Olaria 1991; Delibes *et al.* 1986). Related to this model is the fact that some of these buildings were incorporated into defensive walls, in fortified enclosures, or linked by walls that delimited the interior spaces of some settlements (Los Millares, El Malagón, Cabezo del Plomo: Muñoz 1986; De La Torre and Sáez 1986; Arribas *et al.* 1987; Moreno 1994; Ramos 2004). When they were incorporated into defensive walls, the former houses become bastions, probably maintaining their domestic use. In fact, some bastions, built at same time as the defensive walls, also seem to have been used as dwellings, as suggested by the information that has shed more light on this topic (for example in Los Millares "Fortín 1") (Molina *et al.* 1986).

Figure 6.4. Enclosures with Oval Buildings. South East Iberia (from Castro and Escoriza 2004).

The dimensions of these buildings suggest a rank of greater dimensions than the "pit huts", since their width surpasses 7 m.

Finally, the most limited building typology is the type of angular adjoining rooms, with dividing stonewalls (Fig. 6.5). There are fewer of these buildings, in comparison with other models dealt with here. They are located in Parazuelos (Siret and Siret 1890), Terrera Ventura (Gusi and Olaria 1991) and in the settlement of Los Millares (Arribas *et al.* 1987). In the case of Los Millares, we observed trapezoidal buildings with dividing walls, as well as some unique buildings (Castro and Escoriza 2004), such as the rectangular building in enclosure 3 of Los Millares, which have a difficult chronological adscription, or Building Y, a metallurgical workroom in Los Millares

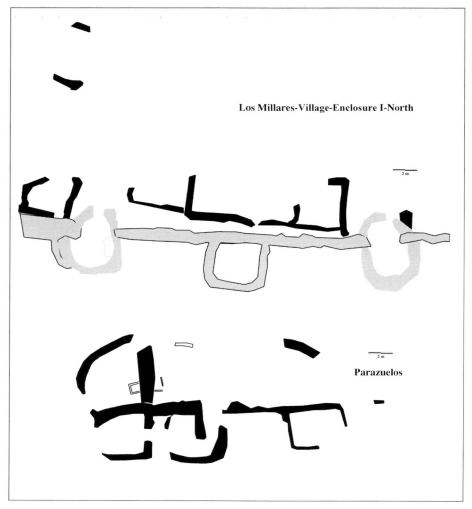

Los Millares-Village-Enclosure I-North

Parazuelos

Figure 6.5. Angular adjoining rooms. South East Iberia (from Castro and Escoriza 2004).

(Arribas *et al.* 1987), the Dwelling C of Campos (Siret and Siret 1890), or the Building A–B in Terrera Ventura (Gusi and Olaria 1991).

From the revision of the different architectonic forms we find in *Millares Horizons*, we can proceed to some general conclusions. Firstly, we documented the existence of a duality of settlements with unlike architectonical forms. There is also the opposition between architecture with stone base-board, which tends to last longer and require less maintenance, although also implying a greater initial investment of labour; and architecture where only clay, vegetables and wood are used, for which materials are easier to access but which do not represent stable edifications. The former are located in bigger, long-term settlements and in all fortified settlements. The latter are present in open settlements or in the first phases of settlements that later adopt stone architecture. Opposition between communities, in a sense that can be related to urban development (urban settlements *versus* rural settlements), is a hypothesis that has already been proposed (Castro *et al.* 2003c).

Secondly, we have the binomial between freestanding buildings, including "pit huts", and buildings with rectangular adjoining rooms with dividing walls. The former suggest the absence of a unitary plan for the domestic groups. We could describe this as independent activity of domestic groups. Only a few cases of enclosures with several huts (Cabezo del Plomo, El Malagón), such as the inclusion of some huts in ramparts of defensive enclosures (Los Millares), can indicate any coordinated politics in the construction of domestic units. For the other form, we must observe that there is a different concept of architecture, one that is conceived as units that enclose several social spaces.

For the moment, this duality can be explained in chronological order, with the type of units with several angular rooms being most recent, but we are still lacking empirical evidence, although in the settlement of Los Millares the architectural stratigraphy indicates that these were the last buildings. If this hypothesis is correct, it may suggest modification in the organisation of politics of the domestic groups, aimed at larger units of greater dimensions, probably new kinship politics, which is surely what is indicated by the domestic enclosures as El Malagón or Cabezo del Plomo also indicate. It is indispensable, therefore necessary to advance proceed by to clarifying the social configuration of the domestic groups and on the base of what is on which groups were added, and led to lead to more extensive units (polygamy or domestic servants could be a hypothesis to take in worth considering). When we know have evidences of the activities carried outperformed in domestic spaces, and with some following as yet inexistent palaeo-anthropological study, still inexistent, of the tombs of multiple burial sites (megalithic graves, *tholoi*), we will be able to advance in the proceed by definition of these hypotheses.

References

Arribas, A., Molina, F., Carrión, F., Contreras, F., Martínez, G., Ramos, A., Sáez, L., De La Torre, F., Blanco, I. and Martínez, J. (1987) Informe preliminar de los resultados obtenidos durante la VI campaña de excavaciones en el poblado de Los Millares (Santa Fe de Mondújar, Almería). In *Anuario Arqueológico de Andalucía 1985*, 245–262. Sevilla, II, Junta de Andalucía.

Augé, M. (1992) *Non-Lieux, Introduction à une Anthropologie de la Surmodernitè*. Paris, Éditions du Seuil.

Ayala, M. M. (1985) Aportación al estudio de los Ídolos Calcolíticos de Murcia. *Anales de Prehistoria y Arqueología* 1, 23–32.

Castro Martínez, P. V. and Escoriza Mateu, T. (2004) Los espacios sociales de las comunidades, de los Lugares a los Territorios. In P. V. Castro Martínez, T. Escoriza Mateu and E. Sanahuja-

Yll (eds) *Soportes Simbólicos, Prácticas Sociales y Redes de Relación. Los "Ídolos Calcolíticos" y los Nexos entre las Comunidades del Sudeste Ibérico, c. 3200–2300 cal ANE*, 394–542. Alicante, Instituto Alicantino de Cultura Juan Gil-Albert.

Castro Martínez, P. V., Escoriza Mateu, T. and Sanahuja-Yll, E. (2003a) *Mujeres y Hombres en Espacios Domésticos: Trabajo y Vida Social en la Prehistoria de Mallorca (c. 700–500 cal ANE): el Edificio Alfa del Puig Morter de Son Ferragut (Sineu, Mallorca)*. Oxford, Archaeopress, British Archaeological Report S1162.

Castro Martínez, P. V., Escoriza Mateu, T. and Sanahuja-Yll, E. (2003b) Trabajo, reprocidad y explotación, prácticas sociales, sujetos sexuados y condiciones materiales. In X. Terradas, J. L. Molina and C. Larrea (eds) *El Recurso a la Reciprocidad, Cultura & Política, IX Congrès d'Antropologia,* CD-ROM. Barcelona, Institut Català d'Antropologia.

Castro Martinez, P. V., Escoriza Mateu, T., Oltra Puigdomenech, J., Otero Vidal, M. and Sanahuja-Yll, E. (2003c) ¿Qué es una ciudad? Aportaciones para su Definición desde la Prehistoria. *Geocrítica-Scripta Nova, Revista Electrónica de Geografía y Ciencias Sociales*, VII, 146(10), http://www.ub.es/geocrit/sn/sn146(010).htm

Castro Martínez, P. V., Escoriza Mateu, T. and Sanahuja-Yll, E. (2002) Trabajo y espacios sociales en el ámbito doméstico. *Scripta Nova, Revista Electrónica de Geografía y Ciencias Sociales* VI, 119 (10), www.ub.es/geocrit/sn/sn119-10.htm

Castro Martínez, P. V., Gili, S., Lull, V., Micó, R., Rihuete, C., Risch, R. and Sanahuja-Yll, E. (1998) Teoría de la producción de la vida social: mecanismos de explotación en el sudeste Ibérico. *Boletín de Antropología Americana* 33, 25–77.

Castro Martínez, P. V., Chapman, R. W., Gili, S., Lull, V., Micó, R., Rihuete, C., Risch, R. and Sanahuja-Yll, E. (1996) Teoría de las prácticas sociales. *Complutum-Extra* 6, 35–48.

De La Torre, F. and Saez, L. (1986) Nuevas excavaciones en el Yacimiento de la Edad del Cobre de "El Malagón". In *Homenaje a Luis Siret (1934–1984)*, 221–226. Sevilla, Junta de Andalucía.

Debord, G. (1961) Perspectives de modifications conscientes de la vie Quotidienne. *Internationale Situationnist* 6, 20–27.

Delibes, G., Fernández-Miranda, M., Fernández-Posse, M. D. and Martín, C. (1986) El Poblado de Almizaraque. In *Homenaje a Luis Siret (1934–1984)*, 167–177. Sevilla, Junta de Andalucía.

Gasull, P., Lull, V. and Sanahuja-Yll, E. (1984a) *Son Fornés I: La Fase Talayótica, Ensayo de Reconstrucción Socio-económica de una Comunidad Prehistórica de la Isla de Mallorca*. Oxford, British Archaeological Reports S209.

Gasull, P., Lull, V. and Sanahuja-Yll, E. (1984b) La Habitación nº 5 de Son Fornés (Montuiri, Mallorca): Modelo de una Vivienda Talayótica. In W. Waldren, R. Chapman, J. Lewthwaite and R. Kennard (eds) *Early Settlement in the Western Mediterranean Islands and the Peripheral Areas, The Deya Conference of Prehistory*, 1259–1297. Oxford, British Archaeological Reports S229.

González, A. (1993) Familia. In A. Aguirre (ed.) *Diccionario Temático de Antropología*, 322–328. Barcelona, Amarcombo.

Gusi, F. and Olaria, C. (1991) *El Poblado Neoeneolítico de Terrera Ventura (Tabernas, Almería)*. Madrid, Ministerio de Cultura.

Jover, F. J., Soler García, M. D., Esquembre, M. A. and Poveda, A. M. (2000–01) La Torreta-El Monastil (Elda, Alicante): un nuevo asentamiento Calcolítico en la Cuenca del río Vinalopó. *Lucentum* XIX–XX, http://Publicaciones.ua.es/LibrosPDF/0213-2338/02.pdf

Kalb, P. (1969) El Poblado del Cerro de la Virgen de Orce (Granada). In *X Congreso Nacional de Arqueología, Mahón, 1967*, 216–225. Zaragoza, Secretaría General de los Congresos Arqueológicos Nacionales.

Lefebvre, H. (1962) *Critique de la vie Quotidienne*. Paris, Arché Editeur, "Le Sens de la Marche".

Leisner, G. and Leisner, V. (1943) *Die Megalithgräber der Iberischen Halbinsel, Der Suden*. Berlín, Madrider Forschungen.

Lévi-Strauss, C. (1956), The family. In H. L. Shapiro (ed.) *Man, Culture and Society*, 333–357. New York, Oxford University Press.

Marx, K. (1857–58) *Grundrisse der Kritik der Politischen Ökonomie*. London, Rohentwurf.

Molina, F. and Cámara, J. A. (2005) *Guía del Yacimiento Arqueológico Los Millares*. Sevilla, Junta de Andalucía.

Molina, F., Contreras, F., Ramos, A., Mérida, V., Ortiz, F. and Ruiz Sánchez, V. (1986) Programa de recuperación del registro arqueológico del Fortín 1 de Los Millares, análisis preliminar de la organización del espacio. *Arqueología Espacial* 8, 175–201.

Moreno, A. (1994) *El Malagón, Un Asentamiento de la Edad del Cobre en el Altiplano de Cúllar-Chirivel*. Granada, Universidad de Granada.

Muñoz, A. M. (1986) El Eneolítico en el Sureste. In *Historia de Cartagena*, t.1, 143–162. Murcia, Mediterráneo.

Ramos, A. (2004) La evolución urbanística del asentamiento Millarense, un texto de historia social y política en la cultura tribal. In *Simposios de Prehistoria Cueva de Nerja. II. La Problemática del Neolítico en Andalucía. III. Las Primeras Sociedades Metalúrgicas en Andalucía*, 404–424. Málaga, Fundación Cueva de Nerja.

Ramos, A., Martínez, G., Ríos, G. and Afonso, J. A. (1991) *Flint Production and Exchange in the Iberian Southeast, III Millennium BC*. Granada, Universidad de Granada.

San Román, T., González, A. and Grau, J. (2003) *Las Relaciones de Parentesco*, Bellaterra, Universitat Autònoma de Barcelona.

Schüle, W. (1986) El Cerro de la Virgen de la Cabeza, Orce-Granada, consideraciones sobre su marco ecológico y cultural. In *Homenaje a Luis Siret (1934–1984)*, 208–220. Sevilla, Junta de Andalucía.

Siret, L. (2001) *España Prehistórica*. Granada, Ed. Arráez-Junta de Andalucía.

Siret, H. and Siret, L. (1890) *Las Primeras Edades del Metal en el Sudeste de España*. Barcelona, Enrich y Cía.

Trotsky, L. (2005 [1923]) *Problemas de la Vida Cotidiana*. Madrid, Fundación Federico Engels.

Val Caturla, E. (1948) El Poblado del Bronce I Mediterráneo del Campico de Lébor, Totana (Murcia). *Cuadernos de Historia Primitiva* III–1, 5–36.

7

Archaeology of the Household. A Swiss Perspective

Nina Künzler Wagner

Introduction

The aim of this short article is to provide an insight into Swiss research on the subject of wetland settlements in particular. Special emphasis will be placed on the history of research and perspectives of household archaeology in Switzerland. The paper is to be seen as an interim report and does not claim to be all-inclusive.

The household – not just in terms of its economic, but also its social components – as a topic of research became a subject, which I felt was worth pursuing further, while studying the finds and features of a small underwater excavation in the area of the Late Bronze Age lakeside settlement Zurich-Alpenquai in lower Lake Zurich (dated to the second half of the 11th to the mid-9th centuries BC), which had been known since the early 20th century (Künzler Wagner 2005). The excavation, while covering only a small area, in its top layers uncovered an indoor hearth and its immediate surroundings, thus revealing traces of a conscious and complex usage of space on the part of the inhabitants. This prompted me to undertake further research into the subject of living space organisation – and I view *households* as part of this subject – within the framework of my doctoral thesis.

The Swiss landscape of finds

It is a feature of the Swiss prehistoric settlement landscape that it not only boasted settlements in dry areas but also numerous Neolithic and Bronze Age wetland settlements. Among these, settlements dating from the 4th and early 3rd millennia BC are found particularly often. The characteristic feature of wetland settlements is that the archaeological layers are deposited in anaerobic conditions and in constant humidity, and ideally are covered by natural lake deposits. Therefore, the preservation conditions for almost all – even uncharred – organic materials are very favourable; however, due to the pH, this does not apply to horn, leather and wool. Another exceptional feature is the possibility of dating the construction timbers and thus indirectly the archaeological layers to the exact calendar year by means of dendrochronology. Consequently, settlements with wetland preservation conditions hold an enormous archaeological potential, of which researchers are becoming more and more aware. Efforts have greatly increased in recent years to protect these special cultural goods (Dunning and Hafner 2005).

Numerous studies of various settlements and off-site climatic data, gathered over the past 20 or more years, have provided Swiss archaeological research with the means to create a mosaic-like image of prehistoric settlement patterns for individual time periods using settlement structures, house constructions, material culture, vegetation *etc*.

Unfortunately, hardly any settlements have been comprehensively and conclusively studied by all the disciplines and published. In addition, the individual results are influenced to various degrees by the following factors: the preservation conditions, the excavation circumstances, and the state of research and publication.

Preservation conditions

Wetland settlements generally offer good to excellent preservation conditions. However, strong lake level fluctuations, recent lake level corrections and the significant force of the wave action due to intensified shipping activities have today accelerated the erosion and destruction of many archaeological layers to such an extent that while in some cases the piles and the structures of the houses and settlements are still visible and sometimes even datable to the exact year, the associated finds and the archaeological layers no longer exist, with the exception of a small number of very resistant materials (Hafner and Suter 2000).

The sizes and structures of the houses allow the reconstruction of approximate numbers of inhabitants, based on which it is possible to draw conclusions about the organisation of the population. However, as regards the archaeology of the household proper, the problem arises that this only enables us to record dwelling units, provided that the structure of a house alone can present enough information to achieve even that. Neither social nor material units can be pinpointed with any degree of certainty and, given the lack of associated material culture, it is even less likely that the joint activities of social units could be identified.

Excavation conditions

The discovery of the Swiss pile dwellings dates back to 1854 (Keller 1854). In subsequent years, characterised by a veritable *pile-dwelling fever* (Flüeler-Grauwiler and Gisler 2004), numerous pile dwellings were literally exploited by avid archaeologists and the finds were sold to interested parties all over Europe (sometimes in order to finance further *excavations*). After the founding of the Swiss National Museum at the end of the 19th century, the first *rescue excavations* took place, for instance at the Zurich-Alpenquai site, which had been badly affected by extensive alterations to the lake promenade (Mäder

2001; Künzler Wagner 2005). However, these excavations largely only differed from their predecessors in as much as they had been officially authorised. Of course, the records compiled at the time by no means reach today's standards. With the newly developed underwater surveying and underwater excavations on one hand and the construction and expansion of the Swiss national road network on the other, the '70s brought new impetus to the field of wetland settlement research. Various major archaeological projects carried out since the late '70s and early '80s have strongly influenced not only excavation techniques, but also the methods used to analyse the findings. For today's researchers this means that, while a lot of finds were accumulated over the past 150 years, only limited observations on the features were made up to the 1970s and the quality of the records compiled since then is still very varied. Today, the excavations carried out on wetland settlement sites are almost exclusively rescue excavations undertaken by the various Cantonal Archaeology Services in connection with building projects or – far more rarely – rescue measures put in place because of a serious threat to the sites. These excavations are often burdened with deadline pressures and funding is usually limited, or it is invested in extending the excavations as opposed to comprehensive subsequent analyses. This leads, for instance, to the conscious decision not to take archaeobiological samples during the excavation, because the financial means for the appropriate analyses could not be raised in the medium or long term.

Based on the analysis of pottery and small finds such as stone and metal artefacts, national and regional phenomena of *cultural groups* can be identified. However, only in association with the archaeological features, can they reveal certain *joint activities* (for example pottery making) of a potential household, which in turn can lead to the interpretation of social units. Depending on the material basis (with or without the archaeobiological analysis), the various functions of households – production, distribution, transmission and reproduction (Wilk and Rathje 1982, 621) – become visible to various extents. In the future, however, this purely functional approach will hopefully be overcome more and more. It should only be seen as the starting point, from which a more extensive analysis is carried out, which in turn will lead to the interpretation of social spaces that can become apparent in activities and material culture.

Analysis and publication conditions

While it is the aim to carry out the (comprehensive) analysis and then publish the findings immediately after the excavation, it is not always possible, due to the lack of funding but also because of inadequate work concepts. Sometimes, smaller assemblages or parts of more substantial analyses are outsourced by the Cantonal Archaeology Services as student projects at universities. Unfortunately, these reports are only rarely published or their publication is significantly delayed, so that the studies actually exist, but their availability is limited. This eventually leads to situations where comprehensive analysis and publication have still not taken place 20 years later. In some cases, certain aspects – in the case of the excavations in the Zurich Seefeld, the archaeobotanical and archaeozoological analyses – have already been published (Schibler *et al.* 1997), while the analyses of the features and of individual finds categories have yet to be brought out.

In general, one can state that it will still take a lot of effort to raise awareness among Swiss archaeologists in order to increase the number of multidisciplinary analyses of wetland and, of course, dryland settlements over the coming years. Against this backdrop, it becomes apparent that the settlement Arbon-Bleiche 3 in Canton Thurgovia is a complete stroke of luck and a milestone within archaeological research (Jacomet *et al.* 2004; Doppler and Pollmann in this volume). Due to the multifaceted analysis carried out there by the various disciplines, households can be discussed in a much more concrete fashion than it was possible up to this point. However, Arbon-Bleiche 3 also provides the impetus to newly evaluate the known Swiss wetland settlements.

Households – then and now

Based on the house sizes and the known range of farm animals and plants and including *site catchments*, various researchers have attempted to simulate the living conditions of the Neolithic population and to calculate numbers of village inhabitants and the population in general as well as estimating the size of the required farmland and of the herds (Gross *et al.* 1990, 97). These reconstructions are based both on ethnographical comparisons regarding the ratio between house size and number of inhabitants, and on the calculation of the daily basic energy requirements of the population.

However, research into the social aspects of prehistoric house and village communities or societies respectively has, to date, been almost exclusively focused on theories regarding hierarchy and religion (for instance Honegger 2005).

It is striking that men, women and children, who constitute households living in these settlements and who form the basis of society, have largely remained invisible in the archaeological finds and features. In my opinion, however, they are not *a priori* invisible, but to date have not or have not enough been the focus of researchers' attention.

It can be stated that within Swiss prehistoric research the term *household* has up to now almost exclusively referred to *economic units* and correspondingly to *houses*, which in turn formed a *village community* or *society* respectively. The interpretation is based on architecture and settlement structure, because the various authors build there analysis on the assumption that each house formed a self-sufficient economic entity. This has resulted in the term *household* staying one-dimensional and purely functional up to now. This is a situation, which of course in future will need to be overcome, if the archaeology of the household from a social archaeological viewpoint is to be developed. In studying the pottery and small finds from the Late Bronze Age settlement Ürschhausen-Horn, Canton Thurgovia, Nagy's (1999) approach also remained purely functional. She discovered a remarkable number of sherds join from two or three houses and the alley in between. Some of the individual houses must have been in closer contact than others (Nagy 1999, 92). This led Nagy to conclude that *houses* must be differentiated in some way from *households*. However, she avoided the use of the term *household* for these houses with *shared courtyard areas*. There are numerous examples of the term *household* being used in connection with pottery and identifiable ensembles (house styles). For instance Seifert (1997, 54–65), in his analysis of the pottery finds from the Late Bronze Age settlement Zug-Sumpf, Canton Zug (dated to the second half of the 11th and 10th centuries BC), which was destroyed by a conflagration, introduced *house styles* based on two vessel assemblages found *in situ*. However, Bolliger (2004, 187) correctly pointed out that even a stack of vessels found *in situ* can contain various decorative styles, *i.e.* potters' hands, thus rendering problematic the use of house styles alone to visualise *households*.

Despite certain reservations, the use of pottery seems to be a good line of approach in order to determine social units based on shared activities by means of the material culture. Together with house and settlement structure data and general thoughts on active spatial organisation (*i.e.* organisation of living space) taken from sociology and cultural anthropology, it should be possible, even in settlements where the conditions are not ideal for analysis, to gather information on joint activities (including the deliberate spatial organisation), which goes beyond the pure calculation of numbers of inhabitants. If this is achieved, more use will be made of the potential contained in Swiss wetland settlements. Moreover, this is the only way to join economic, cultural and social aspects together as a whole, thus providing the basis for the development of the archaeology of the household.

This has prompted me to carry out a more in-depth search, within the framework of my doctoral thesis, for evidence of prehistoric living space organisation, both on the level of house interiors and on the level of the settlement. The research aims to find and apply new lines of approach to the visualisation of social spaces, in terms of their demographic, material and activity-based components within Swiss lakeside settlements (Künzler Wagner in prep.).

It is indeed my opinion that in general not enough attention has been paid to date to the fact that the examined settlements are not just finds and features, but houses and villages – living spaces – built, designed and inhabited by people. Fortunately, the relevance of projects in the area of household archaeology has been recognised by the Swiss National Science Foundation and funding has been granted (Doppler and Pollmann, in this volume). And I hope that it will be possible in the near future to tackle further projects.

Summary

Based on the excellent preservation conditions, even for uncharred organic finds, in the numerous wetland settlements in the region of what is present-day Switzerland, various researchers have, over the past 20 years, attempted to identify households in the archaeological finds and features. It can be stated that these households were viewed mainly from an economic and purely from a functional point of view. However, current research shows that new trends towards social archaeological lines of approach are also possible in the Swiss context and this paves the way for the development of a comprehensive archaeology of the household.

References

Bolliger, S. (2004) Handschriften. In I. Bauer, B. Ruckstuhl and J. Speck (eds) *Die spätbronzezeitlichen Ufersiedlungen von Zug-Sumpf 3/1, Die Funde der Grabungen 1923–37*, 187–216. Zug, Kantonales Museum für Urgeschichte.

Dunning, C and Hafner, A (2005) Das Projekt "Pfahlbauten des Alpenraumes als UNESCO-Welterbe". Information zur Nominierung auf die "liste indicative" der schweizerischen Bundesregierung vom Dezember 2004. In *WES'04 Wetland Economies and Societies. Proceedings of the Conference held at Zurich 10–13 March 2004* ed by Della Casa, Ph and Trachsel, M, Zürich: Chronos, 297–298

Flüeler-Grauwiler, M. and Gisler, J. (eds) (2004) *Pfahlbaufieber – Von Antiquaren, Pfahlbaufischern, Altertümerhändlern und Pfahlbaumythen*. Zürich, Chronos.

Gross, E., Jacomet, S. and Schibler, J. (1990) Stand und Ziele der Wirtschaftsarchäologischen Forschung an Neolithischen Ufer- und Inselsiedlungen im unteren Zürichseeraum (Kt. Zürich, Schweiz). In J. Schibler, J. Sedlmeier and H. Spycher (eds) *Beiträge zur Archäozoologie, Archäologie, Anthropologie, Geologie und Paläontologie, Festschrift für Hans R. Stampfli*, 77–100. Basel, Helbling and Lichtenhahn.

Hafner, A. and Suter, P. (2000) *–3400 v. Chr.– Die Entwicklung der Bauerngesellschaften des 4, Jahrtausends v. Chr. am Bielersee*. Bern, Lehrmittel- und Medienverlag.

Honegger, M. (2005) Les villages littoraux du Néolithique: égalité et autarcie ou complémentarité et mise en réseau? In *WES'04 Wetland Economies and Societies, Proceedings of the Conference held at Zurich 10–13 March 2004*, 185–194. Zürich, Chronos.

Jacomet, S., Leuzinger, U. and Schibler, J. (eds) (2004) *Arbon-Bleiche 3, Wirtschaft und Umwelt*. Frauenfeld, Amt für Archäologie des Kantons Thurgau.

Keller, F (1854) *Die keltischen Pfahlbauten in den Schweizerseen*, Mittheilungen der antiquarischen Gesellschaft in Zürich, Band 9, II. Abteilung, Heft 3, Zürich: Antiquarische Gesellschaft.

Künzler Wagner, N. (2005) *Zürich-Alpenquai V: Tauchgrabungen 1999–2001, Funde und Befunde*. Zürich und Egg, Baudirektion des Kanton Zürich/Fotorotar.

Künzler Wagner, N. (in preparation) *Living Spaces – Prehistoric Spatial Organisation in the 4th and 3rd millennia BC: Developing a New Approach to Research on Social Space via Settlement Structure and Material Culture*.

Mäder, A. (2001) *Zürich Alpenquai I: Die Metallfunde Baggerungen von 1916 und 1919, mit einem Beitrag von M Betschart*. Zürich und Egg, Baudirektion des Kanton Zürich/Fotorotar.

Nagy, G. (1999) *Ürschhausen-Horn, Keramik und Kleinfunde der Spätestbronzezeitlichen Siedlung*. Frauenfeld, Amt für Archäologie des Kantons Thurgau.

Schibler, J., Hüster-Plogmann, H., Jacomet, S., Brombacher, CH., Gross-Klee, E. and Rast-Eicher, A. (1997) *Ökonomie und Ökologie Neolithischer und Bronzezeitlicher Ufersiedlungen am Zürichsee: Ergebnisse der Ausgrabungen Mozartstrasse, Kanalisationssanierung Seefeld, AKAD/ Pressehaus und Mythenschloss in Zürich*. Zürich und Egg, Baudirektion des Kanton Zürich/Fotorotar.

Seifert, M. (1997) *Die Spätbronzezeitlichen Ufersiedlungen von Zug-Sumpf 2/1, Die Funde 1952–54*. Zug, Kantonales Museum für Urgeschichte.

Wilk, R. and Rathje, W. (1982) Household Archaeology. *American Behavioural Scientist* 25/6, 617–639.

Considerations about Possible Household Activities in the Neolithic Lakeside Settlement Arbon Bleiche 3, Switzerland – a Preliminary Approach

Thomas Doppler, Britta Pollmann and Brigitte Röder

Introduction

Our research is part of a larger project that deals with social history in prehistoric archaeology. The project is carried out at the Institute for Prehistory and Archaeological Science at Basel University, Switzerland. It is funded by the Swiss National Science Foundation. The project started in October 2005. For further information see: www.sozialgeschichte.unibas.ch. In the first stage it aims to unveil the epistemological foundations of social interpretations in Swiss prehistoric archaeology. This basis will be used to generate new baselines for research into the interpretation of social issues. These new foundations will integrate the sociohistorical potential of archaeozoology, archaeobotany, biological anthropology, and gender studies in an interdisciplinary approach. Our research team will systematically investigate this potential by researching and compiling innovative approaches on a national and international level, and using them to develop new methodological and theoretical tools. These new approaches will be applied to and tested in case studies of lakeside settlements situated mainly in Switzerland. Thus, in contrast to most of the previous social interpretations centering on burials, the focus of the present project lies on those archaeological sources which reflect the everyday life of prehistoric communities. Using as a starting point the work of Jacomet *et al.* (2004) the present paper is a first attempt to develop a methodological access to the social interpretation of the distribution of archaeobiological sources in lakeside settlements. Since the presentation of this paper, in April 2006, further articles reflect the advancement in our research (*e.g.* Doppler *et al.* 2010; 2011; Röder *et al.* in prep.).

The waterlogged milieu at lakesides and in mires provides excellent conditions for the preservation of organic materials. As a result of this we have at our disposal a rich spectrum of organic remains, both of vegetables and animals, offering optimal preconditions for archaeobiological analyses. In Switzerland many assemblages of organic remains from Neolithic and Bronze Age sites have already been analysed. The resulting data were collected in databases which we can access for our research. In combination with the excavated wooden house constructions dated by dendrochronology, the archaeobiological data offer the best preconditions to search for differences within the distribution of vegetable and animal remains in respect to specific houses. This search was inspired not only by the results from other studies (Jacomet *et al.* 2004; Wullschleger Ms.), but also from our critical position concerning two widespread and opposed views of the social structure of Neolithic and Bronze Age lakeside settlements in the forelands of the Alps. The "row house settlement" structure of the dwellings, with their regularly arranged houses of similar dimensions, gives rise to the interpretation that the architectural homogeneity may reflect social homogeneity – and therefore the assumption that we might be dealing with egalitarian communities. This interpretation is usually connected with the following suppositions: a) that the house as the smallest architectural unit stands for the smallest social unit beyond the individual, ie the household; and b) that households are very homogeneous without any substantial differences – they have more or less the same material culture, the same subsistence strategies, the same eating habits etc (information received from colleagues). The other current interpretation of the "row house structure" of lakeside dwellings considers the absence of architectural differences as evidence for social stratification. The idea associated with this view is that architectural homogeneity, the regular organisation of house rows and lanes as well as communal buildings like palisades require an institutionalised form of power, a central leadership in terms of a village chief (*e.g.* Stöckli 1990, 94–95).

Although in a completely contradictory way, the current social interpretations of lakeside settlements focus on the absence of "differences" in several domains. Therefore, it appears useful to ask the question whether this view of architectural and social homogeneity fits the archaeological record. As already mentioned, recent analyses of the distribution of archaeobiological and archaeological remains demonstrate that, contrary to a common view of lakeside settlements, differences between particular houses do indeed exist. The significance of these differences as well as the determining factors behind them is still not entirely clear. They could be related to differences in the domains of subsistence strategies, eating habits, access to resources, or they could be caused by differing residence rules for women and men. For some phenomena such as the presence of "foreign ceramics" which are produced locally but reflect pottery traditions from distant regions (de Capitani 2002, 209–220; Bonzon 2004, 307–312) one could take into consideration an ethnic interpretation due to migration as well. Anyway – a detailed analysis of the distribution of archaeobiological remains is outstandingly suitable to detect social differences. In our understanding, social differences are not synonymous with hierarchic differences, but can also be related to many other factors, some of which have been mentioned above. With our analysis we intend to shed new light on the everyday lifes of the inhabitants of prehistoric lake dwellings, lifes which obviously were far from being as uniform as assumed so far.

Against this background we intend to develop a methodological approach to detect meaningful distribution patterns of archaeobiological remains. Our starting point does not consist of sociological models or theories, but of the archaeological record. As the reference parameter for the distributions we have chosen the smallest architectural unit, the house. Until we find contrary evidence we identify the house with a social unit and call it a "household". We define "household" as a group of persons living together under the same roof, economising and consuming together, pooling their common resources, ensuring biological reproduction and having close social bonds relying on kinship and partnership.

Working basis and statistical approach

We base our work on Neolithic waterlogged sites with excellent preservation of organic remains. By means of dendrochronology, individual houses and their duration within the settlements can be dated. This individual dating of houses enables us to focus on settlement dynamics and interrelationships between architectural units. An excellent case study in this context is Arbon Bleiche 3 in Switzerland. This waterlogged site is situated in the Northern Alpine foreland, on the Swiss side of Lake Constance in the Canton of Thurgau (Fig. 8.1). The settlement was excavated between 1993 and 1995. During the years to follow the findings of these excavations have been the subject

Figure 8.1. Map of Switzerland with the location of Arbon Bleiche 3 on Lake Constance. © 2004 swisstopo (modified).

of intensive analyses, all of which have been published by now (Leuzinger 2000; de Capitani *et al.* 2002; Jacomet *et al.* 2004).

During the rescue excavation – under the direction of Urs Leuzinger (*Amt für Archäologie Thurgau*) – a very well preserved cultural layer was found. The fact that nearly no shifting of the cultural layer could be observed was of great importance for many investigations (Jacomet *et al.* 2004). Figure 8.2 shows the ground plan of Arbon Bleiche 3: in total 27 houses were (at least partly) excavated, which is a considerable number compared to other settlements in the lake dwelling area.

It is estimated that one-third to a half of the whole settlement was excavated, and that the settlement had 200–300 inhabitants (Leuzinger 2000, 173). In addition to the routine investigations of ceramics (de Capitani 2002), stone artefacts (Leuzinger 2002) and large animal bones (Deschler-Erb and Marti-Grädel 2004b) the excellent preservation allowed in-depth studies of the very well preserved organic material. Without being complete, the following enumeration will give some insights into the broad spectrum of analyses that has been done: dendrochronology (Leuzinger 2000, 51–87; Sormaz 2004), analyses of layer formation processes (Haas and Magny 2004; Brombacher and Hadorn 2004; Ismail-Meyer and Rentzel 2004; Thew 2004; Deschler-Erb and Marti-Grädel 2004a), and the identification and interpretation of small animals such as amphibians and fishes (Hüster Plogmann 2004). The extraordinary preservation also allowed the analysis of parasites in animal dung and human coprolites (Marti 2004; Le Bailly and Bouchet 2004). The analysis of pollen and plant macroremains has disclosed human activities from several years and in different seasons (Brombacher and Hadorn 2004, 63; Hosch and Jacomet 2004, 120). Finally, molecular analysis of cattle dung components has shown that – under good conditions – ancient DNA can be isolated from waterlogged material (Turgay and Schlumbaum 2004).

The analysis that has been done for this paper is based on published data from the site. The huge database permits investigations about archaeobiological distribution patterns within the settlement. A methodological approach for this is the systematic exploration of such patterns by correspondence analysis. This is a statistical method that can be used as an analytical tool in archaeology for unveiling meaningful correlations within a settlement and between individual houses (the software used for our analyses is Canoco: Canoco for Windows 4.0, CanoDraw 3.1 and CanoPost 1.0. For further information: ter Braak and Smilauer 1998). A big advantage of this statistical approach is the fact that several types of data and variables can be analysed at the same time (Brinkkemper 1993, 84). The analysis of archaeobiological remains in general and of food remains specifically can provide interesting insights into a community's daily life, its structure and its functioning, because food, its procurement and production, is an essential part of human life. Distribution studies of hand collected findings such as big bones, ceramics and other artefacts, for which preservation conditions are less important, are possible for almost all houses, whereas smaller finds (such as seeds or fish bones) have to be recovered by flotation of sediment samples, which was not possible for all houses.

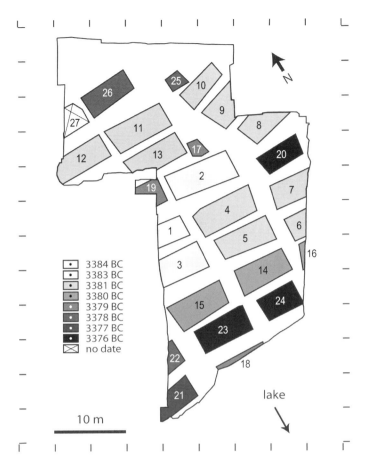

Figure 8.2. Ground plan of Arbon Bleiche 3. The different shadings indicate different years of construction. Each house was dated precisely to its building year by dendrochronology. The numbering of houses does not correspond to the chronological order. After Jacomet et al. 2004 (modified).

Results

While the mathematics of correspondence analysis are complex, the principles of graph reading are quite simple: The greater the distance between two points in the graph, the less correlation exists between these points. The first axis accounts for the largest variance within the data, the second axis for the largest remaining variance, and so on for each further axis. The percentage of variance explained by the axes is given cumulatively (ter Braak and Smilauer 1998, 121).

In order to understand the output of correspondence analysis we will first focus on the analysis of a simple data set consisting of houses and domestic animal bones (Fig. 8.3).

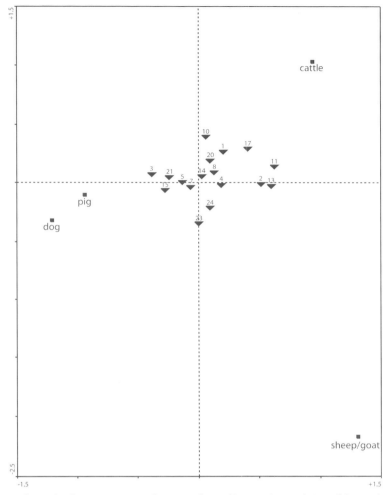

Figure 8.3. Arbon Bleiche 3: Correspondence analysis of houses (triangles) and bones from domestic animals (squares). Analysis is based on the number of bones per year and house (inter-sample distances). Cumulative percentage variance of species data: axis 1 = 67.5, axis 2 = 94.1.

The calculation of this analysis is based on inter-sample distances (ter Braak and Smilauer 1998, 37) and the number of animal bones per year and house ("densities"). Number of finds per year and house means the total number of finds within one house in relation to the time period this house was in use. Squares in this graph represent the domestic animals whereas numbered triangles stand for the houses. The first two axes account for 67.5% and 26.6% of the total variance respectively.

If we focus on the distribution of pigs and cattle one can observe that there is a clear distance between them. This corresponds with the distribution patterns discernible in the classical distribution mapping (Fig. 8.4). Looking at the houses, it is observable

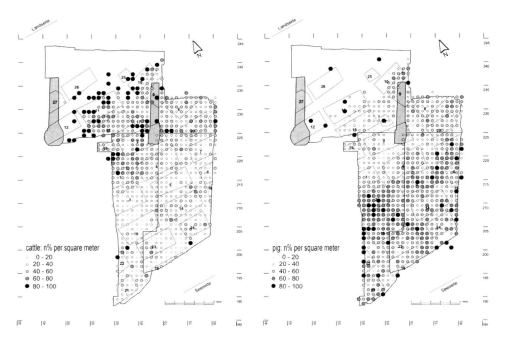

Figure 8.4. Arbon Bleiche 3: The dots indicate bone fragment quantities per square meter. Bigger dark dots reflect the highest quantities. After Deschler-Erb and Marti-Grädel 2004b, 222 Abb. 250 and 252 (modified).

that their plots are all grouped around the diagram's centre. They are clearly closer to each other than the animal samples are. This means that the spectrum of domestic animals – of all considered houses – is quite similar. But at the same time we also notice some kind of division which indicates that some houses tend to have more cattle remains whereas others tend to have more pig remains. These indications demonstrate that there is a noticeable difference between northern landside and southern lakeside houses. What do these differences tell us?

The animal bones primarily reflect settlement waste that comes from food consumption and craft activities. Because analyses of layer formation processes have shown that nearly no post-depositional movement of the cultural layer has occurred we can conclude that the recorded finds are more or less located in their original positions (Jacomet 2004, 102). Thus the differences in bone distribution should indicate differences in consumption, eating habits, subsistence strategies or craft activities. Of course one could assume other explanatory possibilities, for instance ethnic or religious reasons. The northern settlement part shows higher concentrations of cattle bones whereas the southern part presents higher quantities of pigs. Whatever the reasons might be, it is interesting that the north–south separation also is discernible by the analysis of fish remains (Hüster Plogmann 2004, 273, Abb. 322).

As already mentioned this example is a very simple one. We have chosen it to show the functioning of this statistical tool. Of course one can calculate questions of greater complexity with more items considered such as different artefact types. That is what we will do within the scope of our research project (see introduction).

We have seen that there are noticeable differences between two parts of the Arbon settlement. But how about differences between individual houses? In the following we have chosen houses 3 and 20 (Fig. 8.2) whose archaeobiological remains appeared quite conspicuous within the settlement context.

House 3

House 3 was built in 3383 BC and was in use for a minimum of 9 years (Leuzinger 2000, 64). In this house a lot of gathered fruits, like acorns, and beech-nuts, and small parts of mistletoe were found (Hosch and Jacomet 2004, 148). These fruits can be very useful animal fodder. However, it seems unlikely that fruits were used for feeding the animals, as it is assumed, that animal feeding relied on wood pasture in the nearby forests (Hosch and Jacomet 2004, 148). The collected fruits were probably used as human food. The amount of gathered fruits together with a high number of large vessels may indicate that the inhabitants of this house stored such fruits.

House 20

House 20 was built in 3376 BC and is therefore one of the last three buildings constructed in the settlement (see Fig. 8.2). Before its construction the location was an open area that had probably been used as a place for disposing waste and faeces (Hosch and Jacomet 2004, 148). With its dimension of 7 × 3 m it is a little bit smaller than most of the other houses. It was in use for at least 4 years (Leuzinger 2000, 81). In the middle of the house, loam, lots of charcoal and fired clay were found. In addition, many fruits of bur/lesser burdock (*Arctium minus*) have been found being highly over-represented in this house (Hosch and Jacomet 2004, 148). These fruits can be found at ruderal sites and adhere very easily to clothes or fur and fleece. The analysis of animal bones in house 20 has shown that an above-average number of them belonged to wild animals such as marten (*Martes martes*), badger (*Meles meles*), aurochs (*Bos primigenius*) and red deer (*Cervus elaphus*). One explanation for the combination of bur and the bones of wild animals in house 20 could be hunting activities in specific areas from where bur was unintentionally introduced (Hosch and Jacomet 2004, 149), *i.e.* that the inhabitants picked up the bur while they roamed the countryside to hunt and did this much more frequently than the inhabitants of other houses did.

In order to better understand the spectra of archaeobiological remains in houses 3 and 20 as compared to the other houses in the settlement a correspondence analysis was carried out (Fig. 8.5).

The calculation of this analysis is based on inter-sample distances (ter Braak and Smilauer 1998, 37) and the relative percentages of plant remains within houses. The numbered triangles stand for the houses whereas squares and circles indicate

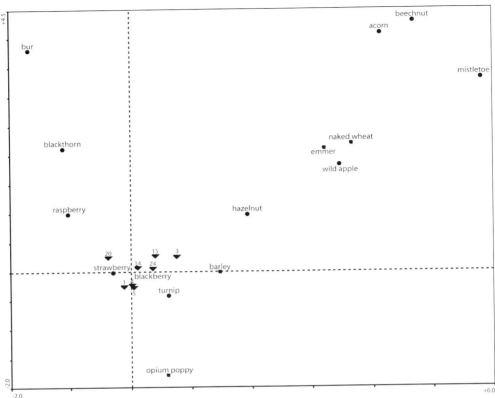

Figure 8.5. Arbon Bleiche 3: Correspondence analysis of houses (triangles), domesticated plants (squares) and gathered plants (circles). Analysis is based on relative percentages of plant remains per house (inter-sample distances). Cumulative percentage variance of species data: axis 1 = 47.5, axis 2 = 76.6.

domesticated plants and gathered fruits respectively. The first two axes account for 47.5% and 29.1% of the total variance respectively. One can observe that all the domesticated plants are grouped around house 3. Some wild plants such as blackberry and strawberry are located around the diagram's centre which means that they are well represented in all analysed houses (Hosch and Jacomet 2004, 140, Abb. 109). Three plants however – raspberry, blackthorn and bur – are located on the plot's left side, near house 20. Another group of wild plants is located in the upper right corner (acorn, beech-nut and mistletoe). These fruits seem to have no correlation with house 20 but are, as already mentioned, typical for house 3.

Discussion

The analysis of Arbon Bleiche 3 is a pilot project that will be of importance for our future research. The present case study points out one of our methodological approaches. It shows that correspondence analysis is a useful tool for detecting differences as well as similarities within and between particular houses on the one hand and within the whole settlement on the other hand. However, correspondence analysis does not explain these correlations. The explanation has to be made by the archaeologist. Of course there are some methodological problems that must be taken into consideration before this statistical tool can be applied to archaeological case studies. A major challenge is finding and defining a common basis for comparison of different data categories, such as archaeological and archaeobiological finds (hand collected objects and macroremains obtained by wet sieving). While working on this paper we still have been looking for and testing possible approaches. In order to avoid methodological problems we limited our first analyses to combinations of houses and plant remains or of houses and animal bones, without mixing up these two biological data groups.

The in-depth analysis of Arbon Bleiche 3 has unveiled an astonishing complexity within this settlement, a complexity further confirmed by evidence of extra regional contacts concerning stone artefacts, ornamental shells (entale tusk, *Dentalium entalis*), copper, ceramics and several plants (Leuzinger 2001, 22–24; 2002, 22–25; de Capitani 2002, 209–216; Hosch and Jacomet 2004, 152–157).

Perhaps such complexity within and between particular houses could be explained in part by specific tasks, division of labour, specialisation etc. Concerning certain activities like the production or use of ceramics one can detect similarities between several houses. Though there is more and more evidence for such similarities (Hafner 1993, 49; Trachsel 2005, 303–308), they have not yet been systematically contextualised within a wider social setting.

In this early state of our research project we cannot yet firmly identify groups of houses which could be considered as a single household. Until we find contrary evidence we shall continue to apply our concept of household to individual houses. Thus, as already mentioned in the introduction, we equate one house with a social unit and call it "household". In this sense we follow the common concept of household as the basis of communal life with a combination of shared residence and the pooling of economic resources at the house level (Düring and Marciniak 2006, 167–168). We are aware that the assumption that a household consists of a single house might be problematic. The same applies to the concept of "household" in general: in Arbon, as mentioned above, there is some evidence of distribution patterns covering several houses. This fact might be interpreted in two ways. On the one hand it could indicate social practices linking the inhabitants of several houses to a single household. On the other hand it could hint at similar social practices of individual houses that act autarkic. This diversity of possible interpretations is in line with numerous ethnographic analyses that have shown the difficulty or even impossibility of arriving at a universal definition of "household"

(Sanjek 2002). Furthermore, studies of recent households in a variety of settings have demonstrated that co-residence and pooling of economic resources do not necessarily overlap (Düring and Marciniak 2006, 168). Third, we have followed recent discussions in social anthropology querying the value of the concept of "household" in principle. In spite of these critical points we have decided to use this concept as an analytical instrument for our research. It will serve to develop working hypotheses for the analysis of the data and to conceive alternative interpretations for the alleged uniformity and homogeneity of social life in prehistoric lake dwellings.

Methodological approaches to social complexity

In the last few years several investigations have revealed social complexity in prehistoric times. Besides the approach shown in this contribution there are numerous other possibilities to look for differences at the house level such as analyses of spatial organisation, architecture and construction dynamics within settlements (Hafner 1993; Trachsel 2005, 303; Düring and Marciniak 2006; Barceló and Maximiano, in this volume; Coupland, in this volume). Further, distribution of hearths (Düring and Marciniak 2006, 173) and house stocks (Hafner 1993, 49; Trachsel 2005, 304–305; Düring and Marciniak 2006, 167) provide continuative indications. Micromorphological analysis (Kovács, in this volume) is also one possible approach.

All the evidence of these analyses shows that social complexity within Neolithic communities is the norm rather than the exception. The understanding and interpretation of Neolithic communities continues to be oversimplified. This places awkward and narrow bounds on scientific insight and hinders us in widening the range of vision for a more detailed perception. For a better understanding of social interrelations we must take into consideration a broader variety of social interactions (Düring and Marciniak 2006, 165–166). Today there should be no doubt that besides settlement analyses one has to focus beyond house and settlement boundaries to detect and recognise complex interrelations (Trachsel 2005, 315 and 318; Düring and Marciniak 2006, 168–169; Briz *et al.,* in this volume). Thus, our upcoming task will consist of continuing the analyses in Arbon Bleiche 3 and broadening them by adopting and testing the approaches developed at other Neolithic waterlogged sites.

Acknowledgments
Our thanks go to Urs Leuzinger, Stefanie Jacomet and Jörg Schibler for their cooperation and the possibility of working with their data. We also are indebted to the collaborators of the archaeobiological department at the Institute for Prehistory and Archaeological Science at Basel University who have been involved in the Arbon project and without whose work we would not have had a working basis. We owe great thanks to Mirjam Wullschleger who – concerning correspondence analysis – has given us very important inputs with her results and ideas developed in a seminar paper. Alexander Gramsch has given us valuable inputs during discussions, for which we are very grateful. Additional

thanks go to Cozette Griffin Kremer and Sandra Pichler for their help with the English language.

This paper was realised within the scope of the project "New foundations for sociohistorical research in prehistoric archaeology" which is funded by the Swiss National Science Foundation.

References

Bonzon, J. (2004) Archaeometrical study (petrography, mineralogy and chemistry) of the ceramics. In Jacomet *et al.* (eds) (2004), 294–312.

Brinkkemper, O. (1993) Indirect correspondence analysis and botanical macroremains: a case study. *Analecta Praehistorica Leidensia* 26, 83–91.

Brombacher, C. and Hadorn, P. (2004) Untersuchungen der Pollen und Makroreste aus den Profilsäulen. In Jacomet *et al.* (eds) (2004), 50–65.

de Capitani, A. (2002) Gefässkeramik. In de Capitani *et al.* (eds) 2002, 135–276.

de Capitani, A., Deschler-Erb, S., Leuzinger, U., Marti-Grädel, E. and Schibler, J. (eds) (2002) *Die jungsteinzeitliche Seeufersiedlung Arbon Bleiche 3 – Funde.* Archäologie im Thurgau 11. Frauenfeld, Departement für Erziehung und Kultur des Kantons Thurgau.

Deschler-Erb, S. and Marti-Grädel, E. (2004a) Hinweise zur Schichterhaltung aufgrund der Tierknochen. In Jacomet *et al.* (eds) (2004), 90–100.

Deschler-Erb, S. and Marti-Grädel, E. (2004b) Viehhaltung und Jagd. Ergebnisse der Untersuchung der handaufgelesenen Tierknochen. In Jacomet *et al.* (eds) (2004), 158–252.

Doppler, T., Pichler, S., Jacomet, S., Schibler, J. and Röder, B. (2010) Archäobiologie als sozialgeschichtliche Informationsquelle: ein bislang vernachlässigtes Forschungspotential. In E. Claßen, T. Doppler and B. Ramminger (eds) *Familie – Verwandtschaft – Sozialstrukturen: Sozialarchäologische Forschungen zu neolithischen Befunden*, 119–139. *Fokus Jungsteinzeit – Berichte der AG Neolithikum I.* Kerpen-Loogh, Welt und Erde Verlag.

Doppler, T., Pollmann, B., Pichler, S., Jacomet, S., Schibler, J. and Röder, B. (2011) Bauern, Fischerinnen und Jäger: Unterschiedliche Ressourcen- und Landschaftsnutzung in der neolithischen Siedlung Arbon Bleiche 3? In J. Studer, M. David-Elbiali and M. Besse (eds) *Paysage – Landschaft – Paesaggio. L'impact des activités humaines sur l'environnement du Paléolithique à la période romaine. Cahiers d'Archéologie Romande* 120, 143–158.

Düring, B. S. and Marciniak, A. (2006) Households and communities in the central Anatolian Neolithic. *Archaeological Dialogues* 12(2), 165–187.

Haas, J. N. and Magny, M. (2004) Schichtgenese und Vegetationsgeschichte. In Jacomet *et al.* (eds) (2004), 43–49.

Hafner, A. (1993) Die neolithische Dorfanlage Lattrigen VI – Riedstation (um 3400 v.Chr.). *Archäologie der Schweiz* 16(2), 46–49.

Hosch, S. and Jacomet, S. (2004) Ackerbau und Sammelwirtschaft. Ergebnisse der Untersuchung von Samen und Früchten. In Jacomet *et al.* (eds) (2004), 112–157.

Hüster Plogmann, H. (2004) Fischfang und Kleintierbeute. Ergebnisse der Untersuchung von Tierresten aus den Schlämmproben. In Jacomet *et al.* (eds) (2004), 253–276.

Ismail-Meyer, K. and Rentzel, P. (2004) Mikromorphologische Untersuchung der Schichtabfolge. In Jacomet *et al.* (eds) (2004), 66–80.

Jacomet, S. (2004) Interdisziplinäres Fazit zur Schichtgenese. In Jacomet *et al.* (eds) (2004), 101–102.

Jacomet, S. and Leuzinger, U. (2004) Einleitung. In Jacomet *et al.* (eds) (2004), 25–39.

Jacomet, S., Leuzinger, U. and Schibler, J. (eds) (2004) *Die jungsteinzeitliche Seeufersiedlung Arbon*

Bleiche 3 – Umwelt und Wirtschaft. Archäologie im Thurgau 12. Frauenfeld, Departement für Erziehung und Kultur des Kantons Thurgau.

Le Bailly, M. and Bouchet, F. (2004) Etude paléoparasitologique des coprolithes humains. In Jacomet *et al.* (eds) (2004), 372–377.

Leuzinger, U. (2002) Steinartefakte. In de Capitani *et al.* (eds) (2002), 22–75.

Leuzinger, U. (2001) *Seesicht verbaut. Leben im Pfahlbaudorf Arbon Bleiche 3 vor 5400 Jahren.* Bozen, Südtiroler Archäologiemuseum.

Leuzinger, U. (2000) *Die jungsteinzeitliche Seeufersiedlung Arbon Bleiche 3 – Befunde.* Archäologie im Thurgau 9. Frauenfeld, Departement für Erziehung und Kultur des Kantons Thurgau.

Marti, H. (2004) Parasitologische Untersuchungen von Wiederkäuer-Exkrementen. In Jacomet *et al.* (eds) (2004), 358–361.

Röder, B., Doppler, T., Pichler, S., Pollmann, B, Jacomet, S. and Schibler, J. (in prep.) *Beyond the settlement grid: investigating social differences through archaeobiology in waterlogged sites.*

Sanjek, R. (2002) Household. In A. Barnard and J. Spencer (eds) *Encyclopedia of Social and Cultural Anthropology*, 285–288. London and New York, Routledge.

Sormaz, T. (2004) Absolute Datierung durch Dendrochronologie und ^{14}C-Analysen. In Jacomet *et al.* (eds) (2004), 105–111.

Stöckli, W. (1990) Gesellschaft und Bevölkerung in der Steinzeit. In Schweizerische Gesellschaft für Ur- und Frühgeschichte (ed), *Gesellschaft und Bevölkerung.* Einführungskurs in die ur- und frühgeschichtliche Archäologie der Schweiz, 6. Kurs, Bern 17./18. November. Basel, Schweizerische Gesellschaft für Ur- und Frühgeschichte, 93–106.

ter Braak, C. J. F. and Smilauer, P. (1998) *CANOCO Reference Manual and User's Guide to Canoco for Windows: Software for Canonical Community Ordination (version 4).* Ithaca (NY), Microcomputer Power.

Thew, N. (2004) The aquatic and terrestrial molluscs from the profile columns. In Jacomet *et al.* (eds) (2004), 81–89.

Trachsel, M. (2005) Feuchtbodensiedlungen als sozialgeschichtliche Quelle. Ergänzungen und Perspektiven nach 150 Jahren Forschung. In P. Della Casa and M. Trachsel (eds) *WES'04 – Wetland Economies and Societies. Proceedings of the International Conference Zurich, 10–13 march 2004*, 299–326. Zürich, Chronos.

Turgay, M. and Schlumbaum, A. (2004) Untersuchung von alter DNA in Koprolithen von Wiederkäuern. In Jacomet *et al.* (eds) (2004), 362–364.

Wullschleger, M. (Ms.) *Netzfischer oder Leinenfischer? – Modellrechnungen zu Haushaltaktivitäten am Beispiel der jungneolithischen Seeufersiedlung Arbon Bleiche 3/TG, Schweiz.* Unpublished seminar paper 2005. Institute for Prehistory and Archaeological Science, University of Basel.

Houses and Domestic Life in the Circum-Alpine Region Bronze Age

Francesco Menotti and Urs Leuzinger

Introduction

The question as to how and where prehistoric lacutrine dwellings in the Circum-Alpine region were built has provoked fierce debate, since Ferdinand Keller (1854, 65–100) published his pile-dwelling theory in 1854 (Stöckli 1979, 50–56; Speck 1990, 9–20; Menotti 2001b). Even today, experts still disagree on how exactly prehistoric lacustrine houses should be reconstructed. However, it is broadly accepted that as well as lakeside settlements built on the ground, pile dwellings with raised floors also existed. Because of the complexity of the archaeological evidence, the variability of anthropogenic layers and the different construction techniques, it is obvious that the adjustment of lake-dwelling architecture to the lakeshores cannot be reduced to a single theory; *e.g.* dry periods equal houses built directly on the ground, or wet periods equal pile dwellings. Waterlogged and unstable subsoils, as well as seasonal sporadic flooding, should also be taken into account (Pétrequin 1997, 104). Therefore, studying human adaptation to environmental change becomes germane to the understanding of the lake-dwelling architecture.

Fig. 9.1. Reconstruction drawing of the Zürich-Mozartstrasse lacustrine village 1b (Office of Archaeology, Zurich City, Underwater Archaeology Unit – Department of Urban Development).

In spite of the rich archaeological assemblage available, we still know very little about the social structures of prehistoric lacustrine communities and how domestic life was organised within the single household. By considering a few well-investigated sites, this chapter provides an overview of the level of research, and the theoretical aspects behind it, in the lake-dwelling studies. It also takes into account advantages and disadvantages of the various methodological approaches within the discipline. The chapter finally argues that, despite the strong empirical functionalist approach to research that has induced environmental deterministic explanations, the archaeological evidence available also has great potential for reconstructing social meaning (Bourdieu 1977; Rapoport 1990) and for detecting cultural change through time (Donley-Reid 1990).

Households: definition and approach to archaeological research

Studies of the social aspect of households span several disciplines, and, their levels of reliability, as well as the results, depend upon the available information. In anthropology, sociology and other social sciences, scholars not only deal with the physical structure of the buildings, but also with the people who occupy them. Research becomes particularly complex and results less consistent when the only evidence available comes from archaeological excavations. Not only are archaeologists faced with the reality of scarcity in the archaeological record, but they also have to be aware of the "transformations" caused by depositional processes after the site was abandoned. The nature of site abandonment creates a series of different situations. For instance, artefacts are usually removed from the site when abandonment is planned in advance, and left in place with sudden abandonment (Cameron and Tonka 1993). As a result, economic and social aspects are preserved in different ways. It is therefore incorrect to assume that all the artefacts found *in situ* reflect activities carried out while the site, or the house, was still in use. This is particularly true with abandonment due to flooding, because artefacts are moved around by water even after rapid evacuation of the site (Menotti 2002). Hence, a distinction is needed between depositional sets and areas, and activity sets and areas, in order to see the role played by depositional processes in creating the archaeological record (Schiffer 1987).

Spatial mapping tools
Despite the myriad of difficulties that one can encounter in studying households, archaeologists have never been discouraged from facing this fascinating territory. But how do we identify the household in the archaeological record? The most obvious answer is to try investigating social organisation using spatial analyses provided by the built environment (Kent 1990). Thanks to tools created by architects, archaeologists have learnt to identify and define spatial cells in material culture. As a result, a few successful cell mapping techniques have been developed in the past two decades or so, with the syntax and grammar methodologies being the most influential ones (Hillier

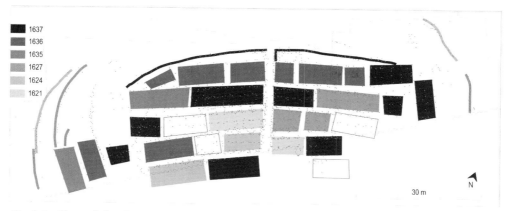

Fig 9.2. Plan of the Concise-sous-Colachoz lake-dwelling, 1637–1621 BC (Courtesy of Ariane Winiger, Archaeology Department of Canton Vaud).

Fig. 9.3. Reconstruction drawing of the Cham-Oberwil, Hof settlement (14th century BC). (Archaeology Department of Canton Zug).

and Hanson 1984). Another well-developed and long-applied methodology in spatial definition is that of artefact distributions and associations, whereby associated artefact patterns are used to spot particular human activities (Binford 1981; Carr 1984).

Social meaning

These approaches have provided important tools with which to address spatial patterning, but they have done little to help us understand the social meaning of the household. The term "house" has a variety of meanings, which change over time according to the people who inhabit the building; it is therefore crucial to consider the term from an etymological perspective in order to comprehend it fully. The study of diachronic or synchronic contexts in which the house is found becomes, therefore, crucial in order to understand social meaning. An invaluable approach to understand "multiple" social meanings is introduced by the work of Amos Rapoport. Rapoport (1990) argues that the built environment, which he calls "setting", delineates a condition that reminds people of a possible behaviour, which is appropriate to a specific situation dictated by the setting itself at a particular time. He furthermore maintains that it is erroneous to consider a setting as a single unit. There are, instead, various and specific "systems of activities" occurring in particular "systems of settings". In other words, the built environment gains or looses multiple and changeable meanings according to specific situations. Another scholar who has been working on similar aspects of environment-behaviour analyses is Pierre Bourdieu. According to Bourdieu (1977), the built environment imposes schemes of social organisation on people, and, at the same time, the organisation of space reflects and generates practices and social structures. As a result, the relationship between spatial organisation and social structure is discursive. Therefore, in defining a household, one should take into account a large range of perspectives within a variety of social and material contexts. Habitations not only reflect social structure, but they determine it (Shanks and Tilley 1987).

There are a number of methods for extrapolating meaning from past and present human-built environments. But whatever view is adopted: behaviour-environmental (Sanders 1985 and 1990), historical (Jameson 1990; Lawrence 1990), or symbolic (Kus 1982), there is an urgent need for integration of these approaches. There is no doubt that none of the above theoretical approaches can be regarded as faultless or infallible. Each serves specific purposes. What has to be kept in mind is that a single archaeological site may require more than one approach, hence archaeologists can make the most of them by integrating them into the archaeological reasoning, regardless of where they might have stemmed from: archaeology, anthropology, ethnoarchaeology, sociology, or other social sciences.

The concept of household in wetland environments

An environmental deterministic approach to the study of human habitations would argue that the space we live in is strongly influenced by the surrounding environment, in terms of shape, size, and building material used (Moran 1990). This can sometimes not be true, for the construction materials might be brought to the site from far away, and the builders or architects might be influenced by external cultural factors. Nevertheless, a good example of when the natural environment literally forces people to adopt specific ways of constructing their houses is found within the wetlands and, in particular, prehistoric wetlands.

Amongst the various hypotheses as to why prehistoric people chose to occupy the lake shores, marshes and other wetland environments, one is certainly a fact: the facility of building a pile dwelling. On top of the unconsolidated organic lake sediments (peat, marl, lake-mud) for instance, vertical wooden piles were much easier to drive directly into the ground (Menotti and Pranckenaite 2008), as opposed to digging

Fig. 9.4. (left) Plan of the Cortaillod-Est lake settlement (1010–955 BC) (Laténium, Archaeological Park and Museum in Neuchâtel).

Fig. 9.5. (below) Plan of the Auvernier-Nord lake-dwelling (878–850 BC) (Laténium, Archaeological Park and Museum in Neuchâtel).

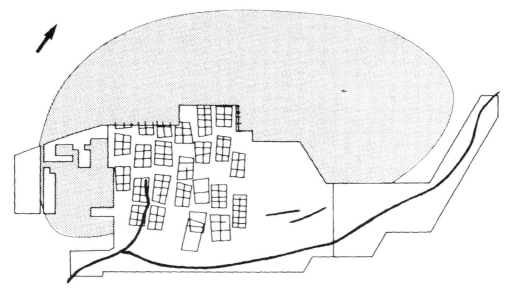

out post holes in the rather tough morainic clay that dominated environments not directly situated on the lakeside. Therefore, the whole architectural tradition of wetland settlements developed in a special characteristic way. One aspect of the lake-dwelling architecture, which has to be noted, is that the buildings were all made almost entirely of wood. Hence, because of the particularly humid conditions in which the houses were constructed, they needed periodical maintenance. Through experimental archaeology, Monnier *et al.* (1991) have been able to prove that the lifespan of a pile dwelling does not exceed 15–20 years, even if the building is properly maintained (Leuzinger

2004). It is therefore vital to consider the house as a living entity, and, as Bailey (1990) suggests, read its actions as a biography. If we consider the house as "alive" within a number of social and material contexts, we "may speak of the life-cycle of a house: the house is born, it lives, it dies, but its spirit is remembered" (Bailey 1990, 28). Similarly, the wetland house retains all these social and material contexts, which are passed on generation after generation, regardless of its short life. And, thanks to the level of preservation of wetland settlements, the socio-cultural aspects of those ancient communities can potentially be extrapolated from the archaeological record.

Wetland archaeological research can even go one step further and detect acculturation processes by analysing material culture and the use of space. Occupational patterns in prehistoric wetland environments have always been irregular (Menotti 1999, 2001a; 2002). It is rare to find continuity in settlements over a long period of time. This is in most cases due to climatic fluctuations (Magny 2004), forcing wetland communities to move to more favourable areas. Displaced groups might encounter and mix with other neighbouring communities, starting different processes of acculturation (Menotti 2003; 2004), which appear in the consistent patterning of the archaeological record as irregularities. Hence, the material culture as well as the built environment has, in this case, the capability of detecting change, proving the presence of acculturation or assimilation processes, and eventually, reconstructing continuity within single cultural traditions (Donley-Reid 1990).

Case studies of prehistoric lakeside village and house organisation in the Circum-Alpine region

Although several plans of Bronze Age lakeside villages and houses are available (some examples of lacustrine village plans from the Early, Middle and Late Bronze Ages are shown in Figures 9.1 to 9.8; and a selection of house reconstructions from Bronze Age lake settlements in Figures 9.9–19), only a few are suitable for the reconstruction of household organisations. It might therefore be useful to start this section of the chapter by stepping back to the Neolithic, in order to discuss one of the most informative sites within the lake-dwelling phenomenon in the Circum-Alpine region: the Late Neolithic lake village of Arbon-Bleiche 3. With a certain degree of prudence, the living conditions at this site could be compared to the Bronze Age period.

The lakeside settlement of Arbon-Bleiche 3
Arbon-Bleiche 3 is located in the eastern part of Switzerland (Canton Thurgau) on the southern shore of Lake Constance. The extensive excavations (over 1100 m²) of the site were carried out by the Archaeology Department of Canton Thurgau, during the summers of 1993–95. A large number of well-preserved artefacts and house features, dating from 3384–3370 BC were recovered. This allowed archaeologists to reconstruct

Fig. 9.6. (left) Reconstruction drawing of the Unteruhldingen-Stollenwiesen lakeside village (975–954 BC) (Lake-dwelling Museum, Unteruhldingen).

Fig. 9.7. (below) Plan of the Greifensee-Böschen lacustrine village (1048–1042 BC) (Office of Archaeology, Zurich City, Underwater Archaeology Unit – Department of Urban Development).

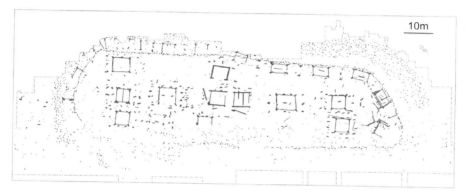

10m

Fig. 9.8. (left) Reconstruction drawing of the Ürschhausen-Horn lakeside village (2nd half of the 9th century BC) (Archaeology Department of Canton Thurgau).

village life and building activities during the transitional period between the Pfyn and Horgen Cultures (Leuzinger 2000; de Capitani *et al.* 2002; Jacomet *et al.* 2004). The ground plans of the houses were detected by analysing the rows of wooden piles and the locations of the lenses of clay and burnt lumps of daub. A total of 27 houses with raised floors were fully excavated.

Francesco Menotti and Urs Leuzinger

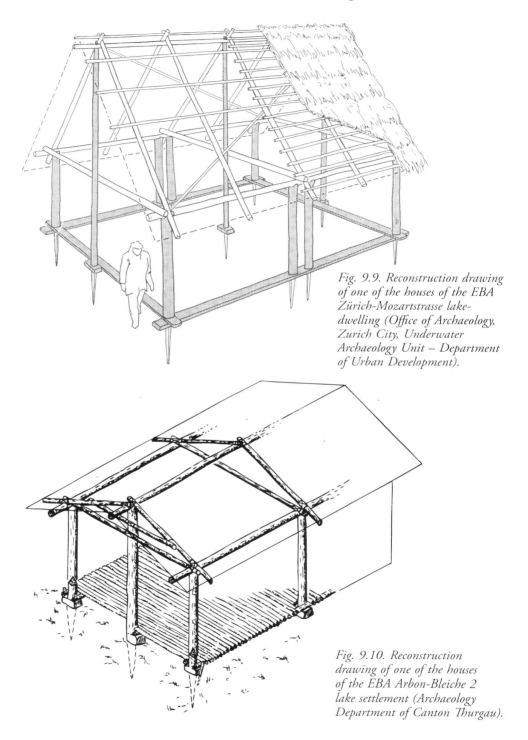

Fig. 9.9. Reconstruction drawing of one of the houses of the EBA Zürich-Mozartstrasse lake-dwelling (Office of Archaeology, Zurich City, Underwater Archaeology Unit – Department of Urban Development).

Fig. 9.10. Reconstruction drawing of one of the houses of the EBA Arbon-Bleiche 2 lake settlement (Archaeology Department of Canton Thurgau).

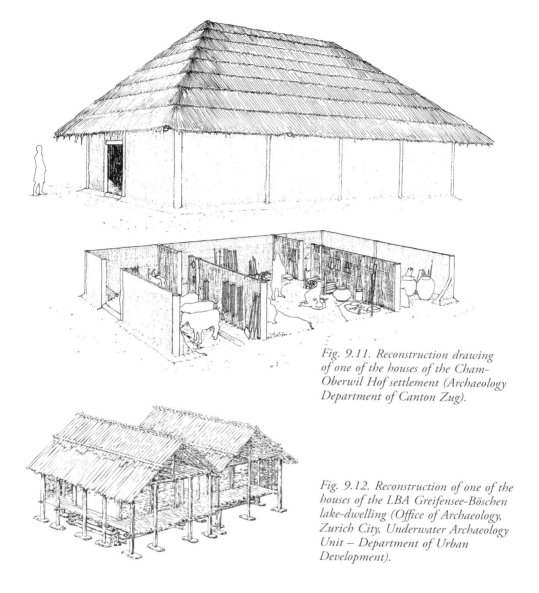

Fig. 9.11. Reconstruction drawing of one of the houses of the Cham-Oberwil Hof settlement (Archaeology Department of Canton Zug).

Fig. 9.12. Reconstruction of one of the houses of the LBA Greifensee-Böschen lake-dwelling (Office of Archaeology, Zurich City, Underwater Archaeology Unit – Department of Urban Development).

Dendrochronological analyses provided the dating of individual houses to the exact year. Eight construction phases identified in the village constituted 15 years of settling, with the first house built in 3384 BC. Two further houses were constructed in the immediate vicinity a year later. No houses were built in 3382 BC, but, the following year, an actual building boom ensued: a total of ten new houses were erected. Rows of houses at right-angles to the shore emerged with alleyways providing access on their sides. A further row of houses was added to the south in 3380 BC. Three

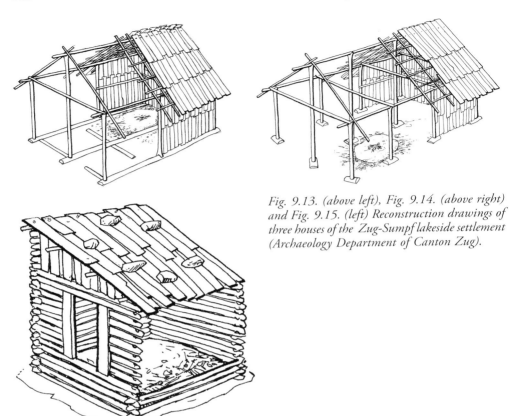

Fig. 9.13. (above left), Fig. 9.14. (above right) and Fig. 9.15. (left) Reconstruction drawings of three houses of the Zug-Sumpf lakeside settlement (Archaeology Department of Canton Zug).

further buildings were erected a year later, one of which, a small house only about 5 squared metres of floor space, exhibited a ground plan that deviated somewhat from the "standard" rectangular (approximately 4 × 8 m) houses. Three more houses were constructed in 3378 BC and, among them there was another little square building. In 3377 BC, an additional row of houses started to emerge in the south-western area of the excavation, which was accessible via a further village alleyway. The last building activity occurred in 3376 BC. No further houses were built after this date; only repair works carried out on the already existing buildings. The latest timber dated was felled in 3370 BC. Therefore, the devastating conflagration, which brought the settlement to an end, probably took place a short while later.

Thanks to an extensive interdisciplinary research project, it was possible to establish a more detailed picture of the village organisation as well as that of the individual households (Jacomet *et al.* 2004). Only a small number of cultivated and gathered plants showed significant differences in their concentrations between house and alleyway areas; this could be connected with the dumping of waste. It is possible that cereal was winnowed in front of the houses, causing a lot of uncharred chaff to be windblown

Fig. 9.16. *Full-size recostruction of one of the houses of the Cortaillod-Est lake-dwelling (Photograph: Urs Leuzinger).*

Fig. 9.17. *Reconstruction drawing of one of the houses of the Ürschhausen-Horn lake village (Archaeology Department of Canton Thurgau).*

Fig. 9.18. *Reconstruction drawing of the inside of one of the houses of the Ürschhausen-Horn lake village houses (Archaeology Department of Canton Thurgau).*

beside and, to a lesser extent, under the houses. No central threshing floor was found in the excavated area. The distribution suggests that each household unit cleaned their own cereal and flax, and presumably also their own poppy crops. Charred cereal remains were concentrated in the areas of the houses and, therefore, represent activities, such as cooking and storing, which took place inside the houses. One can also assume that all households made their own flour, since, with few exceptions, at least one stone quern was found in every building.

Other combinations of plant remains are more difficult to interpret. Positive correlations between berries, rosehips and turnips suggest the presence of faeces; human coprolites were very often found in the cultural layer. However, since they were not mapped systematically, one cannot make statements with any degree of certainty on the locations of the "toilets". High concentrations of berry pips suggest that a small area of house 20, one of the last-built houses, was used as a lavatory zone. An extremely high concentration of hazelnut shells was found in a building constructed in 3381 BC. These may have been dumped under the house through a waste trapdoor. A similar feature was also observed in Risch-Oberrisch (Hochuli *et al.* 1998, 138–139).

The horizontal distribution of the animal bones did not present a clear picture concerning the dumping of waste. Due to the extraordinarily good state of preservation and the extremely small number of joins, one may assume that the animal bones were buried rapidly and experienced hardly any displacement. Bones were found within as well as between buildings, and their horizontal distribution shows clear differences between the individual houses. In houses 1–4, 8, 20 and 24, more than 50% of bones belonged to wild animals. Houses 7 and 23, on the other hand, yielded very small amounts of wild animal bones and high proportions of domestic ones. The distribution of domestic animal species varied from place to place. While domestic cattle bones were dominant in the northern part of the village, domestic pigs were more frequent in the southern part of the settlement.

The bones of wild animal species were also distributed differently among the houses. The largest amounts of deer bones were recovered from houses 3, 8, 20 and 24. Wild cattle were very frequent in houses 3, 8 and 20, while houses 8 and 20 yielded additional concentrations of brown bear, marten/polecat, badger and otter bones. The above-mentioned distribution allowed archaeologists to identify various differences between the households, not only in terms of nutrition, but also in terms of handcraft production – in this case, furs.

Fish remains also show a distributional boundary, previously detected in the cattle and pig bones. The most common species found in the landward area of the village were pike, perch and particularly fish of the carp family, which were caught with nets close to the shore (this is also confirmed by the high number of net sinkers found in the area). On the other hand, whitefish dominated in the lake-ward part of the village. Whitefish are caught from boats, using trawl nets without net sinkers. It is therefore clear that the inhabitants of the northern part of the village pursued a different kind of fishing from those living in the "lake quarter". The former were specialised in near-shore fishing, whereas the latter preferred boat fishing. At the same time, inhabitants of the northern half of the village were responsible for cattle husbandry, while those of the lake-ward half pigs. Sheep and goats were kept in both parts of the village (Jacomet *et al.* 2004).

The distribution patterns show that several households collaborated together in order to use the workforce as efficiently as possible. Such tasks, most likely concerned crop husbandry, harvesting, the provision of winter fodder for the domestic animals, fishing, forest management and possibly also the exploitation of clay deposits for the production of pottery. Gathering plants and hunting were most likely organised individually, and according to spatial distribution, certain households or individual people hunted and gathered more than others.

A division of labour is noticeable throughout the village and within the individual household units. This division of labour is also present in the pottery making. Vessels with similar stylistic characteristics led de Capitani (2002, 222) to believe that one person possibly produced vessels for several households. However, the distribution of the half-finished tools shows that most individual households were generally self-sufficient. This was particularly noticeable, for instance, in the distributions of the stone axe industry, textile and flint production (Leuzinger 2000, 137–139 and 153).

The Early Bronze Age settlement of Zürich-Mozartstrasse
The Department of Urban Development of Zurich carried out an extensive (2700 squared metres) rescue excavation on the Zürich-Mozartstrasse site, from 1981 to 1982 (Gross 1987; Hochuli *et al.* 1998). This resulted in the discovery of several Neolithic and Bronze Age settlements. Unfortunately, artefact analyses of the two Early Bronze Age settlements have not yet been published in full, and only preliminary conclusions can be reached to date. Unfortunately, lack of dendrochronological dates prevents both Early Bronze Age settlements (1a and 1b) from being dated precisely. Nevertheless radiocarbon dating places the massive timber floor overlying the anthropogenic layers of the two villages within the 19th century BC, therefore providing a *terminus ante quem* for the abandonment of both villages (Conscience 2001). The possibility of a much earlier occupational phase is also sustained by typological analyses carried out on the ceramics, which resembles that of the 21th century BC lacustrine settlement of Greifensee-Böschen on Lake Greifen (not to be confused with the LBA one mentioned below).

Village 1a consisted of eight houses, whereas village 1b ten houses (see Fig. 9.1). The buildings were rectangular structures measuring *c.* 3.8 m in width and 6 m in length, and they were oriented north-north-west to south-south-east. The foundations of the houses consisted of sill beams, joined together by square-shaped mortises (ground-joint technique). Both, the corner and the central piles were driven into the ground through these mortises (Fig. 9.20). A partition wall, dividing the building into two halves, was found in house 2. Most rectangular buildings contained a hearth, which was reinforced with either stones, or with a daubed wooden grating. Altogether, the villages yielded about 200 kg of ceramic sherds, a loop-headed pin and several axe blades of the Langquaid type.

Finds distributions, which could provide new insights as to what the individual buildings were used for, have not yet been published. However, the houses with hearths were certainly inhabited dwelling, whereas house 10, a square-shaped building located in the south-eastern part of the village, was probably a storehouse. The numerous questions concerning the internal spatial division and organisation of Zürich-Mozartstrasse houses could only be answered with further extensive scientific analyses.

Fig. 9.19. Scaled model (1:32) of the Neolithic lakeside settlement of Arbon-Bleiche 3, Canton Thurgau (made by Christoph Müller and Daniel Steiner, Archaeology Department of Canton Thurgau).

The Early Bronze Age settlement of Arbon Bleiche 2

A large marshland area of the Bleiche region (near the town of Arbon) was drained in 1944. Mr Otto Meyer-Boulenaz (a local dentist) found numerous Neolithic and Bronze Age objects after a few roadwork trenches had been dug. The discovery triggered a particular interest, because it was one of the first lakeside settlements dating from Early Bronze Age, ever found in the Circum-Alpine region. Under the supervision of Karl Keller-Tarnuzzer, approximately 30 interned Polish soldiers excavated more than 2800 squared metres of the settlement, in 1945. Several test excavations were subsequently carried out by the Archaeology Department of Canton Thurgau in 1983 and from 1990 to 1992, which provided further insights into the Bronze Age settlement.

Based on the dendrochronological dates, pile distribution and the typological analyses, it was demonstrated that the Early and Middle Bronze Age settlement of Bleiche 2 had at least three phases of occupation from 1700–1500 BC. Eighteen houses, about 3.5–4.5 m wide and 4.5–6 m long (all with raised floors) have been located. Several palisades enclosed the village.

Fig. 9.20. Zürich-Mozartstrasse: Early Bronze Age ground plan of house 4 (settlement 1b), with clearly visible sill beam (and ground-joint) construction, (Photograph: Office of Archaeology, Zurich City, Underwater Archaeology Unit – Department of Urban Development).

The abundant archaeological material consisted of more than 15,000 potsherds, 102 bronze objects, including pins, daggers, spearheads and axes (Fig. 9.21), as well as rare items of jewellery made of gold, amber and glass. Some of the ceramic vessels had very fine fabric and were lavishly decorated. The large finds assemblage was used as reference material to define the so-called "Arbon group" of the late Early Bronze Age.

Scientific post-excavation analyses were carried out by Stefan Hochuli in the 1990s. Nevertheless, due to missing parts of the archaeological assemblage excavated in 1945, precise analyses on object spatial distributions (germane for an accurate reconstruction of settlement structures and house organisation), could not be carried out (Hochuli 1994).

However, particular findings such as, two clay tuyères, a casting mould, a piece of pure copper, as well as several bronze chisels show that part of the village was also involved in metalworking, textile manufacturing and pottery production, at a fairly large scale.

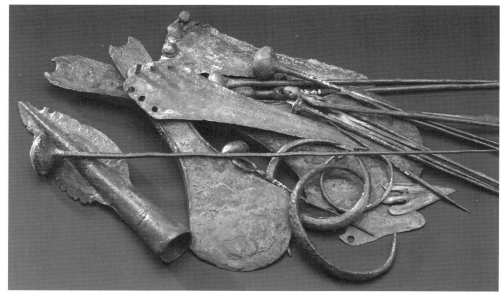

Fig. 9.21. Bronze objects found at the Early Bronze Age settlement of Arbon Bleiche 2 (Photograph: Res Eichenberger, Archaeology Department of Canton Thurgau).

The Middle Bronze Age "settlement hiatus"

The Middle Bronze Age (from the 15th to the 12th centuries BC) is characterised by a complete absence of lacustrine settlements in the northern part of the Circum-Alpine region (Menotti 2001a; 2004, 207–217). Due to a severe change in climatic conditions, the lake water levels increased considerably, forcing people to move away from the shores. However, more recent research has shown that lake-dwellers did not abandon the lacustine environment completely; they simply retreated to higher grounds, keeping their connection to the lakes. Clear evidence of such a climatically triggered inland shift, was found in the Kreuzlingen region (Rigert 2001; Menotti 2003). In fact, a series of settlements dating from the above-mentioned Middle Bronze Age hiatus (15th–12th centuries BC) were found on the gentle slopes adjacent to the lake. Interestingly, these settlements were all situated above the 400 m a.s.l. contour line, which is the maximum expansion of Lake Constance during that period.

The Middle Bronze Age (1450–1350 BC) settlement, most closely located near the 400 m a.s.l. contour line, was Tägerwilen-Hochstross (407 m a.s.l.). All other villages (either contemporaneous, or of later dates) were found in similar topographic settings, but at higher altitude (410–415m a.s.l.). Some examples are those of Tägerwilen-Ribi, Kreuzlingen-Ribi-Brunegg and Kreuzlingen-Ribi-Girsbergtunnel (Rigert 2001; Menotti 2003). The gentle morainic slopes of the Kreuzlingen region continued being settled throughout the entire Middle Bronze Age and part of the Late Bronze Age, reaching also higher altitudes; see for instance Wildenwis-Saubach, Bernrain and Schlossbühl.

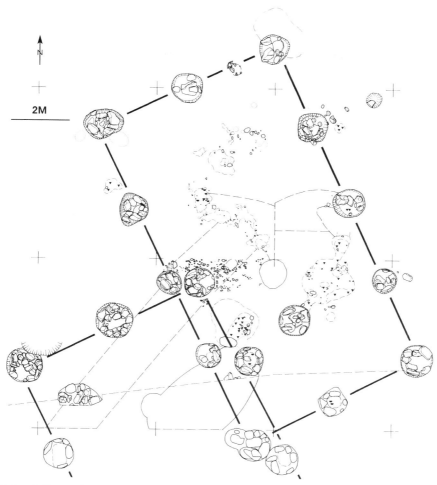

Fig. 9.22. MBA settlement of Cham-Oberwil Hof: ground plan of one of the houses (Archaeology Department of Canton Zug).

Settling more elevated grounds near the lakes was not only confined to the Kreuzlingen region. People moved away from the lake shores all over the northern Circum-Alpine region. Evidence of this "inland" shift is to be found in the northern part of Lake Constance, on Lake Zurich and Lake Zug, and other lakes. One of the best examples is found at Cham-Oberwil-Hof (Lake Zug, Switzerland) (see Figs 9.22 and 9.23), where typical Middle Bronze Age material culture, possibly linked to earlier lacustrine sites was identified. It is important to point out that people did not only move inland because of the threatening waters, but also in search for new tillable land. In fact, not only did the high lake water levels inundate their villages, but also

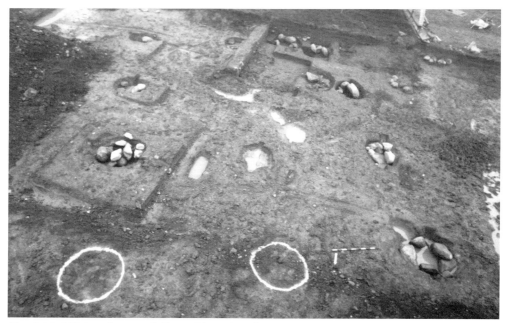

Fig. 9.23. MBA settlement of Cham-Oberwil Hof: in-situ ground plan of one of the houses. The post pits with packing stones are clearly visible (Photograph: Archaeology Department of Canton Zug).

their agricultural fields. Once the lake levels retreated to normal standards in the Late Bronze Age, people returned to the lake shores and the typical lake-dwelling settlements started to appear again.

The Late Bronze Age (HaB1) lakeside settlement of Greifensee-Böschen
The Greifensee-Böschen site is located on the northern shores of Lake Greifen (Canton Zurich). The whole lacustrine village (2500 squared metres) was fully excavated by the Underwater Team of the Zurich Department of Urban Development, between 1984 and 1995 (Eberschweiler 1997, 39–40; and 1998, 21–27; Benkert *et al.* 1998, 193–211; Ruoff 1998: 2–20; Seifert *et al.* 1998: 378–379; Eberschweiler *et al.* 2007). A total of 24 houses were uncovered (Fig. 9.7). The cultural layer was badly disturbed and only partially preserved. Dendrochronology dating placed the village between 1048 and 1042 BC, and the reason of abandonment was probably accidental fire.

The whole agglomerate of houses consisted of 12 buildings in the inner part of the village and 12 small ones (4.5 × 2.5 m) placed in a circle around the main houses. All houses were built using a combination of block-construction technique and vertical posts either driven into the lake marl, or secured with perforated plates (see Fig. 9.12). The whole settlement was enclosed by a fence as well as a dense field of posts.

The 12 central buildings were interpreted as dwellings and workshops, whereas the little buildings around them were probably storehouses. An interesting feature

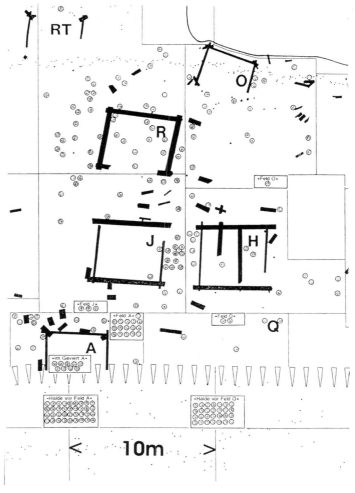

Fig 9.24. Ceramic bowls distribution in the Late Bronze Age lakeside settlement of Greifensee-Böschen, Canton Zurich (Drawing: Beat Eberschweiler and Peter Riethmann – Office of Archaeology, Zurich City, Underwater Archaeology Unit – Department of Urban Development).

was a completely empty area measuring 18 × 8 m located in the north-eastern part of the settlement, directly beside the fence. It still remains unknown whether this was a building plot that had not yet been built, or whether it was a space that was kept empty for a particular purpose.

Given the raised platform on which the buildings were constructed, it is not surprising that no hearths were preserved *in situ*. According to the spatial distribution of the ceramic vessels, the main working space area was probably located outside the buildings, in the porch near the entrance (Eberschweiler 1997, 39–40). The archaeological assemblage (especially pottery) fond in Greifensee-Böschen is extremely varied; in some areas very rich and in others fairly poor. Worth mentioning is the high number of spindle whorls, loom weights, tools and bronze ornaments found in some houses. It is also important to point out that some buildings had specific functions, and no all activities (*e.g.* weaving) were carried out in all houses. For instance, houses J and H apart from

Fig 9.25. Late Bronze Age house floor (with ceramic) of the Ürschhausen-Horn lake-dwelling (Archaeology Department of Canton Thurgau).

huge storage containers, a large number of shouldered beakers and only a few bowls and pots, no other artefacts were found (Fig. 9.24).

Ürschhausen-Horn (Late-Late Bronze Age: HaB3)

The settlement of Ürschhausen-Horn (Canton Thurgau) is located on a peninsula on the Nussbaum Lake in the Seebach Valley. The site dates from the latest part of the Late Bronze Age (HaB3), and was excavated extensively by the Turgau Archaeology Department in 1970 and from 1986 to 1991. A total of 1600 squared metres were examined and 45 house plans were found (Gollnisch-Moos 1999). According to dendrochronological and radiocarbon dates, as well as the typological analyses of the abundant archaeological assemblage (Nagy 1999), the settlement was occupied (probably not continuously) from the second half of the 9th century to the end of the 7th century BC.

Most of the houses at Ürschhausen-Horn were rectangular, but a few square buildings were also found. They usually measure 2–3 × 3–4 m and were built using two techniques together: the block-building and the plank-pillar techniques (see Fig. 9.17). The house floors were reinforced by criss-crossing joists covered by a layer of loam, which, in some cases, consisted of several layers of clay. Hearths, most of which had a simple structure, were identified in 27 houses and they were placed directly on the clay floor without any substructure.

The internal division of the houses was difficult to identify. Some large rooms for instance had several hearths, but dividing walls were not observed. Because of the limited size of the houses and the peculiar artefact distribution, it has been presumed that pottery and other objects were stored on suspended shelves along the walls (see Figs. 9.18 and 9.25), and the same area was used for working and sleeping. Attics, positively identified in some houses, could also have been used as additional storage space. A number of vessels were also left directly around hearths. No furniture was preserved, apart from a particular timber substructure (in house 5), which has been interpreted as a working platform or bedstead (Gollnisch-Moos 1999, 67). A fairly large number of loom weights were also found in several houses. Out of 44 building plans identified in the settlement, 33 could be interpreted as dwellings. The functions of the remaining houses could not be established. A zone in the centre of the peninsula (where the village was located) was left free of buildings and it has been interpreted as a village square (Gollnisch-Moos 1999, 97).

The lake-dwellers' way of living: interpretation

Lacustrine houses and households

Despite the excellent level of preservation in waterlogged environments, identifying the internal division of the lacustrine houses has always been quite problematic. This is mostly due to the formation processes of the archaeological record. The collapsing of the elevated platform (whether on land or in the water), would displace the original position of the floor assemblage, making more difficult for the archaeologists to reconstruct it. Moreover, subsequent flooding (lake level variations) of the site has complicated the matter even further, by moving the artefacts around. As a result, cell mapping techniques to gauge spatial distribution are extremely difficult to apply (Hillier and Hanson 1984).

However, thanks to the development of new methods of analyses, not only the internal division can be identified, but in optimal conditions, also social stratification is recognisable (see for instance Arbon-Bleiche 3: Jacomet *et al.* 2004). What remains very difficult to gauge is demography. We know that the size of the lake-dwelling houses remained fairly similar throughout the Circum-Alpine region from the Neolithic to the Late Bronze Age, as opposed to the size and layout of the villages, which varied considerably according to the period and location (Schlichtherle 2004, 28). Averagely, a house was fairly small (4 × 8 m). But, does a small house mean a small family? It has been assumed that a "mean family size" can be calculated through average house size (Kolb 1985). However, there is no model that explains the relationship between social phenomena and material culture (houses included). The use of average figures for particular level of socio-economic organisation may prevent the recognition of gradual change within a community. This is particularly true within the Circum-Alpine region lake-dwellings, where no evidence of burials are to be found, and therefore demographic calculations and differentiation in social status cannot be easily confirmed.

There are, however, crucial insights to identify internal dynamics and interrelationships of a lacustrine household. Dendrochronology, for instance, allows us to spot repairs or extensions of the house. We can therefore reconstruct the life history of a house, as well as that of the village. It might be difficult to see whether the small internal area of a house was multifunctional, and a single space was used for different purposes, *e.g.* sleeping area at night and working area during the day. But the size, location (within the settlement) and the layout of the village are definitely crucial to identify hierarchical division within the community (see for example Marin: Lake Neuchâtel and Greifensee-Böschen: Lake Greifen – Honegger 2001; Eberschweiler *et al.* 2007). In fact, the limits of a household go often beyond the perimeter of the single house. As a result, if we want to understand the interrelationships of a lake-dwelling household, we need to take into account the whole village.

Households outside houses: the relationship to the village

In trying to recreate the social context and extrapolate meaning from the household, it is important to consider its entire spatial extension. The first question that comes into our mind is therefore: "where does the household end?" And, is there a correlation between the total floor area of dwellings and the settlement (presumed) population? It is understood that not only can a household encompass more buildings, but more households can use the so-called "communal space" to carry out particular activities such as food processing, cooking, artefact manufacture and storage (Whitelaw 1991). Hence, the space used for "private" activities can be reduced considerably. This is particularly true concerning wetland sites, where the amount of space available was quite limited. Of course, space availability varies from site to site, but in the majority of cases, the space used for building the family house was restricted to a few square metres (see previous section). The communal space within the village was much more crucial to the group's social activities!

Studying how households relate to each other and how they are integrated into the wider social landscape (the village and beyond), has become vital within household studies on wetland settlements. Because of the dependability on the natural environment, it is once again, difficult to avoid environmental deterministic explanations. Settlements' location, layout, size and house typology depend upon a combination of natural phenomena within the environment. Villages are built either directly in the water, or on the water basin shore and their house typology depends on a combination of various natural as well as cultural factors (Menotti 2001b). But, regardless of the shape and the particular location of the house, or the settlement, the climate can always influence them directly, or indirectly (Menotti 1999; 2001a). For instance, an increase in humidity and precipitation may alter the hydrologic balance of the basin and inundate the intra-settlement space used for communal activities (see above). In addition to these unpredictable changes, one has to take into account the normal seasonal variability. As a result, activities that are carried out on the "communal ground" outside the houses vary from season to season; the system of activities changes constantly according to the system of settings. Therefore, social activities in relation to the meaning of household within wetland communities are better understood by studying the village as a whole, rather than just the single houses.

The wetland village

The limited building space available to wetland communities has forced them to structure their villages in particular ways. Although most houses were, generally, "self-sufficient" (they had hearths, sleeping space and resting areas), the majority of everyday activities were carried out in the open space, and the facilities (fireplaces, storage and working areas) were shared by the whole community. Depending on the typology of the settlement, the open space might have consisted of a large wooden platform, if the village was a pile dwelling constructed in the water, or just the ground between houses, if the village was built on the shore of a lake. The village would have included horticultural areas and enclosures for cattle or other domestic animals. In the case of large agricultural production, the fields were located outside the perimeter of the village, but still nearby. Sometimes, because of lack of tillable land near the village, the agricultural fields were located fairly far from it. See for instance the Late Bronze Age/Iron Age pile dwellings of Lake Luokesas in Lithuania, where, because of the extensive woodlands around the village, the agricultural fields were located on the other side of the lake (Menotti *et al.* 2005). Both, the village and the adjacent agricultural fields would have been protected by palisades or other sorts of fences. Finally, the number of villages within a single lacustrine region, and the distance between them depended upon the single area and the archaeological period.

Subsistence and economy

According to the rich material culture assemblages commonly found on prehistoric lacustrine sites in the Circum-Alpine region, those wetland groups were a mix between agriculturalists, pastoralists, hunters, and fishermen. The most common artefacts found are: pottery, axes, arrowheads, daggers, spears, fishing gear, and various wooden agricultural tools (also including the plough, from the Late Neolithic and Bronze Age onwards). Although practical tools were more numerous, lake-dwelling sites also yield sophisticated cultic or ornamental objects such as statuettes, beads, amulets, necklaces, bracelets, combs, and even musical instruments (Hochuli 1994; Schlichtherle 1997; Leuzinger 2000; De Capitani *et al.* 2002). Weaving was also part of the lake-dwellers' economic activities, as textiles, mainly from flax and other plant fibres, are not uncommon (de Capitani *et al.* 2002).

An important part of the lake-dwellers economy was trade and exchange. Lacustrine groups in the Alpine region had a fairly complex trade network that not only covered local areas, but also extended over large geographical regions, from the Danube to the Po Plain, and from present-day eastern France to some of the neighbouring eastern

European countries (Menotti 2008). Transportation on lakes and rivers was mainly done by canoes (dugouts) and rafts, whereas, over land, pack animals and sledges were used. From the late 4th millennium BC wheeled carts were also introduced (Schlichtherle 1997; 2004; Sherratt 2006).

The diverse environment and the multitude of activities in which the lake-dwellers were engaged, shaped their diet in a distinctive way. Agricultural activity was fundamental, and that caused extensive woodland clearings throughout the entire lake-dwelling phenomenon. Cereals played a crucial role, with the five main species being naked wheat, emmer, einkorn, barley and millet (Jacomet *et al.* 1989; 1999). Pulses were also present, especially during the Bronze Age. In addition to cereals, the lacustrine people collected berries (raspberries, blackberries and sloes), fruits (apples and plums) and nuts, such as hazelnuts, acorn and walnuts (Jacomet 2004).

The daily intake of protein was mainly obtained from meat, fish and some dairy products. The number of hunted wild animals and exploited domestic ones varies according to the different archaeological periods. The most popular wild game was the red deer (also exploited for its antlers), followed by wild boar, aurochs, elk, various species of birds and fish *e.g.*, pike, whitefish, catfish and perch (Schibler 2004). Among the domestic animals, the main exploited species were cattle, sheep, goats, pigs and dogs. Horses started to appear at the end of the Neolithic, but they were extremely rare even in the Bronze Age, and they were certainly not kept for meat production, but used as pack animals, or for pulling light travois (Hochuli and Maise 1998; Schibler 2004; Pétrequin *et al.* 2006).

Continuity in the lake-dwelling tradition

The lake-dwelling phenomenon within the Circum-Alpine region can certainly be seen as a distinct way of living. However, despite the fact that a number of cultures can be identified within the entire lake-dwelling period (43rd–7th century BC), it is incorrect to separate them from the "inland" groups completely. Scarce archaeological evidence on contemporaneous "terrestrial" settlements, has, so far, prevented us from doing thorough comparative analyses with wetland sites, but different artefacts do not necessarily mean different cultures. A good example is the Luokesas pile-dwellings, where their pottery typology is similar to that of the neighbouring "dryland" communities, but part of the objects are slightly different, more suitable for a wetland environment (Menotti *et al.* 2005). It is nevertheless important to point out that a distinct way of living (*e.g.* wetland settlements) can be perpetuated through time and cultures, even with numerous occupational interruptions.

As pointed out above, dendrochronology allows us to reconstruct the chronology of the settlements on different scales: a single occupation of a site and its abandonment, the spatial expansion of the village in relation to demographic fluctuations, and even the periodical maintenance of the single houses. Hence, as Bailey (1990) remarks, the house (or even the settlement) can be considered as "alive" and its actions read as a biography. A number of social and material contexts are embedded in the life-cycle of a habitation, from the time when the house is born to when it dies, with its spirit being remembered and passed on to following generations. This fine chronological control and detailed architectural evidence not only allows us to reconstruct the chronology of the single settlement, but also to bridge gaps in the archaeological record, *e.g.* the various occupational lacunae within the entire lake-dwelling phenomenon (Menotti 2001a; 2003). Hence, the distinctive settlement-history of this set of environments, and, especially the role of acculturation or assimilation within the overall processes of cultural adjustment, can be identified (Donley-Reid 1990; Menotti 2003; 2004).

Conclusions

Household studies within lake-dwelling research are unfortunately still at an embryonic state. The large amount of archaeological evidence (including its excellent level of preservation) does not always help us shed light on those lacustrine communities' fascinating way of living. We know where and how they built their houses, what they ate and how they interacted with the surrounding environment, but it is still not clear how complex their social organisation and their religious beliefs were. The peculiar site formation processes typical of wetland environments are sometime misleading, and make the identification of the various social aspects of people's life much more difficult. This is unfortunate, but nevertheless an increasingly wide range of new research methods are being developed and some results are expected to appear very soon (Menotti 2012).

Acknowledgements
We would like to thank the editors of this volume for inviting us to write this chapter. We are also very much indebted to a number of our colleagues for providing us with useful insight during the writing of the paper.

References
Bailey, D. W. (1990) The living house: signifying continuity. In R. Samson (ed.) *The Social Archaeology of Houses*. Edinburgh, Edinburgh University Press.
Benkert, A., Carazzetti, R., Gollnisch, H., Rageth, J. and Seifert, M. (1998) *Siedlungswesen*. In S. Hochuli, U. Niffeler, and V. Rychner (eds) *Die Schweiz vom Paläolithikum bis zum frühen Mittelalter. SPM III. Bronzezeit*, 193–211. Basel, Schweizerische Gesellschaft für Ur- und Frühgeschichte.
Binford, L. R. (1981) *Bones: Ancient Man and Modern Myths*. London, Academic Press.
Bourdieu, P. (1977) *Outline of a Theory of Practice*. Cambridge, Cambridge University Press.
Cameron, C. M. and Tonka, S. A. (1993) *Abandonment of Settlements and Regions: Ethnoarchaeological and Archaeological Approaches*. Cambridge, Cambridge University Press.

Carr, C. (1984) The nature of organisation of intrasite archaeological records and spatial analytic approaches to their investigation. In M. B. Schiffer (ed.) *Advances in Archaeological Method and Theory* (vol. 7)*,* 103–222. New York, Academic Press.

de Capitani, A., Deschler-Erb, S., Leuzinger, U., Marti-Grädel, E. and Schibler, J. (2002) *Die jungsteinzeitliche Siedlung Arbon-Bleiche 3. Funde.* Frauenfeld, Amt für Archäologie des Kantons Thurgau. Archäologie im Thurgau 11.

Conscience, A-C. (2001) Frühbronzezeitliche Uferdörfer aus Zürich-Mozartstrasse – eine folgenreiche Neudatierung. *Jahrbuch der Schweizerische Gesellschaft für Ur- und Frühgeschichte* 84, 147–157.

Donley-Reid, L. W. (1990) A structuring structure: the Swahili house. In Kent (ed.) (1990), 92–113.

Eberschweiler, B., Riethmann, P. and Ruoff, U. (2007) *Das spätbronzezeitliche Dorf von Greifensee-Böschen. Dorfgeschichte, Hausstrukturen und Fundmaterial.* Zürich und Egg, Baudirektion Kanton Zürich, Monographien der Kantonsarchäologie Zürich 38.

Eberschweiler, B. (1997) *Zur Nutzung von Häusern und Plätzen in der Spätbronzezeit. Beispiel Greifensee.* In NIKE-Nationale Informationsstelle für Kulturgüter-Erhaltung (ed.) *Das Haus als Lebens- und Wirtschaftsraum. Wissenschaftliche Fachtagung vom 22./23. August 1997 auf Schloss Münchenwiler BE,* 39–40. Bern, NIKE-Nationale Informationsstelle für Kulturgüter-Erhaltung.

Eberschweiler, B. (1998) Greifensee-Böschen. Keramik und Kleinfunde im Siedlungskontext. *Helvetia Archaeologica* 29/113, 21–27.

Gnepf Horisberger, U. and Hämmerle, S. (eds) (2001) *Cham-Oberwil, Hof (Kanton Zug). Befunde und Funde aus der Glockenbecherkultur und der Bronzezeit.* Basel, Schweizerische Gesellschaft für Ur- und Frühgeschichte, Antiqua 33.

Gollnisch-Moos, H. (1999) *Ürschhausen-Horn. Haus- und Siedlungsstrukturen der spätestbronzezeitlichen Siedlung.* Frauenfeld, Amt für Archäologie des Kantons Thurgau, Forschungen im Seebachtal, 3. Archäologie im Thurgau 7.

Gross, E. (1987) *Zürich «Mozartstrasse». Neolithische und bronzezeitliche Ufersiedlungen 1.* Zürich, Orell Füssli Verlag, Berichte der Zürcher Denkmalpflege Monographien 4.

Hillier, B. and Hanson, J. (1984) *The Social Logic of Space.* Cambridge, Cambridge University Press.

Hochuli, S. (1994) *Arbon-Bleiche. Die neolithischen und bronzezeitlichen Seeufersiedlungen. Ausgrabungen 1885–1991.* Frauenfeld, Amt für Archäologie des Kantons Thurgau, Archäologie im Thurgau 2.

Hochuli, S. and Maise, Ch. (1998) Verkehr und Transport. In Hochuli *et al.* (eds) (1998), 299–306.

Hochuli, S., Niffeler, U. and Rychner, V. (eds) (1998) *Die Schweiz vom Paläolithikum bis zum frühen Mittelalter. SPM III. Bronzezeit.* Basel, Schweizerische Gesellschaft für Ur- und Frühgeschichte.

Hochuli, S., Schaeren, G. and Weiss, J. (1998) Ein Dorfbrand in Oberrisch am Zugersee vor 5700 Jahren und die Folgen. *Archäologie der Schweiz* 21, 134–141.

Honegger, M. (2001) Marin NE - Les Piécettes au Néolithique: une station littorale d´exception. *Jahrbuch der Schweizerischen Gesellschaft für Ur- und Frühgeschichte* 84, 29-42.

Jacomet, S. (2004) Archaeobotany: a vital tool in the investigation of lake-dwellings. In F. Menotti (ed.) (2004)*,* 162–177.

Jacomet, S., Brombacher, C. and Dick, M. (1989) *Archäobotanik am Zürichsee. Ackerbau, Sammelwirtschaft und Umwelt von neolithisch en und bronzezeitlichen Seeufersiedlungen im Raum Zürich. Ergebnisse von Untersuchungen pflanzlicher Makroreste der Jahre 1979–1988.* Zürich, Orell Füssli, Zürcher Denkmalpflege, Monographien 7.

Jacomet, S., Brombacher, C. and Schraner, E. (1999) Ackerbau und Sammelwirtschaft während der Bronze- und Eisenzeit in den östlichen Schweizer Alpen – vorläufige Ergebnisse. In P. della Casa (ed.) *Prehistoric Alpine Environment, Society, and Economy. Papers of the International Colloquium PAESE, 97 in Zürich*, 231–244. Zürich, Universitätsforschungen zur prähistorischen Archäologie, Universitätsforschungen zur prähistorischen Archäologie 55.

Jacomet, S., Leuzinger, U. and Schibler, J. (eds) (2004) *Die jungsteinzeitliche Seeufersiedlung Arbon-Bleiche 3. Umwelt und Wirtschaft*. Frauenfeld, Amt für Archäologie des Kantons Thurgau, Archäologie im Thurgau 12.

Jameson, M. H. (1990) Domestic space in the Greek city-state. In Kent (ed.) (1990), 92–113.

Keller, F. (1854) Die keltischen Pfahlbauten in den Schweizerseen. *Mitteilungen der Antiquarischen Gesellschaft* 9(3), 65–100.

Kent, S. (1990) *Domestic Architecture and the Use of Space. An Interdisciplinary Cross-Cultural Study*. Cambridge, Cambridge University Press.

Kolb, C. (1985) Demographic estimates in archaeology: contributions from ethnography on Mesoamerican peasants. *Current Anthropology* 26, 581–599.

Kus, S. (1982) Matters, material and ideal. In I. Hodder (ed.) *Symbolic and Structural Archaeology*, 47–62. Cambridge, Cambridge University Press.

Lawrence, R. J. (1990) Public collective and private space: a study of urban housing in Switzerland. In Kent (ed.) (1990), 73–91.

Leuzinger, U. (2000) *Die jungsteinzeitliche Siedlung Arbon-Bleiche 3. Befunde*. Frauenfeld, Amt für Archäologie des Kantons Thurgau, Archäologie im Thurgau 9.

Leuzinger, U. (2004) Experimental and applied archaeology in lake-dwelling research. In F. Menotti (ed.) (2004), 237–250.

Magny, M. (1995) *Une histoire du climat. Des derniers mammouths au siècle de l'automobile*. Paris, Errance.

Magny, M. (2004) The contribution of palaeoclimatology to the lake-dwellings. In Menotti (ed.) (2004), 237–250.

Maute-Wolf, M., Quinn, D. S., Winiger, A., Wolf, A. C. and Burri, E. (2002) La station littorale de Concise (VD). Premiers résultats deux ans après la fin des fouilles. *Archäologie der Schweiz* 25(4), 2–15.

Menotti, F. (1999) The abandonment of the ZH-Mozartstrasse Early Bronze Age lake-settlement: GIS computer simulations of the lake-level fluctuation hypothesis. *Oxford Journal of Archaeology* 18(2), 143–155.

Menotti, F. (2001a) *The "Missing Period": Middle Bronze Age Lake-dwelling Occupational Hiatus in the Northern Alpine Region*. Oxford, Archaeopress, British Archaeological Report S968.

Menotti, F. (2001b) The "Pfahlbauproblem" and the history of the lake-dwelling research in the Alps. *Oxford Journal of Archaeology* 20(4), 319–328.

Menotti, F. (2002) Climatic change, flooding and occupational hiatus in the lake-dwelling central European Bronze Age. In R. Torrence and J. Grattan (eds) *Natural Disasters and Cultural Change*, 235–249. London, Routledge.

Menotti, F. (2003) Cultural response to environmental change in the Alpine lacustrine regions: the displacement model. *Oxford Journal of Archaeology* 22(4), 375–396.

Menotti, F. (2004) Displacement, readaptation and cultural continuity: a lake-dwelling perspective. In Menotti (ed.) (2004), 237–250

Menotti, F. (ed.) (2004) *Living on the Lake in Prehistoric Europe*. London, Routledge.

Menotti, F. (2012) *Wetland Archaeology and Beyond: Theory and Practice*. Oxford: Oxford University Press.

Menotti, F. and Pranckenaite, E. (2008) Lake-dwelling building techniques in prehistory: driving wooden piles into lacustrine sediments. *EuroREA* 5: 3-7.

Moran, E. F. (ed.) (1990) *The Ecosystem Approach in Anthropology*. Ann Arbor, University of Michigan Press.

Nagy, G. (1999) *Ürschhausen-Horn. Keramik und Kleinfunde der spätestbronzezeitlichen Siedlung. Text und Tafeln*. Frauenfeld, Amt für Archäologie des Kantons Thurgau, Forschungen im Seebachtal 2, Archäologie im Thurgau 6.

Monnier, J-L., Pétrequin, P., Richard, A., Pétrequin, and Gentizon, A-L. (1991) *Construire une maison 3000 ans avant J.C.: le lac de Chalain au Neolithique*. Paris, Editions Errance.

Pétrequin, P. (1997) *Ufersiedlungen im französischen Jura: eine ethnologische und experimentelle Annäherung*. In H. Schlichtherle (ed.) *Pfahlbauten rund um die Alpen*, 100–107. Stuttgart, Konrad Theiss Verlag.

Pétrequin, P., Arbogast, R-M., Pétrequin, A-M., Van Willigen, S. and Bailly, M. (2006) La traction animale au Néolithique: diversité des documents, diversité des approches. In P. Pétrequin, R-M. Arbogast, A-M. Pétrequin, S. van Willigen and M. Bailly (eds) *Premier Chariots, Premier Araires*, 11–20. Paris, CNRS Éditions.

Rapoport, A. (1990) Systems of activities and systems of settings. In Kent (ed.) (1990), 9–20.

Rigert, E. (2001) *A7 – Ausfahrt Archäologie. Prospektion und Grabungen im Abschnitt Schwaderloh–Landesgrenze*. Frauenfeld, Amt für Archäologie des Kantons Thurgau, Archäologie im Thurgau 10.

Ruoff, U. (1998) *Greifensee-Böschen, Kt. Zürich. Die Unterwasser-Rettungsgrabung*. Helvetia Archaeologica 29/113, 2–20.

Sanders, D. H. (1985) Ancient behaviour and the built environment: applying environmental psychology methods and theories to archaeological contexts. In S. Klein, R. Wener and S. Lehman (eds) *Environmental Change/Social Change*, 296–305. Washington, DC, EDRA.

Sanders, D. H. (1990) Behavioural conventions and archaeology: methods for the analysis of ancient architecture. In Kent (ed.) (1990), 43–72.

Schibler, J. (2004) Bones as a key for reconstructing the environment, nutrition and economy of the lake-dwelling societies. In Menotti (ed.) (2004),144–161.

Schiffer, M. B. (1987) *Formation Processes of the Archaeological Record*. Albuquerque, University of New Mexico Press.

Schlichtherle, H. (ed.) (1997) *Pfahlbauten rund um die Alpen*. Stuttgart, Konrad Theiss Verlag.

Schlichtherle, H. (2004) Lake-dwellings in south-western Germany: history of research and contemporary perspectives. In Menotti (ed.) (2004), 22–35.

Seifert, M. (1996) *Die spätbronzezeitlichen Ufersiedlungen Zug-Sumpf. Band 1. Die Dorfgeschichte*. Zug, Kantonales Museum für Urgeschichte Zug.

Seifert, M., Schibler, J. and Jacomet, S. (1998) Greifensee ZH, Böschen. In Hochuli *et al.* (eds) (1998), 378–379.

Shanks, M. and Tilley, C. (1987) *Social Theory and Archaeology*. Cambridge, Polity Press.

Sherratt, A. (2006) La traction animale et la transformation de L'Europe Néolithique. In P. Pétrequin, R-M. Arbogast, A-M. Pétrequin, S. van Willigen and M. Bailly (eds) *Premier Chariots, Premier Araires*, 329-360. Paris, CNRS Éditions.

Speck, J. (1990) *Zur Geschichte der Pfahlbauforschung*. In M. Höneisen (ed.) *Die ersten Bauern* 1. Schweizerische Landesmuseum, 9–20.

Stöckli, W. E. (1979) Das Pfahlbauproblem heute. *Archäologie der Schweiz* 1, 50–56.

Whitelaw, T. (1991) Some dimension of variability in the social organisation of community space among foragers. In C. S. Gamble and W. A. Boismier (eds) *Ethnoarchaeological Approaches to Mobile Campsites*, 139–188. Ann Arbor, International Monographs in Prehistory.

10

Locating Household Activities on a Bronze Age Tell

Marie Louise Stig Sørensen and Magdolna Vicze

Background reflection on tell settlements and their households

The construction of tells in Bronze Age temperate Europe is an extremely interesting phenomenon. It is arguably an intrusive settlement form, coming into Europe during the Neolithic and having close affinities to the settlements of the Near East. Furthermore, as a settlement form it may be interpreted as relating to proto-urban social organisation, although administrative or religious structures as well as other clear evidence of a social hierarchy seem generally absent from the European tells and certainly absent from the ones built during the Bronze Age. This settlement form disappears in the course of the Bronze Age, with some of the latest ones being the groups of tells in Hungary. Amongst the tells continuing well into the Middle Bronze Age is Százhalombatta-Földvár, on the west side of the Danube some 30 km south of Budapest, see Figure 10.1.

Bronze Age tells are extremely important for our understanding of socio-political developments in later European prehistory. One of their foremost characteristics is that they are densely packed constructions, suggesting, amongst others, that the space and activities of individual household had to be closely correlated and that mechanisms for reducing tensions between households were in place. In the absence of strong central administrative structures the management of such relationships must have been expressed

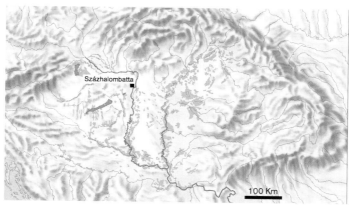

Figure 10.1. Map of the Carpathian Basin showing the location of Százhalombatta-Földvár.

at the level of the individual household; with the household here understood as the smallest social unit of social and economic decisions and activities. Thus, on tell sites the household was a formative element for the nature of community and its impact ranges from being central in the sustenance of the cohabiting group to the negotiation of the relationships that enable the larger community to coexist within the restricted space. The impact of the household, as a social and economic entity, can therefore be traced not just in the form of houses but also in the very layout of the settlement and the various traces of activities and the use of space within its boundaries. Using the concept of the household is therefore essential for any attempt to further our understanding of the organisation and political structures that made this type of cohabitation possible without overt public offices and social ranking.

Several excavations of Bronze Age tells in Hungary (*e.g.* Bóna 1992) have revealed how they were occupied by uniformly laid-out houses with narrow paths between them. Accordingly, one of the central questions that has emerged is the separation between public/communal and private activities and how they were organised and managed within such sites, or in other words what was the relationship between the individual household and the community? Following from this comes a concern with how the tell, or specific parts of it, were maintained and what factors determine how it is regeneration through time. Were decisions to rebuild or move structures made at a communal level or in a more haphazard organic manner in response to needs and pressures, or, alternatively, is the actual layout of the site only comprehendible as the result of centralised decisions even if we do not recognise their archaeological correlates? Finding ways of responding to such questions and concerns is a significant challenge to tell investigation, but one that is needed to unlock the information about Bronze Age societies found within them.

Hungarian tells investigation has a long history and can roughly be divided into three phases based on the aims of research (see also Bóna 1975). During the first phase, which lasted until the 1970s–80s, research was concentrated upon establishing the relative chronology of the different cultural groups (*e.g.* Banner *et al.* 1959; Bóna 1979–80; Banner and Bóna 1974). Tells were looked upon as layered chronology-books. The sequencing of ceramic types and their development through time were the primary research questions with the aim of establishing the relative chronological order of the numerous local variations of tell forming cultures and their neighbouring cultural complexes. These works helped to establish that the tell forming communities in Hungary evolved during the second half of the Early Bronze Age and that they lasted till the end of the Middle Bronze Age. It also became evident that there is certain chronological and territorial overlaps between the different local groups or cultures. During the second phase, which began during the 1980ties, the focus shifted towards house types and other structures (*e.g.* Csányi and Stanczik 1982; Bóna 1982; Csányi and Tárnoki 1992). As a third phase one can identify current attempts at developing ways of investigating tells that aim to analyse how the tell works and where and what happened within its space and therefore how society was organised and run.

Introduction to Százhalombatta-Földvár

The Vatya Culture is the western most representative of the tell-forming way of life within the Carpathian Basin (and thus within Europe), and it can be thought of as a kind of buffer zone between non-tell forming and tell forming communities. In addition, it covers a key geographical area insofar as it occupies both sides of the Danube along the stretch where Europe's largest river changes from its west to east course to take a direct north–south direction. This location is most likely one of the reasons for the distinctive settlement pattern of this culture (Kovács 1982; Vicze 2000). It was partly due to the unique character of the Vatya Culture and partly due to the fact that almost all tell research was concentrated on the eastern tells in Hungary, that a research-group dedicated to the Vatya Culture was formed at the end of the 1960s and the beginning of the 1970s (Bándi and Petres 1969). The main aim was to understand the role of the apparently high status, fortified settlements which, on one hand, surround the Vatya territory and, on the other hand, create a chain of "forts" along the western bank of the Danube (Kovács 1975; Vicze 2000). It was within this framework that the first "modern" archaeological investigation of Százhalombatta took place in 1969 (Kovács 1977).

Százhalombatta is one of a series of fortified settlements located on the western bank of the river Danube. The tell is located on a natural, loess promontory approximately 150 m high. Along the eastern side the site boundary was the Danube, while along its southern and western sides it was encircled by a creek created by a natural water flow and possibly at times still containing running water. On the northern side there was a small natural cut, which the Bronze Age settlers deepened into a 5 m deep ditch. The site was thus defended along its perimeter, and could only be approached from the northwest, along a narrow strip of land, see Figures 10.2 and 10.3.

The initial investigation in 1969, in accordance with the custom of the time, involved two small trenches, neither of which larger than 5 × 5 m (Kovács 1969). The result of that investigation was a clear understanding of the chronological sequence of the site, according to which Százhalombatta has been settled from the second half of the Nagyrév (Early Bronze Age) period until the end of the MBA, *i.e.* the end of the Koszider phase. This excavation also clearly established that a substantial stratigraphy including at least six layers was present on the site.

The next phase of excavation (coinciding with the second phase of Hungarian tell research generally) took place from 1989 to 1993 and was focussed upon investigating the house structures on the site (Poroszlai 1992a; 2000). Two large trenches, one 10 × 5 m and the other 10 × 20 m, were excavated (for details see Poroszlai 1992a; 2000). Amongst the results were details about three houses and paths between them as well as an area of hearths. This work also resulted in experimental investigations including the construction of an Early Bronze Age house in the Archaeological Park of the Matrica Museum (Poroszlai 1998).

In response to recent developments in archaeology, including new methods and

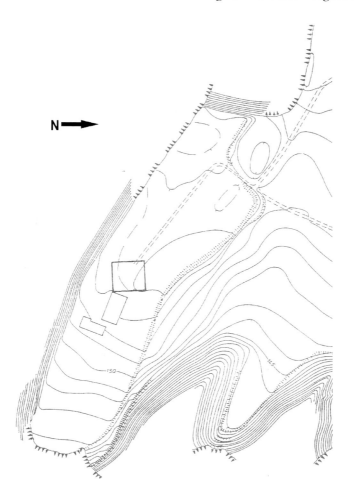

Figure 10.2. Site plan of Százhalombatta-Földvár, showing the location of trenches.

N➡

techniques, such as GIS, and the emergence of social, and environmental archaeology, the need for new approaches and techniques came into view. Therefore, a new phase of research began in 1998 and is still ongoing. This phase of research aims at the following three distinct but very closely linked aims. One is focusing upon understanding the diversity and the significance of the Vatya settlement system, and especially investigating the role of the Százhalombatta settlement within that system (Vicze 2000). The second is to reach a detailed comprehension of the inner settlement layout, household structures, and changes in the uses of space during the lifetime of the tell and with regard to its compact settlement structure. The third is a more detailed knowledge of both the immediate and wider natural environment.

This broad and complex set of aims needed an equally complex and detailed excavation strategy, involving several interdisciplinary sciences, very precise excavating techniques, and documentation methods. Some of the general characteristics expected

Figure 10.3. Százhalombatta Földvár: view of the site from the south, where formerly there would have been a small creek.

of the site, such as the sizes of houses and their location in relationship to each other, were already known, although no complete Vatya house has been excavated (Bóna 1982; Poroszlai 1988; 1992a; 1992b; 2000a; 2000b; Vicze 1992). In addition, the excavation strategy had to take into account the large number of pits usually found on Vatya sites. The detailed research questions therefore focussed on the house as the initial scene for the basic economic and social life of the prehistoric society. Activities connected to the everyday life and the social organisation of each household would have affected the construction of space both inside and outside houses, and the excavation procedure was designed to identify and record the remains of such activities.

Taking into account the size of the area excavated on other Bronze Age tells (for detailed information about tell excavations see Bóna 1992), it was decided that the 20 × 20 m trench is an optimal size for recovering data in accordance with our aims. It was important to be able to gain a large as well as systematic, detailed and precisely documented data set (for a general discussion of the excavation strategy see Vicze 2004). A 2 × 2 m grid system was used for the excavation and sampling of all fills. The exception to this is the excavation of features (such as hearths, ovens, special working areas, house-floor or house-debris fragment) and houses (which are excavated in 1 × 1 m squares). Based on the earlier excavation it was known that the site is rich in charred remains, and an intensive programme of sampling was therefore initiated. On average this means 300–600 soil samples have been taken annually. In addition, soil-micromorphological samples have been taken in order to investigate the structure of the matrix at particular points.

The open area

Tell excavations have tended to focus singularly upon the individual structures, and any attempt at understanding the household has been constrained by a simple and unquestioned equation between the house and the household. Therefore, while important new insights into the house *per se* is emerging from the ongoing excavation, the aim of this paper is to explore how the space outside the houses themselves and their immediate surroundings may have been used for the activities of the household. In short, how was the household, as the smallest unit of sustenance and maintenance activities, defined and contained spatially?

During the first seasons of excavation the northwestern part of the trench appeared as an area without clear house structures and with apparently very low finds density. Such open areas have not been commonly associated with the habitation of tells, and the aim of this paper is, therefore, to focus upon this area of the excavation as such empty spaces are usually disregarded in terms of the functionality of the site thus leaving the house separated from the area in which it functioned as a household. This paper is therefore somewhat experimental and explorative and at its core sits the question of how we can investigate the household beyond the walls that sheltered it. In pursue of such answers we have had to pay almost forensic attention to the details of the make-up of layers as we attempt to make visible and tangible activities that are now only faintly preserved. In order to make transparent the procedures through which we have traced the household activities we shall in the following sections provide rather minute details – this is of necessity as it is through the minute remains of daily and routine activities that the household emerges as a real aspect of the life on the tell.

The further excavation of the open area revealed a thick stratigraphic sequence that had accumulated while the area was not used for housing while there nonetheless appeared to be some changes in what had taken place within it. It is this sequence we shall now try to disentangle. At the highest level, further excavation revealed feature 225, this appeared as a very clean, pale compact yellow sandy loam surface with high clay content. While it shared physical characteristics with house floors it had no associated postholes or hearths, and it ran as a band 9–10 m wide, 5–20 cm thick and more than 15 m long throughout the trench. It appeared to be an area that was used substantially (thus the compactness) but also continuously kept clean. As a preliminary interpretation it was proposed that this was an *open area* (platform or open plaza). The rest of the trench was at this level quite disturbed and full of later inclusions although there were possibly the remains of a wall in the northeastern corner. Feature 225 gave way to fill 1323, which went beyond the limits of 225 as it covered most of the trench. 1323 was distinctly different from 225; it was less compact and was composed of a sandy loam with low clay content but with clay lumps scattered throughout, and it was pale grey. There were no features associated with this layer, and the finds density was higher than in 225 while still comparatively modest. The interpretation put forward was of this being a *general fill* with the recognition that this term needed further investigation.

The fill was around 20–25 cm thick in the western part of the trench, while in the eastern part a second spit (labelled 1623) added another 10–20 cm to its thickness (in the western part there was in addition an extensive fill (fill 1745) composed of several layers of clay lumps without any obvious structures. 1623 and 1745 will not be further discussed in this paper). Next were fills numbers 3019 and 3077, which were separate excavation spits of basically the same fill. These fills were found only in the western and particularly the southwestern part of the trench and they may represent a *dumping episode* immediately after the destruction of the burnt house, the outline of which has now been located as a central structure in the trench. This was a considerable layer, and the thickness of the two fills together averaged 40–45 cm. These fills were quite loose sandy loams, darker brown than the layers above and without clay lumps, they also appeared to have a much higher organic content than the layers above. The finds density was also considerably higher, and in particular they contained large amounts and a great variety of bones.

These features and fills, which collectively constitute a series of areas outside the houses, are interesting for several reasons. Firstly, as already indicated, open areas have not previously been investigated in their own right within Bronze Age tells of Central Europe, although they, of course, provide an important insight into the layout of the tell. In particular such areas can give clues to the organisation of activities within the densely settled area and help to establish the relationship between the house and the areas of domestic activities. Secondly, the observation that these fills cover earlier houses, suggests that a reorganisation of the lay-out of the tell took place even if its main lines of orientation were maintained during these changes. Further detailed analyses of how the open area (represented by 225) and the underlying fills (represented by 1323 and 3077) were composed and used provide the only means of establishing what was going on within this part of the site. To maximise the effectiveness of such an analysis, we designed a comparative study of the range of debris that one may associate with different types of activities in order to investigate their presence within these levels.

The potentials of small find analysis

As there were neither considerable finds nor structures associated with this area its analysis had to focus upon other elements of the archaeology and use both inferences and negative evidence to establish what role and uses this area had within the site. The small finds recovered during systematic sampling and sieving was therefore used as the basis for investigating what activities were associated with this area. This analysis was then supplemented with and compared to the evidence from the macrofossils sampled at the same sampling points. On this basis a fine tune interpretations of what was going on in this area could be put forward.

In addition to clarifying the character of this particular area, we believe analysing contexts that are part of the site matrix but which do not classify as structures is also

Figure 10.4. Százhalombatta Földvár: the site from the opposite eastern bank of the Danube River.

Figure 10.5. Százhalombatta Földvár: view from the north of the tell situated on the Danube River.

Levels	Pottery weight in % of total from level	Bone weight in % of total from level	Weight of other materials in % from level
225	78%	18%	3%
1323	49%	31%	19%
3077	58%	31%	10%

Table 10.1. The relative weight of the main categories of materials within each level.

Levels	Total weight of pottery (gram)	Average weight of pottery (gram)	Total weight of bone (gram)	Average weight of bone (gram)
225	596.05	4.17	141.45	0.24
1323	253.97	2.44	161.93	0.17
3077	278.9	1.90	149.25	0.26

Table 10.2. Total and average weight of pottery and bone from each level.

significant for reasons fundamental to how we investigate settlements and in particular households. Firstly, this approach confirms the entire site rather than merely finds and features as the historic environment, which we must attempt to comprehend. Secondly, it serves as a pilot project of how the information and potentials contained within dense settlement data may be harvested using new methods of analysis and explicit research design.

Heavy fraction analysis
Samples for heavy fraction analysis were extracted from each context being analysed with the aim of creating a coherent coverage both horizontally and vertical. A total of 13 ten litre samples were selected from 225, another 16 from 1323, and seven from 3077. The material was weighed, counted, and sorted after size. The sorting was based on the following categories: ceramics, bones, charcoal, vitrified clay, shell, seeds, lithics, bronze, coprolites and others. On this basis various comparisons became possible, and we therefore selected to focus upon horizontal and vertical patterns within, on one hand, the most frequent heavy fraction categories and, on the other hand, the rare materials. In addition, comparison was made with the patterns found within the macrofossil remains. As one would expect the frequency of the inclusions of different types of material vary considerably, see Table 10.1 and Table 10.2. It was, therefore, decided to analyse the distribution of pottery and bones, which together constitute more than 80% of the inclusions.

There was little material of any kind in the open area (225), but even so there was some horizontal variation. In particular, there were a very high number of pottery fragments in the northern part of the trench, and there was greater horizontal variation in weight than in the number of pot fragments. This means that the average size of the fragments vary quite considerably. This suggests that the material included was less abraded in some parts of the trench than in others. The bone remains showed less distinct patterning insofar as the material overall was less homogeneous than the pottery.

In comparison, the pottery remains in the general fill (1323) made up 49% of the material overall with the amount of bone increasing compared to the context above, the open area, and with a distinct inclusion of other materials. This level was clearly different by its greater admixture of materials. This layer was also interesting insofar as all the samples were rather similar with regard to the low weight of bones, which contrasts to their numbers, which varied and in some samples was very high. These peaks in the number of bones are due to some samples containing large amounts of fish bones and bones that have been smashed up. Overall, and somewhat surprising, there was less abundance of finds in the general fill than in both the open area and the dumping episode below and the material was also more homogenised. The proportion of bone was similar to that from the dumping episode, but higher than in the open area. Taken together, the pottery fragments and bones suggested that the material from the general fill had been affected by processes through which it had become heavily fractured and abraded and that a large amount of very small bones were present.

The bone remains from the dumping episode (3077) showed similarity with the general fill in terms of both the number of bones and the considerable fluctuation in this. It is also the level in which the average weight of bones was highest (*i.e.* there was less abrasion). The pottery fragments, which contributed 65% of the total remains from this level, showed similarity with the pattern seen in the open area insofar as there was horizontal variation in both the number and weight of the fragments. There was also a tendency towards pottery being found along the eastern edge of this layer.

Overall the analysis of bone and pottery suggested that the pottery fragments in the open area and from the dumping episode are similar in terms of their relative dominance within the samples (75% and 65% respectively) and in terms of the distribution of their weight horizontally; both also show considerable variation in the weight of pottery fragments. This suggests that the sources of the fragments in both cases are too varied for uniform sized fragments to emerge. At the same time, the number within each sample is generally larger in the dumping episode than in the open area. Both of these levels also show some horizontal clustering. In comparison with both, the pottery from the general fill is surprisingly uniform in numbers and weight. This is also the case for the weight of bones, while in terms of the number of bones the general fill has similarity with the dumping episode as both show considerable variation between samples and have individual samples with extremely high numbers.

Overall the remains suggests that the pottery fragments from the open area and the dumping episode were already abraded but in a range of sizes when they became included in the level, and that they were not subjected to further *in situ* abrasion in a manner that caused homogeneity of size. There were also differences between the two levels, however, and the dumping episode contained higher numbers overall. This suggests that the levels are made up of material brought from other places and dumped here, and that, furthermore, the inclusions were somewhat protected from further abrasion. This could result either from substantial dumping through which much of the material would be immediately buried within the matrix and thus not subject to trampling, sweeping or other abrasive activities, or in could reflect that this area only saw limited and inconsistent use. In contrast, the remains from the general fill are very homogenised, *i.e.* the size of fragments is very similar throughout the samples. This is due to consistent abrasion of the pottery fragments, which could have happened either prior to or/and after the material was left in this place. As one can expect considerable variability in the size of pottery fragments included in primary middens or refuse dumping (for the characteristics of midden debris see Needham and Spence 1996), the homogeneity of the material suggests this was not a midden or dumping area as such but rather an open surface which had considerable and consistent movement on it, such as a yard or a communal activity area. Consistent trampling (or sweeping) is, for example, a mechanism that could have caused the observed uniformity. The bone material basically supports this suggestion while it adds to the observation that the number of bones is highly varied and increases in the lower levels. The very high number of very small bone and bone fragments suggests closeness to food processing areas including possibly the boning of fish.

The range of other materials found is wide including pebbles, bronze and amber. Meanwhile, as some materials, such as bronze, appear only once, only those materials, which can be used to discern horizontal and vertical similarities, and differences will be considered further. On a general level the remains clearly show much less inclusion (in terms of weight) in the open area than in the other two levels and a greater range of remains in the general fill than in the other two. Two interesting small concentrations of materials were noted. One was the presence of lithics, which were found in the same restricted area down through all three levels. Although the evidence is very limited, this could suggest that lithics were consistently used or collected in a place or structure neighbouring this area. The other observation is the spatially limited concentration of lime in 1323. This material may be associated with house-building material and its presence may relate to the preparation of such material possibly hinting at this being a work area.

The analysis of the heavy fraction material suggests subtle but nonetheless distinct changes in the composition and thus potentially the use of this area during the accumulation of the three levels. Or, in other words, the use of this area of the settlement changed three times during the accumulation of these levels. The lowest level, 3077, may indeed have been part of a dumping area, rather than directly a midden, with material brought from other contexts rather than gradually accumulated there. The material included in the matrix was not subjected to further heavy abrasion possible because the layers were build up over a short time period. The reason for constructing such an area is still unclear but amongst possibilities that could be considered are the need to make up a new surface or to cover up abandoned structures. The use of the area seemed to have been restricted and there are no direct association to either movement, sweeping or specific activities. It does not seem likely that such an area was a major communal activity area or thoroughfare nor that it was directly linked to the entrance area of a house. Rather, the qualities of the finds suggest that this area was a kind of back-space slightly removed from the main activity areas around the houses and probably used occasionally rather than continuously and by different household rather than directly linked to only one of them. 1323 is a quite different place; the material is throughout grounded into small fragments while at the same time they suggest the presence of distinct activity areas, such as the high numbers of small bones and their possible link to the preparation of fish. When this level accumulated the area seems to have become a major place for activities, and we can tentatively suggest that it was used as a yard or a communal working area, through which people moved constantly and which may also have been kept clean through sweeping. Thus, while we may not be able to associate this level with a particular household we may suggest that the responsibility of households, such as cleaning and sweeping, were extended into this area and that during the accumulation of this level it acted as the extended activity area for a number of households. Some of these characteristics, such as the cleaning, continue into the top level, 225, which had few finds generally. This level nonetheless shows less homogenisation of the inclusions and it seems that while it was used or constructed in a manner that caused considerable compaction, the inclusions were not affected to the degree one may have expected. One reason for this may be that the level was deliberately constructed of relatively clean material and only thereafter used in a consistent manner causing the somewhat contradictory appearance of a very clean level with some horizontal difference in the amount and size of its inclusions. These qualities seem to suggest that the area was deliberately made-up and used for consistent movement, while there is little evidence to support an interpretation of this as a working area. This could suggest that the activity area of a number of households were replaced by other needs; the impression of this being a well prepared communal action may even hint at a situation where the need of a few households were overwritten by the needs of the larger site. These tentative interpretations can be further assessed by comparison with other data from the same sampling points, as outlined below.

Macrofossil analysis

The macrofossil analysis aimed to establish whether specific stages in food processing activities were represented within the area and whether there was any clustering or concentration of such traces. These aims were formulated in direct response to the potential interpretation of this being a part of the site where certain dirty activities, such as threshing, would be carried out, or the possibility that this was an area where various foodstuff would be brought before divided up between households or even that some type of plant remains would be stored here.

The archaeobotanical investigation of 255, 1323 and 3077 was therefore carried out with the aims of investigating horizontal and vertical variation in the presence of plant remains relating to different activities (*e.g.* crop processing, food preparation and consumption). The proposal of a correlation between different macrofossil remains and distinct stages of, for instance, food processing and preparation is based on ethnographic models (Hillman 1981). Of particular interest to this study is that during parching

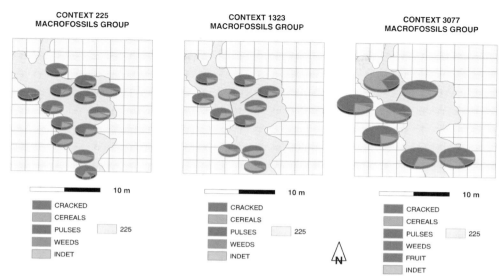

CONTEXT 225
MACROFOSSILS GROUP

CONTEXT 1323
MACROFOSSILS GROUP

CONTEXT 3077
MACROFOSSILS GROUP

10 m   10 m   10 m

	CRACKED
	CEREALS
	PULSES	225
	WEEDS
	INDET

	CRACKED
	CEREALS
	PULSES	225
	WEEDS
	INDET

	CRACKED
	CEREALS
	PULSES	225
	WEEDS
	FRUIT
	INDET

Figure 10.6. Distribution of Macrofossil remains within the three levels.

and pounding each spikelet breaks up into light chaff, spikelet fork, glume bases and grains. As a result, these important stages in the processing can be separated out and used as a basis for analysing the samples.

Thirty-two samples chosen from the same locations as the heavy fraction samples were analysed (14 samples from 225, 11 from 1323, and seven from 3077; see Fig. 10.6). With regard to food crops, carbonised grains of hulled species of wheat were present in most samples from all three levels, with the quantity of einkorn being considerably higher in the general fill than in either of the others. This is primarily due to the presence of particularly large amounts in two squares. The concentration of seeds in these two locations is especially interesting in view of the suggestion made in the section above that this level may have been a working area. In addition, the weed species found are common on fields highly affected by human activities, and there does not appear to be any significant differences between the samples in terms of the types or quantity of weeds present although some localised concentrations can be observed, such as the higher amount of weed in the south-eastern part of the trench in the general fill, possibly a further confirmation of this being a working courtyard. The samples from the open area contained spikelet forks and glume bases but no chaff. Spikelet forks and glume bases were also found in the general fill, but in considerably higher quantities (around 10 times more). It is interesting to note that the largest count was recorded in a sample where 80% of the total amount of spikelet forks from the level was found, and that this was the same sample that produced the very high amount of grain. This suggests fine sieving and hand sorting of the grain-taking place close to where the sample was taken. Overall, the analysis suggests that the macrofossil remains are the result of the final cleaning stages of crop processing as well as fragments of grinded grain. The small amount of spikelet forks and glume bases are likely to be the result of fine sieving and hand sorting applied immediately prior to the grain being prepared for food; remains from earlier stages of processing are absent including any evidence for winnowing. It was also interesting to note that the open area contained fewer grains and their fragments than the general fill and the dumping episode. The general fill contained the largest amount of plant species, and also had the lowest percentage of grain fragments from the smallest size group. The sample with extreme high numbers of spikelet fork and glume bases within this layer may represent either a single dumping event or it is accumulated due to this being a place (or near to a place) where grain was regularly hand sorted. The fact that this sample also has one of the largest seed count supports the latter interpretation.

In summary, a large number of cereal grain and fragments were recorded. Most samples contain broken grains and the largest amount was found in the dumping episode. The presence of charred hulled prime grain (einkorn, emmer, barley, spelt), and a small amount of free threshing wheat (bread wheat) probably represent final cleaning stages, and the peak of these remains in the south-eastern end of the trench may suggests that grain were processed there or nearby. Finally, it should be noted that the open area contained fewer grains and their fragments than the other two levels, while there were only slight differences between the others.

While the evidence from the macrofossil data cannot be used to definitively discriminate between the proposals put forward in the section above, they do confirm that food processing activities took place in or near to these areas. It is also suggested that some spots within the general fill were used for the fine hand sorting of grain, supporting the suggestion that at this level the area functioned as a working area in a manner that may have created close links to the nearby households.

Soil-micromorphological analysis

Soil-micromorphology provides a method for constructing a data set with unique resolution that can be used to trace some of the workings of densely packed settlements, such as tells. For instance, recognition of living surfaces, identification of particular activities and the pattern of the spatial organisation of these activities is possible (*e.g.* Matthews 1995; Boivin 2000). This technique has been used to good effect in analysis of the use of domestic space within urban and semi-urban sites in the Near East (Matthews *et al.* 1997), but has not previously been used for Bronze Age tells in temperate Europe. The sampling from Százhalombatta suggests that the household remains reflect choices made regarding the creation and maintenance of domestic space, as discussed by G. Kovács (this volume).

The soil-micromorphological analysis was carried out in order to shed more lights upon two aspects of the area. One was how it was made, what material was it composed of and what can we tell about how it was deposited? The other aim was to characterise the inclusions within the matrix and the processes through which they have become incorporated. A detailed account of these samples can be found in G. Kovács (this volume), and only the discussions directly relevant to the interpretation of these levels will be provided here.

Five samples were taken from the general fill and five from the dumping episode while none exist from the open area. Collectively the samples suggest that the dumping episode at some point in time was transformed into a much cleaner area (the general fill). Neither of these levels has so far been found to have sharp borders, and refuse material occur throughout although to different degrees. The general fill is a cleaner layer, and may have accumulated through a gradual process involving both further relatively clean deposits and reintegration of refuse from the layer below. Despite some problems regarding the representativeness of the samples, as they were collected early in the research project and aimed at more limited questions, it is without doubt that the samples linked to the general fill although not a clean layer contain less refuse/ human-related material than those from the dumping episode. No definite patterns were observed that would suggest that this layer can be related to any specific activity. However in some cases observations suggest (*e.g.* high compaction, pattern of cracks and voids) that parts of layer 1323 might have contained remains of "living" or intentionally prepared surfaces, or at least remnants of such surfaces, which got incorporated into this layer. In contrast, the dumping episode contained significant amounts of anthropogenic inclusions, dung fragments and decayed plant matter. Their spatial organisation does not show any pattern, except from one sample, where a fine plant layer was observed, but as none of the other samples show this pattern it is likely that this was an isolated patch. The high amount of finely fragmented organic matter (dung, plant matter) and anthropogenic inclusions, and their random orientation supports the interpretation of this being an area where refuse was dumped. To identify separate dumping events is very difficult since the samples were collected randomly. With this limitation in mind it is, nonetheless, possible to suggest that at least two separate dumping events can be distinguished. Between these events some cleaner soil material accumulated. Since the samples are from different locations and only partly overlapping in terms of their absolute depths, the interpretation of the cleaner intervals is difficult, and it is in particular impossible to tell whether this material was brought in intentionally or whether it was just accumulated on the spot as wind blown material, for example. The only observable difference between the two phases is the amount of anthropogenic inclusions. None of the investigated samples contained any material that could not be found on the site, and there is therefore no evidence for soil or any other distinctive sediment brought in to make up these layers.

The most important microscopic observation is the significant amount of dung fragments, which can be identified as herbivore dung in most of the cases. The biggest size of these fragments is only a couple of millimetres, which makes it impossible to detect them visually on the site. They would most probably not survive the flotation procedure either; hence they are missing from both the heavy and light fraction.

Moreover, most of the organic matter (which at least would cause the matrix to have a darker colour) is decayed and in most cases only the inorganic components of the dung can be traced, and these are only a couple of microns in size. The fine dung fragments suggest that animals were kept close to the people, otherwise dung would have been found only in forms of bigger lumps if, for example, it was stored close to the houses for firing or for tempering. Since the small dung fragments are almost everywhere in the sediment matrix, this suggests that animal waste was dumped, probably regularly, at the investigated area together with other domestic refuse. A limited amount of bigger aggregates were also found, and their compaction and the horizontal orientation of the phytoliths suggest that this waste originated from stabling or penning area. Searching for bigger fragments of dung and/or the identification of the stabling/penning area would be a highly desirable aim for future work, as the present of stabling within tell is a disputed topic.

No specific activity can be related to the general fill. Part of its "refuse" content was most probably inherited from the dumping episode, although some of the refuse material might also be the result of continuous use of the area. Layer 1323 is cleaner than the other layers, but it is not significantly clean. Unfortunately, the micromorphological investigation of soils did not make it possible to link any specific activity to it, and a multifunction-area seems to be the most feasible term for it, since a wide range of human related material was identified.

Interpretation and discussion of results – moving from small finds to households

The three types of evidence outlined above each suggests further characterisation of the levels that we, based on the excavation, had interpreted as respectively a dumping episode, a general fill, and an open area. Starting at the lowest level, the dumping episode, the heavy fraction as well as the macrofossil data showed this to be the level with the highest amount of inclusion, but also with a high degree of variation between samples in terms of size and composition. The highly fragmented state of the material at the same time suggests dumping rather than a regular midden and the amount of bone, pottery, and grain fragments suggest that the material dumped may have come from working areas or/and domestic contexts. This interpretation is clearly supported by the soil-micromorphological samples, which suggested at least two dumping events and the possible accumulation of a thin layer of soil between them (for instance wind blown). There is no evidence in any of the data for substantial compaction or abrasion and it is unlikely that the dumping of material was due to the construction of working surfaces or pathways. Rather, during the period of dumping this area may have been slightly peripheral to the main activity areas or domestic structures (*i.e.* at the back of the houses rather than at their entrances) and it does not show evidence of any particular or consistent use. This may suggest that the area was used occasionally by several households rather than being physically part of or assigned to a single household. The most surprising results arising from the analysis was, therefore, the characterisation of the next fill in the sequence, the so called general fill. The heavy fraction data stressed the homogenised nature of the samples in general while they also pointed to the localised very high numbers of very small bones. This suggest that this fill may have been a working area, where residues from localised activities were mixed-in with fragments already present in the soil matrix or accumulated during use. The lithics and lime concentrations suggest some of the activities (tool preparation, building work) that were going on. The macrofossil data supports this interpretation and augmented it by demonstrating the localised presence of possible *in situ* hand sieving/cleaning of grain, while the high present of weed also suggest some processing of crops. These, furthermore, were remains related to the final stages of crop processing immediately prior to food preparation. It is, therefore, extremely gratifying that the soil-micromorphological samples suggest a similar interpretation while adding the possibility of there having been particularly prepared working surfaces in this level. While the soil-micromorphological data alone cannot securely establish whether such surfaces were constructed *in situ* or as a result of secondary inclusion, the overall characteristics of the finds collectively make the presence of prepared, however informally, work surfaces very likely. The amount of compaction and the range of activities suggest that during the time when the general fill accumulated this area became either an intensely used yard or a communal work area, which was also a thoroughfare. We may imagine this as an area of regular, probably daily, use, and that it functioned as a kind of extension of the household – during the phase when the general fill developed the activities areas of the individual households fused together or overlapped in the large open space in front of them. We do unfortunately not have any soil-micromorphological data to characterise the compactness of 225, and this feature remains, maybe, the most enigmatic of the three levels studied. It clearly appears much cleaner than it actually was, probably because much of its inclusions were clearly embedded within the fill rather than appearing on its surface; its compactness also suggests either deliberate compaction or consistent use. It seems most likely that this feature was constructed by the laying of a relatively clean soil matrix taken from other parts of the site (with the possibility of localised patching as the surface wore down), which contained a limited range of already fragmented material. There is no suggestion of specific activities being associated with this level, and while the appearance of its uppermost part may suggest consistent movement and possible sweeping (causing the initial impression of this being a house floor) the inclusions within its matrix were not extensively abraded and homogenised. It is likely that during the accumulation of 225 this area continued being used as a thoroughfare but that the simultaneous use as a working area had ceased. It is in this context interesting to notice that this level appears as a band running over the area while the general fill below it seemed to have covered a much larger part of the trench; clearly when this area became used for movement and passage it became different in many ways and its intimate links to the households may have been broken.

The finds and soil characteristics make it possible to propose, very tentatively, a sequence of change in the use of this particular area within the settlement. From being a back-space with dumping but little activities otherwise, it took on a more central role becoming an open area with considerable movement back and forth and with a range of activities going on; activities, such as the preparation for meals that linked it directly to the household. Thereafter its surface seems to have been remade at the same time as its size is reduced so that it becomes a wide corridor running through the area rather than a small square. These different characteristics all impacted upon how and where activities were organised and how people interacted through this time period.

The study shows that the different types of spaces within the tell can and should all be investigated in terms of the practices (and thus decisions) that affected how they were constructed and maintained. Through increased attention towards the different areas that make up a site, and how they are transformed through time, we begin to identify and develop avenues of research that will enable a more full exploration of the decisions being made within a densely settled Bronze Age social space and how through this the relationship between individual households and the community were managed. Such investigations will make it possible to add to traditional research concerned with establishing phasing, cultural horizons, and cultural contacts, insight into how life was lived within the tell. We feel this study begins to show these potentials, and we trust that through such analysis the social dynamics of tell communities will begin to be thought about at a range of scale including that of the cooperation and tension between the cohabiting households. In other words, through forensic investigation of the mundane material found through sieving and systematic sampling an analysis of how life was lived within this type of settlement can be attempted.

Acknowledgements
We are grateful for the comments that various members of the SAX project have made on this work. British Academy Small Grants funded the analyses. We are very grateful for this support as it made possible detailed studies which otherwise could not have been carried out: the macrofossil analysis, carried out by Brigitta Kulcsárné-Berzsenyi while studying for a PhD at the University of Cambridge under the supervision of Prof. M. Jones; and the soil-micromorphological analysis, carried out by Gabriella Kovács under the supervision of Dr. C. French, while studying for a PhD at the University of Cambridge. We would also like to thank the staff at the Matrica Museum for their help in finding and organising samples, and Brigitta Kulcsárné-Berzsenyi, Gabriella Kovács, and Ulla Rajala for carrying out the different analyses. In particular, we want to thank Dr I. Poroszlai (Ildikó) for help and support. It is important to us that Ildikó, shortly before she died, read the initial analysis, and it is good to remember her excitement about how our knowledge about tells may be progressed.

References

Bándi, G. and Petres, É. (1969) Ásatás Lovasberény-Mihályváron. *Archaeologiai Értesítő* 96, 170–177.

Banner, J. and Bóna, I. (1974) *Mittelbronzezeitliche Tell-Siedlung bei Békés*. Budapest, Akadémiai Kiadó, Fontes Archaeologici Hungariae.

Banner, J., Bóna, I. and Márton, L. (1957) Die Ausgrabungen von L. Márton in Tószeg. *Acta Archaeologica Academiae Scientificarium Hungarica* 10, 1–140.

Boivin, N. (2000) Life rhythms and floor sequences: excavating time in rural Rajasthan and Neolithic Catalhöyük. *World Archaeology* 31(3), 367–388.

Bóna, I. (1975) *Die mittlere Bronzezeit Ungarns und ihre Südöstlichen Beziehungen*. Budapest, Akadémiai Kiadó, Archaeologia Hungarica, 49.

Bóna, I. (1979–80) Tószeg-Laposhalom (1876–1976). *A Szolnok Megyei Múzeumok Évkönyve* 1979–1980, 83–100.

Bóna I., (1982) Alpár Bronzkori Rétegei. In I. Bóna and Gy. Nováki (eds) *Alpár Bronzkori és Árpád-Kori Vára. Cumania* 7, 17–117.

Bóna, I., (ed.) (1992) *Bronzezeit in Ungarn. Forschungen in Tell-Siedlungen an Donau und Theiss*. Frankfurt am Main, Walter Meier-Arendt and Main Museum f. Vor- u. Frühgeschichte Frankfurt.

Csányi, M. and Stanczik, I. (1982) Előzetes jelentés a Tiszaug-kéménytetői bronzkori tell-telep ásatásáról. *Archaeologiai Értesítő* 109, 239–254.

Csányi, M. and Tárnoki, J. (1992) Túrkeve-Terehalom. In Bóna (ed.) (1992), 159–165. Frankfurt am Main, Walter Meier-Arendt and Main Museum f. Vor- u. Frühgeschichte Frankfurt.

Hillman, G. C. (1981) Reconstructing crop husbandry practices from charred remains of crops. In R. J. Mercer (ed.) *Farming Practice in British Prehistory*, 123–162. Edinburgh, Edinburgh University Press.

Kovács, T., (1969) A százhalombattai bronzkori telep. *Archaeologiai Értesítő* 96, 161–168.

Kovács, T. (1975) Historische und chronologische Fragen des Überganges von der mittleren- zur Spätbronzezeit in Ungarn. *Acta Archaeologica Academiae Scientiarum Hungariae* 27, 297–317.

Kovács, T. (1977) Funde der Metallkunst der Koszider-Periode aus Siedlungen und Gräber- feldern. *Folia Archaeologica* 28, 41–65.

Kovács, T. (1982) Befestigungsanlagen um die Mitte des 2. Jahrtausends v. u. Z. in Mittelungarn. In B. Chropovsky and J. Herrmann (eds) *Beiträge zum bronzezeitlichen Burgenbau in Mitteleuropa*, 279–291. Berlin-Nitra, Archeologický Ústav Slovenskej Akadémie Vied- Zentralinstitut für alte Geschichte und Archäeologie der Akademie der Wissens[c]haftn der Deutscher Demokratischer Republik.

Kovács, T. (1984) Die Vatya-Kultur. In N. Tasić (ed.) *Kulturen der Frühbronzezeit das Karpatenbeckens und Nordbalkans*, 219–233. Beograd, Institut for Balkan Studies.

Kovács, T. (1988) Review of the Bronze Age settlement research during the past one hundred and a half centuries in Hungary. In T. Kovács and I. Stanczik (eds) *Bronze Age Tell Settlements of the Great Hungarian Plain* I, 17–25. Budapest, Magyar Nemzeti Múzeum.

Matthews W. (1995) Micromorphological characterisation and interpretation of occupation deposits and microstratigraphic sequences at Abu Salabikh, Iraq. In A.J. Barham and R. I. Macphail (eds) *Archaeological Sediments and Soils: Analysis, Interpretation and Management*, 41–76. London, University College Press.

Matthews, W., French, C. A. I., Lawrence, T., Cutler, D. F. and Jones, M. K. (1997) Microstratigraphic traces of site formation processes and human activities. *World Archaeology* 29(2), 281–308.

Needham, S.P. and Spence, T. (1996) *Refuse and Disposal at Area 16 East, Runnymede'. Vol 2. Runnymede Bridge Research Excavations*. London, British Museum Press.

Poroszlai, I. (1988) Preliminary report about the excavation at Nagykőrös-Földvár (Vatya culture): Stratigraphical Data and Settlement Structure. *Communicationes Archaeologicae Hungariae* 1988, 29–39.

Poroszlai, I. (1992a) Bölcske-Vörösgyír. In Bóna (ed.) (1992), 141–145.

Poroszlai, I. (1992b) Százhalombatta-Földvár. In I. Bóna (ed.) (1992), 153–155.

Poroszlai, I. (1998) Régészeti Park és vaskori halomsír rekonstrukció. In I. Poroszlai and M. Vicze (Eds.) *Százhalombatta története. Állandó kiállítás vezetője*, 48–50. Százhalombatta, Matrica Múzeum.

Poroszlai, I. (2000a) Excavation campaigns at the Bronze Age tell site at Százhalombatta-Földvár I: 1989–1991; II. 1991–1993. In I. Poroszlai and M. Vicze (eds) *Százhalombatta Archaeological Expedition, Annual Report* 1, 13–74.

Poroszlai, I. (2000b) Die Grabungen in der Tell-Siedlung von Bölcske-Vörösgyűrű (Kom. Tolna) (1965–1967). *Acta Archaeologica Academiae Scientificarium Hungarica* 51, 111–145.

Poroszlai, I. and M. Vicze (2000) SAX. *Százhalombatta Archaeological Expedition. Annual report 1 – Field Season 1998*. Százhalombatta, Matrica Museum.

Vicze, M. (1992) Baracs-Földvár. In Bóna (ed.) (1992), 146–148.

Vicze, M. (2000) Background to the Benta-valley field survey. In I. Poroszlai and M. Vicze (eds) *Százhalombatta Archaeological Expedition (SAX) Annual Report* I. 119–133. Százhalombatta, Matrica Museum.

Vicze, M. (2004) Excavation methodology on the Százhalombatta Project. In J. Kisfaludi (ed.) *Archaeological Investigations in Hungary 2002*, 131–146. Budapest, Kulturális Örökségvédelmi Hivatal.

11

Soil Micromorphology of the Household at Százhalombatta-Földvár Bronze Age Tell Settlement, Hungary

Gabriella Kovács

Introduction

Since many papers of this book revise the concept of household from several perspectives, with a broad selection of references, I will turn to introduce the technique of *soil thin section micromorphology* – a method through which household can also be studied – and demonstrate its application through the case study of Százhalombatta-Földvár Bronze Age tell settlement in Hungary. After a brief review of the use of soil micromorphology in archaeology and its relation to household archaeology, a well preserved house (House 3147) of the so-called Vatya Culture will be investigated.

Archaeological soil micromorphology

It seems reasonable to start this chain of thoughts with the definition of "micromorphology" since this field of research constitutes the base of this study. This term embraces a vast and complex amount of knowledge, which cannot be summarised easily. Therefore, I will use the comprehensive definition offered by G. Stoops (2003, 5):

> *Micromorphology* ... "is a method of studying undisturbed soil and regolith samples with microscopic and ultramicroscopic techniques in order to identify their different constituents and to determine their mutual relations, in space and time. Its aim is to search for the processes responsible for the formation or transformation of soil in general, or of specific features, whether natural (*e.g.* clay skins, nodules) or artificial (*e.g.* irrigation crusts, plow pans). Consequently it is an important tool for investigations of soil genesis, classification, or management of soils and regoliths".

After the definition, the following brief historical review of this research area will hopefully shed light on the importance and necessity of such studies.

From the 1970s onward, the evolving field of geoarchaeology (*Geoarchaeology* "... is the contribution of earth sciences, particularly geomorphology and sedimentary petrography to the interpretation and environmental reconstruction of the archaeological context" (Gladfelter 1977, 519)) introduced new scientific methods to archaeology, which were adapted from the earth sciences (*e.g.* sedimentology, geomorphology, pedology, petrology, geochemistry, geophysics, etc). These fields were not only adopted but were also refined and redefined to answer specific archaeological questions (Rapp and Hill 1998). Soil micromorphology became one of the highly specialised techniques of geoarchaeology as it became a specialised field of archaeology itself. Over the decades archaeological questions started to become more and more complex. To provide accurate answers to the multiple questions greater specialisation began following two major trends. While the major concern of *environmental archaeology* (Shackley 1981; Evans and Connor 1999) is to understand the formation of different landscapes and to detect its changes over the timeframe of human existence, the focal point of *settlement archaeology* (Barham and Macphail 1995) is the characterisation and localisation of human activity, which is considered to be a reflection of social, economic and political organisation. Obviously the two fields are overlapping as human occupation is strongly determined by natural circumstances (landscape, available resources, *etc*) while human influence can be the inducing force of landscape changes. Geoarchaeological investigations also point towards these directions and soil micromorphology has been proven to be an effective technique to be adopted in both cases (*e.g.* Courty *et al.* 1989; Goldberg 1992; Matthews *et al.* 1996; Simpson and Barrett 1996; Canti 1998; French 2003; *etc*). Geoarchaeological investigations of environmental issues are based on the study of *soils* [pedogenetic processes; *Soil*: a natural body composed of minerals, organic compounds, living organisms, air and water in interactive combinations produced by physical, chemical and biological processes (Gerrard 2000)] while *anthropogenic sediments* [*Anthropogenic sediment*: the built-up of human (activity) related matters, which can also provide scene for soil development but not necessarily (Limbrey 1975)] are the fundamental sources for indicators of human activity, which needs to be clearly distinguished. Although anthropogenic sediments are clearly distinct from natural soils, they both share many of the formation processes and are subject to the same formative factors (Middleton 2004). In this study emphasis will be placed on settlement archaeology.

The word "morphology" generally refers to a specific shape, form, characteristic or position of an object and this is not any different in the case of geoarchaeological soil micromorphology. Interpretations are derived from the measurement of components, and from the observations of features, fabrics and human induced inclusions of the soil/sediment (Bullock *et al.* 1985; Courty *et al.* 1989; Stoops 2003). The "micro" prefix of micromorphology only highlights that observations are made beyond the visibility of the naked eye, at a microscopic level.

Thin sections are produced from consolidated blocks of undisturbed, oriented soil/sediment, which constitute the basis of soil micromorphological studies (Murphy 1986).

Environmental micromorphology

Environmental soil micromorphology is a valuable tool in the hands of environmental archaeologists. This trend is focusing on natural processes, such as soil-formation, signs of climate change, impact of freezing-thawing activity, effect of flooding, glacial processes, slope processes, animal disturbance *etc*, and of course on the role of humans in environmental changes at a microscopic level (for detailed explanation and more reference see Courty *et al.* 1989 or French 2003, for example).

The soil micromorphology of settlements

As illustrated above, soil micromorphology can contribute to the investigation of a broad range of environmental problems. However, since this paper aims to investigate human activity, especially how space was created and used during the Middle Bronze Age by the so-called Vatya Culture, the fundamental work of Wendy Matthews has to be highlighted. Her work (*e.g.* Matthews 1992; 1995; 2003; Matthews *et al.* 1994; 1996; 1997a; 1997b; 1998; 2000) is of great importance for two major reasons. She was one of the first to use micromorphological thin sections to study how space was used and how different activities can be detected at a microscopic level. She was also the one who focused on Near Eastern tell settlements, which are in the closest association with my own study, the study of the Bronze Age tell of Százhalombatta in Hungary.

Detection of domestic activities

Soil micromorphology is a unique technique employed in tracing human activities. Before the discussion of the different *domestic* activities, and their micromorphological indicators, it is important to define what we mean by "domestic".

One would think that the definition of this term is very simple and straightforward. Words such as "family, house, household, home and private" are all listed as synonyms of domestic (O. D. 1999, 119). Although all of these terms are closely associated with each other, they can all be defined individually in several ways and with different meanings. What is a house? Is it a mere functional unit or is it more than a physical structure? Is it a social institution or should it be looked at as a dynamic entity (Carsten and Hugh-Jones 1995)? Is it a hut, a thatched house, a villa, or a mansion? Does the household mean one single family or several families? Is it the fundamental unit of production, consumption, and social and biological reproduction (Wilk and Rathje 1982)? Does family mean house or home, let alone being private? Parker Pearson and Richards write (1994, 5–6) that:

> "For many people the house is synonymous with the home. The word "home" … may be filled with emotional meaning – reminders of childhood and the roots of our being, or concept of privacy, freedom and security'. But … home may not mean house; it might also mean the ancestral land. Home is a concept of order and identity".

And what about private? Should the house by itself be looked at as private space or only part of it that is hidden from visitors?

Although there is an extended amount of literature regarding the house (Hillier and Hannson 1984; Watkins 1990; Wilk 1990; Allison 1999; Parker Pearson and Richards 1994; *etc*), no universal definition exists. To simplify the problem the easiest way is to create my own definition that describes what I mean by domestic.

Domestic space is the scene of domestic activity. Domestic activities are embracing all those activities that are the products of everyday life (firing, food preparation, cooking, sweeping/cleaning, maintenance, and building) and furthermore all those actions that serve the survival and comfort of human beings (*e.g.* consumption, sitting/sleeping, resting). Therefore, in my understanding, domestic represents everything that is connected to the everyday life and to its major and most obvious scene, to the house and its immediate surroundings.

Activities and their associated micromorphological indicators

Tables 11.1–11.5 gathers those activities and their micromorphological indicators that are in some way associated with households. It must be emphasised that the review here is highly selective with no claim to offering a comprehensive history or inventory of all the works or even all the significant works that have been done so far. To do so would obviously exceed the limits of this paper. The author's sole intention here is to highlight issues that are closely related to her own research in some respect. It also has to be noted that the listed indicators and the derived interpretations are based on specific contextual information for specific environments and that they individually and even in groups can also represent other processes and activities. For example it is obvious that amorphous organic staining alone does not indicate matting or that the lack of insect activity is the result of food storage.

The research site

The site was established during the Early Bronze Age (*c.*1800 BC) (Poroszlai 1996) some 30 km south from the present day capital of Hungary, Budapest. The settlement is situated on the right (west) bank of the Danube River, which served as the main east–west communication channel in prehistoric times.

The settlement is located on a natural loessic elevation, surrounded by valleys, and it can only be entered across a narrow promontory (see Figs 11.1 and 11.2).

The present dimensions of the site are approximately 200 m long and 100 m wide. The coring probes revealed that the greatest thickness of the settlement is some 3.5–4 m in the central area (Varga 2000). This area is only the remaining one-fifth of the

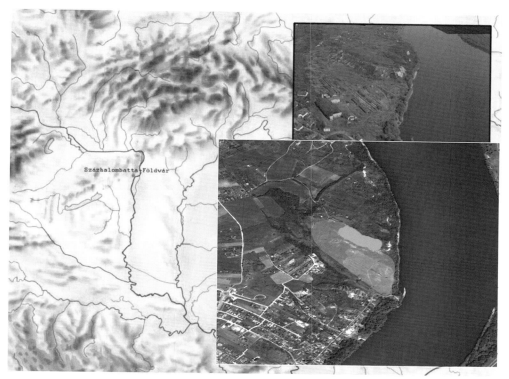

Figure 11.1. Location and aerial view of Százhalombatta-Földvár site (Photos: archive of the 'Matrica' Museum).

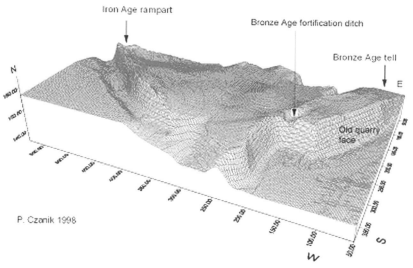

Figure 11.2. 3D picture of the site (after Füleky 2005).

	Activity	Associated micromorphological indicators	Site	Reference
Consumption/diet	Cooking	Intensive biological activity, charred remains, burnt bone, phytoliths, burnt aggregates, calcitic ashes.	Abu Salabikh (Iraq)	Matthews 1995
	Food preparation and grinding	Lenses of basalt grains, vegetal voids from grinding plant foodstuffs, pottery, bitumen fragments, unburned bone, phytoliths, charred remains, organic staining, microbial filaments and hyphae.	Abu Salabikh (Iraq)	Matthews 1995
		Layers of fish scales.	Hazendonk (Dutch)	Exaltus and Miedema 1994
		Fruit remains (blackberry/raspberry, strawberry).	Swiss lake village	Wallace 2000
	Crop-processing	Plant remains, grinding stone fragments.		Matthews et al 1994
	Food storage	No insect activity.		Matthews 1995
Sitting/sleeping	Matting	Strongly layered articulated phytoliths, occasional charred remains, void pattern suggesting decayed matting.	Abu Salabikh (Iraq)	Matthews et al 1994
		Amorphous organic staining.		Matthews 1995
		Peaked boundaries and fine lenses of dust.	Çatalhöyük (Turkey)	Matthews et al 1996
		Date palm leaflets.	Saar (Bahrain)	Matthews et al 1997b
		Charred/unheated elongated grass remains (placed as floor cover).	Ohalo II (Israel)	Tsatskin and Nadel 2003
Cleaning	Sweeping	Sub-rounded components, moderate-poor orientation and layering.	Abu Salabikh (Iraq)	Matthews 1995
	Discard and maintenance	Burnt oven plaster aggregates, cereal grains (from cooking, parching accidents), obsidian flakes, fragments of bone and subrounded aggregates of plaster (from sweeping).	Çatalhöyük (Turkey)	Matthews et al 1997a
		Loosely packed fragments of mollusc shells, bones, mixed organic and mineral matter, overall angularity of the fragments, loose, porous nature.	Potterne (England)	Courty et al 1989

Table 11.1. Activities and their associated micromorphological indicators.

Activity	Associated micromorphological indicators	Site	Reference
Firing (hearths, ovens)	Phytoliths, calcium oxalates, charred remains, calcitic ashes, burned plant matter, reddening and alteration of sediment particles by heat.	Abu Salabikh (Iraq)	Matthews et al 1994
	Date palm leaflets and rachis as fuel, articulated siliceous and desiccated remains.	Saar (Bahrain)	Matthews et al 1997a
	Wood, grass, leaf and dung ashes.	The Cave of the Pigeons (Morocco), Les Rivaux, Massif Central (France), Cave of Arene Candide (Italy), Fort Harrouard (France), Potterne (England), Kebara Cave (Israel)	Courty et al 1989; Macphail et al 1990
	Ash, phytoliths, charcoal.	Israel	Albert et al 1999, 2000, 2003
	Ash residues, rubified minerals, burnt turf, peat, wood and dung.	Hofstadir, Sveigakot (Iceland)	Simpson et al 2003
	Wood ash (rhombic calcite crystals, charcoal, partially burnt woody tissue with Ca-oxalate druses, red-burnt sediment).	AB1 (Kenya)	Shahack-Gross et al 2004
	Burnt dung.	Tell Brak (Iraq)	Matthews 2003
	Bone as fuel.	Hohle Fels Cave (Germany)	Schiegl et al 2003
	Sooth residue (internal use of fire).	Çatalhöyük (Turkey)	Matthews 1992
	Glass-like slag (from melting of phytolith) and charcoal.	Hoge Andjoen (Belgium), Flixborough (England)	Gebhardt and Langohr 1999; Canti 2003

Table 11.2. Activities and their associated micromorphological indicators.

Activity		Associated micromorphological indicators	Site	Reference
Building/construction	Building practises	Mudbricks, mortar, wall/floor plasters.	Abu Salabikh (Iraq)	Matthews 1995
		Mudbrick (elongated, tubular shaped voids, remnants of plant matter, phytoliths), daub (soil matter including soil organic matter fine charcoal, dung, refuse, coarse temper and plant fragments), walls (pure geological material, with very little or no mixing), thatched roof (large amount of wood plant matter, concentration of large fragments of straw, mixed with other construction material), mortar, plaster, cement (calcitic nature).	Southwark (England), Deir al-Balah, Netiv Hagdud (Israel), Castellaro di Uscio (Italy)	Courty et al 1989
	Floor/wall preparation and maintenance	Plastering/re-plastering of floors with different types of plaster (specific event or period of life, arguing that regular 'maintenance' activity has a deeper meaning then mere functionality).	Rural Rajasthani village (India)	Boivin 2000
		Dung, leaves, straw, chaff and other organic matter (for tempering). The absence of plant pseudomorph voids (vegetal voids) (lack of chaff or straw in the floor material-shortness of plant matter (seasonal effect, specific utilization of various species etc.) or temporal use of the floor.	Abu Salabikh (Iraq), Çatalhöyük (Turkey)	Matthews et al 1996; Matthews 1995
		Lime (whitewash).	Çatalhöyük (Turkey)	Matthews et al 1996
Crafts	Metalwork	Metallurgic slags, hammerscale.	Winchester Palace (England)	Courty et al 1989
	Flintwork	Fragments of flint debitage.	Boxgrove (England)	Macphail et al 1990
Bioturbation		Channels, chambers, mixing.	Abu Salabikh (Iraq)	Matthews 1995
		Channels, faunal excrement, vertiforms, crumb structure, biogenic calcium carbonate granules.	Rushen Abbey (Isle of Man)	Milek 1999
		High porosity dominated by large voids and reworked microfabric.	Netiv Hagdud (Israel), Jubilee Hall (England)	Courty et al 1989

Table 11.3. Activities and their associated micromorphological indicators.

Activity		Associated micromorphological indicators	Site	Reference
Pits	Ash pit	Phytoliths, reed and grass stem and leaves, charred remains.	Abu Salabikh (Iraq)	Matthews et al 1994
		Intensive biological activity, charred remains, burnt bone, phytoliths, burnt aggregates, calcitic ashes.	Tel Dor (Israel)	Shahack-Gross et al 2005
	Cremation	Bone remains, ashes, fuel.	Azirou (France)	Courty et al 1989
	Ritual activities	Painted/pigmented walls, burnt fuel with a lens of red ochre.	Çatalhöyük (Turkey)	Matthews et al 1997a
	Trampling	Horizontal crack structure, surface disaggregation, compaction.	Abu Salabikh (Iraq), Netiv Hagdud (Jordan Valley), Bronze Age alley (India), Potterne (England)	Gé et al 1993; Courty et al 1994
		Sub-horizontal cracks, irregular surface boundaries with cavities from dislodged aggregates.	Abu Salabikh (Iraq)	Matthews et al 1994; Matthews 1995
	Passage activity	Trampling effect (accessibility patterns, high/low traffic areas).	Piedmont (Italy)	Courty et al 1989, 1994
Agricultural activities and land use	Cultivation	Spade mark cuts.	Wandlebury (England)	Lewis 1998
		Ard marks, mixing (tillage).	Welland Bank Quarry (England)	French 2003
	Clearance and devegetation	Strongly, heterogeneously mixed fabric, occurrence of wood charcoal and flint (uprooting), burning (finely mixed charred organic matter, ash).	Hazelton (England)	Courty et al 1989
	Tillage	Disrupted fabric, mixing.	Papa Stour (Shetland), Welland Bank Quarry (England)	Davidson and Carter 1998; French 2003
	Vegetation burning	Abundant charcoal fragments and phytoliths, red soil fragments.	Carn Brae (England), Brittany (France), Cornish peninsula (England)	Courty et al 1989; Macphail et al 1990
	Grazing	Elongated platy pores, dense fabric.	Chisone Valley (Italy)	Courty et al 1989

Table 11.4. Activities and their associated micromorphological indicators.

Activity	Associated micromorphological indicators	Site	Reference
Animal keeping/ Animal husbandry	Excremental wastes of herbivores, carnivores and omnivores (composition, shape)		Courty et al 1989; Macphail and Goldberg 1995
	Herbivore dung (faecal spherulites)		Canti 1997, 1998, 1999
	Cattle dung (horizontally bedded organic matter, mineral particles)	Arbon Bleiche 3 (Switzerland)	Akeret and Rentzel 2001
	Laminated plant fragments, phytoliths, moss sporangia (dung, bedding and folder)		Davidson et al 1992
	Layers of trampled uncharred dung pellets, organic staining	Çatalhöyük (Turkey)	Matthews et al 1997a
Stabling/ penning	Organic microfabrics, decalcification of calcareous substrates, destabilisation of fine calcareous fabric and the formation of void infills, impregnation by amorphous organic material, microcrystalline calcium carbonate pedofeatures associated with organ	Butser Ancient Farm, Gordon's Barn Stable, Dove House Stable, Windy Hose Pens, Mount Roman Villa, West Heslerton	Heathcote 2002

(Agricultural activities)

Table 11.5. Activities and their associated micromorphological indicators.

original extent (Vicze 2005) as it has been highly truncated due to the activity of the nearby brick factory.

The investigated area

Due to the difficulties of working with the material of an ongoing excavation, where the majority of the samples are still under analysis, this paper will only investigate one of the Middle Bronze Age houses (House 3147) of the early to mid-2nd millennium BC, primarily from the soil micromorphological point of view.

House 3147 is one of the exposed Middle Bronze Age houses with two distinctive building phases (M. Vicze, pers. comm.), defined by internal architectural changes, while the enclosing walls remain in their original place. Unfortunately, as Figure 11.3 shows, the limits of the house exceed the dimension of the excavation trench, so only part of the building will be under inspection.

During the excavation an area approximately 5 m wide and 9 m long has been unearthed, which was encircled by walls. Figure 11.3 shows that the enclosing walls are only partially preserved. The intrusive pits of the later periods further prevent the detection of the entrance and obviously it is also impossible to detect windows as no standing walls were found. Although no partition wall was found within the house, differences in the use of the internal space can be observed between the northern and southern areas, as will be demonstrated below.

It must be pointed out that the plans of the two phases illustrate the floor rather idealistically. As stated above, the intrusive

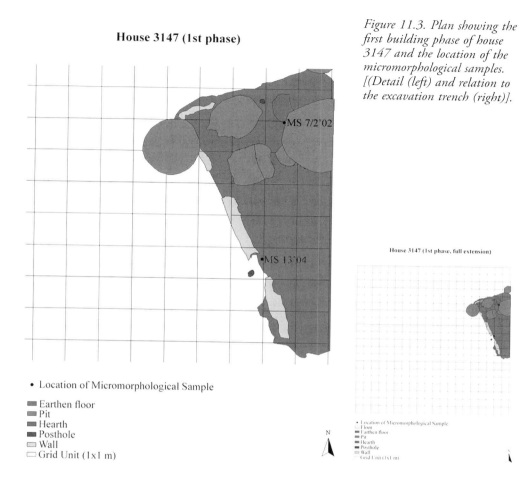

Figure 11.3. Plan showing the first building phase of house 3147 and the location of the micromorphological samples. [(Detail (left) and relation to the excavation trench (right)].

pits very much destroyed the northern section, while the middle and part of the southern area appeared to be worn out/away, with only fragments of the original floors remaining. Since the remains made it possible to reconstruct the floors, and since the destruction is not limited to specific locations but are occurring throughout the surface, it seemed to be more appropriate to illustrate the change with such plans. It also has to be noted that obviously there was no point in sampling the destroyed areas.

1st Building Phase
The initial building phase of the house is exemplified in two micromorphological samples (samples MS 7/2 '02 and MS 13 '04) as Figure 11.3 shows.

Building techniques and space use of the 1st phase
FLOORS (NORTHERN AREA)
An earthen floor was detected in relation to the 1st building phase. Although field

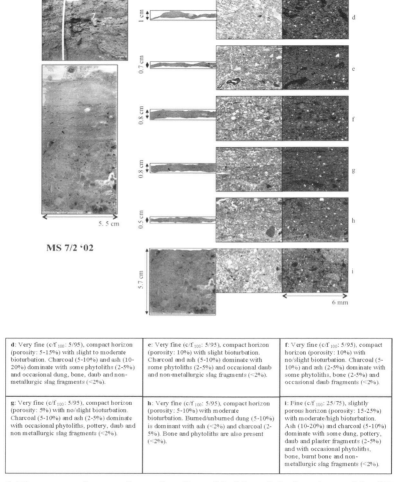

Figure 11.4. Thin section showing the earthen floors ('d'–'h') and the foundation ('i') of House 3147 (1st phase, northern area).

documentation registered the possibility of several earthen floors, they could not be distinguished securely with traditional archaeological techniques.

The microscopic analysis not only confirmed the initial field impression, but also revealed additional details. The earthen floor was not the result of a single occupation event, but the result of several renovation phases.

As Figure 11.4 shows five earthen floors ("d"–"h") were prepared on an initial foundation surface ("i") at the northern area of the house. The foundation surface, compared to the rest of the earthen floors, is less compact. The somewhat higher rate of porosity (15–25%) seems to be the result of enhanced bioturbation. This horizon

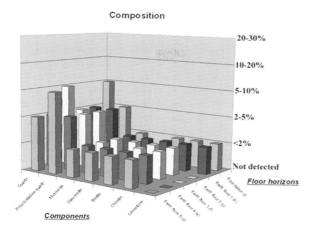

Figure 11.5. Basic mineral composition and limestone contents of the earthen floors ('d'–'h') and the foundation layer ('i') in sample MS 7/2 '02.

contained decomposed plant matter in the forms of phytoliths (<2%) and dung fragments (in forms of articulated phytoliths and calcite spherulites) (2–5%), which seems to be the subject of faunal attacks. The foundation layer is a mixture of domestic waste (*e.g.* dung, charcoal, bone, burned bone, ash, pottery, daub and plaster fragments) and sediment particles (*e.g.* quartz, polycrystalline quartz, muscovite, biotite, chlorite and limestone), which does not show any sign of intentional preparation, except for some levelling, which is indicated by the sharp boundary between the foundation layer and the overlying floor.

It seems that the previously accumulated settlement material served as a foundation. The plan of this building phase (Fig. 11.3) shows that the sample (sample MS 7/2 '02) was taken near the hearth, which seems to correlate nicely with the enhanced amount of ash and charcoal all the way through the various horizons. However, the horizons are not clear ash zones, which suggest that they are not the pure results of hearth rake-out activity, but only remnants of such events. Charcoal and ash fragments became captured in the earth floors as the result of firing and trampling activity.

As Figure 11.5 shows, there is no significant difference between the mineral compositions of the five earthen floor horizons. Quartz and polycrystalline quartz are the dominant minerals in all floor layers with additional muscovite, glauconite, biotite and chlorite. Limestone fragments were only observed in the foundation layer and in the oldest floor layer, suggesting that the limestone was only derived from the general sediment matrix on which the house was built. The small number of fragments does not suggest intentional use of this material or any specific activity (fragments of grinding stone or craftworks, for example).

It must be emphasised here that proportions of all of the mineral compounds were not calculated due to time limitations. Only the most abundant and therefore, the more representative minerals were documented. Identical methods of estimating (visual estimate, Stoops 2003, 48–49) the amount of these minerals were used to illuminate differences in the investigated horizons.

Figure 11.6. Anthropogenic inclusions of the earthen floors ('d'–'h') and the foundation layer ('i') in sample MS 7/2 '02.

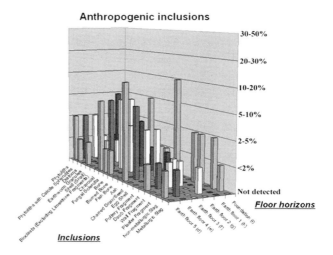

Feldspar and zircon were also noticed with relatively low frequency, but there occurrence did not seem to be indicative of anything. Flint was also counted during the initial phase of the research, but was later eliminated, because only a few mineral grains were registered. It appeared in all the investigated horizons but no significant pattern could be recognised. Nonetheless, flint has no natural occurrence in the research area. There is only one region in Hungary (*i.e.* the Tokaj region) where flint is found. However, as the research site is located near the River Danube, flint could have been transported there from a wide area. Therefore, provenance analysis of this matter holds no promising potential in the investigated area. Unfortunately, no elevated amounts of flint have been registered in the analysed samples, therefore, flint working is not an issue here.

USE OF SPACE (NORTHERN AREA)
There is no debris accumulation between the floors. This suggests either regular cleaning and maintenance, or short periods between their formations, which did not allow time for the accumulation of debris. Lack of use can be excluded since the incorporated anthropological inclusions signals domestic activity.

Figure 11.6 shows the abundance of the various anthropogenic inclusions within the matrix of the earthen floors. Charcoal and ash are the most abundant inclusions, as was implied above. Phytoliths are also frequent, which seems indicative of the high intensity of faunal activity (see rates of bioturbation). The rest of the anthropogenic inclusions are less common and this does not seem to be surprising. The fine (0.5–1 cm), thin floors have no physical capacity to capture macro-finds and it seems that floors were generally laid with care and only "clean" building matter was employed. The floor plasters below will demonstrate this.

The absence of accumulated debris makes it impossible to detect the range of activities that may have taken place, with the exception of fire making and possible

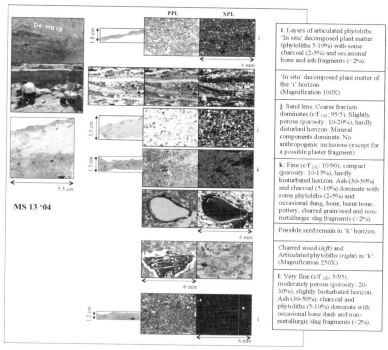

Figure 11.7. Thin section showing the earthen floors ('l' and 'k') and the floor build-up materials ('i' and 'j') of House 3147 (1st phase, southern area).

cleaning. The occurrence of non-metallurgic slag is also an indicator of heat/firing. The bone, pottery and daub fragments are indicators of domestic context (*i.e.* remnants of everyday life). However, as they occur only infrequently, they cannot be used as solid proof of specific domestic activity such as food preparation, cooking or consumption. The foundation layer (horizon "i") shows higher amounts of inclusions on a wider scale, which suggests that the house was built on a surface that enclosed various refuse elements, as mentioned earlier.

FLOORS (SOUTHERN AREA)

Figure 11.7 captures the last two earthen floors ("k" and "l") in the southern part of the house. The composition of these horizons is very similar to the ones observed in sample MS 7/2 '02. The mineral composition (Fig. 11.8) exhibits quartz and polycrystalline quartz with a higher frequency, just as in the case of sample MS 7/2 '02.

It is obvious that the same technique was applied both in the northern and southern area of the house during the initial phases of the building. Some of the Vatya houses, where partition walls were detected show differences between the northern and southern areas, both in terms of building techniques and space-use. It seems that during the initial building phase, an earthen floor was laid in the northern area while the southern

*Figure 11.8. Basic
mineral composition
and limestone contents
and the anthropogenic
inclusions of the earthen
floors ('k' and 'l') and
the above-laying layers
('i' and 'j') in sample
MS 13 '04.*

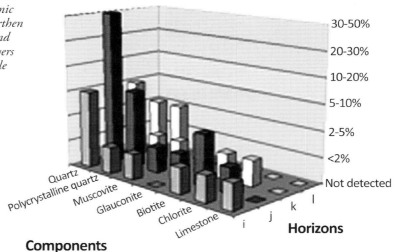

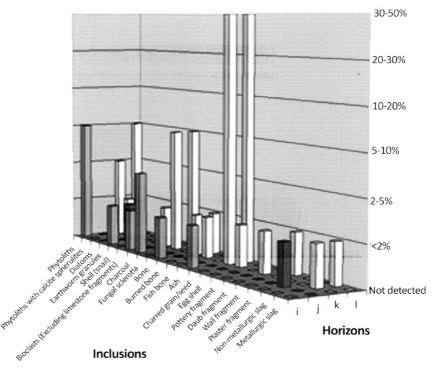

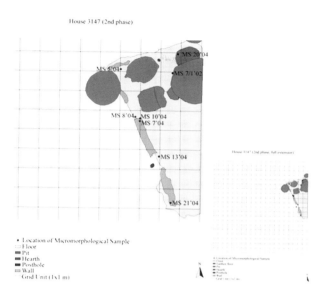

Figure 11.9. Plan showing the second building phase of House 3147 and the location of the micromorphological samples [(Detail (left) and relation to the excavation trench (right)].

area was plastered. However, during the 2nd phase both areas were plastered, showing differences in the building practise and most likely in the space useage as well (M. Vicze, forthcoming).

USE OF SPACE (SOUTHERN AREA)

The most outstanding difference is detected between the ash content of the earthen floors in the northern and southern areas. The southern area has higher amounts of ash (Fig. 11.8), which either indicates a lower frequency of cleaning, or the deliberate disposal of ash to this area. The first assumption is further supported by the appearance of the decomposed plant matter ("i"), which does not show any sign of disruption. However, as the sample was taken immediately next to the wall, it is also possible that some of the debris accidentally survived the sweeping. This is not surprising in areas that are not affected by heavy use, and which are more "protected" due to their sheltered position. Unfortunately, none of these hypotheses can be confirmed because no additional samples were taken from this area.

2nd Building Phase

The second building phase of House 3147 is illustrated in Figure 11.9 which indicates that, during the 2nd phase, the entire house was plastered. Three soil micromorphological samples (samples MS 5 '04, MS 7/1 '02 and MS 13 '04) were taken to characterise this phase of the building with respect to the nature of the flooring. Another four samples (samples MS 7 '04, MS 8 '04, MS 10 '04 and MS 21 '04) will reveal the wall structure, and one sample was taken from the hearth of this phase (sample MS 20 '04).

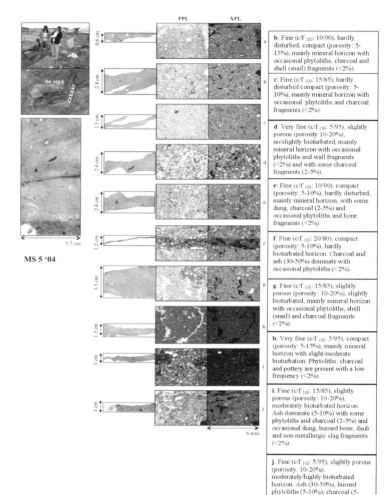

Figure 11.10. Thin section showing the plaster floors ('g' and 'h') of house 3147 (2nd phase, northern area). Note the last two phases of the earthen floors ('i' and 'j') of phase 1.

b: Fine (c/f $_{100}$: 10/90), hardly disturbed, compact (porosity: 5-15%), mainly mineral horizon with occasional phytoliths, charcoal and shell (snail) fragments (<2%).

c: Fine (c/f $_{100}$: 15/85), hardly disturbed compact (porosity: 5-10%), mainly mineral horizon with occasional phytoliths and charcoal fragments (<2%).

d: Very fine (c/f $_{100}$: 5/95), slightly porous (porosity 10-20%), no/slightly bioturbated, mainly mineral horizon with occasional phytoliths and wall fragments (<2%) and with some charcoal fragments (2-5%).

e: Fine (c/f $_{100}$: 10/90), compact (porosity: 5-10%), hardly disturbed, mainly mineral horizon, with some dung, charcoal (2-5%) and occasional phytoliths and bone fragments (<2%).

f: Fine (c/f $_{100}$: 20/80), compact (porosity: 5-10%), hardly bioturbated horizon. Charcoal and ash (30-50%) dominate with occasional phytoliths (<2%).

g: Fine (c/f $_{100}$: 15/85), slightly porous (porosity: 10-20%), slightly bioturbated, mainly mineral horizon with occasional phytoliths, shell (snail) and charcoal fragments (<2%).

h: Very fine (c/f $_{100}$: 5/95), compact (porosity: 5-15%), mainly mineral horizon with slight/moderate bioturbation. Phytoliths, charcoal and pottery are present with a low frequency (<2%).

i: Fine (c/f $_{100}$: 15/85), slightly porous (porosity: 10-20%), moderately bioturbated horizon. Ash dominate (5-10%) with some phytoliths and charcoal (2-5%) and occasional dung, burned bone, daub and non metallurgic slag fragments (<2%).

j: Fine (c/f $_{100}$: 5/95), slightly porous (porosity: 10-20%), moderately/highly bioturbated horizon. Ash (30-50%), burned phytoliths (5-10%), charcoal (5-10%) and daub (5-10%) dominate with some pottery and non-metallurgic slag (2-5%) and occasional burnt bone fragments (<2%).

Building techniques and space use of the 2nd phase
FLOORS

It is evident that the building technique employed did not change during the 1st phase of building, and since no partition wall was detected in the 2nd phase either, it does not seem to be viable to further test the differences between the northern and southern areas in terms of building techniques. The composition of the plaster floor in the northern and southern parts is also very similar, so it is not necessary to discuss the building technique using such a division any longer. During the 2nd phase, the previous practice of renovating the earthen floor ceased and the whole floor was renewed with

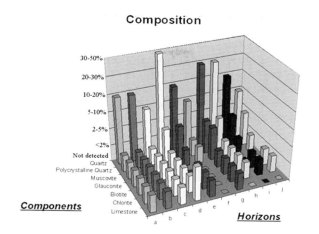

Figure 11.11. Basic mineral composition and limestone contents of the plaster floors ('g' and 'h') and the layers above ('a–f') and below ('i' and 'j') in sample MS 5 '04.

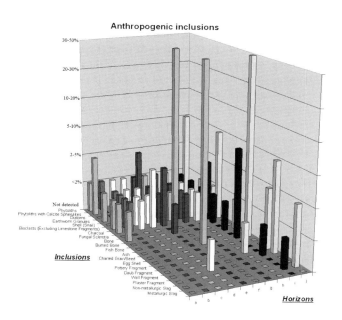

Figure 11.12. Anthropogenic inclusions of the plaster floors ('g' and 'h') and the layers above ('a-f') and below ('i' and 'j') in sample MS 5 '04.

yellow plaster to a thickness of *c.* 3 cm. Samples MS 5 '04 ("g") (Fig. 11.10), MS 7/1 '02 ("c") (Fig. 11.13) and the upper horizons of MS 13 '04 ("f") (Fig. 11.16) show this phase of the building.

The floor is composed primarily of fine mineral matter (Figs 11.11, 11.14 and 11.17) and it contains almost no anthropogenic inclusions (except for the occasional phytoliths and charcoal fragments) in any of the three samples. The samples illustrate that "clean", very fine matter was used to build the floor and care was taken to exclude any debris from the surroundings. The floor plasters contain only a few phytoliths. The absence of vegetal voids (empty space that remains after the decomposition of the various plant matters), and organic staining, or any other form of plant material, clearly shows that no vegetal tempering was present. The floors exhibited a low frequency of pore spaces and high compaction. This suggests that only moderate mixing of the raw material took place, which prevented too much air from being captured in the floor horizons. This is quite frequent when temper is added.

In samples MS 5 '04 ("i" and "j") (Fig. 11.10) and in MS 7/1 '02 ("d") (Fig. 11.13) the previous earthen floors are clearly visible, and are illustrative of the changes in the floor building practise. "Clean" clay matter is recognisable beneath the proper plastering in the case of sample MS 5 '04 ("h") and MS 13 '04 ("h"). However, this is not the case in sample MS 7/1 '02.

Since no plaster-floor renovation was detected, either micromorphologically or archaeologically, it seems reasonable to believe that what appears as clay patches was used to eliminate surface unevenness prior to the flooring. This hypothesis seems to be further supported by the fact that both samples exhibiting these "extra" clay horizons were taken near the walls. The plaster floors were slightly raised-up to the walls to join the two elements, where the use of more building matter was necessary to create the slight slope between the wall and the floor plaster. The "extra" clay might have served this purpose. The sandy horizon ("g") on top of the clay matter in sample MS 13 '04 also suggests some packing material, which served as foundation.

Use of space in the 2nd phase

The accumulated debris in sample MS 5 '04 (Fig. 11.10) is represented by a 1–2 mm thick horizon ("f") that is composed of pure ash and charcoal with some phytoliths, suggesting that this layer represents the remains of hearth rake-out. The sample contains only a thin layer of ash and no other remnants of domestic waste, which might indicate regular cleaning, just as we have seen in the case of the 1st phase in this area. The rest of the horizons on top of this layer represent fallen in debris (mainly wall fragments ("b", "c", "d" and "e")). One of the fallen-in wall fragments ("e") contains some dung, which might indicate that it was used as temper. Although no dung was registered in any of the other wall fragments, it does not necessarily mean that such matter was excluded from the plaster. It should be noted here that the detection of dung in such fine and compact matter is rather problematic due to the poor visibility of the microscopic elements. (Faecal spherulites are 5–15 microns in size). The chemical analysis of plasters is a way of testing this hypothesis. However, the abundance of dung is small as is the amount of plant matter – features associated with animal waste. This suggests that dung was not a significant element in the plaster matter.

The "b" horizon of sample MS 7/1 '02 (Fig. 11.13) shows the accumulated debris on top of the floor (horizon "c"). It is evident after the first glance that this sample does not contain an ash layer similar to the one observed in the previous sample. This

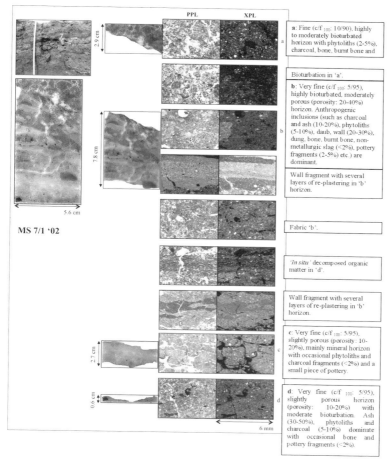

MS 7/1 '02

a: Fine (c/f $_{100}$: 10/90), highly to moderately bioturbated horizon with phytoliths (2-5%), charcoal, bone, burnt bone and

Bioturbation in 'a'.

b: Very fine (c/f $_{100}$: 5/95), highly bioturbated, moderately porous (porosity: 20-40%) horizon. Anthropogenic inclusions (such as charcoal and ash (10-20%), phytoliths (5-10%), daub, wall (20-30%), dung, bone, burnt bone, non-metallurgic slag (<2%), pottery fragments (2-5%) etc.) are dominant.

Wall fragment with several layers of re-plastering in 'b' horizon.

Fabric 'b'.

'In situ' decomposed organic matter in 'd'.

Wall fragment with several layers of re-plastering in 'b' horizon.

c: Very fine (c/f $_{100}$: 5/95), slightly porous (porosity: 10-20%), mainly mineral horizon with occasional phytoliths and charcoal fragments (<2%) and a small piece of pottery.

d: Very fine (c/f $_{100}$: 5/95), slightly porous horizon (porosity: 10-20%) with moderate bioturbation. Ash (30-50%), phytoliths and charcoal (5-10%) dominate with occasional bone and pottery fragments (<2%).

Figure 11.13. Thin section showing the plaster floor ('c') of House 3147 (2nd phase, northern area). Note the last earthen floor ('d') of phase 1 below the plaster floor ('c').

sample was taken very close to the hearth – an area that might have been kept extremely "clean" – and this might account for the lack of floor build-up. Just as in the case of sample MS 5 '04, this sample also contains a considerable amount of wall fragments that seem to be collapsed debris after the abandonment and destruction of the house. However, the presence of charcoal, ash, organic matter (in the form of phytoliths), bone and pottery fragments demonstrate the domestic context. The southern area (sample MS 13 '04, Fig. 11.16), nonetheless shows, a different picture. Three ash layers (horizons "c", "d" and "e"), which vary between 11–17 mm, are visible on top of the plaster floor (horizon "f"). These consecutive ash layers and the orientation (parallel to the floor level) of their various components, together with the sharp boundaries between the horizons suggest deliberate placing. The exact aim of this action is hard to discern but it might have served hygienic purposes. Ash is highly calcareous (Karkansas *et al.* 2000), that is to say alkaline, so it can be used as disinfectant (Hakbijl 2002). Furthermore, ash has a high capacity of water absorption, which makes it useful to reduce dampness (Milek

Figure 11.14. Basic mineral composition and limestone contents of the plaster floor ('c') and the layers above ('a' and 'b') and below ('d') in sample MS 7/1 '02.

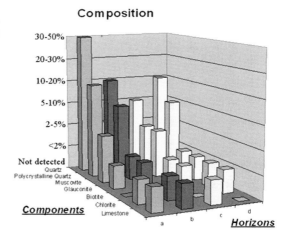

Figure 11.15. Anthropogenic inclusions of the plaster floor ('c') and the layers above ('a' and 'b') and below ('d') in sample MS 7/1 '02.

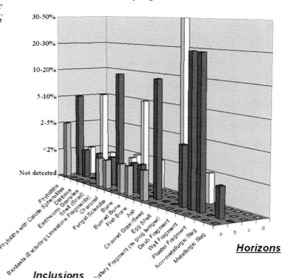

2006). There is no other type of debris accumulation between the ash layers, which hints at regular maintenance or short periods of time between their formations. The practise of regular maintenance is further supported by the presence of floor build-up ("b") on top of the last ash layer ("c"). The floor build-up contains charcoal, phytoliths, ash, bone and non-metallurgic slag, all of which indicates domestic activity. A fallen-in wall fragment ("a") occupies the majority of the floor build-up suggesting that horizon "b" was the last occupation surface after which the house was abandoned.

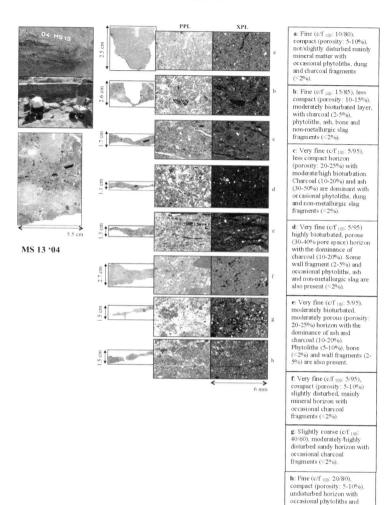

PPL   XPL

a: Fine (c/f ₁₀₀: 10/80), compact (porosity: 5-10%), not/slightly disturbed mainly mineral matter with occasional phytoliths, dung and charcoal fragments (<2%).

b: Fine (c/f ₁₀₀: 15/85), less compact (porosity: 10-15%), moderately bioturbated layer, with charcoal (2-5%), phytoliths, ash, bone and non-metallurgic slag fragments (<2%).

c: Very fine (c/f ₁₀₀: 5/95), less compact horizon (porosity: 20-25%) with moderate/high bioturbation. Charcoal (10-20%) and ash (30-50%) are dominant with occasional phytoliths, dung and non-metallurgic slag fragments (<2%).

d: Very fine (c/f ₁₀₀: 5/95) highly bioturbated, porous (30-40% pore space) horizon with the dominance of charcoal (10-20%). Some wall fragment (2-5%) and occasional phytoliths, ash and non-metallurgic slag are also present (<2%).

e: Very fine (c/f ₁₀₀: 5/95), moderately bioturbated, moderately porous (porosity: 20-25%) horizon with the dominance of ash and charcoal (10-20%). Phytoliths (5-10%), bone (<2%) and wall fragments (2-5%) are also present.

f: Very fine (c/f ₁₀₀: 5/95), compact (porosity: 5-10%) slightly disturbed, mainly mineral horizon with occasional charcoal fragments (<2%).

g: Slightly coarse (c/f ₁₀₀: 40/60), moderately/highly disturbed sandy horizon with occasional charcoal fragments (<2%).

h: Fine (c/f ₁₀₀: 20/80), compact (porosity: 5-10%), undisturbed horizon with occasional phytoliths and charcoal (<2%).

Figure 11.16. Thin section showing the plaster floor ('f') of House 3147 (2nd phase, southern area).

MS 13 '04

5.5 cm

6 mm

WALL

Three soil micromorphological samples were used to characterise the wall-building technique (samples MS 8 '04, MS 10 '04, MS 21 '04), and one of the postholes was also (sample MS 7 '04) sampled. As demonstrated above, the inner structure of the house has two distinctive phases while the enclosing walls remained the same.

MS 21 '04 (Fig. 11.19) represents the inner structure of the wall. Its main composition can be characterised with the abundance of sediment particles. Various refuse elements (such as charcoal, ash, bone, organic matter, *etc*) were also identified in the horizon (see Fig. 11.20). Although the sample contains some coarser (a couple of millimetres in size) inclusions (charcoal and bone, for example), it can be characterised as rather fine and compact. The material under investigation did not accumulate *in situ*. This is clearly indicated by the bone fragment (see Fig. 11.19) and the brown material

*Figure 11.17. Basic mineral
composition and limestone contents
of the plaster floor ('f') and the layers
above ('a'–'e') and below ('g' and 'h') in
sample MS 13 '04.*

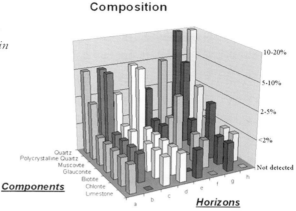

Composition

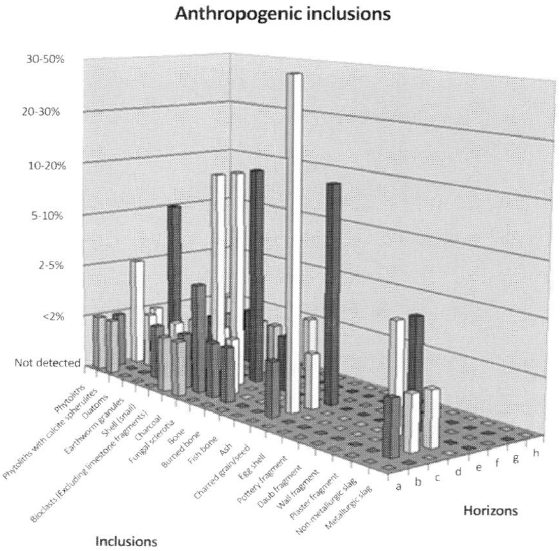

*Figure 11.18. Anthropogenic inclusions
of the plaster floor ('f') and the layers
above ('a'–'e') and below ('g' and 'h') in
sample MS 13 '04.*

Anthropogenic inclusions

surrounding it. The bone was originally deposited elsewhere and the brown material surrounding it represents the original deposit in which it was lying. Later on, it was transported and incorporated into the matter that was used to prepare the wall. The same is true for the ash fragment (see Fig. 11.19). No reddening of the enclosing matrix is visible, which clearly indicates that the actual burning took place somewhere else. This fragment, like the bone, later became mixed into the wall matter. The reason for this is that the "base" of the wall was created from the general fill matrix of the site, which was highly compacted. (For the characterisation of the general fill, see Kovács 2008). This compact general fill contained the posts, which supported the roof. The posthole was lined inside with fine plaster, as sample MS 7 '04 shows (Fig. 11.21).

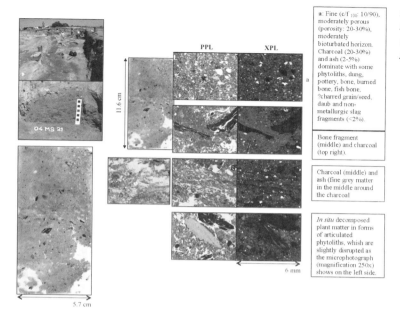

a: Fine (c/f ₁₀₀: 10/90), moderately porous (porosity: 20-30%), moderately bioturbated horizon. Charcoal (20-30%) and ash (2-5%) dominate with some phytoliths, dung, pottery, bone, burned bone, fish bone, ?charred grain/seed, daub and non-metallurgic slag fragments (<2%).

Bone fragment (middle) and charcoal (top right).

Charcoal (middle) and ash (fine grey matter in the middle around the charcoal

In situ decomposed plant matter in forms of articulated phytoliths, whish are slightly disrupted as the microphotograph (magnification 250x) shows on the left side.

Figure 11.19. Thin section showing the wall 'base' of House 3147.

MS 21 '04

The plaster (horizon "a") is very similar to that used for the flooring, thus suggesting a shared origin for the two materials. Sample MS 7 '04 also exhibits the compact wall "base" ("b") in which various refuse elements are present (Fig. 11.22).

The final phase of the wall construction was the application of a fine yellow plaster, which was periodically renewed during the lifetime of the house (see sample MS 10 '04 (Fig. 11.23) further down). It seems that houses constructed with such walls only had their fine plaster layers applied from the inside. The application of this fine plaster by itself suggests concerns about hygiene, and this is further indicated by the sealing of the incorporated refuse elements of the wall "base" from the living area.

As can be seen in the case of sample MS 10 '04, the wall fragments are not *in situ* but in a secondary position surrounded by fallen-in debris.

Sample MS 10 '04 will not be discussed in detail as the other soil micromorphological samples more clearly demonstrate the building technique. The only importance of this sample is to show the fine wall plasterings (see Fig. 11.23) that seem to be typical in some of the Vatya houses. It clearly demonstrates that the plaster layers are very fine, compact and contain no anthropogenic inclusions. They show no sign of any kind of tempering, which is also true of the floor plasters. It is also evident that the first layer is slightly thicker than the rest of the renovation layers, which are only a couple of millimetres thick. The pore spaces are parallel to the main horizon, which is indicative of the smoothing effect with which the plaster was most likely applied.

Sample MS 8 '04 (Fig. 11.24) also demonstrates wall plaster fragments (horizons

Figure 11.20. Basic mineral
composition and limestone content
and the anthropogenic inclusions of
the wall 'base' of House 3147.

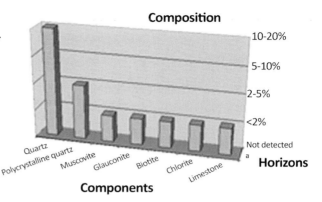

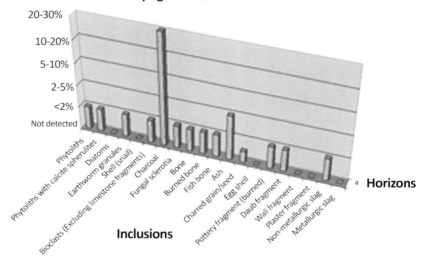

"a", "b", "d" and "f") that were most likely mixed with the wall 'base' ("c" and "e")
matter during the later destruction of the house.

The wall plaster fragments are very fine, compact and composed of primarily mineral
elements, excluding anthropogenic inclusions, such as in the rest of the analysed
plaster materials (Fig. 11.25). The wall "base" (horizon "e") captured in this section is
almost identical to sample MS 21 '04, with the pre-dominance of small anthropogenic
inclusions.

The detection and characterisation of such walls are very important because so far
only wattle and daub walls were considered typical of the Vatya Culture (see for example
Kovács 1977). Although wattle and daub walls are also present at Százhalombatta-
Földvár site, the recent excavation and the micromorphological analysis revealed that

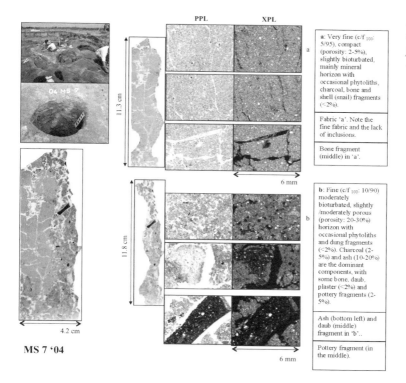

Figure 11.21. Thin section showing the plastered posthole of House 3147.

there is much more variation in terms of building techniques than it was previously thought. It was even proposed that there might be variation between the walls of the same house (Sørensen and Vicze, pers. comm.). Only systematic sampling and analysis of the wall fragments can shed light on this assumption.

HEARTH

Hearths are the most obvious installations that we find in the Vatya houses and soil micromorphological investigations of them can reveal details that might be overlooked by other methods, such as field observations or content analysis.

Two hearths have been unearthed in House 3147: one for each of the two building phases as shown in Figures 11.3 and 11.9. Both of them are situated in the northern area of the house close to the wall. They are almost at the same position, which clearly indicates the significance of the location. Even though the floor has been renewed, using a different technique (from earthen floors to plaster floor), the location of the hearth remained the same. The latter hearth partially destroyed the older one. Only the wall of the latter hearth was subject to micromorphological investigation. Unfortunately, the content of the hearth was not sampled, thus, it is impossible to make conclusions regarding the fuel type.

Figure 11.22. Basic mineral composition and limestone contents and the anthropogenic inclusions of the posthole plaster ('a') and its 'foundation' ('b').

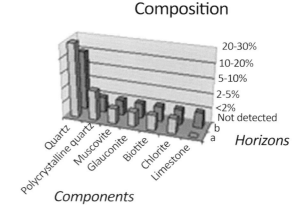

Figure 11.22. Basic mineral composition and limestone contents and the anthropogenic inclusions of the posthole plaster ('a') and its 'foundation' ('b').

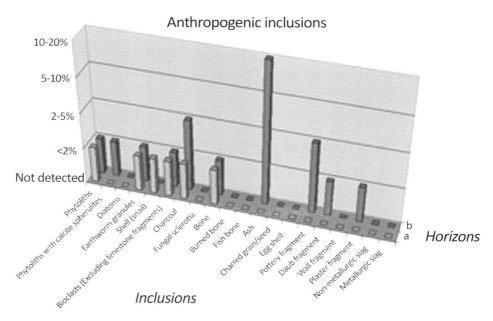

However, the ash layers detected on the plaster floor surface in sample MS 13 '04 suggests that wood (indicated by the charcoal fragments), grasses (indicated by the burnt phytoliths that are most characteristic of grasses) and possibly dung (in forms of phytoliths and calcitic spherulites) were also used for firing.

The macroscopic observations during the excavation revealed that the hearth was renovated several times – suggesting regular maintenance – which could not be captured in one sample.

Fine, compact, primarily mineral material was used to create the hearth (Fig. 11.27), just as it was used for the wall or floor plasters. The most significant difference to wall/floor plasters is the abundance of organic matter (in forms of phytoliths and charred

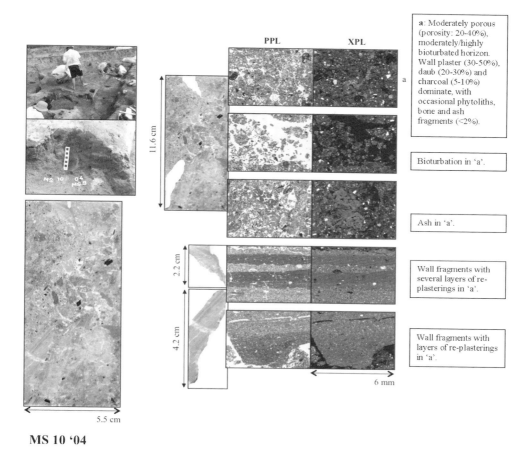

PPL   XPL

a: Moderately porous (porosity: 20-40%), moderately/highly bioturbated horizon. Wall plaster (30-50%), daub (20-30%) and charcoal (5-10%) dominate, with occasional phytoliths, bone and ash fragments (<2%).

Bioturbation in 'a'.

Ash in 'a'.

Wall fragments with several layers of re-plasterings in 'a'.

Wall fragments with layers of re-plasterings in 'a'.

6 mm

11.6 cm

2.2 cm

4.2 cm

5.5 cm

MS 10 '04

Figure 11.23. Thin section showing the re-plastered wall fragments of House 3147.

organic material) and the higher frequency of anthropogenic inclusions such as daub, bone and pottery fragments (Fig. 11.27). The abundance of organic matter suggests that it was used as temper and the rest of the inclusions might be indicative of the refuse elements around the hearth, which became mixed into the material during the renovation phases, while the used raw material was deposited in the hearth surroundings waiting to be applied. The majority of the clay matter used during the construction was rather "clean" and the small amount of anthropogenic inclusions suggests that they were not used intentionally.

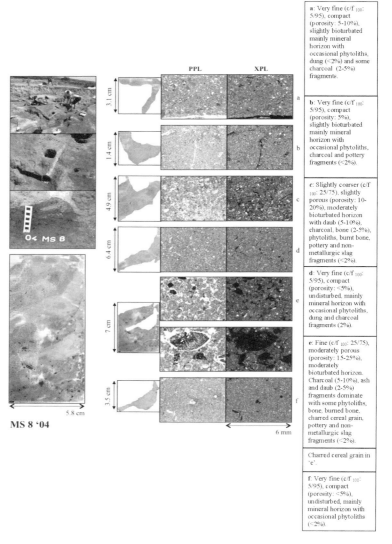

Figure 11.24. Thin section showing fragments of the wall of House 3147.

*Figure 11.25. Basic
mineral composition
and limestone contents
and the anthropogenic
inclusions of the wall
fragments ('a', 'b', 'd'
and 'f') of House 3147
and their framing
matrix ('c' and 'e') in
sample MS 8 '04.*

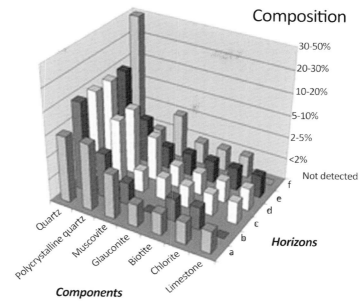

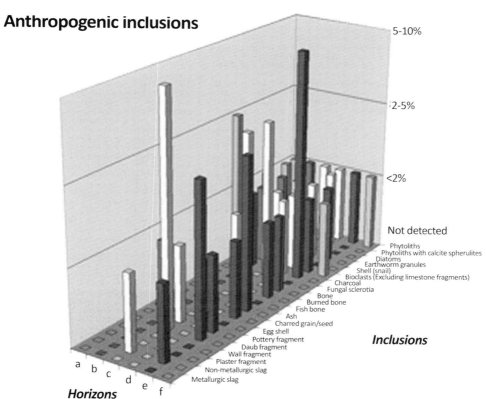

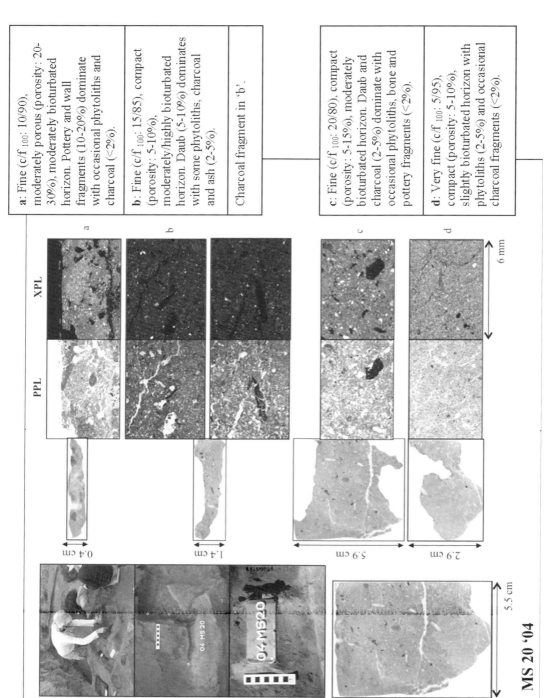

Figure 11.26. Thin section showing the hearth-wall in House 3147.

Figure 11.27. Basic mineral composition and limestone contents and the anthropogenic inclusions of the hearth-wall in House 3147.

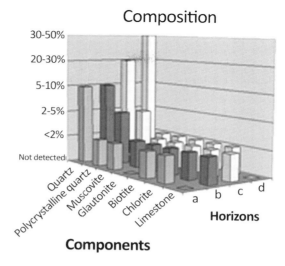

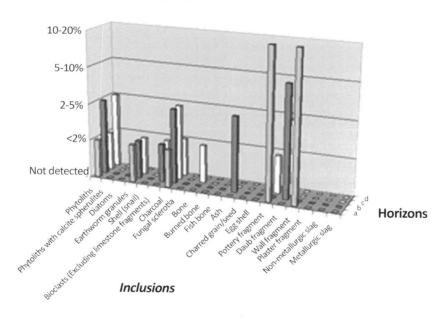

Conclusions

During the lifetime of House 3147 a major change took place regarding the floor building practice. The initial earthen floors were subsequently replaced by plaster. In terms of the use of space, regular cleaning and maintenance is clearly detectable throughout the life-span of the house, except for the last occupation surface just before it was abandoned. There is a clearly visible pattern between the two building phases: the southern area contains higher amounts of ash and charcoal in both cases. There are at least two possible explanations for this: the hearth area (northern part) was kept cleaner than the rest of the house; and it seems that ash was deliberately placed in the southern part, possibly to disinfect and absorb dampness.

The wall of House 3147 revealed new techniques applied during wall construction. The previously believed wattle and daub walls are not the only ways of wall preparation. The compacted general fill material of the settlement was used to create the foundation of the wall that incorporated the posts, and only the inner side of the wall was plastered to seal the living area. Continuous re-plastering of the walls reveals that regular maintenance was practised.

The hearth was renovated several times (suggesting regular maintenance) and stayed almost at the same location during both phases. Although no micromorphological sample was taken from the inside of the hearth, the accumulated ash most probably derived from the hearth indicated that wood, grasses and possibly even dung was used for firing.

Overall, it has to be realised that construction was well thought out and material of different quality was applied to the various elements (for example fine, "clean" matter for inner wall and floor plaster *vs.* general fill with waste fragments for the wall foundation). Regular maintenance and cleaning, together with remnants of domestic activities such as firing, cooking, and consumption, were identifiable throughout the various horizons. The absence of any hints of craftwork, metalwork or any other activity (*e.g.* animal keeping, sacrifice) reveals that the house was only used for living. Only activities that are strongly connected to everyday life took place in this locale.

Finally, it must be pointed out that neither the extent nor the frequency of cleaning and maintenance can be judged at this stage based on the soil micromorphological analysis of one house. Further micromorphological analysis of contemporary houses of the tell (and other tells) together with analysis of the macro-level findings offers a tremendous potential for understanding such practices. The aim of this paper was to highlight those patterns that are visible through the eyes of a soil micromorphologist.

Acknowledgment
Special thanks to Professor Kristian Kristiansen (University of Göteborg) for setting up the EU funded "Emergence of European Communities" research project under whose jurisdiction the preparation of this paper (part of my PhD thesis) became possible. I would also like to thank the dig directors, the late Dr Ildikó Poroszlai and Dr Magdolna Vicze ("Matrica" Museum), who provided the archaeological background and who endlessly encouraged my work, both academically and personally, over the years. The micromorphological guidance of Dr Charles French (Department of Archaeology, University of Cambridge) is also very much appreciated. Finally, I wish to thank Dániel

Fűköh ("Matrica" Museum) for his assistance in the preparation of the plans used in this paper.

References

Akeret, Ö. and Rentzel, P. (2001) Micromorphology and plant macrofossil analysis of cattle dung from the Neolithic lake shore settlement of Arbon Bleiche 3. *Geoarchaeology: An International Journal* 16(6), 687–700.

Allison, P. M. (1999) *The Archaeology of Household Activities*. New York, Routledge.

Barham, A. J. and Macphail, R. I. (1995) *Archaeological Sediments and Soils: Analysis, Interpretation and Management*. London, Archetype Books.

Boivin, N (2000) Life rhythms and floor sequences: excavating time in rural Rajasthan and Neolithic Çatalhöyük. *World Archaeology* 31(3), 367–388.

Bullock, P., Federoff, N., Jongerius, A., Stoops, G., Tursina, T. and Babel, U. (1985) *Handbook for Soil Thin Ssection Description*. Wolverhampton, Waine Research Publications.

Canti, M. G. (1998) The micromorphological identification of faecal spherulites from archaeological and modern materials. *Journal of Archaeological Science* 25, 435–444.

Canti, M. G. (1997) An investigation of microscopic calcareous spherulites from herbivore dungs. *Journal of Archaeological Science* 24, 219–231

Canti, M. G. (1999) The production and preservation of faecal spherulites: animals, environment and taphonomy. *Journal of Archaeological Science* 26, 251–258.

Carsten, J. and Hugh-Jones, S. (1995) Introduction: about the House – Lévi-Strauss and Bbeyond. In J. Carsten and S. Hugh-Jones (eds) *About the House, Lévi-Strauss and Beyond*, 1–46. Cambridge, Cambridge University Press.

Courty, M. A., Goldberg, P. and Macphail, R. I. (1989) *Soils and Micromorphology in Archaeology*. Cambridge, Cambridge University Press.

Courty, M. A., Goldberg, P. and Macphail, R. I. (1994) Ancient people – lifestyles and cultural patterns. Micromorphological indicators of anthropogenic effects on soils, symposium of the subcommission B. In J. B. Etchevers (ed.) *Transactions of the 15th World Congress of Soil Science*, 250–269. Mexico DF, Sociedad Mexicana de la Ciencia del Suelo, International Society of Soil Science 6a.

Davidson, D. A. and Carter, S. P. (1998) Micromorphological evidence of past agricultural practices in cultivated soils: the impact of a traditional agricultural system on soils in Papa Stour, Shetland. *Journal of Archaeological Science* 25, 827–838.

Davidson, D. A., Carter, S. P. and Quine, T. A. (1992) An evaluation of micromorphology as an aid to archaeological interpretation. *Geoarchaeology: An International Journal* 7(1), 55–65.

Evans, J. and Connor, T. O. (1999) *Environmental Archaeology, Principles and Methods*. Stroud (UK), Sutton.

Exaltus, R. P. and Miedema, R. (1994) A micromorphological study of four Neolithic sites in the Dutch coastal provinces. *Journal of Archaeological Science* 21, 289–301.

French, C. A. I. (2003) *Geoarchaeology in Action: Studies in Soil Micromorphology and Landscape Evolution*. London, Routledge.

Füleky, Gy. (2005) Soils of the Bronze Age tell in Százhalombatta. In I. Poroszlai and M. Vicze (eds) *SAX, Százhalombatta Archaeological Expedition, Annual Report 2 – Field Season 2000–2003*, 89–110. Százhalombatta, "Matrica" Museum.

Gebhardt, A. and Langohr, R. (1999) Micromorphological study of Cconstruction materials and living floors in the medieval motte Werken (West Flanders, Belgium). *Geoarchaeology* 14(7), 595–620.

Gerrard, J. (2000) *Fundamentals of Soils*. London, Routledge.

Gé, T., Courty, M. A., Matthews, W. and Wattez, J. (1993) Sedimentary formation processes of occupation surfaces. In P. Goldberg, D. T. Nash and M. D. Petraglia (eds) *Formation Processes in Archaeological Context*, 149–163. Madison (WI), Prehistory Press, Monographs in World Archaeology 17.

Gladfelter, B. G. (1977) Geoarchaeology: the geomorphologist and archaeology. *American Antiquity* 42, 519–538.

Goldberg, P. (1992) Micromorphology, soils and archaeological sites. In V. T. Holliday (ed.) *Soils in Archaeology*, 145–167. Washington, Smithsonian Institution Press.

Hakbijl, T. (2002) The traditional, historical and prehistoric use of ashes as an insecticide, with an experimental study on the insecticidal efficacy of washed ash. *Environmental Archaeology* 7, 13–22.

Harding, D. W. (1986) *Az Őskori Európa*. Budapest, Helikon Kiadó.

Heathcote, J. L. (2002) *An Investigation of the Pedosedimentary Characteristics of Deposits Associated with Managed Livestock*. Unpublished PhD thesis, University College London.

Hillier, B. and Hanson, J. (1984) *The Social Logic of Space*. Cambridge, Cambridge University Press.

Kovács, T. (1977) *A Bronzkor Magyrországon*. Budapest, Corvina.

Kovács, G. (2008) Geoarchaeological investigation of Százhalombatta-Földvár Bronze Age tell settlement in Hungary, unpublished PhD thesis, University of Cambridge.

Lewis, H. A. (1998) *The Characterization and Interpretation of Ancient Tillage Practises Through Soil Micromorphology: a Methodological Study*. Unpublished PhD thesis, University of Cambridge.

Limbrey, S. (1975) *Soil Science in Archaeology*. Waltham (MA), Academic Press.

Macphail, R. I. and Goldberg, P. (1995) Recent advances in micromorphological Interpretations of soils and sediments from archaeological sites. In A. Barham and R. I. Macphail (Eds.) *Archaeological Sediments and Soils: Analysis, Interpretation and Management*, 1–24. London, Architype Books.

Macphail, R. I., Courty, M. A. and Gebhardt, A (1990) Soil Micromorphological Evidence of Early Agriculture in North West Europe. *World Archaeology* 22, 53–69.

Matthews, W. (1992) *The Micromorphology of Occupational Sequences and the Use of Space in a Sumerian City*. Unpublished PhD thesis, University of Cambridge.

Matthews, W. (1995) Micromorphological Characterisation and Interpretation of Occupation Deposits and Microstratigraphic Sequences at Abu Salabikh, Iraq. In Barham and Macphail (eds) (1995), 41–76.

Matthews, W. (2003) Microstratigraphic sequences: indications of uses and concepts of space. In R. Matthews (ed.) *Excavations at Tell Brak, Vol. 4: Exploring an Upper Mesopotamian Regional Centre, 1994–1996*, 377–388. Cambridge, McDonald Institute Monographs, British School of Archaeology in Iraq.

Matthews, W., French, C. A. I., Lawrence, T. and Cutler, D. F. (1996) Multiple surfaces: the micromorphology. In I. Hodder (ed.) *On the Surface: Çatalhöyük 1993–95*, 301–342. Cambridge, British Institute of Archaeology at Ankara, McDonald Institute.

Matthews, W., French, C. A. I., Lawrence, T., Cutler, D. F. and Jones, M. K. (1997a) Microstratigraphic traces of site formation processes and human activities. *World Archaeology* 29(2), 281–308.

Matthews, W., French, C. A. I., Lawrence, T., Cutler, D. F. and Jones, M. K. (1997b) Activities inside the temple: the evidence of microstratigraphy. In H. Crawford, R. Killick and J. Moon (eds) *The Dilmun Teple at Saar, Bahrain and its Archaeological Inheritance*, 31–46. London and New York, Kegan Paul International.

Matthews, W., Postgate, J. N., Payne, S., Charles, M. P. and Dobney, K. (1994) The imprint of living in an early Mesopotamian city: questions and answers. In R. Luff and P. Rowley-Conwy (eds) *Whither Environmental Archaeology?* 171–212. Oxford, Oxbow Monograph 38.

Middleton, W. D. (2004) Identifying chemical activity residues on prehistoric house floors: a methodology and rationale for multi-elemental characterization of a mild acid extract of anthropogenic sediments. *Archaeometry* 46, 47–65.

Milek, K. (2006) *Houses and Households in Early Icelandic Society: Geoarchaeology and the Interpretation of Social Space.* Unpublished PhD thesis, University of Cambridge.

Milek, K. (1999) Soil micromorphology. In P. J. Davey (eds) *Rushen Abbey, Ballasalla, Isle of Man: First Archaeological Report*, 77–93. Liverpool, Centre Fox Manx Studies, University of Liverpool.

Murphy, C. P. (1986) *Thin Section Preparation of Soils and Sediments.* Berkhamsted, A. B. Academic.

O. D. (1999) *Oxford Dictionary of Synonims and Antonyms.* Oxford, Oxford University Press.

Parker Pearson, M. and Richards, C. (1994) *Architecture and Order. Approaches to Social Space.* London, Routledge.

Poroszlai, I. (1996) Aspects of Bronze Age tells in Hungary. In *Proceedings of the XIII Congress*, 183–193.

Rapp, G. and Hill, C. (1998) *Geoarchaeology: The Earths Science Approach to Archaeological Interpretation*, New Haven (CT), Yale University Press.

Schiegl, S., Goldberg, P., Pfretzschner, H. U. and Conard, N. J. (2003) Paleolithic burnt bone horizons from the Swabian Jura: distinguishing between in situ fireplaces and dumping areas. *Geoarchaeology* 18(5), 541–565.

Shackley, M. (1981) *Environmental Archaeology*, Sidney, Allen & Unwin.

Shahack-Gross, R., Albert, R. M., Gilboa, A., Nagar-Hilman, O., Sharon, I. and Weiner, S. (2005) Geoarchaeology in an urban context: the uses of space in a Phoenician monumental building at Tel Dor (Israel). *Journal of Archaeological Science* 32, 1417–1431.

Shahack-Gross, R., Marshall, F., Ryan, K. and Weiner, S. (2004) Reconstruction of spatial organization in abandoned Maasai settlements: implications for site structure in the Pastoral Neolithic of East Africa. *Journal of Archaeological Science* 31, 1395–1411.

Simpson, I. A. and Barrett, J. H. (1996) Interpretation of midden formation processes at Robert's Haven, Caithness, Scotland using thin section micromorphology. *Journal of Archaeological Science* 23, 543–556.

Simpson, I. A., Vésteinsson, O., Adderley W. P. and McGovern, T. H. (2003) Fuel resource utilisation in landscapes of settlement. *Journal of Archaeological Science* 30, 1401–1420.

Stoops, G. (2003) *Guidelines for Analysis and Description of Soil Regolith and Thin Section.* Madison (WI), Soil Science Society of America Inc.

Tsatskin, A. and Nadel, D. (2003) Formation processes at the Ohalo II submerged prehistoric campsite, Israel, inferred from soil micromorphology and magnetic susceptibility studies. *Geoarchaeology* 18(4), 409–432.

Varga, A. (2000) Coring results at Százhalombatta-Földvár. In I. Poroszlai and M. Vicze (eds) *Sax, Százhalombatta Archaeological Expedition, Annual Report 1-Field Season 1998*, 75–81. Százhalombatta, "Matrica" Museum.

Vicze, M. (2005) Excavation methods and some preliminary results of the Sax Project. In I. Poroszlai and M. Vicze (eds) *Sax, Százhalombatta Archaeological Expedition, Annual Report 2–Field Season 2000–2003*, 65–80 Százhalombatta, "Matrica" Museum.

Wallace, G. (2000) *A Microscopic View of Neolithic Lakeside Villages on the Northern Rim of the European Alps*. Unpublished PhD thesis, University of Cambridge.

Watkins, T. (1990) The origins of house and home? *World Archaeology* 21, 336–347.

Wilk, R. R. (1990) The built environment and consumer decisions. In S. Kent (ed.) *Domestic Architecture and the Use of Space: an Interdisciplinary Cross-Cultural Study*, 34–42. Cambridge, Cambridge University Press.

Wilk, R. R. and Rathje, W. L. (1982) Household aArchaeology. *American Behavioral Scientist* 25, 617–639.

Willey, G (1956) *Prehistoric Settlement Patterns in the New World*, Fund Publications in Anthropology 23. New York, Viking.

Yanigasako, S. (1979) Family and household: the analysis of domestic groups. *Annual Review of Anthropology* 8, 161–206.

House 1, Monte Polizzo, Sicily: from Excavation of a Ruin to Steps Towards an Interpretation of a Household

Christopher Prescott and Christian Mühlenbock

From 800 BC and on, the Mediterranean enters a process of accelerating social, political and cultural transformation and regional interaction. Though research has most strongly focused on groups familiar from historical records, such as the Greeks, Phoenicians and Etruscans, transformations were initiated in a much wider context. The situation is culturally complex and socially dynamic. Although this process has often been studied in terms of large scale political and economic terms (*e.g.* Kristiansen 1998; Morris 1989), the impact of this historical situation can also be profitably studied in archaeological terms through the concepts of "material culture" and "the household".

The present study starts with an analysis of the ruin of "House 1" within the Archaic Period settlement (*c.* 600–525 BC) of Monte Polizzo (MP) in Salemi, Western Sicily (Fig. 12.1). The settlement is associated with a people known from historical sources (Thucydides 6.2.1–5) as "Elymian", and is situated north of the westernmost Greek colony Selinus, east of the Phoenician city of Motya, south-east of Elyminan Eryx and south-south-west of the Doric-Elymian city of Segesta. The concepts of material culture in combination with the historical setting creates a valid platform for regarding the Monte Polizzo site, and especially the House 1 household(s), as an arena for the integration and negotiation of cultural streams (as the term is developed in Barth 1983) from the wider Mediterranean – especially from the east – and the impact of these streams on social practice.

The present article presents some background information, and outlines relevant features of the MP settlement. It then describes the House 1 site and proposes an internal chronology based on architectural and constructional evidence. More than a ton of ceramics were collected from House 1, *i.e.* vessels with various functions (storage, tableware and cooking) as well as of various origins (local, regional, Corinthian, Etruscan, and Punic) (cf. Mühlenbock and Prescott 2004). Other finds include bone and metal tools, jewellery and weapons.

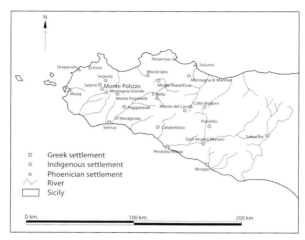

Figure 12.1 Map of Western Sicily at the time of the Monte Polizzo settlements. (fig. by Hege Vatnaland).

The distribution of artefacts in House 1 is plotted within the various rooms (Figs 12.4 and 12.6). On the basis of this data, interpretations are generated and explored concerning the function of various rooms, the social constitution of space (private *vs.* public, banqueting and rituality), and the make up of one or two households. These interpretations are briefly related to what is otherwise known concerning the MP-settlement. The particular nature of household practices in House 1 is discussed in light of this settlement's context, and the complex political and cultural historical situation.

Site background

The Monte Polizzo site is a large urban development in Salemi, Trapani Western Sicily. Located on a 700 masl hilltop, the settlement represents a built-up area approximately 30,000 sq metres large (Johansson and Prescott 2004; Mühlenbock and Prescott 2004). Although the mountain top of Monte Polizzo was utilised before the Archaic period, and was also used after this period, the primary urban phase seems to have been within a short period: the urban settlement seems to have been quickly established around 600 BC and was probably abandoned around 530–525 BC (perhaps relocated to present-day Salemi). The settlement is "indigenous", *i.e.* tied to local Iron Age groups in this region referred to with the elusive ethnic tag of "Elymians".

The localisation of an urban settlement on the Monte Polizzo hilltop must primarily be seen as a response to political, military and visual-symbolic factors. Monte Polizzo is visible from nearly anywhere in the region (and must have been even more prominent when a living city was found on top of it), the highest point – the "acropolis" – commands a view of most of the region, while the steep hillsides provide a degree of natural fortification. On the other hand, the agro-pastoral potential and other natural resources in the immediate vicinity are meagre, so the inhabitants must have cultivated the valley bottom to attain necessary commodities (Kolb 2004; Hjelle 2004).

The location of the Monte Polizzo urban settlement could be seen in relation to cultural influences, strands of cultural streams from the Greeks and Phoenicians (*c.f.* discussions in Leighton 1999,: 219ff; Tusa 1983, 662f; 2004), so clearly demonstrated in the archaeological finds. However, changing constellations of tension between "indigenous groups", Greek colonist and Phoenicians would have created a very real competitive and conflict situation that would have promoted a settlement pattern like that at Monte Polizzo. And indeed, Monte Polizzo was surrounded by powerful neighbours: Greek Selinus (*f.* 628 BC) to the south, Punic Motya to the west, Elymian-Doric Segesta to the north-east and Elymian Eryx to the north.

Although, indigenous developments are quite often attributed to Greek and to a lesser degree Phoenician/Punic influences, it is certainly reasonable to see the Western Sicilian urban developments not only as acculturation (*c.f.* Dietler 1999), but a semi-autonomous, if somewhat late, expression of the general Mediterranean trajectory at this time: towards urbanisation, hierarchy, states and military intensification (Kristiansen 1998, 124ff). As such, developments in Western Sicily are probably specific, localised responses to more general, regional socio-political forces (Tusa 1983, 663).

This short summary of the cultural-political context indicates that this was a tumultuous era of socio-political and cultural transformation. It also demonstrates that the cultural, political and social sources of "capital" provided by broad Mediterranean events could be utilised not only in relations between groups, but also internally in Elymian society. The sources of this cultural-political capital were variable and changing, but in general terms arguably – based on the material found at Monte Polizzo – referred back to tradition, to internal socio-political developments, to specific external networks, as well as the more eastern Mediterranean hero cult.

The present article is concerned with a single (set of) household(s), at the site of House 1 in the Monte Polizzo settlement. The study has as a fundamental premise that the internal (Elymian and Monte Polizzo) socio-political processes, the external networks and the ideals expressed through myths must certainly lead to new forms of social practice – of which the urban settlement itself is a telling expression. These practices would have impregnated the whole society – down to the single household, the domestic layout, the architecture, the activities and the social relations. We also lean heavily on the premise that there were competing modes of practice, differentially emphasising and capitalising on elements from the varied set of potential sources of socio-cultural capital. This article thus aims at not only outlining the internal makeup of House 1, but also exploring why this unit seems to be *different*; different both in reference to the ritual acropolis centre, but also different in relation to what we tentatively regard as the dominant mode of architectural style. The features of House 1 – position within the settlement, the architectural layout and the makeup of the finds material – and the elements of household practices that can be inferred from the archaeological record, suggest that there were competing practices and competing bids to interpret reality. These competing practices and interpretations – based on the Monte Polizzo data – conceivably drew on variable emphasis in the cultural-political capital, also in reference to spatial practices: example of the latter could be emplacement in relation to the highest point withn the settlement (the acropolis), the architectural layout or the spacing of practices within a household.

The Monte Polizzo settlement

The layout of the Archaic Monte Polizzo settlement can briefly described in reference to a handful features. It was a hilltop settlement (Fig. 12.2) that seems to "open" up along its less steep side towards the south-east, *i.e.* to the valley bottom (Kolb and Tusa 2001; Johansson and Prescott 2004); it is here the main access roads were probably located.

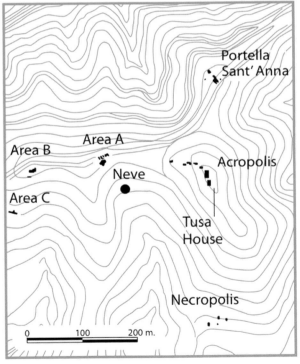

Figure 12.2 Map of the Archaic Monte Polizzo settlement. House 1 is located in "Area A". (fig. by Hege Vatnaland).

Towards the west and north, below the hill's steepest slopes and in the direction of the neighbouring Elymian settlements, there does not seem to have been as significant economic activities or infrastructural features.

Within the settlement, attention is immediately drawn to the highest point of the Polizzo hill, the "acropolis". We assume that this highest point was also important in the urban settlement and that it was ritually and symbolically referential. Excavations so far support this view, and ritual activity seems to have been an important feature on and around the acropolis (Morris et al. 2001; 2002; 2003; Vretemark 2003). Indeed, more than at any other place at Monte Polizzo, the acropolis has attracted activity, construction and visits throughout a very long stretch of history. We have therefore assumed that this highest point within the settlement is the conceptual place of reference, and have as a thereto-linked premise that the settlement's construction and layout is in deference to this acropolis. We furthermore have assumed that the most prestigious parts of the city were located closest to the acropolis and that the traditional elite lived here or at least dominated the place.

Around the acropolis, evidence so far (Johannson and Prescott 2004; Mühlenbock and Prescott 2004) suggested a built up area that spilled out towards the west and north. An excavation implemented by Vincenzo Tusa (1973) unearthed what we believe is probably the most commonly recurring type of domestic architecture: Non-composite structures dug into the slopes (Fig. 12.3). Along the sides of these houses there was probably drainage, while on the terrace in front there were streets.

Figure 12.3 The house structure excavated in early 1970's by Vincenzo Tusa, re-excavated 2000. The structure is characteristically constructed into the hill slope.

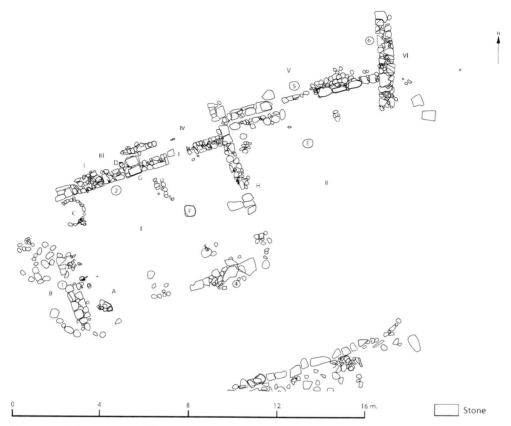

Figure 12.4 Constructional features house 1. Roman numerals I through VI refer to rooms. Numerals in rings refer to wall sections. Letters refer to other constructional features. Note feature "C", interpreted as a platform for a loom. In addition to the features marked here, a pit with animals bones was later uncovered east of wall section 6 in room VI. (fig. by Hege Vatnaland).

House 1 in the settlement

House 1 is located on the northern outskirt of the Monte Polizzo settlement, on a relatively level strip of shoulder that runs east–west along the northern slope. It is c. 600 m from the acropolis (Fig. 12.2, area A).

House 1 itself is a single-level, multi-room structure, built on one of the few level patches within the settlement, and indeed excavations have demonstrated that this level surface is artificial. The plot was created by filling in along the northern slope of a rock outcrop. This suggests that the construction of House 1 was not solely adapted to landscape features, but had a high degree of intentionality. Recent excavations (Mühlenbock 2004) have uncovered structures in the slope immediately below and to the south of House 1.

These are built in the same manner as the "Tusa house" mentioned above, but seem to be built in relation to, and have a final phase of usage contemporaneous with, House 1.

In summary we may conclude that House 1 is not located in the most prestigious part of the settlement, that the House 1 layout is not typical for the Polizzo settlement, and that the layout is the result of an intentional architectural plan on an artificial plot.

House 1: the structure

The Monte Polizzo land is owned by the Italian Forest Service, and includes a reforestation project. House 1 is located in one of the Forest Service's fire breaks that criss-cross the region. These breaks are annually maintained by light bulldozers that scrape away surface vegetation and, in the process, part of the surface soil. This entails that, during the initial mapping of the site, constructional features here were readily accessible and cleared down to just above the floor level. Unfortunately, fire break maintenance also entails that the site is damaged. The House 1 ruin also sustained some damage in connection with boundary fences built before the property was acquired by the government.

Due to this damage we do not have a complete layout and must reconstruct the ground plan at the time House 1 was abandoned (Fig. 12.4). Based on architectural features, the landscape and the distribution of artefacts we believe that there were two smaller rooms (room nos III and IV) in the north-east corner. Doorways lead from each of these rooms to a larger room (no. I). This room might have been partially open towards the south, and it might have had a light wall-division running north–south down the middle of (part of) the room. East of rooms I and IV were two more rooms (nos II and V). These were delimited to the east by a wall, and on the other side of this wall there is an important collection of material that indicates that there was a room or activity area here (VI). All in all there are at least six rooms. Within these rooms there are several lines of evidence that say something about the constructional features:

- Foundations were built out of limestone (transported to the site) and rounded boulders (probably attained from the conglomerate that geologically creates the Monte Polizzo hilltop).
- The northern part of the house plot was artificially created by fill-in along an east–west rock ridge, the southern half is simply levelled with soil to even out the rock and create a floor. Most of the infill has been removed by bulldozers, so we primarily find remnants along the ridge.
- Room nos I, III and IV exhibit a red burnt clay material, running through the doorways from one room to another, indicating that these rooms were destroyed by fire. The red clay lies immediately over the in situ find-bearing floor level, indicating that clay was used in part of the superstructure. Some clay with vegetation imprints and a few "bricks" indicate that the structure (roof and walls) above the limestone foundation was of wattle-and-daub and mud brick. Burnt

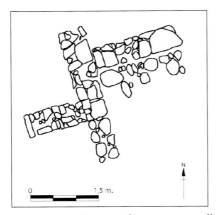

Figure 12.5 Integrated interstice, wall between rooms I and IV (wall sections 1 and 3). (fig. by Hege Vatnaland).

branches and poles indicate that some construction (internal divisions, beams and roofing?) used wooden materials.

- There was some sort of oven or hearth, probably the source of the fire that burned or smouldered under debris in rooms I, II and IV. It was located in the south-west corner of room I. This would support the conclusion that this room was not necessarily fully enclosed or even completely covered by a roof.

- In rooms II, V and VI, there is no such red burnt clay. We have thus little evidence of a superstructure, but assume that clay was

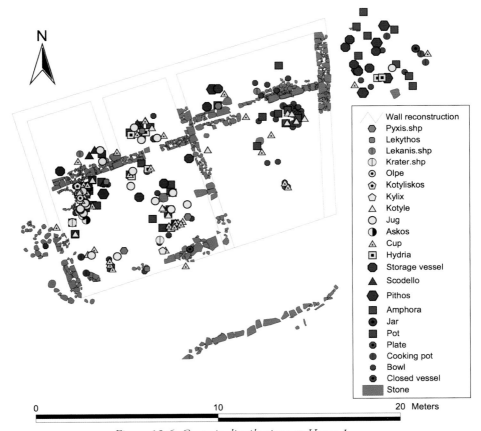

Figure 12.6. Ceramic distributions at House 1.

also used in the walls and roof her, but as it was not fired it is not preserved or
readily identifiable. This might indicate that there was a slightly different history
of use and destruction for these rooms, and that there was no opening through the
wall dividing rooms I and II. This also suggests that the fire was not particularly
intense, perhaps is best described as smouldering in the ruins of rooms I, II and
IV.

- In the same room I, but against the northern wall, there was a small (*c.* 1 m
  diameter) raised (15–20 cm) platform. The platform was lined with rounded
  cobbles, covered with pebbles. On top of the platform more than 20 terracotta
  weights were found.

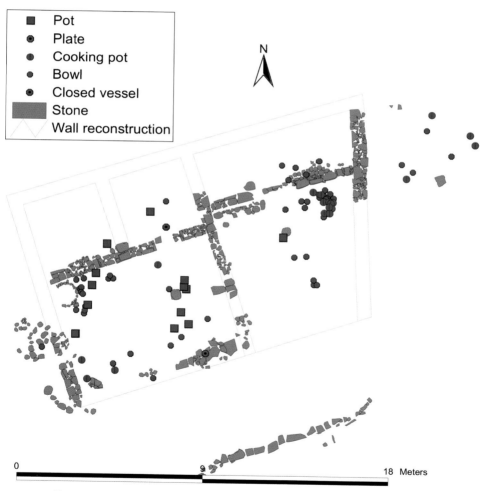

Figure 12.7. Distribution of cooking vessels and eating wares at House 1.

- The situation indicates that this was an area or facility designated for weaving.
- Along the wall that divides rooms II and V, there is cobblestone foundation, along the eastern section in V, and the western in II.
- In room VI there was pit dug close to the wall.

Internal chronology

The layout of House 1, as described above, is an expression of the final stage of the house's use – the layout on the day it was destroyed. However, there are some elements that illuminate the internal relative chronology, and thus the "developmental" history.

In the infill used to level out the northern half of the plot on which House 1 is built, there were rounded ceramic sherds that are probably from the Bronze Age. Thus, before the Elymian/Archaic settlement there was some kind of Bronze Age settlement located in the vicinity.

Turning to the House 1 structure itself, the artefact material is not suited for a concusive and detailed resolution of the chronological development. There are, however, some structural features that indicate a rather complex relative chronology. Various interstices between wall sections, as well as construction materials, base levels and angles indicate that the House 1 structure developed over time. The south-east corner of room IV contains an integrated corner interstice (Fig. 12.5) that was constructed as a unit. The thereto connected walls between rooms I and II, as well as between II and V, were clearly added later; they are not constructionally integrated, and they are constructed in a different fashion. This would indicate that rooms III and IV are the rooms first constructed, with room 1 taken in use concurrently, conceivably as a more open activity area. The wall foundations between rooms I and II were probably built later.

The wall between rooms V and VI lies at an angle at odds with the rest of House 1's foundations, is broader than most walls and has a deeper base. We originally interpreted this wall as older – part of a solid structure that was reused. However, the southern part of the wall, between rooms II and VI has a shallower base and the nature of the northern part of the construction may therefore be a function of the topography of the underlying ground, the levelling of the floor in room V and a lower floor level in room VI, and perhaps also the burdens the foundation carried (a roof bearing wall). Though we have previously entertained the idea that a *capeduncola* (ritual drinking bowl, Fig. 12.11) found in room might be substantially older (see previous discussion of such bowls in Tusa 1983), there is no firm evidence to sustain this suggestion. We therefore conclude that no significantly older elements have been recorded in room VI.

In summary, this review of construction features would indicate a growth of the complex towards the east within an archaeologically short time span. The questions then arise: are we dealing with a single household in an expanding composite structure? Or are we dealing with a composite structure with two households, one slightly older than the other?

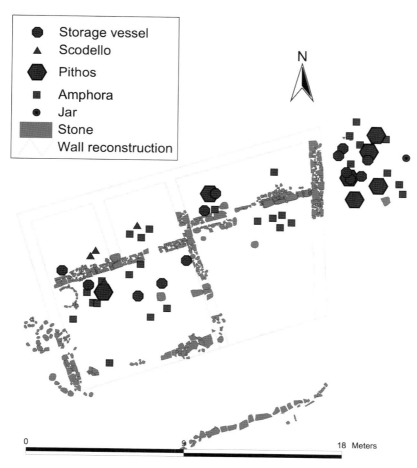

Legend:
- ⬟ Storage vessel
- ▲ Scodello
- ⬡ Pithos
- ◼ Amphora
- ● Jar
- ▨ Stone
- ⌃ Wall reconstruction

N

0   9   18 Meters

Figure 12.8. Distribution of storage vessels at House 1.

The rooms and finds

House 1 clearly has a history, even though this history spanned a short period in archaeological terms, probably a generation or two. This history was brought to an abrupt end when the house was destroyed and abandoned – probably more or less at the same time as the rest of the city. In general it would seem that the house was kept clean, and there was little deposition over time in or immediately around the house (perhaps with the exception of the pit in room VI). This means the study below represents an arbitrary point in the use of the settlement, a day among others, preserved due to sudden destruction/abandonment.

In general, the ceramics demonstrate storage, cooking and consume, and thus a superficial glance (Fig. 12.6) indicates that all the rooms – or sets of rooms – project a

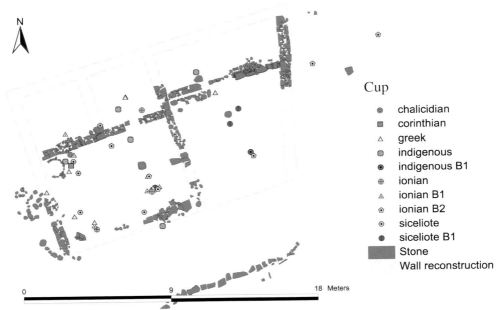

Figure 12.9. Distribution of drinking vessels at House 1.

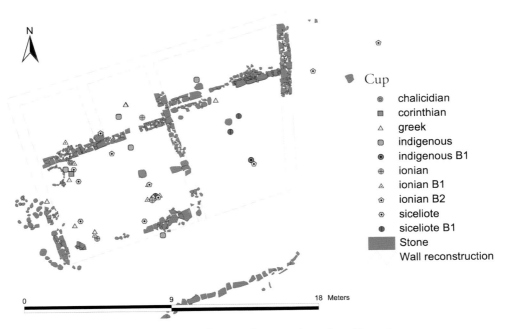

Figure 12.10. Distribution of imported vessels at House 1.

comparable impression, based on the finds. However, within the general finds categories there are interesting variations (compare Figs 11.6–11.10):

1)   Room VI contains a large amount of storage vessels (*amphora, pithoi*), but also elements perhaps of a more ritual character: a pit with bones (Vretemark 2003; Mühlenbock and Prescott 2004, 181), an Attic cup, possibly a bronze cauldron, and an anthromorphic capeduncola. Such vessels are arguably related to a Mother Goddess cult that spread from Mesopotamia via the eastern Mediterranean (Panglese 1994).

2)   Room V also contains some storage vessels and also elements tied to consume. This room may be seen in connection with room II. These rooms contain a significant amount of cooking vessels, plates and some drinking cups. It would therefore seem that room II was tied to the preparation and consume of food. An important aspect of the ceramics here is that it is mostly local grey wares. Despite the cooking ware, it is interesting to note that no ovens or hearths were found in these rooms, and indeed, there are no significant traces of fire here. Based on the ceramics, the room was related to consume, but not on imported status wares.

3) Room I is previously tied to weaving and to a hearth/oven. The assumed location of the hearth/oven was in the south-west corner, and it is here the cooking wares were found. Towards the north and east there are also some plates and bowls. Most interesting are the many elements tied to drinking: amphoras, kraters and cups. Importantly, this room exhibits the largest and most comprehensive collection of drinking wares. Significantly, the majority of imported wares come from this context. The indications of preparation of food and consume are prominent (partly with imported wares), there are indications of weaving (terracotta loom weights and the associated round platform) – an activity of major symbolic importance, also in the highest social echelons in the Greek world, virtually the symbolic opposite to warriors (Brandt 2003).

Interpretations of households

The above observations concerning relative chronology, architectural features and distribution of finds allows for interesting comparisons between rooms. The crux of an argument rotates around rooms I, II and IV vs. II and V vs. VI, and concerns the number and nature of households in House 1 – an indeed even if House 1 represents household units?

We have considered the option that House 1 does not represent a household at all, that the structure was a ritual or political compound. Supporting this idea would be the large amounts of pots, the emphasis on drinking and what at the moment seems like an unusual type of architecture. To this might be added potential ritual features like weaving, sacrifice (faunal material in pits), and cult (the capeduncola; Fig. 12.11)

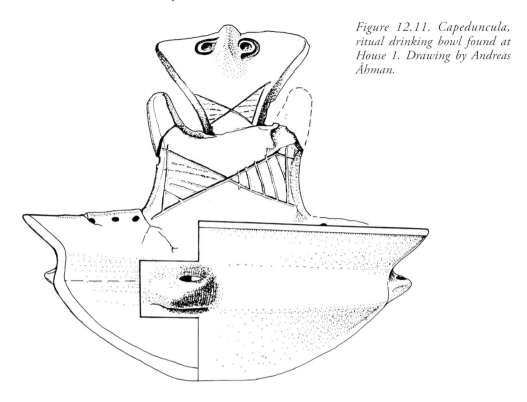

Figure 12.11. Capeduncula, ritual drinking bowl found at House 1. Drawing by Andreas Åhman.

and feasting (banquet equipment, an indigenous parallel to the Greek *symposium*?). However, all these elements may be explained in terms of household rituality and functionality. For example, according to Vretmark (2003) compared faunal remains from the ritual acropolis contexts with those of House 1, and found the latter to be more in accordance with what one would expect in a household context. We therefore interpret House 1 as a household locality/ set of localities.

If this premise of (a) household(s) is accepted, we can envision two interpretative avenues. Both interpretations accentuate that this is a house, a dwelling place for households. Both assume that the household space contains variable spaces, a semi-public stage, but also spaces designed to provide privacy (Allison 1999 in reference to Carsten and Hugh-Jones 1985) – but the relative emphasis on private-public space, and the social implications, are radically different in the two interpretations; one developing a high degree of social complexity, the other moderately non-complex. The implications for gender ideologies and gender relations – not developed in this paper – are also dramatically different.

In the first interpretation, the House 1 situation represents the development of two households, one being older and more affluent (rooms I, III and IV), the other later and less socially prominent (V and II). This could indicate social difference between to independent households, or it could represent a hierarchical relationship of dependence. The extreme version would be one part representing a dominant family, the other a subservient family. The building chronology and social ordering could conceivably reflect a genealogical chronology.

In the second interpretation, the situation represents a single unified household, where the variations in space represent variable use of different rooms. These variations reflect and spatially order some age, gender and activity differentiation, but a prominent feature would seem to be public areas of social display versus secluded private space. The public social rooms would reflect a high, virtually ritual status (or aspirations to attain such status), with public weaving, drinking and feasting. Here, consume of wine, the ritualistic enactments of such consume (from amphora via mixing to cups) and the use of referential Greek wares, are essential to the public display. We thus see an indigenous banquet institution, perhaps with a function and form analogous to the Greek symposium. Other parts of the building – not immediately accessible from the "symposium arena" were perhaps more private. This would suggest a degree of segregation of men and women, or perhaps a degree of seclusion of many women from the outside world. This interpretation is not without problems, as it is partly based on direct interpretations of archaeological material in combination with an analogy to Nevett's study of later Greek material, which again rests on analogy to modern ethnography (Nevett 1999, 30f)

If weaving and the banqueting activities may be termed as social rituals, further features are the indications of household cult suggested by the anthromorphic drinking vessel, the capeduncula, and the pit with bones.

The household and the world

"The dwellings and dwelling spaces we inhabit house the attitude and traditions through which we both conform to and confront the world beyond … That world has the potential to bring innovation into dwelling spaces but the dwelling spaces also provide the security through which we learn to negotiate acceptable relationships with these ideas, and to act as a medium through which the outside world (…) can exercise control over the activities within. At the same time the physical structures provide the means to separate these activities from the direct influence of that wider world." (Allison 1999, 1)

The above quote serves to refresh a central premise for this article: the archaeological ruin of a dwelling place is a source of insights into the anthropological phenomena of the household. Insight into the household is a potentially fine-tuned source for understanding the development and impact of the larger scale historical process. It is an arena for the reproduction of institutions, practices, but also an arena for rejection and mediation of larger scale influences. It is an arena where to a varying degree the dialectics between practice and ideology, private and public are played out. Influenced by the changeable and multi-stream epoch we have studied, we would emphasise the potential political nature of the arena of the households location and expression as a symbol directed out to the urban community it is located in.

In this respect, the House 1 household utilised and displayed variable cultural capitals, and mediated various cultural streams. The capital was involvement in a network with expansive external groups (as historically attested by sources like Thucydides and archaeologically indicated by a map of settlements of the Archaic period) – Greeks and Punic – as well as the local Elymian institutions. In Anthony Giddens' sense of the word:

> "Structural properties exist in time-space only as moments of the constitution of social systems. None the less, we can analyse how "deeply layered" structures are in terms of the historical duration of then practices they recursively organise and the spatial "breadth" of those practices: the most deeply layered practices in this sense are *institutions.*" (Giddens 1982, 36).

In the different public and more private spheres of the household the material culture displays, and is used in the mediation of, various cultural streams – external and Elymian – in this very unsettled era. The historical trajectories towards a pronounced elite, whether in reference to adopted Greek ideals or in reference to broader Mediterranean socio-ideological development, and the ideals for elite behaviour are displayed through the domestic loom and the banquet-*symposium* consume.

As the material from Monte Polizzo stands today, the patterns generated from the House 1 data may seem to express paradoxes. Our proposed patterns and interpretations are based on premises, for example about social standing and urban geography, and these of course may be erroneous. Another approach regarding the contradictions that seem to arise from practices at House 1 is to see them as inherent to an ongoing socio-political process in a turbulent era. If House 1 was the site of an elite's household, it was peripheral to the ritual acropolis centre. And if so, at this periphery we have interpreted an Elymian elite's prestige goods (imported table and drinking wares) and practice (banqueting, weaving, cult and architecture) in an urban zone that otherwise seems to be characterised by traditional practices (based on interpretations of data in Mühlenbock 2004). Can household practices at House 1 be interpreted as political bids to redefine power schemes in a traditional society, bids that rely on a household using its network, material goods and its elite practices to negotiate an elite social position within the community?

Given the premises that material culture and household practices both reproduce institutions, express ideals, but also can be used to renegotiate social reality, it is not an unreasonable premise that variations in the archaeological remains we interpret as the result of variable household practices, represent part of the socio-political tug of war in a unsettled and dynamic historical epoch. Further investigations will uncover a greater material to allow more representative comparative studies. Hopefully, this will provide a context in which better to understand House 1. The starting point for the *Scandinavian-Sicilian Archaeological Project* was, and should continue to be, that cultural streams, political turbulence and historical events were expressed on different spatial scales, and that analyses of the household level in combination with material culture and landscape is a profitable strategy for illuminating the historical, anthropological and political developments.

References

Allison, P. M. (1999) *The Archaeology of Household Activities*. London, Routledge.

Barth, F. (1983) *Sohar: Culture and Society in an Omani Town*. Baltimore, John Hopkins University Press.

Brandt, J. R. (2003) Krigere og veversker. Om Parthenonfrisen, Panatheneerfesten og initiasjon. In J. W. Iddeng (ed.) *Antikke samfunn i krig og fred. Festskrift til Johan Henrik Schreiner*. Oslo, Novus Forlag.

Carsten, J. and Hugh-Jones, H. (1995) *About the House: Lévi-Strauss and Beyond*. Cambridge, Cambridge University Press.

Dietler, M. (1997) Consumption, cultural frontiers, and identity: anthropological approaches to Greek colonial encounters. In *Confini e Frontiera nella Grecità d'Occidente. Atti del XXXVII Convegno di Studi sulla Magna Grecia, Taranto, 3–6 ottobre 1997*, 475–501. Napoli, Arte tipographica.

Giddens, A. (1982) *Profiles and Critiques in Social Theory*. Berkeley, University of California Press.

Hjelle, K. L. (2004) Pollen analytical investigations in the Scandinavian-Sicilian Archaeological Project (SSAP) 1999–2000. In Mühlenbock and Prescott (eds) (2004), 123–138.

Johansson, L. G. and Prescott, C. (2004) Surveying and mapping the Monte Polizzo site 1998. In Mühlenbock and Prescott (eds) (2004), 27–32.

Kolb. M. J. (2004) Regional survey report Monte Polizzo region. In Mühlenbock and C. Prescott (eds) (2004), 34–38.

Kolb, M. J. and Tusa, S. (2001) The Late Bronze Age and Early Iron Age landscape of interior western Sicily. *Antiquity* 75(289), 503–504.

Kristiansen, K. (1998) *Europe Before History. New Studies in Archaeology*. Cambridge, Cambridge University Press.

Leighton, R. (1999) *Sicily before History. An Archaeological Survey from the Palaeolithic to the Iron Age*. London, Duckworth.

Morris, I. (1989) Tomb, cult and the "Greek renaissance": the past in the present in 8th century BC. *Antiquity* 62(237), 750–761.

Morris, I. (2002) Mediterraneanization. *Mediterranean Historical Review* 18(2), 30–55.

Morris, I., Jackman, T., Blake, E. and Tusa, S. (2001) Stanford University excavations on the Acropolis of Monte Polizzo, Sicily I: Preliminary report fn the 2000 season. *Memoirs of the American Academy in Rome* 46, 197–279.

Morris, I., Jackman, T., Blake, E. and Tusa, S. (2002) Stanford University excavations on the Acropolis of Monte Polizzo II: preliminary report on the 2001 season. *Memoirs of the American Academy in Rome* 47, 153–198.

Morris, I., Jackman, T., Blake, E., Garnand, B. and Tusa, S. (2003) Stanford University excavations on the Acropolis of Monte Polizzo III: preliminary report on the 2002 season. *Memoirs of the American Academy in Rome* 48, 243–315.

Mühlenbock, C. (ed.) (2004) *The Scandinavian Sicilian Archaeological Project. Excavations at Monte Polizzo Sicily. Reports 2002–2003*. Göteborg, Göteborg Universitet, Inst för Historiska Studier, Gotarc serie C 57.

Mühlenbock, C. and Prescott C. (eds) (2004) *The Scandinavian Sicilian Archaeological Project.*

Archaeological Excavations at Monte Polizzo Sicily. Reports 1998–2001. Göteborg, Göteborg Universitet, Inst för Historiska Studier, Gotarc serie C 56.

Mühlenbock, C. and Prescott, C. (2004) Survey report 2000. In Mühlenbock and Prescott (eds) (2004), 139–170.

Nevett, L. (1999) *House and Society in the Ancient Greek World. New Studies in Archaeology*. Cambridge, Cambridge University Press.

Panglese, C. (1994) *Greek Myths and Mesopotamia*. London, Routledge.

Thucydides (1972) *History of the Peloponnesian War*. Translated by Rex Warner. London, Penguin Books.

Tusa, S. (1983) *La Sicilia nella preistoria*. Palermo, Sellerio editore.

Tusa, S. (2004) Historical reference frame in western Sicily since the end of II to the beginning of I millenium b.c. In Mühlenbock and Prescott (eds) (2004), 17–26.

Tusa, V. (1973) L'attività archeologica della soprintendenza alle antichità della Sicila occidentale nel quadrienno 1968–1971. *Kokalos* 1972–73, 392–410.

Vretemark, M. (2003) Djurbenen från Hus 1, Monte Polizzo Sicilien. Report available at: www.hf.uio.no/iakk/sicilia/ostrapport2003.htm

13

Households in Context. Cosmology, Economy and Long-Term Change in the Bronze Age of Northern Europe

Kristian Kristiansen

Cosmology and economy – A theoretical outline

In this paper I propose that economy and cosmology represent dominant domains of action in Neolithic and Bronze Age society, in so far as they shaped and constrained what at any time was considered possible. It raises a series of new questions as to their relationship, such as that between the rationality of economic practice and the rationality of cosmological practice. Linking cosmology to economy enables us to analyse their relationship through time, which promises to open up a deeper and more dynamic understanding of how the rules of the gods (cosmology) shaped and at times constrained the rules of nature and people (economy) and *vice versa*.

The main idea behind this proposition is the role cosmologies play in organising the physical landscape and the way it is inhabited and used (Bradley 2000). In traditional religious and cosmological thinking this is done according to the rules of the gods "to organize space is to repeat the paradigmatic work of the gods" (Eliade 1987, 32). Consequently the placing of settlements, barrows, cemeteries, sanctuaries or rock art can be understood as meaningful in relation to the cosmological and religious order of society. In this way we may be able to detect important aspect of cosmology and religion by studying the repetitive or paradigmatic structure of the organisation and use of landscape, especially those activities linked to ritual production and consumption. And, *vice versa*, we may employ cosmological principles from Bronze Age and Indo-European texts on religion as a way of understanding the meaning of such paradigmatic structures. Once we are able to establish the cosmological principles governing the organisation of landscape we can more profitably begin to understand and interpret the role of settlements, barrows, cemeteries, ritual bogs, sanctuaries etc within this larger framework. And we have a platform for evaluating local variations and their meaning.

However, the reproduction of the physical landscape, its settlements, burials and households also depends on the political organisation of the economy (Earle 2002a). "The political economy is the material flows of goods and labour through a society, channelled to create wealth and to finance institutions of rule" (Earle 2002b, 1). This is an arena for social and political competition, which may lead to the formation of unequal access to productive resources, their distribution and consumption. At the local level this may be reflected in different sizes of farms, specialisation of production between settlements and communities at large, elements that can be analysed and studied in the archaeological and environmental record. Finally the deposition of prestige objects in burials and hoards represent a ritualised aspect of how to study unequal access to wealth and its disposition/consumption. In the political economy political and religious institutions with a set of rules that governed the production and distribution of resources and wealth would integrate these domains. Institutionalisation is thus a prerequisite for obtaining and maintaining power (Kristiansen 2004); while it at the same time serves to regulate and constrain individual's attempt to increase their power. Institutions are thus the building blocks of society. Their rituals legitimised the power of office holders, whether ritual chiefs or war chiefs, through visible performance and participation that engaged and integrated all members in society in its reproduction (Fig. 13.1).

Many of the actions and transactions that define the political economy had to pass through the household. Therefore the household economy, as it can be reconstructed through archaeological excavations of farmsteads, fences, fields, *etc,* and its impact upon the environment, constitute an important point of departure for our study. It is from the production of individual households and their participation in, and subordination to, the political economy and its institutions that wealth and surplus were created, that allowed the maintenance of a chiefly elite with attached specialists, warriors, chariots, and boats for long-distance trade. However, both wealth (mainly bronze objects) and monuments (houses, barrows) would be produced and used according to the cosmological traditions that governed religious and ritual practice. Thus investments were made not only in fields and farming, cattle and sheep (economy), but to similar degree in non-utilitarian ritual objects, such as lurs (blowing horns), helmets, ritual axes, golden rings, *etc* and in the construction of a monumental barrow landscape of chiefly ancestors and their genealogies (religion/cosmology), that materialised and memorised the institutions of chiefly power in the landscape (DeMarrais *et al.* 1996).

Thus the reproduction of the political economy and its religious institutions were increasingly linked to a landscape of memory, cosmological and genealogical power (Gröhn 2004, ch. 4.2). As power resided in the history of the landscape, colonising groups would occupy an inferior position and, over time, centres of cosmological and economic power would preside over peripheries of attached communities. It corresponds to Thomas Larsson's demonstration in Scania of the difference between local centres of accumulation, characterised by barrow concentrations, surrounded by larger areas of production with few barrows. In his model their relationship is regulated through forms of tribute (Larsson 1986, fig. 7). These structures were institutionalised, as they

Figure 13.1. Conceptual relationship between practice and social institutions, tradition and material worlds.

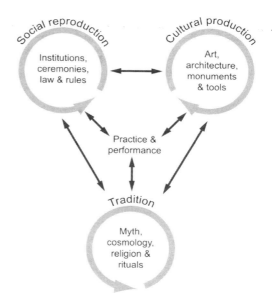

persisted for several hundred years (Strömberg 1982; Olausson 1993; Gröhn 2004, ch. 4.1). The long term economic and cosmological investments in the landscape also meant that contradictions would develop between cosmological and economic power, if the economy could not continue to sustain the chiefly elites and their population, as has been demonstrated for the Thy region (Kristiansen 1998b). I will now proceed to analyse these relationships for the Bronze Age of Scania and south Scandinavia. Before doing that it is necessary to briefly describe the institutions of chiefly government in the Bronze Age.

Institutions and rulership in the Bronze Age

During the 1990s and early 2000s interest has increasingly focused on defining social identities and institutions in the Bronze Age (Sørensen 1997; 2004; Kristiansen 1996; 2004; Earle 2001) and their role in social organisation.

Institutions are the building blocks of society, and have been ever since the rise of more complex societies during the Neolithic. To trace them is, therefore, a central interpretative task. Although institutions are invisible, they often materialise in specific and recurring ways that allow us to infer the cultural and institutional significance of the evidence (Earle 2001; Kristiansen 2001; 2004). The interpretative task is to single out, from among the different objects and contexts available to us, those which formed a specific relationship defined by a set of symbolic meanings, actions and transactions that once linked them together in an institution.

In several studies I have been able to demonstrate on empirical grounds that different sword types are meaningfully linked to different forms of social roles and, ultimately, institutions. It has thus been possible to demonstrate that leadership was divided between a ritual leader with highly decorated full-hilted swords unsuited for practical use, and a war leader with functional swords for practical use, where the ritual leader represented the highest authority (Kristiansen 1984; 2001). War leaders could have been linked to ritual leaders in a form of a decentralised retinue that he would mobilise in times of need. This institutional structure is most clearly materialised in Montelius Period 2 in hundreds of male burials (1500–1300 BC), after that time the rules of its material representation become less strict, as burial rituals change.

It can further be demonstrated that twin chiefly leaders corresponds to the major gods of the Bronze Age: the Divine Twins. Chieftainship in the Bronze Age was theocratic, and ritual chiefs would therefore perform in the role of the Divine Twins in the re-enacting of central myths, as testified in rock art, ritual hoards and bronze figurines. In doing so they employed the material attributes of the Divine Twins: elaborately decorated ritual axes, lurs, helmets and shields, all of bronze and all displaying the most sophisticated technical skills. These were divine objects never associated with burials, but occasionally deposited in sacred bogs, illuminated in rock art and occasionally on decorated bronzes (Kaul 1998; 2005; Kristiansen 2004). Figurines and models were employed as ritual sets, perhaps in the context of learning and in other now lost ritual acts. Ritual chiefs were thus semi-divine and their authority must have been immense.

These institutions exhibit a *longe-durée* throughout the whole Bronze Age. Beginning in Period 1, they are formalised from Period 2 onwards with a standardised set of social and ritual paraphernalia, consisting of elaborate full-hilted swords, razor and tweezers, while the ritual gear consists of ritual axes, lurs and figurines. This recurring set of objects, defining the institution of ritual (twin) leaders, shows unbroken continuity until the end of Period 5, possibly persisting even into Period 6, during a period of almost 1000 years, or 33 generations. This latter perspective makes it easier to comprehend how tradition could be handed down through the generations, which makes a much shorter genealogical period. It speaks of a highly persistent social and cosmological tradition, whose institutions were inherited as a rule from within the highest-ranking families, as they demanded the most exclusive social and religious qualifications (Kristiansen and Larsson 2005, ch. 6).

Timothy Earle has further linked social and economic institutions to the institutionalised organisation and use of the landscape (Earle 2001), which corresponded to a paradigmatic model of Bronze Age cosmology (Kristiansen 1998b; 2004). Thus social life in the Bronze Age was ritualised, and it took place in an equally ritualised landscape. In this way economy and ideology were unified in the reproduction of society.

Households, settlement and economy

Each historical problematic and interpretative strategy demands corresponding theoretical reflections. How do we balance knowledge at a general regional level – *e.g.*

about landscape history and cultural traditions – with the detailed knowledge at the micro-level of individual households and their local articulation with landscape and with other households (Cornell and Fahlander 2002)?

In this article I employ a long-term perspective of the household in the Bronze Age, to see how changes at the micro- level of life articulate with ecological and economic changes at a wider regional and interregional level. How do local changes articulate with regional changes? How do actions and decisions taken in the household at any given time articulate with actions and decisions taken by past households? I shall thus employ the notion of genealogies from Julian Thomas (1999). In doing so I wish to confront it with unintended changes imposed from social and economic actions of the past, to see how households cope with their obligations towards tradition, as this tradition forces changes and new decisions upon them. And how do individual households articulate with other households during this long-term process of small scale changes from generation to generation. Finally: when does the accumulation of changes reach a critical point that forces or motivates a break with past traditions and genealogies? Can we describe the various factors at work confronting families and communities in the Bronze Age, before they decided to break with tradition, leave their farmsteads and move together in a village community?

The interpretative concepts at play are summarised in Figures 13.2 and 13.3. They demonstrate the heuristic value of organising theoretical concepts according to a set of fundamental variables. In Figure 13.2, I have chosen scale as a defining parameter. How do the temporal and spatial dynamics between long term/short term and macro-/micro- affect decisions in the Bronze Age present based on tradition, ecology, economy *etc?* In Figure 13.3 I have chosen functional relationships as the defining parameter. The two figures demonstrate the number of factors at work when explaining changes of the organisation of the household. In the following text I shall apply these two interpretative strategies in a series of case studies. I shall analyse long-term changes in ecology and economy against household size and organisation. My hypothesis is that they are closely inter-linked, and secondly that the productive potential of the economy and ecology defines barriers to the size and complexity of households. According to this hypothesis I expect that it is possible to define thresholds for maintaining household structures and traditions. I shall finally discuss what happens when thresholds are passed forcing communities to take fundamental decisions about their future. This is about the nature and conditions of social transformation.

Households, burials and cosmology

Most religions share basic ideas about the otherworld and the creation of the universe. The forms its takes, and not least the way these other worlds are inhabited and related to each other may vary. In IE religion the three realms of the otherworld are the upper, middle and lower realm. They were inhabited by gods with different functions

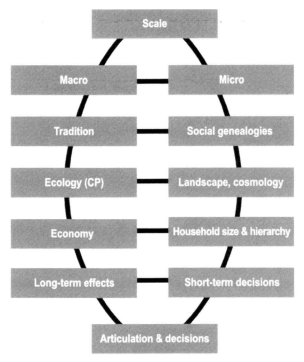

Figure 13.2. Theoretical model of the dynamics between macro/micro and short term and long term change in households.

who, over time, competed with each other over power, and thereby added change and dynamic to the pantheon. Many myths are about these power struggles between the gods (Olmstead 1994). According to our model we would expect the different realms to be situated in the real world as well, represented by ritual places and monuments where the gods could be approached through rituals and sacrifice, or through other means of communication. Let us first consider a typical decentred Bronze Age landscape from such a perspective (Fig. 13.4).

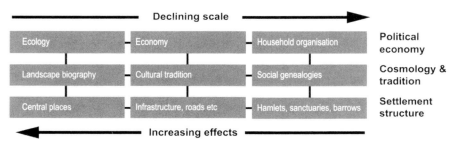

Figure 13.3. Theoretical model of the relationships between political economy, cosmology and settlement structure.

Upper realm

Middle realm

Lower realm

Figure 13.4. The cosmological cycle of the three realms: A model.

On hilltops, or grouped in lines in flat landscapes, we find the round barrow. Its construction is a paradigmatic model of the major symbols of the upper realm – the sun wheel and the rising sun, in combination with the world tree (the oak coffin). Ox sacrifice and libation to the sky god accompanied the rituals. Let us, however, decompose the rituals of the barrow into its religious and cosmological components.

First a ritual ploughing encircled the place of the barrow, where a stone ring was constructed to represent the sun wheel. In some barrows the spokes of the wheel are constructed too, in others several circles of concentric stone rings are employed. The symbolic meaning, however, remains the same, the sun wheel, with the barrow itself rising from the ground as the rising sun. During the rituals the stone circle was open, serving as a ritual entrance (Goldhahn 1999, ch. 10.1). Based on the uniquely preserved oak coffin burials from Denmark we can further detail the ritual process. A huge tree was now felled and used as coffin (the world tree unifying upper and lower realms), an ox sacrifice took place, and the freshly skinned hide was employed as a shroud to cover the inside of the coffin, where the deceased was placed in his or her clothes. Finally it was wrapped around the dead body and all the accompanying grave goods. The body was now inside the ox (the sky god) and the world tree (life/afterlife), carried away in the sun wheel and covered by grass turfs from neighbouring fields to lay out in the otherworld as eternal meadows for the herds, as known from Hittite burial ritual (Hass 1994, 224). Often a libation stone covered with cup marks was placed near the coffin to finalise the sacrifices. After passing these liminal phases towards the otherworld the barrow would be covered with a final layer of earth (Goldhahn 1999, ch. ix). Soon the deceased would take his or her place among the ancestors that communicated directly with the gods.

Communications with the gods and the playing out of central myths mostly took place at the middle realm, linked to chiefly halls and to places where central symbols and scenes were carved on rocks that separated the world of the dead/sky god from the world of the living. Thus rock art is often situated between realms; it represented liminal rituals necessary to cross between different realms or territories, whether at land or sea (Ling 2005). Their functions were thus linked to travels between realms and travels in the real world between foreign territories, which represented the same type of dangerous liminal crossings (Helms 1988). On rock art one will therefore find the central symbols of the upper realm (sun crosses), as well as symbols of the major gods linked to liminal crossings and travels, such as ships (Kristiansen 2001). Here, at the middle realm, we also find long cult houses or temples; they appear to be a recurring and paradigmatic feature of death rituals in local settlement centres throughout Scandinavia (Victor 2002).

Finally the lower realm was approached through sacrifice and ritual depositions in lakes, rivers and moors/or caves – doors to the netherworld where, among others, the snake goddess of the dead resided and where the sun spent the night on its journey and was held imprisoned. The gods of the netherworld were approached through sacrifice and depositions of both personal goods, such as ornaments, weapons and tools, and of ritual gear employed by the priests in ritual performances, such as lurs, helmets, shields, *etc*. The depositions to the gods of the netherworld in moors and waters were often different from those deposited in burials. In periods and regions of cremation burials in urns, the larger personal ornaments of women or weapons of men were deposited separately in the natural sanctuaries of moors and lakes and caves. We can detect a hierarchy of such depositions in the Bronze Age, as exemplified in Figure 13.5. But throughout the Bronze Age the ritual equipment employed by divine priests during ceremonies belonged to the gods and could only be deposited in their sanctuaries/holy places. It could not be owned by mortal chiefs and is therefore never found in burials.

Priests/priestess, warriors and farmers would all make depositions according to their social standing at specially selected places in the landscape. In recent years new excavations of such wet environments in England have revealed the highly complex and organised nature of these depositions and sacrifices to the netherworld also found in other parts of Europe (Scwenzer 1997, Abb. 5). They could be occasioned by initiation rituals, combats between chiefs, *etc*, and as a conclusion of some highly important rituals. But we should also envisage life cycle changes in rules of deposition, linked to changes in social identity (Fontijn 2002, ch. 11 and fig. 11.3; Sørensen 2004; Thedéen 2005). Likewise chiefly houses might be abandoned at death and buried under the barrow, an indication of the connection between the farmhouse and the barrow as monuments for the living and the dead. Only under certain conditions would they become unified, perhaps suggesting that the house could accompany the deceased on the journey to the otherworld as well as fields for grazing the chiefly herd (grass turfs of the barrow).

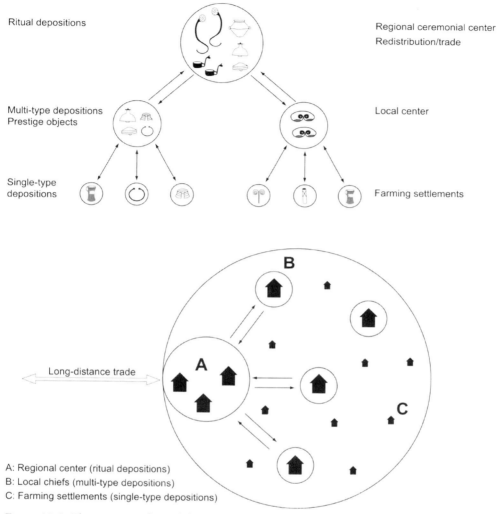

Figure 13.5. The structure of ritual deposition and settlements in the Late Bronze Age in northern Europe (after Kristiansen 1996).

It can thus be demonstrated that the decentred Bronze Age landscape of temperate Eurasia repeated the paradigmatic cosmological structure of the three realms of the gods. Together they represent a cosmological cycle characterised by different rituals and sacrifices throughout the year and throughout the life of people. Power resided in the chiefly control of cosmological/religious institutions that were used to mobilise wealth, which could be employed in political strategies. I will therefore discuss how these processes were played out in practice.

Power structures and decentralised complexity

The Bronze Age has been characterised as a networked chiefdom, based upon a political economy of wealth finance/prestige goods (Earle 2002b). It represents a variety among complex societies also described as corporate versus networked, collective versus individualising societies (Feinman 2001). I have chosen the term-decentralised complexity (Kristiansen 2007), as it adds an important geographical dimension to the distribution of power. However, before approaching the question of power structures it is necessary to discuss theoretical concepts linked to practice: what social processes operate in decentralised and yet complex societies and how can we transform them into theoretical tools of interpretation?

In his famous work: *Outline of a Theory of Practice*, Pierre Bourdieu exemplifies the processes operating in establishing symbolic power (Bourdieu 1977, ch. 4). He is concerned with the conversion of symbolic capital back into economic capital.

> "Thus we see that symbolic capital, which in the form of prestige and renown attached to a family and a name is readily convertible back into economic capital, is perhaps the most valuable form of accumulation in a society in which the severity of the climate (the major work-ploughing and harvesting – having to be done in a very short space of time) and the limited technical resources (harvesting is done with the sickle) demand collective labour" (Bourdieu 1977, 179).

What are the mechanisms by which a local chief or renowned person can mobilise labour? In Bourdieu's words:

> "Thus this system contains only two ways (and they prove in the end to be just one way) of getting and keeping lasting hold over someone: gifts or debts, the overtly economic obligations of debt, or the "moral", "affective" obligations created and maintained by exchange" (Bourdieu 1977, 191).

However, this mobilisation needs to be socially or ritually sanctioned:

> "The endless reconversion of economic capital into symbolic capital, at the cost of a wastage of social energy which is the condition for the permanence of domination, cannot succeed without the complicity of the whole group … As Mauss put it, the whole society pays itself in the false coin of its dream" (Bourdieu 1977, 195).

Finally:

> "To these forms of legitimate accumulation, through which the dominant groups or classes secure a capital of "credit" which seems to owe nothing to the logic of exploitation, must be added another form of accumulation of symbolic capital, the collection of luxury goods attesting to the taste and distinction of their owner" (Bourdieu 1977, 197).

Bourdieu's description of the mechanisms of power in a peasant society corresponds well to what we know of Bronze Age society, and in Figure 13.6 I have therefore summarised his argument into a dynamic theoretical model, which over time may transform gift obligations into tribute and slavery.

We have now added some of the basic social mechanism through which chiefly institutions are maintained and eventually strengthened over time. Thus we can proceed

Figure 13.6. Dynamic historical model of the potential transformation of gift obligations into tribute and slavery.

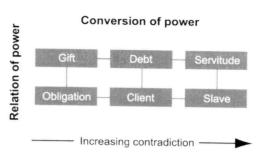

to combine the institutional and economic realities of the Early Bronze Age with the processes through which they operated to build barrows, exchange metal and prestige goods.

In a recent excavation of a large Bronze Age barrow, Skelhøj in southern Jutland, it has been possible to demonstrate that it was constructed with cut out sods (grass turfs) from up to 4–5 different fields (Holst *et al.* 2004, fig. 7). The work was further highly organised, so we should envisage the mobilisation of several households or kin groups, which contributed to its construction. These observations were used by Johansen, Laursen and Holst (2004) to construct a model of a rather egalitarian, self-organising society during the Middle Bronze Age, only to become permanently ranked and hierarchical during the Late Bronze Age, when barrow construction was terminated (also Thedéen 2005 for a different argument). In opposition to this I consider the notion of self-organisation to be an arbitrary, analytical concept without a theory to account for the underlying social processes involved (for a discussion, see Kristiansen 2007). If we take the Skelhøj barrow as a paradigm for the mobilisation of labour for at least the larger barrows, it corresponds to the model of gift obligations and tributary relations between higher and lower status persons/families in Figure 13.5. Which again was part of a larger network of exchanges and obligations linked to metal and prestige goods.

A network analysis of several thousand Bronze Age barrows and burials from Jutland by Johansen, Laursen and Holst (2004), corresponds well to a similar analysis of Trobiand networks and the distribution of chiefly power during the early 20th century in the Trobiand islands (Irwin 1983, maps 1–6). Centrality and ecological resources played an important role for the maintenance of rank locally within the islands, whereas the kula exchange added external dynamics that could be used to sustain or challenge power (Irwin 1983, pt 2 and map 7). In this the Trobiand chiefdoms and their engagement in interregional exchange may serve as a minimal model for understanding the much larger and more elaborate political economy of Bronze Age Europe (Johnson and Earle 2000, ch. 9). The fact that prestige goods (solid hilted swords/gold) could be accumulated in nodal points in the network during several hundred years, as demonstrated by Johansen, Laursen and Holst (2004, figs 9–13), points to chiefs abilities to exploit their central position in the network. Geographical centrality in the network would permit chiefs to extend the number and range of trade partners and clients. It consequently secured them a more powerful and permanent position allowing them to demand labour, war service *etc* in return.

The continuous accumulation and consumption of chiefly prestige goods in burials was the outcome of – and the motor in – these social and economic processes. It should be realised that the three centuries of Montelius Periods 2 and 3 (1450–1150 BC) saw the construction of at least 40,000 barrows within present day Denmark (44,000 square km), This staggering investment of labour and soil (the barrows were constructed with grass turfs, and each barrow consumed *c.* 3 hectares) was accompanied by grave goods of bronze and sometimes gold. Among the excavated burials, which amount to several thousand, there were more than 2000 swords, if we include Schleswig-Holstein (Thrane 2005). We are speaking of a political and economic activity, and a level of metal consumption, without parallel in other parts of Europe.

These observations from Denmark correspond quite well to Thomas Larsson's demonstration in southern Sweden of centre–periphery structures where local centres of wealth accumulation were surrounded by larger areas of production. In his model their relationship is regulated through forms of tribute (Larsson 1986, fig. 7). Thus in Scania areas of barrow concentrations would correspond to centres of accumulation and power competition, whereas surrounding areas with less barrows and less burial wealth were areas of production, that the centres were able to exploit in an unequal tributary relationship sanctioned by ritual and cosmological authority. These structures were institutionalised as they persisted over several hundred years (Strömberg 1982; Olausson 1993; Gröhn 2004, ch. 4.1). They represent the institutionalisation of a cosmological order upon the landscape, which persisted throughout the Bronze Age (Kristiansen 1998b).

It is also clear, however, that whereas the chiefly institution of ritual chiefs represented the highest level of chiefly power, only enjoyed by a relatively small group among the upper chiefly clans, access to the warrior groups was more open, and could probably be recruited from a larger segment of the chiefly clans. We should envisage that barrows belonged only to members of chiefly clans, as argued above. These groups, however, were both numerous and highly diversified in terms of power and prestige, the lowest ranks being close to commoners, as indeed demonstrated by variations in burial wealth and the huge differences in farm sizes. We should thus envisage a society with institutionalised ranks and with fierce competition and negotiations over positions. It meant that the social role of different sword types and the rules of accompanying grave goods gradually eroded (Kristiansen 1984). Already during Montelius Period 3 we see how the strictly observed roles of warriors with full hilted swords and priestly chiefs with Nordic swords, razors and tweeters become blurred, to disappear from Period 4 (Thrane 2005). The sword simply lost its typological meaning as a social indicator of warriors and chiefs.

In his classic book *How Chiefs come to Power* Timothy Earle makes an interesting attempt to explain the relationship between power, wealth and production:

"I argue that control over the ideology of social ranking rested on control over the system of wealth finance. Wealth finance has a major advantage over staple fiancé. Its highly valued objects are easily transported over considerable distance and can be used to exert long-distance control over people" (Earle 1997, 73).

He then suggests that the pastoral economy of Early Bronze Age Thy was used as mobile wealth, linking production of cattle to the production and distribution of prestige goods and control over people.

"The primary advantage of cattle ... would have been the ease with which they could have been managed and owned as currency in the political economy. An animal is a convenient unit of ownership and production. In herding chiefdoms, the preponderance of animals is owned by the local chief, who lends them out to individual households for their subsistence in return for support" (Earle 1997, 100).

Here is sketched the mechanism for exerting power in a decentralised, networking Danish Early Bronze Age chiefdom. In subsequent case studies I shall demonstrate that new farm architecture allowed the stalling of cattle, thus supporting Earle's scenario. Ownership of cattle was therefore one of the defining criteria of the chiefly lineages of "free farmers", and cattle were also necessary for being correctly buried in the barrows. To be buried under a barrow was thus another prerogative for the chiefly lineages, in opposition to commoners without cattle, as you had to control land in addition to cattle in order to build a barrow. This bundle of rights and privileges defined the chiefly class of free farmers, but their positions could probably be contested from below, just as there were substantial differences in wealth and prestige even within the group.

Which other carrier paths were open for young ambitious male members of the chiefly clans of lower ranks? The most obvious way was to become a warrior, serve for a prestigious chieftain and take part in raids to acquire fame. But warriors were part of a brotherhood of warriors stretching far outside the Nordic realm, as demonstrated by the distribution of flange hilted and octagonally hilted swords. It allowed warriors to travel long distances to take war service at distant or famous chiefly houses. Having achieved fame they may return with this new symbolic capital. It could then be transferred in prestige and power, perhaps giving access to compete for local chieftainship (Harrisson 2004; Kristiansen and Larsson 2005, ch. 5.5). In this way local chiefs would constantly have to compete to attract warriors to secure their own power base from being contested. The Early Bronze Age was thus a dynamic society characterised by a web of changing, competitive alliances, but regulated by the institution of ritual chiefs and war chiefs (Kristiansen 2001). These and other institutions lasted throughout the Bronze Age, although they probably became increasingly powerful in a process that ultimately separated chiefs and commoners, and created a large group of enslaved commoners, according to the dynamic of Figure 13.6. Towards the end of the Bronze Age these processes had generated the conditions for the collapse of Bronze Age society when its lifeblood – metal supplies – declined and were finally cut.

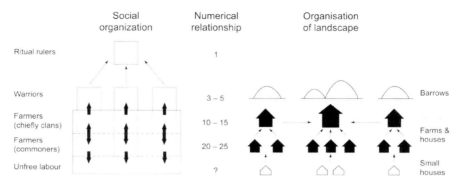

Figure 13.7. Model of Bronze Age society, defined by the relationship between barrow, farms and social organisation.

In Figure 13.7, I have summarised the evidence of Early Bronze Age social and economic organisation, its political economy (Earle 2002a, ch. 1), as a point of departure for future research and discussions. Chiefly clans served as recruitment for warriors/war chiefs and from among the highest ranked clans ritual rulers were appointed. Every local community would have local chiefs and war leaders, but their power and status varied as in Trobiand society. Rank and power represented a *continuum*, although high ranked clans would set themselves apart, and could probably periodically mobilise alliances and support to create confederations of power covering larger areas. But as stated by Earle:

> "The control of wealth exchange in the Danish case illustrates how difficult and unstable were network strategies and how problematic was finance based on wealth exchanges. The role of metal was apparently critical for the emergence of stratification in the EBA, but metals also proved problematic to control" (Earle 2002, 313).

So far my attempt to quantify the relative numbers of rulers, warriors, farmers and commoners is qualified guesswork. As to ritual leaders and warriors the number of swords gives an indication, but the division between chiefly clans and commoners cannot yet be demonstrated in the archaeological record. One indication mentioned earlier, would be the occurrence/non occurrence of stalling for cattle. Slave labour is perhaps easier to demonstrate, as we have large chiefly farms that presuppose labour service whether volunteer or not. Very small farms could testify to both commoners and slave labour, but here is an area of research to be pursued in the future.

Households, economy and society: the case of Scania

Ecological and environmental change
In what follows I shall discuss the theoretical models from Figures 13.2 and 13.3.

In doing this I employ the concepts of centre and periphery to account for local processes of expansion and interaction. How are we to understand the relationship between intensively settled and exploited landscapes and more extensively settled and exploited landscapes, as indicated by the pollen and settlement record. In Norway marked ecological differences and the close proximity between coastal and upland settlements favoured an early development of transhumance (*Sæterdrift*) from the Bronze Age onwards (Prescott 1997). However, in southern Sweden distances are often longer between central and marginal areas, which allow other economic models to come into play.

Berglund, Lagerås and Regnéll recently summarised the rich pollen-botanical evidence from southern Sweden (Berglund *et al.* 2002, figs 4 and 5). They demonstrate that the historically well-established dualism between an open coastal farming landscape and a forested inland with an extensive farming economy based mainly on grazing appeared during the Bronze Age. A more intensified farming regime with new crops (Lagerås and Regnéll 1999) and further opening of the landscape took place from the Late Bronze Age and continued into the Iron Age. During this period the forest region developed a full farming economy, and became a permanent settlement area. How does these findings relate to the evidence from western Scania?

We have in the pollen diagram from Sjögungan for the first time a well dated vegetation history that demonstrate a full opening of the landscape from the Early Bronze Age onwards. It corresponds to other coastal diagrams from Halland (Wallin 2004), Bohuslän (Ekman 2002, fig. 5), and from north-western Jutland (Bech and Mikkelsen 1999, fig. 2), where opening of landscape starts with the Single Grave Culture, to be completed during the Early Bronze Age. Grazing and herding were dominant subsistence strategies, but a new practice of deep-sea fishing and maritime explorations began with the Bronze Age (Berntsson 2005). The late opening of the landscape in some pollen diagrams from south eastern Scania dated to the Late Bronze Age (Berglund *et al.* 1991, figs 5 and 13, 5) must be due to local variation, as the selected pollen sites were not coastal; alternatively I propose that the Late Bronze Age opening of landscape should be moved back into the earlier Bronze Age, as the dating of the pollen diagrams in the Ystad project was difficult (see discussion in appendix A in Berglund *et al.* 1991). But even if the dating is correct the diagrams indicate that grazing, burning and grain-growing increased during the Early Bronze Age, as in Gudme on Fuen (Thrane 2003, fig. 8). However, the evidence from the Ystad project otherwise demonstrate the economic variation between coastal and inland areas, as seen also in western Scania.

From the Late Bronze Age onward grazing pressures increases, as well as some agrarian practices, which led to the introduction of new crops throughout southern Scandinavia (Gustafsson 1998; Robinson 2000, fig. 2). It corresponds to similar changes in the household and the political economy to be discussed. We can assume that all densely settled landscapes with many barrows were open grazed landscapes from at least 1500 BC onwards, but with forest reserves available in the inland and on the less densely settled heavy moraine. These were areas that could be exploited for a variety of economic purposes, and also represented areas for some colonisation, especially from the Late Bronze Age onwards. The nature and the dating of this colonisation in Scania and Småland has been debated (Lagerås and Regnell 1999; Berglund *et al.* 2002). A more recent series of radiocarbon dates of clearance cairns date the first expansion to the earlier Bronze Age (Skoglund 2005, 76), with some intensification during the Late Bronze Age. This new evidence has been confirmed by palaeo-botanical work (Lagerås pers. comm.). Leif Häggström has recently summarised the published evidence, which shows that grazing was predominant during the Early Bronze Age. The role of farming increased through time, and developed mostly during the Iron Age (Häggström 2005, table 2; Lagerås 2000). From the Early Bronze Age we can document a diversified economy and settlement pattern that combined intensive and extensive farming practice in southern Sweden to be continued throughout the period. We can further substantiate the often-observed trend in the Late Bronze Age of south Scandinavia towards degrading environments and agrarian intensification, which culminated with the introduction of Celtic fields and controlled crop rotation in many regions throughout northern Europe. These general trends in settlement and economy during the Bronze Age were, of course, locally adopted and resulted in slightly different solutions in different environments, just as different time trends operated in western and eastern Scandinavia; western Scandinavia being earlier in the process (Kristiansen 1978). Much of this variation has been studied locally in recent years with interesting results (Skoglund 2005; Thedéen 2005), but they remain variations within a Bronze Age world that was shared throughout southern Scandinavia.

We can thus distinguish between central and more marginal settlement areas already from the beginning of the Bronze Age, and this raises a series of question as relating to the political economy: did there exist a geographical division of labour that was politically controlled and secured that central areas received tribute in a system of unequal exchange due to their superior social and cosmological position? Or were the two ecological zones part of a single economic system where cattle and herders moved between coastal and inland areas during summertime? In some coastal regions along the Swedish west coast a similar division can be observed between a maritime economy that employed cairns on outlying islands and farming settlements on the more fertile lands with barrows of grass turfs close to farms (Skoglund 2005, table 11). Along the coast rock art depictions of ships demonstrate the connection of the maritime people to long distance sea journeys as well as deep-water fishing (Ling 2005). Again economic specialisation and division of labour between neighbouring ecological zones raises questions about their relationship. Did the farming economies control the maritime economy at the coast? Or should we rather see these different economies as representing independent polities (chiefdoms) that interacted with each other, but employed different ritual strategies (rock art versus metal depositions), as suggested by Skoglund (2005, 155). It can be documented that wealth was unevenly distributed and mainly consumed in the grass turf barrows of the central farming areas (Skoglund

2005, 150), and I take this to represent an underlying system of tributary relations. The maritime economy was integrated into the dominant economy of south Scandinavia, which marks a major difference in social and economic complexity compared to the later Neolithic with its separate cultural and economic groups, such as Pitted Ware and Battle Axe Culture.

To summarise: during the Bronze Age a diversified economy developed that integrated a coastal maritime economy, an extensive forest economy and an intensive herding and farming regime in the central settlements through various forms of trade, gift exchange and tribute. Central meeting places with hundreds and even thousands of fire pits in long lines become a regular feature during the Late Bronze Age (Martens 2005; Thörn 2005) The ability to create a unified perception of cosmos and culture throughout northern Europe from the beginning of the Bronze Age was linked to two phenomena: the introduction of metal and a concomitant introduction of new forms of prestige and social hierarchies, that were exemplified not only in barrow burials and new social identities, but also in a new household economy with a new architecture. We have recently seen two important studies on farmhouses and households in the Bronze Age, which introduce new interesting interpretations of their social and economic roles.

The house(hold) as social institution

In a recent work Anna Gröhn makes an in depth analysis of the social role of Bronze Age house architecture (also Streiffert 2005, for an important contribution). Ethnographical and archaeological research on houses and households suggest that investments in house constructions of some complexity is linked to a similar complex use of and investments in the landscape forming a political economy (Earle 2002a; Gröhn 2004, 282). Within such a theoretical context the house becomes a social and political institution, and its biography is linked to the life history of the household and its head (Gerritsen 1999). The death of the head of the household marks a critical moment of transmission and negotiations of power. In the Early Bronze Age such an occasion was sometimes used to take down the house and construct a barrow over it to unify the dead chief with his household in the afterlife (Svanberg 2005). In this way cosmology and political economy was unified and would serve as a genealogical and mythological starting point for the descendents of the now heroic lineage. A visible claim had been made to legitimise a chiefly lineage. In this way genealogies of chiefly lineages were anchored in the landscape and handed down through the generations by bards retelling the accumulating mythical genealogies and heroic deeds of dead, yet still acting chiefly agents. Hero cults of such outstanding chiefly lineages might then later become institutionalised through rituals at cult houses during the Late Bronze Age (Victor 2002), but beginning in the Early Bronze Age (Clemmensen 2005). From this we may conclude that the house(hold) during the Bronze Age was an important social, economic and symbolic (metaphorical) institution. Settlement structure and architectural variability is therefore an important point of departure for understanding the role of the household as a social institution.

During the Neolithic all houses were two aisled constructions of rather moderate size (Nielsen 1999, figs 2–7). The transition between the Middle Neolithic B and Late Neolithic A (Dagger Period, early metal) around 2300 BC marks a significant change in house architecture. Variability increases between small and large houses, suggesting a corresponding variability in the political economy (Björhem 2003, fig. 4; Gröhn 2004, table 10), and this development accelerated during Late Neolithic B, when copper came in more regular use. Some farmsteads after 2000 BC are highly elaborate and their size, architectural regularity and internal complexity correspond to new economic and political needs of a group that we may assume represents a new chiefly institution (Nielsen 1999, fig. 9). Length increases up to 30–50 m, but most significantly the new large houses are also wider than the smaller houses: 8–10 m, compared to 5–7 m. This is perhaps the most visible and important change, as it adds space to the houses more effectively than increased length and it adds monumentality to the internal space/rooms. The new architecture was introduced from the Unetiće Culture in Central Europe, and used solid timber in the wall construction (Nielsen 1999, 10). The houses now exhibit a functional division of the internal space between a western living section, a middle section and an eastern barn or byre (the byre is rather inferred) that was to continue.

The new large long houses introduce a whole new concept of housing and households. The house now became a social and political institution for the economically leading, chiefly lineages, here they boasted external and internal monumentality; new capacity for storage and animals signalled new forms of ownership and control of production. This corresponded to the potential for a much larger household than the average farmsteads. Also new forms of social behaviour and etiquette could be displayed inside the house. Thus, the new house architecture and a new social institution of chiefly households signalled important social changes that were introduced from Central Europe, where metal was already in use, especially after 2000 BC. We should observe, however, that the introduction of metal and its imitation in flint dagger production introduced social changes before the systematic use of metal, which followed a few hundred years later (Apel 2005; Lekberg 2004; Varberg 2005). It meant that a more ranked society was already in place when a full metal economy was introduced from around 1700 BC, leading to a major social and economic transformation after 1500 BC.

The high degree of regularity in house constructions, despite variations in size, is seen to reflect an institutionalised use of space that became more complex and hierarchical with the introduction of the three aisled houses around 1500 BC (Middle Bronze Age in Central Europe; late Early Bronze Age in Scandinavia; Montelius 2). This goes hand in hand with a more structured land-use, where it can be demonstrated in some areas that farm units, fields and cattle tracks were demarcated with fences (Fokkens 2005a, figs 18.15–16; Knippenberg and Jongste 2005, fig. 6 and p. 23). Some researchers see this as being part of a complete restructuring of society that was implemented also economically in a new farm lay out and land-use (Kristiansen 1998b). While this is undoubtedly true of north-western Europe, the more fertile moraine landscapes of southern Scandinavia exhibit more continuity in settlement structure, and a slightly different land-use characterised by the use of central and marginal areas in the local economy, as discussed above. We may have to deal with two ecological/economic trajectories in northern Europe, which shared the basic components of social and religious organisation, but whose long-term economic and demographic conditions differed, as expressed in different strategies of land-use (Kristiansen 1978, fig. 11).

However, there is also continuity in the use of space/activity areas in the Bronze Age farms from the two aisled houses to the three aisled houses. Thus the division into living section, middle room/barn/entrance and byre can now be more safely documented in some houses, such as Bdr. Gram (Ethelberg 2000, 192), and in the Netherlands (Fokkens 2005a). However, variability increased, both functionally and in terms of size. The largest houses are now 10 × 50 m, best documented in southern Jutland (Ethelberg 2000, fig. 29), economy building are increasingly added, just as interior divisions show great variability (Gröhn 2004, table 17). Some farms, mostly middle sized or small, clearly had no byre, while others, especially the larger houses, most often do, at least in well-documented cases. Thus internal complexity in the use of space increased, as well as variability between households (Gröhn 2004, table 12). Timothy Earle used the well documented evidence from Thy to suggest that large households with byres, such as Legård, were chiefly farms controlling cattle, while middle sized houses without byres belonged to the warrior group, and the quite small houses to commoners/farmers (Earle 2004, fig. 14.1). This identification with social groups or institutions was based upon very well preserved houses. In the case of the warriors' farm the house had been fully preserved under sand, including wooden posts, and the activities inside the house demonstrated that amber collecting had been important, as well as grinding and hide and wood working (Bech and Mikkelsen 1999, figs 3 and 4). An amber hoard was buried under the floor. Although all activities took place throughout the house, they were most frequent in the western part. Two bronze objects: a fibula and a double stud belong with male dress, the double stud with the sword strap of leather, from which the interpretation was deduced of a warrior house (Bech 2003, fig. 10). This would correspond with the colleting of amber for trade, as this was most probably an activity linked to warriors, who travelled and traded (Kristiansen and Larsson 2005).

Whether or not this interpretation can be sustained in other cases, the internal and external variability in farm size and functions demonstrate a highly stratified social and economic structure throughout northern Europe from 1500 BC, whose manifestations included the whole landscape, that was controlled both in cosmological and economic terms. It was also a period of fierce competition between local chiefly lineages, trying to outdo each other, thus tapping the ecological resources in the landscape in terms of timber for houses and grassland for barrows. Several of the large farms have been extended, reflecting the social and economic dynamic of individual households.

Period 2, 1500–1300 BC, represents the climax period in terms of farm size and monumentality, from Period 3 the large farms become smaller, and from the beginning of the Late Bronze Age the medium sized farm becomes the norm, just as they are more numerous (Welinder 1998, 121). Thus the transition from Period 3 to 4 represents yet another social, religious and economic change. The ordinary farmer, the commoner, has apparently become the largest group, and chiefly lineages were fewer and probably more powerful. However, ecological and economic changes were also at play, and their role will now be discussed.

The house(hold) as economic institution

After this discussion of the house as social institution we shall now turn to its economic functions. This has been facilitated by a major reinterpretation of the Bronze Age farmstead as a social and economic unit by Magnus Artursson (2005a; 2005c; also Björhem 2003; Thrane 2003). The prevailing interpretation of the last 30 years has it that houses/farms were individual farmsteads, which were rebuilt once per generation. This would explain the often numerous house plans from archaeological excavations within a smaller area that often spanned the whole Bronze Age. However, better house typologies and series of radiocarbon dates has made it possible to demonstrate that several farm houses often existed side by side (Ängeby 1999; Gröhn 2004, 213) and thus had a life span closer to three generations than one. It would make sense also from an economic point of view, as the larger farms represented a major economic investment of timber, just as the craftsmanship behind them that was probably shared within a community or even between communities. This is clear from the common architectural standards employed throughout Scandinavia, and is also revealed by close up comparisons of similar houses (Gröhn 2004, fig. 61).

There is a further social and economic implication to be drawn from these new findings. The co-existence of several farms, often one larger and two smaller, suggests that they all belonged to the same household. The relations between them would be both economic and social; economically the smaller farms helped to support the large, chiefly farm, socially they were probably of the same lineage, but with a subordination or client relationship between large and smaller farms. Such an extended definition of a chiefly household, or rather a chiefly hamlet, would explain its economic basis, which could not have been provided and maintained by its own household. While the construction of the large hall like house could be done through temporary, lineage based mobilisation, like barrow construction, the mobilisation of timber and grassland resources for such endeavours would demand some form of control. For the largest longhouses a group of client farms would be needed to maintain their social and economic position on a year-to-year basis, which must have demanded labour, warriors and production far beyond that of one or two farms.

A central issue in the discussion about the introduction of large three aisled farms is the importance of stalling cattle (Rasmussen 1999; Roymans 1999; Zimmerman 1999; Årlin 1999). Here Marianne Rasmussen demonstrates the connection between the three aisled farms, and the importance of cattle, although not all farms would have byres. She stresses a new form of cattle management, where also new forms of enclosures and pens belong, although some of these could just as well be for sheep management. Cattle and especially draught animals gained new importance when farming was intensified, but also short distance transport to and from the farm increased many times when cattle was stalled and storing facilities had to be expanded. In addition there were seasonal transports of dung, grass turfs for barrows and timber for house constructions, furniture, wagons etc. We should therefore consider the introduction of stalling, especially after 1500 when it is systematically evidenced, as being part of a new more labour demanding farming economy that implied a better and more controlled management of fields, grasslands and forests as well (Zimmerman 1999, 315). A further intensification was introduced during the Late Bronze Age, when some of the storing facilities were moved out from the main farm building into economy buildings, and thus in part explains why the farm becomes smaller. This, however, was also due to forest management and lack of solid timber in some regions, such as Thy.

While economy may form the foundation for these changes, it cannot explain why some farms had cattle stalled and others not, why some farms became irrationally large, only comparable with royal farms of the later Viking Period. Here the social and political processes have to be taken into account – in short the political economy.

Most researchers now agree that stalling of cattle was part of an economy where cattle played an important role in social transactions. Therefore the most valuable had to be stalled, cared for and protected. Harry Fokkens has put it this way:

> "Thus, to posses and to exchange cattle means to be able to acquire and maintain social relations, to enter into strategic and nuptial alliances. From this perspective the longhouse is a symbol of what Roymans calls a "pastoral ideology" ".

Fokkens is thus in agreement with Earle in the statement I referred earlier. To this we might add, that cattle raids was a popular sport of war, as indicated by both Homeric and Irish sagas, the most famous of course being *The Tain*, where two kings goes to war over a famous bull. Cattle raids were mostly long distance, as you do not raid your neighbours and close allies. Such patterns of long distance raids have been documented for Irish King *Toirhealbhach Ó Conchobhair* during the early medieval period (Roymans 1999, fig. 6), but they have old Indo-European (Bronze Age) origins, as demonstrated by Lincoln (1981). In Figure 13.8 the Indo-European Cattle Cycle is reproduced, which represents the mythical blueprint for the practice of cattle raiding.

Thus warfare in the form of cattle raids was a regular seasonal activity for young aspiring warriors, and it explains the large group of (re)-sharpened flange hilted swords throughout the Middle Bronze Age in Northern and Central Europe. Roymans summarises the significance of cattle raids:

> "The importance of cattle as a medium of exchange and as the main object of raiding parties meant that cattle circulated in society much more intensively than is generally assumed. The practice of raiding need not result in accumulation of cattle on the homesteads of successful warrior elites. In Northeast Africa as well as in ancient Ireland the cattle captured in raiding was often directly redistributed by elites to their followers or clients. Especially in Ireland, clientship networks were closely connected with a system

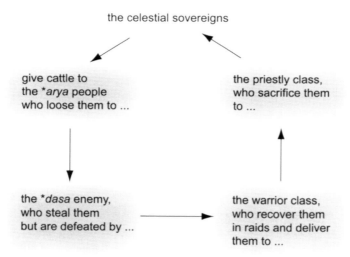

the celestial sovereigns

give cattle to
the *arya* people
who loose them to ...

the priestly class,
who sacrifice them
to ...

the *dasa* enemy,
who steal them
but are defeated by ...

the warrior class,
who recover them
in raids and deliver
them to ...

Figure 13.8. The Indo-European cattle raid cycle, according to Lincoln (1981). Here reproduced after Roymans (1999).

of cattle loans. The existence of such redistributive practices makes it almost impossible to reconstruct the cattle ownership of tribal leaders on the basis of archaeological evidence" (Roymans 1999, 298).

Both the economy of ancient Ireland, as well as its historical evidence would seem to correspond most clearly with the situation during the Bronze Age of north-western Europe, where the client relations are archaeologically evidenced in other forms of activities, such as barrow constructions, and in the economic power of the large chiefly farmsteads.

The institution of the warrior and the cattle raids probably declined with the Late Bronze Age when the classical flange hilted swords disappear, just as cattle become less frequent and is monopolised and protected in fewer chiefly farms. We may assume that warriors as well were now more firmly attached as retines to such regional chiefly courts. When wealth and power is concentrated so are warriors.

At Bjerre in Thy it can be documented that manuring of the Early Bronze Age fields was practised (Robinson *et al.* 1995). Thus, a cluster of factors interacted in the process that led to the formation of three aisled longhouses with byre. The significance of cattle can also be read from the fact that their frequency in bone assemblages is very high, in the "warrior's house" in Bjerre around 80%, followed by sheep and horse but no pig bones (Bech and Mikkelsen 1999, fig. 8). Here a significant change takes place during the Bronze Age, when cattle are reduced in number at the expense of sheep. During the pre-Roman Iron Age sheep then takes over as the dominant animal. This transformation is also evident in other settlements throughout southern Scandinavia. What we observe, however, is that cattle remained dominant at the large chiefly settlements such as Voldtofte on south-western Funen. Cattle had now become monopolised at fewer chiefly courts while wool production became a main activity among common farmers. It is yet another indication of an increasing division of labour in the political economy during the Bronze Age.

The picture of an intensified farming economy during the Bronze Age is completed when the macro-botanical evidence is added. Here the Late Neolithic marks the introduction of a more varied grain production directed at specialised production of *e.g.* beer and bread. From the beginning of the Bronze Age proper (Period 1–2) weeds from annually cultivated fields become more numerous. This trend continues during the Late Bronze Age, when also new forms of barley are introduced (Robinson 2000, fig. 2). When we dissolve the generalised picture into its components, as evidenced in specific households/farms, we note that the storing of cleaned grain is common in the larger chiefly farmsteads, such as Brd. Gram in southern Jutland or the warrior's house in Thy. In house IV at Brd. Gram only cleaned grain was found in the western section intended for cooking. Rest products from the cleaning of the grain were found throughout the house, and might indicate its use in the floor. It further demonstrates that storing of un-threshed grain must have taken place in the house. Concentrations of seeds from wetlands in the central and eastern section may suggest storing of hay. When considering all of southern Scandinavia, changes in grain cultivation follow the same pattern, just as the frequent occurrence of weeds from the Middle Bronze Age that point to an intensified, annual use of fields that corresponds to the introduction of the three aisled farm house and a new system of land-use. Grain cultivation was further intensified during the Late Bronze Age, when more robust barley types became popular. This trend continued into the Iron Age, where the management of agrarian production was further formalised with the introduction of Celtic Fields.

Households and the political economy – a temporal model

From Holland to northern Germany and Scandinavia the historical and environmental processes of change were more or less similar. Through networks of exchange that originated in the 3rd millennium BC (Single Grave Culture and later Bell Beaker/ Dagger Culture) the Bronze Age societies of this vast region shared many traits of social and economic organisation as well as burial rituals and cosmology. It is therefore meaningful to compare and discuss developments in household economies and cosmologies during the Bronze Age within this larger north European/Nordic region (Assendorp 1997). In the following I delimit the major temporal phases of changes in the political economy.

The Late Neolithic or Dagger Period: starting 2300 BC marks the beginning of a Nordic/north European metal age through the adaptation of metal models for flint dagger production and through a major intensification of exchange and farming, leading to a series of innovations from dress to burial ritual (Apel 2004; Vandkilde 1996). Late Neolithic expansion and reorganisation of the late 3rd millennium BC into more marginal forested landscapes such as Småland and Värmland is indicated by the building of stone cists and by pollen-botanical evidence of small scale farming and grazing that opened up the forest (Berglund and Börjesson 2002; Lagerås 2000; Heimann 2002, fig. 6). This settlement expansion mainly includes areas with closer proximity to central settlement areas, such as southern Småland. In Norway the Late Neolithic or Dagger Period represents the systematic introduction of farming proper and the opening of the landscape for grazing (Prescott 1996; 2005). Two aisled houses/farmsteads were scattered in the landscape. Around or shortly after 2000 BC large chiefly farmhouses for extended families are introduced from Central Europe accompanying the first more systematic use of metal (Nielsen 1999, fig. 9). During the Late Neolithic the Nordic area was, for the first time, integrated into a common cultural and social model of society through the long-distance exchange of flint daggers and metal (Lekberg 2004). To this was added a new social organisation of leadership linked to large chiefly clan houses after 2000 BC with one or two smaller farms being part of the household. It was from this basis that a Bronze Age economy was extended through southern Scandinavia. We should envisage a political economy of settlement expansion and the rise of chiefly families that were able to extract tribute and labour from closer kin.

Middle Bronze Age: expansion and re-organisation of landscape and society (Arnoldussen and Fontijn 2005). Massive opening of the forest and transformation of landscape into pastures and scattered fields took place from around 1700–1500 BC, some regions earlier some slightly later. A new organisation of households, farm architecture and landscape is introduced. Ownership of cattle is formalised just as strict regulations of land-use were introduced, in the Netherlands in the form of fences and other demarcations of land-use. This represent the transformation of northern Europe into a more complex and ranked society characterised by physical boundaries to regulate the behaviour of people and animals, from interior divisions of houses to fences and field boundaries. The political economy saw the first division of labour between farms and communities that were linked together in a chiefly polity through exchange, tribute and communal projects of barrow building, trade expeditions, raids, *etc*. This was a period of fierce competition between chiefly lineages, with some consolidation from Period 3 onwards. Chiefly families were now able to extract tribute, warriors and labour from a wider network beyond the kin group. Slaves or dependent labour became a feature of chiefly households.

The Late Bronze Age: represents yet another transformation of economy and society. Throughout Scandinavia larger farmhouses are reduced in size from 200–400 square metres to 100–150 square metres and become more standardised. Or rather – the smaller farmstead of the Early Bronze Age becomes dominant, while the large farmsteads disappear, or are replaced by chiefly settlements, whose structure is still in need of systematic excavation. Small farms of 50–100 square metres existed throughout the Bronze Age. This development represented a further transformation of society into a large group of commoners or peasants (the smaller family farm house), and a much smaller chiefly elite, sometimes buried in huge barrows with rich burial goods, such as Lusehøj near Voldtofte, and living in elaborate residences where they controlled the production and distribution of prestige goods and ritual gear (Thrane 1994). Chiefly leaders were now able to extract tribute from a larger chiefly polity, and command labour and other services from this larger region. This represents complex chiefdoms or archaic decentralised states.

End of Bronze Age/Beginning of Iron Age: The fall of the Bronze Age chiefdoms was the result of a complex interplay of factors to be discussed in conclusion. That it was a period of dramatic change and internal unrest is demonstrated by the massive deposition of costly ritual gear, especially lurs, a majority of which took place during this period. We may note, however, that changes followed different trajectories in different parts of Scandinavia. In Jutland a major reorganisation of the whole settlement structure took place. The Bronze Age farmsteads were left and their households moved together in villages with an apparent egalitarian organisation (Rindel 1999). Also, cemeteries in the form of village urn-fields under low barrows exhibit the same lack of differentiation. In southern Scandinavia, Norway and Sweden, there seems to be continuity in the settlement structure. Single farms of hamlets of farms continue to be the norm (Streiffert 2005).

The whole pre-Roman Iron Age is characterised by a cultural and religious fragmentation of the former rather hegemonic Nordic Bronze Age culture into local and regional variation. It marks a decline in international trade and in Nordic interaction that was only reopened towards the end of the period.

Cosmology and economy – the long term trends

It can be demonstrated that the accumulation of short-term decisions of individual households in a region create long-term unintended consequences beyond the predictive horizon of individual communities. In this way societies pave the way for necessary adjustments and changes in households to maintain their strategies and traditions. In the small scale from one generation to the next slight adjustment are made to maintain prestige and tradition. At Legård in Thy the first massive chiefly farm of (early) Period 2 was later replaced by one of exactly similar construction and size – except that timber for both wall posts and central posts were scaled down in size. It testifies to the increasing shortage of building timber and mature forest, which over the next generations led to a downsizing of the houses (Bech 2003, fig. 9). At the transition to the Late Bronze Age this development reached a critical limit leading to a complex social, religious and economic transformation that defined the close family as the household unit, whereas chiefs retained more power, at least in some regions. Thus, we observe a direct line from decisions and adjustments made on a year-to-year basis to their impact upon long-term changes in the size of households. Compromises had to be made facing ecological overexploitation, yet the overall social and economic framework remained intact, as far as we can judge. Here a mixture of contradictory factors and forces are at work. Tradition in the form of ritual places, ancestor barrows, must have had a strong impact on decisions to stay rather than move when economic conditions worsened, as it happened in Thy. Here settlements even moved into economically non- viable habitats, as in Bjerre, but with good grass production. We can demonstrate the worsening conditions in the use of smaller timber of bad quality for house construction, the use of bog turf for heating. The ecology had been overexploited timber resources became scarce as grazing pressure increased (Bech and Mikkelsen 1999; Kristiansen 1998a).

However, these conditions known from Thy already during the Early Bronze Age (Period 3) became widespread throughout Scandinavia in the course of the Late Bronze Age. Households and farms were reduced in size, individual farms and small hamlets of the Early Bronze Age became larger hamlets, and some settlement expansion took place. But generally speaking the old inhabited areas of the Bronze Age remained unaltered until some fundamental thresholds were passed. Factors at work were a combination of population expansion and economic intensification that reached a first threshold by the end of Period 2 around 1300 BC in Thy, somewhat later in the rest of south Scandinavia. However, Period 3 already witnessed many local adjustments towards a more intensified economy, by taking in new fertile land (Kristiansen 1978, 11; Poulsen 1993). Many new primary barrows were still erected in new locations, suggesting continued competition for resources and power. By the early to middle Period 3 supplies of metal from central Europe came to a temporary halt due to revolutionary social and religious changes (the Urnfield expansion). Consequently, over the next one or two generations chiefly swords throughout northern Europe were kept in circulation until their hilts were worn through and the clay core lay bare. This exceptional phenomenon, which could have meant the end of the Bronze Age, was terminated by new supplies of metal towards the end of Period 3, and the old worn out swords were put into the graves as tradition proscribed – for the last time on such a massive scale. From now on barrow building ceased, having taken its toll of good grazing land, metal was ritually economised as urn burials took over, instead ritual hoarding took precedence. We should of course not underestimate the religious meaning of these changes, but on the whole the changing rituals that were introduced by the beginning of the Late Bronze Age were part of a social and economic consolidation of the ruling elite, that included a conservation of economic resources.

A series of adjustments took place throughout the Late Bronze Age to intensify the economy – from the introduction of the composite ard for more efficient ploughing to new more resistant crops. Manuring was practised to some extend just as the more tolerant and wool-producing sheep became the dominant animal in many regions (Fig. 13.8). We should see the reduction of farm size as being part of these adjustments, more and smaller households replaced the earlier larger farmsteads. The social changes accompanying these adjustments in physical properties are illuminated in Appalle in Sweden (Ullen 1994). The house became increasingly the domain of a single, multi-generational family with their animals. Chiefly households seem to have become bigger and fewer during this period, whereas the ordinary farming family household becomes

"Early group"

	Haag	Bulbjerg	Voldtofte	Kirkebjerget	Hötofta	Kvarnby	Fosie IV	Veddelevvej
Cattle	54,5	63,0	69,3	82,35	55,8	58,5	54,5	54,5
Horse	–	0,6	2,8	1,9	27,7	1,8	(–)	8,8
Pig	28,6	0,6	18,6	11,0	8,0	13,2	11,5	24,1
Goat/sheep	15,6	35,8	9,2	4,7	7,4	24,3	25,3	17,6
Dog	1,3	–	0,04	0,2	1,1	2,2	(–)	2,9
Total %	100	100	99,9	100	100	100	100	99,9
Total number	(77)	(165)	(2381)	(1867)	(375)	(292)	(87)	(171)
Goat + sheep + pig	44,2	36,4	27,8	15,7	15,4	37,5	38,8	41,7

"Late group"

	Abbetved	Hasmark	Kolby	Veddelevvej	Fosie IV	Ängdala
Cattle	33,9	43,1	46,8	45,3	44,3	46,2
Horse	7,1	7,6	14,4	2,7	(–)	3,0
Pig	28,6	16,3	20,0	13,3	7,7	24,5
Goat/sheep	30,4	31,1	18,4	37,7	47,9	20,4
Dog	–	2,0	0,3	1,3	(–)	6,0
Total %	100	100	99,9	99,9	99,9	100
Total number	(56)	(541)	(374)	(75)	(194)	(1100)
Goat + sheep + pig	59,0	47,4	38,4	50,6	55,6	44,9

Figure 13.9. Table showing changes in the composition of domestic animals during the Late Bronze Age (after Hedeager and Kristiansen 1988 Det danske landbrugs historie).

the norm. Using the evidence from south-western Funen this has been interpreted as a development of more hierarchical forms of rulership, where regional chiefs were in control of a much larger territory than in the Early Bronze Age (Thrane 1994). A new type of local and regional ritual meeting place defined by rows or groups of cooking pits, sometimes several hundred, emerge (Gustafson *et al.* 2005; Henriksen 2005).

Causes of change: increasing population pressure in old settlement areas and a degradation of the environment should, from a rational economic perspective, have caused a major colonisation to release the pressure. However, this did not happen, but to a limited degree, as in Småland, while in western Jutland and Thy some regeneration of forests suggest local migrations to more fertile regions. In most of southern Scandinavia, and Scania, more farmsteads were constructed in the old inhabited areas. The reason can only be the cosmological force of tradition and power inherent in the old settlement areas. A landscape of memory and genealogical power had been constructed through several centuries, and heavy economic investments in land had also been made. To compensate for the increased internal competition caused by more people and households, farms and households became smaller. More farmers became dependent on the chiefly households, according to the model of Figure 13.5. Indeed the economic

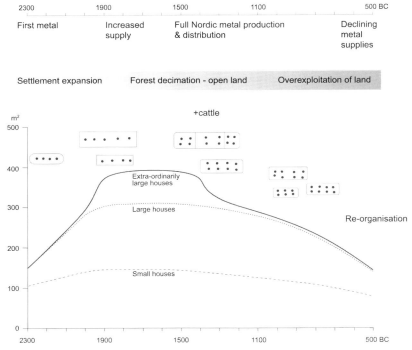

Figure 13.10. Long term model of the rise and decline of the Bronze Age farm, compared to changes in metal supplies and ecology.

degradation and intensification of the Late Bronze Age would have served as an ideal catalyst for the processes towards dependency for larger groups of farmers exemplified in the model. Old chiefly lineages are still honoured by employing the barrow for urn burials, but in some regions, such as Scania urn cemeteries are emerging, suggesting a new ritual status dislocated from the old barrow for larger groups. Thus, religious change to cremation and urn burials are in Scandinavia integrated into the existing social framework, and helps to introduce necessary changes in ritual practice that would conserve the ecology and lower the consumption of metal in burials.

What we see is an economic and social adjustment of Bronze Age households over the long term perhaps in combination with increased regional settlement hierarchy (Fig. 13.10). During the Early Bronze Age households were generally bigger and richer. Differences in scale were gradual, although small dependent households did exist. During the Late Bronze Age households are generally reduced in size, to conform to single-family households, probably under the protection of a chiefly household. This paved the way for the reorganisation taking place at the beginning of the Iron Age, when suddenly all hamlets were left, and everybody moved together into small villages in some regions, such as Jutland. It represented a significant break with a 1000 year-old settlement pattern with a corresponding cosmology carved out in the landscape and its infrastructure. It must have demanded negotiations and decisions that deliberately broke with traditions and created a new ideology for coming together under a new social and economic order as it was accompanied by the introduction of regulated field systems. Was it a rebellion of numerous ordinary farmers against an outdated chiefly culture, economically undermined and lacking legitimacy? Or was it the result of the chiefly elite's capacity to reinvent them under a new banner of collective village life? We don't know, but there is little sign of chiefly elite's in the settlement evidence, so I am rather inclined to the first alternative – a widespread revolution linked to a new social ideology of collective farmers. It is further reflected in the introduction of collective cemeteries that are much larger than those existing in the Late Bronze Age. In other regions in Scandinavia the break in settlement structure was not so drastic, and some Bronze Age traditions were continued. It corresponds to a pattern of regional and local diversion during the earlier pre-Roman Iron Age, as the intensive interaction of the Bronze Age fell apart (Jensen 1994).

These changes took place at a time when similar revolutionary changes undermined and erased the royal Hallstatt courts in Central Europe, paving the way for the first Celtic migrations. And in Greece tyrants were overthrown and democracy introduced for the free farmers and citizens. It was thus a turbulent period in Europe where new social and religious ideas spread and in some regions found that conditions were ready for change. In Denmark, however, it was the result of a nearly 1000 year-long period of a rather stable social formation, whose trajectory had finally come to its historical end. Thus it is the accumulating historical forces of the long term that pave the road for social transformations. It was only when the potential for change and adjustments within the social and cosmological formation of Bronze Age society, had been exhausted, that it was possible – and perhaps necessary – to break with that tradition. It therefore became a fundamental break – the creation of a new social order, which over the next 1000 years, would run through the same type of cycle of economic growth, expanding households, and final decline with the reorganisation into the medieval village. But that is another story.

References

Apel, J. (2004) From marginalisation to specialisation: Scandinavian flint-dagger production during the second wave of Neolithisation. In H. Knutsson (ed.) *Coast to Coast – Arrival, Results and Reflections, Proceedings from the Final Coast to Coast Conference 1–5 October in Falköping, Sweden*, 295–309. Uppsala, University of Uppsala. Dept. of Archaeology and Ancient History.

Apel, J. (2005) Flinthandverk och Samhälle I södra Skandinavien under Senneolitikum och tidig Bronsålder. In Goldhahn (ed.) (2005), 1–12.

Arnoldussen, S. and Fontijn, D. (2005) Towards familiar landscapes? On the nature and origin of Middle Bronze Age landscapes in the Netherlands. *Proceedings of the Prehistoric Society* 72, 289–317.

Artursson, M. (2005a) Byggnadstradition. In P. Lagerås and B. Strömberg (eds) *Bronsåldersbygd 2300–500 f.Kr.*, 20–83. Stockholm, Skånska Spor-arkeologi langs Västkustbanan, Riksantikvarämbetet.

Artursson, M. (2005b) Gårds-och Bebyggelsestruktur. In P. Lagerås and B. Strömberg (eds) *Bronsåldersbygd 2300–500 f.Kr.*, 84–155. Stockholm, Skånska Spor-arkeologi langs Västkustvanan, Riksantikvarämbetet.

Artursson, M. (2005c) Byggnadstradition, Bebyggelse och Samhällsstruktur I Sydksandinavien under Senneolitikum och Alder Bronsålder. In Goldhahn (ed.) (2005), 13–39.

Assendorp, J. J. (1997) *Forschungen zur Bronzezeitlichen Besiedlungen Mittel- und Nordeuropas.* Espelkamp, Internationales Symposium vom 9.11. Mai 1996 in Hitzacker, Internationale Archäologie 38.

Bech, J. H. (2003) The Thy Archaeological Project – results and reflections from a multinational archaeological project. In Thrane (ed.) (2003), 45–60.

Bech, J. H. and Mikkelsen, M. (1999) Landscapes, settlement and subsistence in Bronze Age Thy, NW Denmark. In C. Fabech and J. Ringtved (eds) *Settlement and Landscape. Proceedings of a Conference in Århus, Denmark May 4–7, 1998*, 69–78. Århus, Jutland Archaeological Society.

Berglund, B. and Börjesson, K. (2002) *Markens Minnen*, Lanskap och Odlingshbistoria på Smålänska Höglandet under 6000 år. Stockholm, Riksantikvarämbetets Förlag.

Berglund, B., Lagerås, P. and Regnéll, M. (2002) Odlingslanskpaets Historia I Sydsverige – en Pollenanalytisk Syntes. In B. Berglund and E. Börjesson (eds) *Markens Minnen. Lanskap och Odlingshbistoria på Smålänska Höglandet under 6000 år*, 153–196. Stockholm, Riksantikvarämbetets Förlag.

Berglund, B., Malmer, N. and Persson, T. (1991) Landscape-ecological. Aspects of long-term changes in the Ystad area. In B. Berglund (ed.) *The Cultural Landscape during 6000 Years in Southern Sweden – the Ystad Project*, 153–195. Copenhagen, Munksgård, Ecological Bulletin 41.

Berntsson, A. (2005) Fiske och Resor – ett nyt sätt at se på Kommunikation. In Goldhahn (ed.) (2005), 241–252.

Björhem, N. (2003) Settlement structure in south-western Scania – a Local Perspective. In Thrane (ed.) (2003), 29–44.

Bourdieu, P. (1977) *Outline of a Theory of Practice*. Cambridge, Cambridge University Press.

Bradley, R. (2000) *An Archaeology of Natural Places*. London, Routledge.

Clemmensen, B. (2005) Bronzealderens Kultanlæg – en Undersøgelse af Anlæggene uden for Gravhøjene. In Goldhahn (ed.) (2005), 291–305.

Cornell, P. and Fahlander, F. (2002) *Social Praktik och Stumma Monument, Introduktion till Mikroarkeologi*. Göteborg, Göteborg Universitet, Inst för Historiska Studier, Gotarc Serie C 46.

DeMarrais, E., Castillo, L. J. and Earle, T. (1996) Ideology, materialization, and power strategies. *Current Anthropology* 37, 15–31.

Earle, T. (1997) *How Chiefs Come to Power. The Political Economy in Prehistory*. Stanford, Stanford University Press.

Earle, T. (2001) Institutionalization in Chiefdoms, why landscapes are built. In J. Haas (ed.) *From Leaders to Rulers*, 105–124. New York, Kluwer Academic, Plenum Publishers.

Earle, T. (2002a) *Bronze Age Economics: The Beginnings of Political Economies*, Boulder (CO), Westview.

Earle, T. (2002b) Political economies of chiefdoms and agrarian states. In Earle (ed.) (2002a), 1–18.

Earle, T. (2004) Culture matters: why symbolic objects change. In E. Demarrais, C. Gosden and C. Renfrew (eds) *Rethinking Materiality. The Engagement of Mind with the Material World*, 153–165. Cambridge, MacDonald Institute Monographs.

Ekman, S. (2002) Hääristningar under Vatten? *In situ* 2001–2, 81–97

Eliade, M. (1987 [1957]) *The Sacred and the Profane. The Nature of Religion*. San Diego, New York and London, Harcourt Brace.

Ethelberg, P. (2000) Bronzealderen. In P. Ethelberg, E. Jørgensen, D. Meier and D. Robinson. (eds) *Det Sønderjyske Landbrugs Historie, Sten- og Bronzealder*, 135–270. Haderslev, Haderslev Museum og Historisk Smafund for Sønderjylland.

Fabech, C. and Ringtved, J. (eds) (1999) *Settlement and Landscape. Proceedings of a Conference in Århus, Denmark May 4–7, 1998*. Århus, Jutland Archaeological Society.

Feinman, GM (2001) Mesoamerican political complexity, the corporate-network dimension. In J. Haas (ed.) *From Leaders to Rulers*, 151–176. New York, Kluwer Academic/Plenum Publishers.

Fokkens, H. (2005a) Longhouses in unsettled settlements. Settlements in the Beaker period and Bronze Age. In Louwe Kooijmans *et al.* (eds) (2005), 407–428.

Fokkens, H. (2005b) Mixed farming societies: synthesis. In Louwe Kooijmans *et al.* (eds) (2005), 463–474.

Fontijn, D. R. (2002) *Sacrificial landscapes. Cultural biographies of persons, objects and "natural" places in the Bronze Age of the southern Netherlands, c 2300–600 BC*. Leiden, *Analecta Praehistorica Leidensia* 33/34.

Gerritsen, F. (1999) The cultural biography of Iron Age houses and the long-term transformation of settlement patterns in the southern Netherlands. In Fabech and Ringtved (eds) (1999), 139–148.

Goldhahn, J. (1999) *Sagaholm, Hällristningar och Gravritual*, Jönköping, Umeå University, Studie Archaeologica Universitatis Umensis, 11, Jönköping Läns Museums Ark. Rapportserie 41.

Goldhahn J. (2005) (ed.) *Mellan sten och järn. Del I and II, Rapport från det 9:e Nordiska Bronsålderssymposiet, Göteborg 2003-10-09/12*. Göteborg, Göteborg Universitet, Inst. för Historiska Studier, Gotarc Serie C, Arkeologiska Skrifter 59

Gröhn, A. (2004) *Positioning the Bronze Age in Social Theory and Research Context*. Lund, University of Lund, Acta Archaeologica Lundensia Series, 8, 47.

Gustafson, L., Heibreen, T. and Martens, J. (2005) *De Gåtefulle Kokegroper*. Oslo, Kulturhistorisk Museum, Fornminnesektionen, Varia 58.

Gustafsson, S. (1998) The farming economy on south and central Sweden during the Bronze Age, a study based on carbonised botanical evidence. *Current Swedish Archaeology* 6, 63–71.

Haas, V. (1994) *Geschichte der Hethitischen Religion*. Leiden, Brill.

Harrisson, R. (2004) *Symbols and Warriors. Images of the European Bronze Age*. Bristol, Western Academic and Specialist Press.

Hedeager, L. and Kristiansen, K. (1988) Oldtid o. 4000 f.Kr.-1000 e.Kr. In C. Bjørn, J. Dieckmann, S. P. Jensen, J. Christensen, T. Dahlerup and E. H. Pedersen (eds) C. *Det danske landbrugs historie*, 11–203. Odense, Landbohistorisk Selskab.

Heimann, C. (2002) Neolitisering i Västvärmland, Boplatser, Näringsfång och Landskap. *In situ* 2001–2, 27–55.

Helms, M. (1988) *Ulysses Sail. An Ethnographic Odyssey of Power, Knowledge, and Geographical Distance*. Princeton (NJ), Princeton University Press.

Henriksen, M. B. (2005) Danske Kogegruber og Kogegrubefelter fra Yngre Bronzealder og ældre Jernalder. In L. Gustafson, T. Heibreen and J. Martens (eds) *De Gåtefulle Kokegroper*, 77–102. Oslo, Kulturhistorisk Museum, Fornminnesektionen, Varia 58.

Holst, M. K., Rasmussen, M. and Breuning-Madsen, H. (2004) Skelhøj, Et Bygningsværk fra den ældre Bronzealder. *Nationalmuseets Arbejdsmark* 2004, 11–25.

Häggström, L. (2005) Et Jungfrueligt Land – om Bronsålderns Markutnyttjande i Norra Småland. In Goldhahn (ed.) (2005), 689–705.

Irwin, G. J. (1983) Chieftainship, Kula and trade in Massim prehistory. In J. W. Leach and E. Leach (eds) *The Kula, New Perspectives on Massim Exchange*, 32–72. Cambridge, Cambridge University Press.

Jensen, J. (1994) The turning point. In K. Kristiansen and J. Jensen (eds) *Europe in the First Millennium BC*, 111–124. Sheffield, Sheffield Archaeological Monograph 6.

Johansen, K. L., Laursen, S. T. and Holst, M. K. (2004) Spatial patterns of social organization in the Early Bronze Age of south Scandinavia. *Journal of Anthropological Archaeology* 23, 33–55.

Johnson, A. W. and Earle, T. (2000 [1987]) *The Evolution of Human Societies. From Foraging Group to Agrarian State*. Stanford, Stanford University Press.

Kaul, F. (1998) *Ships on Bronzes. A Study in Bronze Age Religion and Iconography*. Copenhagen, Publications of the National Museum, Studies in Archaeology and History 3.

Kaul, F. (2005) *Bronzealderens Religion. Studier af den Nordiske Bronzealders Ikonografi*. København, Det Kgl. Nordiske Oldskriftsselskab.

Knippenberg, S. and Jongste, P. B. F. (2005) *Terug naar Zijderveld. Archeologische Opgravingen van een Bronstijdnederzetting Langs de A2*. Leiden, Archol, Archeologisch Onderzoek Leiden, Archol Rapporten 36.

Kristiansen, K. (1978) The consumption of wealth in Bronze Age Denmark, a study in the dynamics of economic processes in tribal societies. In K. Kristiansen and C. Paludan-Müller (eds) *New Directions in Scandinavian Archaeology*, 158–190. Copenhagen, National Museum of Denmark.

Kristiansen, K. (1984) Krieger und Häuptlinge in der Bronzezeit Dänemarks. Ein Beitrag zur Geschichte des Bronzezeitlichen Schwertes. *Jahrbuch des Römisch-Germanisches Zentralmuseums* 31, 187–208.

Kristiansen, K. (1996) Die Hortfunde der Jüngeren Bronzezeit Dänemarks, Fundumstände, Funktion und Historische Entwicklung. In P. Schauer (ed.) *Archäologische Forschungen zum Kultgeschehen in der Jüngeren Bronzezeit und frühen Eisenzeit Alteuropas*, 255–271. Regensburg, Universitaetsvlg. Regensb.

Kristiansen, K. (1998a) *Europe Before History*. Cambridge, Cambridge University Press.

Kristiansen, K. (1998b) The construction of a Bronze Age landscape, cosmology, economy and social organisation in Thy, Northwest Jutland. In B. Hänsel (ed.) *Mensch und Umwelt in der Bronzezeit Eropas*, 281–293. Kiel, Oetkers-Voges Verlag.

Kristiansen, K. (2001) Rulers and warriors: symbolic transmission and social transformation in Bronze Age Europe. In J. Haas (ed.) *From Leaders to Rulers*, 85–104. New York, Kluwer Academic/Plenum Publishers.

Kristiansen, K. (2004) Institutions and material culture, towards an intercontextual archaeology. In E. Demarrais, C. Gosden and C. Renfrew (eds) *Rethinking Materiality. The Engagement of Mind with the Material World*, 179–193. Cambridge, McDonald Institute Monographs.

Kristiansen, K. (2007) The rules of the game, decentralised complexity and power structures. In S. Kohring and S. Wynne-Jones (eds) *Socialising Complexity. Structure Interaction and Power in Archaeological Discourse*, 60–75. Oxford, Oxbow Books.

Kristiansen, K. and Larsson, T. B. (2005) *The Rise of Bronze Age Society. Travels Transmissions and Transformations*. Cambridge, Cambridge University Press.

Lagerås, P (2000) Gravgåvor från Växtriket, Pollenanalytiska Belägg från en Senneolitisk Hällkista I Hamneda. In P. Lagerås (ed.) *Arkeologi och Paleoekologi I Sydvästra Småland. Tio Artiklar från Hamnedaprojektet*, 65–83. Stockholm, Riksantikvarämbetet, Avdelingen för Arkeologiska Undersökningar, Skrifter 34.

Lagerås, P. and Regnell, M. (1999) Agrar Förändring under Sydsvensk Bronsålder. En Diskussion om Skenbare Samband och Ulösta Gåtor. In M. Olausson (ed.) *Spiralens Öga – Tjugo*

Artiklar Omkring Aktuell Bronsåldersforskning, 263–276. Stockholm, Riksantikvarämbetet, Avdelingen för Arkeologiska Undersökningar, Skrifter 25.

Larsson, T. B. (1986) *The Bronze Age Metalwork of Southern Sweden. Aspects of Social and Spatial Organization 1800–500 BC.* Umeå, University of Umeå, Archaeology and Environment 6.

Lekberg, P. (2004) Lives of axes – landscapes of men, on hammer axes. Landscapes and society of the Late Neolithic in eastern central Sweden. In H. Knutsson (ed.) *Coast to Coast – Arrival. Results and Reflections, Proceedings from the Final Coast to Coast Conference 1–5 October in Falköping, Sweden*, 259–295. Uppsala, University of Uppsala, Department of Archaeology.

Lincoln, B. (1981) *Priests, Warriors, and Cattle, A Study in the Ecology of Religion.* Los Angeles and London, Berkley.

Ling, J. (2005) The fluidity of rock art. In Goldhahn (ed.) (2005), 437–460.

Louwe Kooijmans, L. P., van den Broeke, P. W., Fokkens H. and Van Gijn, A. (2005) *The Prehistory of the Netherlands.* Amsterdam, Bert Bakker.

Martens, J. (2005) Kogegruber I syd og Nord-samme sag? Består Kogegrubefelter bare af Kogegruber? In L. Gustafson, T. Heibreen and J. Martens (eds) *De Gåtefulle Kokegroper*, 37–56. Oslo, Kulturhistorisk Museum, Fornminnesektionen, Varia 58.

Nielsen, P. O. (1999) Limensgård and Grødbygård, Settlements with House Remains from the Early, Middle and Late Neolithic on Bornholm. In Fabech and Ringtved (eds) (1999), 149–166.

Olausson, D. (1993) The Bronze Age barrow as a symbol. In L. Larsson (ed.) *Bronsålderns gravhögar. Rapport fra et Symposium*, 91–115. Lund, University of Lund, Inst. of Archaeology, Report Series 48.

Olmsted, G. S. (1994) *The Gods of the Celts and the Indo-Europeans.* Budapest, Archaeolingua, Innsbrucker Beiträge zur Kulturwissenschaft.

Poulsen, J. (1993) Nyt om ældre Bronzealders Gravhøje i Danmark. In L. Larsson (ed.) *Bronsålderns Gravhögar*, 59–68. Lund, University of Lund, Inst. of Archaeology, Report Series 48.

Prescott, C. (1997) Aspects of early pastoralism in Sogn. *Acta Archaeologica* 66, 163–190.

Prescott, C. (2005) Settlement and economy in the Late Neolithic and Bronze Age of southern Norway: some points and premises. *AmS-Varia* 43, 123–134.

Rasmussen, M. (1999) Livestock without bones. The long-house as contributor to the interpretation of livestock management in the southern Scandinavian Early Bronze Age. In Fabech and Ringtved (eds) (1999), 281–290.

Rindel, P. O. (1999) Development of the village community 500 BC–100 AD in West Jutland, Denmark. In Fabech and Ringtved (eds) (1999), 79–99.

Robinson, D. (2000) Det Slesvigske Agerbrug I Yngre Stenalder og Bronzealder. In P. Ethelberg, E. Jørgensen, D. Meier and D. Robinson (eds) *Det Sønderjyske Landbrugs Historie, Sten- og Bronzealder*, 281–298. Haderslev, Haderslev Museum og Historisk Samfund for Sønderjylland.

Robinson, D. E., Moltsen, A. and Harild, J. A. (1995) *Arkæobotaniske Analyser af Bronzealder Gårdsanlæg og Marksystemer ved Bjerre Enge, Hanstholm, Thy.* København, Nationalmuseets Naturvidenskabelige Undersøgelser, NNU Rapport 15.

Roymans, N. (1999) Man, cattle and the supernatural in the Northwest European Plain. In Fabech and Ringtved (eds) (1999), 291–300.

Skoglund, P. (2005) *Vardagens lanskap. Lokala Perspektiv på Bronsålderns Materielle Kultur.* Lund, University of Lund, Acta Archaeologica Lundensia Series 8, 49.

Streiffert, J. (2005) Boningshusets Rumsbildningar, Tolkningar av de Halländska Boningshusens

Rumsliga Funktioner under Yngre Bronsålder och Alder Järnålder. In J. Streiffert (ed.) *Gårdsstrukturer i Halland under Bronsålder och Alder Järnålder*, 13–157. Göteborg, Göteborg Universitet, Inst för Historiska Studier, Riksantikvarämbetets Arkeologiska Undersökningar Skrifter 66/ Gotarc Series B 39.

Strömberg, B. (1982) *Ingelsstorp, Zur Siedlungsentwicklung eines Südschwedisches Dorfes*. Bonn, Lund, University of Lund, Acta Archaeologica Lundensia Series 4, 14

Svanberg, F. (2005) Kulthus, Tempel och Aristokratiske Husgravar. In Goldhahn (ed.) (2005), 307–331.

Sørensen, M. L. S. (1997) Reading dress: the construction of social categories and identities in Bronze Age Europé. *Journal of European Archaeology* 5(1), 93–114.

Sørensen, M. L. S. (2004) The interconnection of age and gender: a Bronze Age perspective. *Ethnographisch-Archäolog. Zeitschrift* 45, 327–338.

Thedéen, S. (2005) Till Fågan om Hövdingadömet under Bronsåldern. In Goldhahn (ed.) (2005), 385–401.

Thomas, J. (1999) *Understanding the Neolithic*. London and New York, Routledge.

Thrane, H. (1994) Centres of wealth in northern Europe. In K. Kristiansen and J. Jensen (eds) *Europe in the First Millennium BC*, 95–110. Sheffield, Sheffield Archaeological Monograph 6.

Thrane, H. (2003) Diachronic settlement studies in the south Scandinavian lowland zone – the Danish persepctive. In Thrane (ed.) (2003), 13–27.

Thrane, H. (ed.) (2003) *Diachronic Settlement Studies in the Metal Ages, Report on the ESF Workshop Moesgård, Denmark, 14–18 October 2000*. Århus, Aarhus University Press, Jutland Archaeological Society.

Thrane, H. (2005) Sværd i tal og Tolkning. In Goldhahn (ed.) (2005), 621–626.

Thörn, R. (2005) Kokgropsrelationer. In L. Gustafson, T. Heibreen and J. Martens (eds) *De gåtefulle kokegroper*, 67–76. Oslo, Kulturhistorisk Museum, Fornminnesektionen, Varia 58.

Ullen, I. (1994) The power of case studies, interpretation of a Late Bronze Age Ssttlement in central Sweden, *Journal of European Archaeology* 2(2), 249–262.

Vandkilde, H. (1996) *From Stone to Bronze. The Metalwork of the Late Neolithic and Earliest Bronze Age in Denmark*. Århus, Jutland Archaeological Society Publications 32.

Varberg, J. (2005) Flint og Metal – Mellem Stenalder og Bronzealder I Sydskandinavien. In Goldhahn (ed.) (2005), 67–79.

Victor, H. (2002) *Med Graven som Granne*. Uppsala, Om Bronsålderns Kulturhus, AUN 30.

Wallin, J. E. (2004). Människan och landskapet I Halland—En miljöhistorisk studie i Brons- och järnåldersbygd, baserad på pollenanalyser. In L. Carlie, E. Ryberg, J. Streiffert, and P. Wranning (eds) *Landskap i förändring. Hållplatser i det förgångna*. Volym 6. Halmstad och Kungsbacka, Hallands Länsmuseer och Riksantikvarieämbetet.

Welinder, S. (1998) Neoliticum-Bronsålder 3900–500 f.Kr. In S. Welinder, E. A. Pedersen and M. Widgren (eds) *Jordbrukets Första Femtusind år. 4000 f. Kr.-1000 e.Kr.*, 11–236. Stockholm, Natur och Kultur/ LTs Förlag, Det Svenska Jordbrukets Historia.

Zimmermann, W. H. (1999) Why was cattle-stalling introduced in prehistory? The significance of byre and sStable and of outwintering. In Fabech and Ringtved (eds) (1999), 301–328.

Ängeby, G. (1999) Långhusets Livstid – en diskussion kring järnåldershusets brukningstid och sociala funktioner utifrån ett månghundraårigt halländskt exempel. In T. Artelius, E. Englund and L. Ersgård (eds) *Kring västsvenska hus – Boendets Organisation och symbolik I förhistorik och historisk tid*. Göteborg, Institutionen för Arkeologi, Gotarc Serie C 22.

Årlin, C. (1999) Under Samma tak, Om "Husstallets" Uppkomst och Betydelse under Bronsåldern ur et Sydskandinavisk perspektiv. In M. Olausson (ed.) *Spiralens öga. Tjugo artiklar kring aktuell bronsåldersforksning*, 291–309. Stockholm, Riksantikvarieämbetet.

14

Endurance of Household Constructional Systems in Castilla-La Mancha (Spain) from the Protohistoric Period to the Middle Ages

Rosario García Huerta, Francisco Javier Morales Hervás and David Rodríguez González

Introduction

The natural landscape

The present-day Ciudad Real, one of the five provinces of the region of Castilla-La Mancha, is located in the southwestern part of the Southern Plateau (in Spanish: Meseta Sur), between 38° 21´ and 39° 35´ of latitude, with a surface of over 19,000 km². About 87.5% of the province territory is situated at an altitude of more than 600 m, surrounded by mountains on the outskirts (*e.g.* the Toledo Mountains, in the north). The province can be divided into five natural regions (Ferreras and García Rayego 1991, 113) whose denominations are Sierra Morena (a mountanious region), Campo de Calatrava, Campo de Mudela, Campo de Montiel and La Mancha. The two main types of soils in the province of Ciudad Real are ones developed on siliceous (rankers and grey-brown soils) and calcareous (rendzinas and grey-brown soils) rocks, and also pockets of Mediterranean red soils and saline soils. Climatically that area is part of the *Csa* type of Köppen's classification. The general climate is arid continental, with a significant annual thermal variation: an intensely cold winter and a hot summer. The average temperature is between 5°C and 14°C, for the cold months, and between 18°C and 24°C, for the hot months. The main fluvial basin is that of the Guadiana River, which has its source in Lagunas de Ruideras and whose main tributaries are the Gigüela, Záncara and Jabalón rivers. The vegetation is typical of the Mediterranean region.

The cultural landscape: Protohistory

During Protohistory, settlements were part of the *Oretano* culture, one of the ethnicities of the pre-Roman Iberian people. The *Oretanos* population is not cited in the classical sources until relatively late (2nd century BC) being called *Oretano* by the Latin authors and *Orissios* by the Greek authors. Some authors consider that the term "*Oretanos*" is composed by the root "*or*" and the suffix "*tanos*" (that is frequent in the tribes of the Iberian-Tartessian area) and it means "highlander", a name referring to the link with Sierra Morena.

Generally, the *Oretano* people were to be found between the valley of the Guadiana and Guadalquivir rivers, with a central territory, which represents the nuclear *Oretano* area, around which there was an area of influence (of larger or smaller extent, depending on the period) called *Oretania*. The nuclear area is the central axis of Sierra Morena, of vital importance for its economic (mining industry) and religious (sanctuaries) components. These mountains also act as a watershed between the northern *Oretanos*, of present-day Ciudad Real, and southern *Oretanos*, of the area of Jaén (Andalucía).

In the northern part of *Oretania*, about 200 settlements are known and several have been the focus of archaeological excavations: La Bienvenida (situated in the village of Almodóvar del Campo), Peñarroya (Argamasilla de Alba), Calatrava La Vieja (Carrión de Calatrava), Alarcos (Ciudad Real), Oreto (Granátula de Calatrava), Las Nieves Hill (Pedro Muñoz), Las Cabezas Hill (Valdepeñas) and Villanueva de la Fuente. The Iberian culture was mainly urban even though the urbanization process was not the same in all areas. The *Oretano* towns show a great variety in terms of location, size, town planning, etc. The documented large towns are situated next to important communication routes. The major settlements (over 14 ha) that can be considered to be like *oppida*, such as Las Cabezas Hill (Valdepeñas) or Alarcos (Ciudad Real), are set along major communication routes while smaller size towns are dispersed in all the area, highlighting the existence of a hierarchical occupation of the territory. This settlement pattern is similar to those of other Iberian areas.

The location of the Iberian settlements was conditioned by topography and proximity to basic resources, such as water. However, development of the larger *oppida* must have been connected to economic factors, as the prosperity of the settlement would have depended on them. Indeed, we can observe that towns such as Alarcos, El Cerro de Las Cabezas, Oreto or Calatrava La Vieja are situated in areas that were very important for farming and mining, and La Bienvenida has rich mining resources. The layout and dispersal of settlement is obviously conditioned by the morphology of the territory, however there is a general standard in town organization in the pattern of occupation of the territory of northern *Oretania* and this was probably planned by aristocracy economic interests. This eventually resulted in a structure of four types of settlements, differentiated in terms of their size: *oppida*, towns, medium-size villages and small villages (Morales 2003).

Oppida (over 6 ha)
These are significant towns that are generally separated by a distance of between 20 and 30 km. The *oppida* tend to be located on elevated places and this location has a double function: for defense and for control, not only of the surrounding resources but also of the communication routes. These settlements are close to water resources and they are located less than 5 km (but often less than 1 km) from a major route (Morales

2003). In this group are two of the main archaeological sites we will discuss within our study: Alarcos (Ciudad Real; see Figure 14.1), and Las Cabezas Hill (Valdepeñas).

Towns (1–5 ha)

These settlements are normally linked to an *oppidum,* which is normally at a distance of 6–10 km. The towns can be on high promontories, on top of some modest elevations or in the plains.

Medium-size villages (0.2–0.9 ha)

These constitute the most numerous type of settlements. About 100 settlements are present in northern Oretania but they are concentrated in the eastern half of Ciudad Real province. The average distance between

Figure 14.1. Alarcos (Ciudad Real, Spain), aerial sight.

these villages is 2–5 km. However, in areas with more intense surveys (areas of the Jabalón, Gigüela and Guadiana rivers) the average distance becomes 1.5–3 km. With a few exceptions, most of the settlements are to be found on moderate relief or flat areas, generally those suitable for farming. Some of the excavated settlements show incipient town planning; this aspect is clearly evident in the case of Peñarroya (Argamasilla de Alba). In the case of Cerro de Las Nieves (Pedro Muñoz), there is also a clear functional differentiation between different areas of the site.

Small villages (less than 0.2 ha)

The only data currently available for the characterization of these settlements comes from surveys. These small villages are mostly found on fluvial terraces and they are small agglomerations of houses from which a small population would make good use for cultivation of the fertile river valleys (Figure 14.2).

Cultural landscape: the Middle Ages

During the Middle Ages, the present-day province of Ciudad Real was part of what the Muslim population, who settled in the Iberian Peninsula in the 8th century, called *La'a Mansha*: the "land without water". After the collapse of the Caliphate of Córdoba (929–1031) and the fragmentation of Muslim power in several political entities, the area was under the administration of the *Taifa* of Toledo. But the area was a focus of conflict between Toledo and the nearby *taifas* (a *taifa* is an independent Muslim-ruled principality). The Christian Kingdom of Castilla intervened in this situation at request of the *Taifa* of Toledo, conquering the city of Toledo in 1085 and controlling the territory to the south, all the way to Ciudad Real. This pressure from the Christian

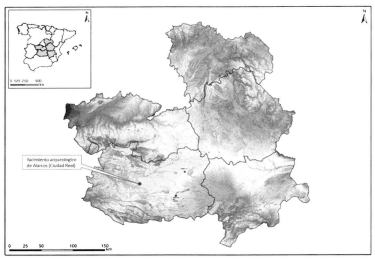

Figure 14.2. Settlements in the province of Ciudad Real (Spain) mentioned in the text.

kingdom was counteracted by the other *taifas* of the region that asked for assistance to the *Almorávides* (a Berber dynasty from Morocco). In 1158, Castilla began again to undertake its expansion on the lands in the south of the Tajo River and reconquered La Mancha. These new territories were assigned for safekeeping, administration and exploitation to the Military Order of Calatrava (this is the reason for the presence of several castles in the area, including those in Calatrava la Vieja and Alarcos). This clerical and military order kept control of the territory until the 15th century, with a short interval between 1195 and 1212. During these years, the territory was under Muslim control thanks to a new Muslim contingent, the Almohades, who arrived in the Peninsula from Morocco and it was successful in conquering Alarcos. In 1212, Alfonso VIII regained this territory in the Battle of the Navas de Tolosa, and returned it to the Order of Calatrava. In 1255, Alfonso X, to counteract the growing power of the Order, founded a settlement in Villa Real (nowadays Ciudad Real), the town that also gives the name to the province that is the object of our research.

Description of the households

Protohistoric
Pre-Iberian period (Período Preibérico)
In spite of the scarcity of data, we can begin by discussing the transition from the Late Bronze Age to the Iron Age I (pre-Iberian) mostly focusing on the northern *Oretania*. In layers 12 and 11 of the deposit of La Bienvenida, dated from the mid-7th century BC to the beginning of the 6th century BC, there is the presence of habitation areas

attested by the remains of rectangular structures with clay and cobbled pavements. Also, there is a hearth constructed with a base of (average to small size) stones and repetitive clay layers. The walls are composed of a skirting made with small to average size irregular stones bonded with soil, upon which sit an upper part in adobe or rammed earth. The exact dimensions of these structures and the hearth are not clear, as they are not preserved in their totality (Fernández Ochoa *et al.* 1994, 42–43). In the settlement of Alarcos there are also habitation structures that are dated to the pre-Iberian Period (8th–7th century BC). During the unfinished excavations of sector III, other structures of this period have also been uncovered. Specifically, these are adobe walls and a circular hearth of a diameter of *c*. 50 cm, delimited by average-size stones and with a plate of refractory mud. In the levels corresponding to the pre-Iberian phase of Las Cabezas Hill (Vélez Rivas and Pérez Avilés 1987, 173) several rectangular domestic structures have been documented, with walls formed by a skirting of 3–4 courses of rough stones, clay and small lime nodules. On the skirting, there are some remains of clay and straw adobe (10 cm thick, 15 cm high and 25 cm long). In some dwellings it was possible to observe the remains of floors made of a layer of sand and lime.

Early Iberian period (Período Ibérico Antiguo)

This period is represented in the deposits of La Bienvenida in levels 9b and 10 of trench A1, dated between the mid-6th century and the early 5th century BC (Fernández Ochoa *et al.* 1994, 147–148). On these levels there are two, more or less, square rooms with walls made of a stone base and adobe or rammed earth. One of these structures has an access or threshold and, on the left of this access, there is a hearth formed by several strata of clay on a base of small stones and fragments of pottery. Both structures have a floor made of irregular size stones. The Early Iberian deposit of Cerro de las Cabezas offers certain modifications in respect to the pre-Iberian (Vélez Rivas and Pérez Avilés 1987, 176), especially in the kind of material used. For example, the limestone is now replaced by the more resistant quartzite and the mortar is of better quality so that the joining of foundations, and adobe offer better consistency. The walls have a skirting of roughly worked stones on which rows of adobes were constructed. The pavements have not been regularly preserved, but it seems that they were formed by superimposed layers of clay, lime and hardened ash. The kind of habitation structures did not substantially change from the previous period (they continue to be rectangular in shape with dimensions of about 4–5 m long and 2 m wide); nevertheless, the rooms are now attached to each other, forming wider compounds. It is, however, difficult to clarify if this new pattern fits a specific plan (Figure 14.3).

This phase is still poorly known from the deposit of Alarcos but it seems that some quadrangular dwellings with walls of stones/rammed earth with plaster and whitewash, as well as red clay floors, may pertain to this period (Fernández Rodríguez and Serrano Anguita 1995, 212–213). The two houses excavated in the deposit of Peñarroya also belong to the Early Iberian (García Huerta *et al.* 1999). These two houses (Enclosure 1 and Enclosure 2) each consist of a single rectangular enclosure. However, Enclosure

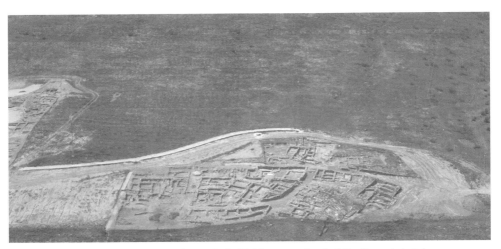

Figure 14.3. Las Cabezas Hill (Valdepeñas, Ciudad Real), aerial sight.

1was rebuilt and assumed a semi-squared shape during the Old Iberian period, with dimensions of 4.75 m in length and 4.35 m in width (20.6 m²). The southern, eastern and northern walls show the same constructional system consisting of a base/skirting made of two external parts of medium rough stones and an internal core filled with smaller stones and clay. The width of the base varies between 0.50 m and 1 m and the height of the remaining sections between 60 cm and 70 cm. The elevation of the walls was probably constructed with adobe, as the large amount of this material, especially by the southern wall, seems to suggest. In the northern wall there is a 1.10 m opening that would have provided access to the house and which was placed in the middle of the wall of the original plan of the enclosure, although after the enlargement, the door was moved to the northwest. The further extension of the eastern wall to the north seems to point to the existence of a porch or threshold. A small wall made with adobe and medium-sized stones, probably plastered with mud, was present along the eastern wall but at a noticeably lower level. This is *c*. 50 cm wide by *c*. 20 cm high, and could have functioned as a bench or kitchen shelf.

In Enclosure 1 two floors have survived to the present day: the oldest of which consists of a relatively thin, rammed earth floor, a fact that seems to suggest infrequent use of this surface. Next to the southern wall, the slabs of calcareous bedrock are used as floor. When the room was enlarged, another rammed earth with lime floor was made. In the middle of the dwelling, and basically lined up with the door, there is an roundish hearth plate with a diameter of about 60 cm, made of several superimposed grayish clay layers without any specific structure as base. In Enclosure 2 there was a rectangular floor that was 5 m long and 3.5 m wide, which meant a surface of 17.5 m². All the walls in this structure showed the same construction technique consisting of a course of rough large-sized stones externally and small and medium-sized stones mixed with earth in the inner cavity of about 50 cm width. The door of the house opens in

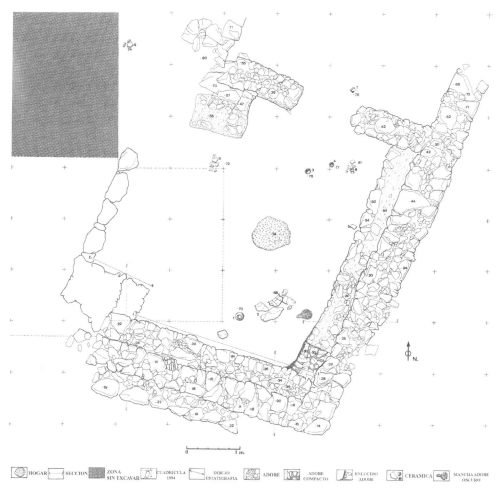

HOGAR · · · · SECCION · ZONA SIN EXCAVAR · CUADRICULA 1994 · DIBUJO ESTATIGRAFIA · ADOBE · ADOBE COMPACTO · ENLUCIDO ADOBE · CERAMICA · MANCHA ADOBE OSCURO

Figure 14.4. Housing of the settlement of Peñarroya (Argamasilla de Alba, Ciudad Real).

the southern wall and consists of a 1 m opening, which is located in the middle of the wall. The inside of this enclosure was much damaged and did not preserve remains of floors or hearths (Figure 14.4).

Middle Iberian period (*Período Ibérico Pleno*)

In La Bienvenida, this period is documented in the levels 9a, 8 and 7 of trench A1, which are dated between the mid-5th and late 4th century BC. Here several walls were uncovered pertaining to a quadrangular construction that underwent various changes over time. The structure of these walls is similar to those of the older levels: a base of small and medium-sized rough stones with adobe/rammed earth above. In some cases hearth plates and floors were documented, consisting of hardened clay (Fernández

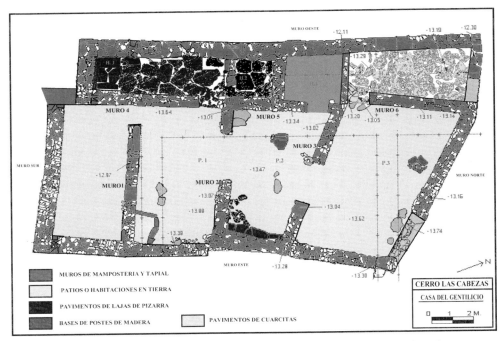

Figure 14.5. Gentilicio's house. Las Cabezas Hill (Valdepeñas, Ciudad Real).

Ochoa *et al.* 1994, 39–40). In the Cerro de las Cabezas two occupation phases of the Middle Iberian have been identified (Vélez Rivas and Pérez Avilés 1987, 176). The first is dated between the late 5th and the 4th century BC. It is clear that the settlement was organized around a main axis represented by a street with a maximum width of 4 m, from which other, secondary perpendicular streets arise. One of these streets leads directly to the entrance of the town and another, after making a turn, is parallel to the main one. The land is terraced and the corners are open in order to discharge rainwater, which would run down the slope of the hill towards the Jabalón River.

The structures of the settlement are again similar to those of the previous period: the shape is basically rectangular with 50–60 cm wide walls comprising four or five rows of worked stones with clay and lime mortar. On this stone base would have rested an upper part made of adobe and straw. The most usual kind of pavement was of hardened clay; in one room a more elaborated cobbled floor of small river pebbles was uncovered. The second phase of occupation in Cerro de las Cabezas pertains to the Middle Iberian Period and it was the last level of occupation of the town after which the population settled in the plain, near the Jabalón River. This phase is dated between the 4th and late 3rd centuries BC and it is characterized by clear planning of the built space with groups of houses or blocks, and by an improvement in constructional techniques. Perfectly cut stones were now also used for the construction of walls, which sometimes still bear remains of the mortar. In many rooms remains of the roofs were uncovered, which burnt down during the period of abandonment of the *oppidum*. There were remains of poles that were used as the uprights for the wooden framework of wattle and daub structure. The floors are also improved, but the archaic types made of hardened clay, small pebbles or flagstones continued to be present. There are some documented hearth plates with a diameter of about 50 cm with a base of ceramic fragments on which a clay and lime mixture was layered (Figure 14.5).

The reconstruction of Middle Iberian Period town planning in the *oppidum* of Alarcos is based on the excavation in sector IV-E (Fernández Rodríguez and García Huerta 1998), where four occupation phases were identified. The better-known phase, and that to which most parts of the structures belong, is phase 4. This represents the height of *oppidum* development and dates to the mid-4th to the late 3rd centuries BC, when an important part of the area of the Alarcos Hill was occupied, as reflected by the structures that appeared in other sectors of the excavations (*e.g.* IV and III). This is the time when the urban structure of the settlement reached its greatest complexity with areas of habitation, a sanctuary, a necropolis, warehouses, etc. Moreover, the residential area becames clearly differentiated according to the social status of the people, with an elite living in the area of the acropolis; the characteristics of which are unfortunately unclear as this is located below the medieval fortifications. The rest of the population resided lower on the slopes of the hill where, during the excavation of sector IV Entrada, there came to light a well-planned, terraced area with retaining walls and houses laid down along the sides of a north–south main street. This street was *c.* 5 m in width and paved with slabs of calcareous rock. On the western side of the street were uncovered 12 dwellings articulated around two streets which were perpendicular to the main road and surfaced with small stones cobbles. Both dwelling structures, on the west and east of the main street, offer a degree of architectural complexity. The ground plan was rectangular with one or two rooms whose size varied between 9 and 23 m². Some houses in the western area had a kind of porch or open place in which some domestic activities could have been carried out. The floors of the houses in the eastern side were at a lower level compared to the street, a fact that might suggest the possible presence of stairs to access the houses. The walls of the houses were made using a stone base/skirting upon which adobe elevations were laid out. The floors consisted of hardened reddish clay, although in some cases stone floors of quartzite have been documented. There are also round or oval hearths encircled by stones. A dwelling in the eastern district can shed some light on the roofing system because the remains of the wooden beams, branches and mud were found (Figure 14.6). The excavations carried out between 1975 and 1978 in Oreto (Nieto *et al.* 1980) documented several wall structures belonging to the Middle Iberian Period, but no complete houses came to light. However, the basic constructional characteristics weare again very similar to those so far described: walls with a base made of medium and small regular stones on the external side mixed with mud grouting, upon which adobe elevations were set in place. Rammed reddish earth floors have been found and also the remains of paved areas made with perfectly fitting stone slabs.

Figure 14.6. Ideal reconstruction of a house of Iberian houses in Alarcos (Ciudad Real). Archaeological Park of Alarcos©.

Up to now we have discussed data from settlements such as La Bienvenida, Cerro de las Cabezas and Alarcos. These are Middle Iberian Period major towns in our study area. In order to be able to reconstruct the characteristics of town-planning organization when referring to smaller settlements there is the need to discuss the evidence from Cerro de las Nieves. This is a town of about 2000 m² rising 6 m over the surrounding land. One-third of the total extension was excavated during six excavation seasons (Fernández Martínez 1994). The habitation structures in Cerro de las Nieves are rectangular, with areas of 13–18 m², and masonry or adobe walls. In some cases, the existence of plasters in clear colours found on the adobe points to the presence of painted decoration in the form of red vertical bands. In almost every excavated enclosure there is a round or oval hearth consisting of a hardened clay plate with fragments of ceramic and cobbles. In some enclosures, and especially in those situated in the eastern area, there is the presence of small curled rims containers (cuvettes), whose function is unknown but that they might be related to the preparation of bread (Fernández Martínez and Hornero del Castillo 1990, 169). The floors consisted of several hardened clay layers intercalated, sometimes, with ash layers, and some enclosures had adobe or stone benches embedded in one of the walls. There is not much data to reconstruct the roofing system as only some burnt beams in Enclosure 1 and post-holes lined up along the middle of Enclosure 9 were discovered. However, these elements suggest that the roof consisted of wooden beams supporting a wood framework. From a detailed study of the structures uncovered in Cerro de las Nieves it was possible to identify different functional units, made up by more than one building (Fernández Martínez and Hornero del Castillo 1990, 173–175):

- Unit 9–11: shows ritual and functional characteristics (child inhumation burials, a decorated door, a great number of whorls for spinning, etc.) suggesting a special setting as a meeting point and an area of textile working.

- Unit 7–8–10: shows elements connected the preparation of food (hand-operated mills, containers with curled rims, a possible oven, etc.), from which we deduce a connection with the processing of cereals.
- Unit 2–6–16: shows the presence of a large quantity of coarse pottery with signs of fire, as well as a hearth and a large container, which suggest that this might have been a kitchen area.

In broad outline, this functional distribution let us interpret the enclosures as complementary spaces of the same domestic group, that because of population growth needed a reorganisation of the living structures as Fernández Martínez and Hornero del Castillo suggest:

> "At the beginning, the enclosures could have been independent and multifunctional habitation units, holding small family groups … At a later date maybe the growth of the population or the higher complexity of the family groups caused the use of all of these enclosures by one group only." (1990, 176).

A kind of settlement similar to the one found in Cerro de las Nieves is to be found in the Bronze Age: the *motilla* is a type of site (mound) reoccupied by Iberian towns. In this respect we have to highlight the Motilla de las Cañas, in which an Iberian occupation from the mid-4th century to the early 3rd century BC has been documented (López Rozas 1987, 345). The Iberian habitation is not distributed in a uniform way on the extension of the *motilla*, as only some areas are terraced (mostly in the lower parts of the mound) and it is here that some structures were built. There is however no apparent town-planning organization. The enclosures have walls of whitewashed stones and rammed earth. Motilla de los Palacios, with an occupation from the Iberian Period, dated between the early 4th and the late 3rd century BC, has similar characteristics. According to Nájera and Molina (1977), rectangular or square dwellings were built with wall with interlocking stones and mud grouting skirting/base more than 1 m high, on which adobe extensions were constructed. In the site El Llano, in the deposit of the fan area near the Fresnedas River, there is an Iberian town (Middle Phase) of less than 1 ha, which is set *c.* 50 m above the riverbed. During a rescue excavation some structures that belonged to different rooms of the same house – made with stone stone-based, adobe walls – came to light. The floors were of cobbles from the riverbed and there was probably a hearth (Fernández Rodríguez and López 1995).

Late Iberian period

This period is still scarcely documented and the town-planning aspects are not an exception. We can only make reference to isolated data. In Villanueva de la Fuente, the excavations carried out in the site Callejón del Aire (Benítez de Lugo and Galindo 2001) provided the opportunity to document a wall belonging to the Late Iberian, which was built with tuff stones but was very ruinous due to later building works. In Oreto (Nieto *et al.* 1980), walls dated to the 2nd century BC presented constructional features similar to the Middle Iberian and, in some cases, lime and sand pavements were associated with them. On the other hand, for this period we can also discuss the town of Valderrepisa (Fernández Rodríguez and García Bueno 1993), with an extension of about 4 ha, that was related to metallurgical activities of Roman mining in Sierra Morena. Because of the contacts with the Roman world, this settlement has characteristics that are more related to this external connection than to the typical Iberian settlements. Indeed, this exogenous character is highlighted by the presence of new constructional materials, such as tiles and bricks. The excavations carried out in this town documented the existence of quite developed town-planning organisation with the presence of a street axis around which the settlement was organised. The walls consisted of a base of quartzite and slate mixed with mud grouting up to 60 cm in height. On this base were laid courses of bricks, as it can be understood from the great quantity of fallen brick fragments by the walls. The floors consisted of hardened clay layers; although in some cases large slate stone slabs have also been found. Internal hearths were present, in some cases quite elaborate examples were found, such as a rectangular hearth built from very large bricks. Regarding the roofing, it seems that tiles were used, as it can be deduced from the "*imbrices*" found in some deposits.

Middle Ages

For the purposes of discussing medieval households, we have decided to examine the excavated structures of sector III in Alarcos. Once these medieval households have been described they are compared with the Iberian esamples (protohistoric) discussed above.

So far, in the medieval levels of sector III in Alarcos, two enclosures separated by a 3.5 m wide street have been documented. The first of these (Enclosure 1) has been completely excavated. It had a rectangular plan 16 m in length and 2.7 m wide (43.2 m²). In the southern part of the enclosure there was a small dwelling that could be entered through a small opening. Inside this enclosure, in the centre, was a circular pit with a diameter of 110 cm and a depth of 95 cm, the last function of which, highlighted from the analysis of the deposits, was as a rubbish dump. The western, eastern and southern walls revealed the familiar construction system consisting of a stone base/skirting made using medium-sized rough stones to form the inner and outer faces of the base, while the inner space was filled with smaller stones mixed with mud. The width of this base was 70 cm, and still present is only one of the upper courses of about 20–30 cm height. The northern wall employed the same constructional technique but had foundations of 70–80 cm, which cut through the Iberian levels. Although only the stone base of the wall survived, we know that the elevation of the walls was made with adobe because of the large amount of adobe blocks (also containing piece of Iberian ceramic as temper) that were found inside the enclosure. A 3.5 m wide street was located to the west, which separated this enclosure and the following one (Enclosure 2). Enclosure 2 was similar to Enclosure 1 both in size and rectangular plan (16 m long and 2.6 m wide).

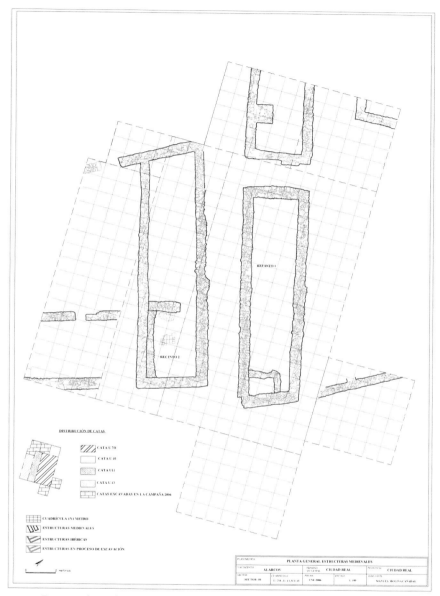

Figure 14.7. Planning of the medieval houses in Alarcos (Ciudad Real).

The construction system was also similar: middle-sized stones for the outer and inner faces of the base/skirting and a cavity filled with small stones and mud. The width of the base was 60–70 cm. However, the walls differed from those of Enclosure 1 because the height ws 65–95 cm and some of the stones were reused from Enclosure 1. Enclosure 2 was partitioned in the southern area by an east–west wall with a small

Figure 14.8. Interior of the medieval housing "Enclosure 2" in Alarcos (Ciudad Real), with benches and the central hearth.

door that provided an entrance to a 4.6 × 2.5 m room (11.5 m²). This room ws very well preserved with a hearth and a running bench. The hearth, set in the middle of the room, was constructed using a rectangular base plate of 85 × 70 cm and 11 adobe bricks of 26 × 18 cm. Two vertically placed cut bricks were also found but it seems that there must have been more bricks of this kind surrounding the central plate. Attached to the western wall of the room and at a slightly lower level, was a small structure built using the same constructional system as the other walls. It was 50 cm wide and 20 cm high and could have served as a bench or kitchen shelf. Enclosure 2 had a poorly preserved eastern wall and it appeared that the northern part of the wall had been partially removed because of a sharp incline (Figures 14.7 and 14.8).

Comparative analysis

The domestic space is part of both the materiality and symbolism of human groups. Indeed, the domestic space is an element of the visible world but its significance is imbued with symbolic meanings that go beyond the tangible.

Therefore, the domestic space needs to be studied both as visual and symbolic elements. In our case, these arguments are difficult to develop but it is certain that in terms of the relationship of the household with the domestic space, the group of people and their homes, it is precisely the settings and the social, economic and symbolic factors that allow the appearance of constraints or limitations to enter the structuring of the domestic space and that are ultimately the key to understand the very limited variability of the domestic space between the Iberians and medieval periods. In this view, the key limitations for the human groups are already set by:

a)   the "environment and geography" (resources available such as stones, wood, etc.);
b)   the "economy" (the exploitation strategies of the natural resources);
c)   the "social" (the technological knowledge, which is similar).

Rappaport (1969), in his studies of domestic space, focused on the physical and social influences which affect the organisation of human groups, reaching the conclusions that the above-mentioned factors (*e.g.* environment, resources, technology, etc.) restrict and limit more than determine. The key point of his argument is that the physical factors (*e.g.* the resources available), the economic factors (the local economy) and the social factors (*e.g.* technical knowledge, typology of the domestic unit or family) never determine the configuration of the household; they simply restrict the possibility of having a different morphology to the one we can observe nowadays (Rappaport 1969). Moreover, we have to be conscious that the historical, economical and social factors are at least as important as the edaphological and climatological ones (Laburthe-Tolra and Warnier 1998, 78). Sharing, ourselves, the ideas of Rappaport, we will discuss in our reflection the conditioning role of these factors to argue about the similitude between the prehistoric and medieval domestic structures.

One of the clearest factors to consider is the geographical setting that offers a limited variety of available materials. In fact, Iberian construction materials were often reused to build medieval houses. It is very commonly observed that some of the limestone blocks, used during the Iberian period to lay the foundations of the houses, were later reused in the medieval period. Our discussion will focus on the same three kinds of conditioning or limiting factors that we believe have favoured the similarities between the Iberian and medieval domestic unit structures: geographical, economical and social.

The corpus of environmental evidence shows that the landscape during both periods was similar; for example, in respect to the hydrography, we know that the present-day fluvial setting considerably differs from that of the pre-Roman, Roman and medieval periods. This is because of human activity, which has been especially intensive from the beginning of the 20th century, when many riverbeds were constrained and some dammed. Rodríguez-Picavea's (1996) interesting study discusses the spread of the hydraulic mill in the region of the Field of Calatrava during the Middle Ages, pointing out that (considering the high concentration of hydraulic mills around the Alarcos Hill) river discharge must have been higher than today. This fact is supported by other data such as the existence of structures related to hydraulic functions in Calatrava la Vieja (Retuerce 1994) and the recovery from medieval levels of fishes native of the Guadiana river, such as the catfish, chub and bogue (Retuerce 1996, 218). From the archaeofaunal analysis of the Iberian levels in Alarcos, catfish was also recovered, supporting the idea that the modern Guadiana environment is different from the Iberian/medieval. The consequences of human activities on the vegetation and the deep transformation undergone is made evident by the analysis of both written and archaeological sources, which highlight the past presence of a fauna associated with wooded areas. For example the *Libro de la Montería*, by Alfonso XI, says that bears could be hunted in some areas of Ciudad Real (Gutiérrez de la Vega 1877). Also, the faunal analysis we have carried out in our excavations at Alarcos reveals the presence of deer and wild boar during the Iberian Period. Species today are present only tens of kilometres from the site. Therefore, it is quite clear from the available data that the landscape transformations started in modern times and that during the Iberian and medieval periods this land had very similar characteristics. This means that the Iberian and medieval domestic units developed under similar environmental conditions.

Regarding the kind of economy that sustained the inhabitants of these households, it can be said that agricultural activities were the basis of subsistence. From the archaeological and archaeobotanical data we can deduce that agriculture was founded on the cultivation of cereals and legumes. In the case of the medieval Ciudad Real, cereal crops – the staple products – are attested in many written sources. According to Villegas Díaz (1993, 92–93), during the Middle Ages cereal crops were most commonly cultivated with mainly wheat and barley. In the written record of this period are commonly mentioned certain plots called *heredades de pan llevar* (it can be translated as "estates of take away bread") that were specifically dedicated to cereal crops. This land was clearly different from the *quiñones*, a denomination for more general farming land. The cultivation of cereals was well suited to be combined with the cattle raising. Another fact that supports the importance of cereals in the agriculture of this area is the abundance of hydraulic mills. For the proto-historic period the classical written sources offer some information about the kind of agriculture of the towns of pre-Roman Iberia. Bread was made using cereal flour (Caro Baroja 1976, 165) but also other products were used, such as acorn (Estrabón III, 3, 7). Bread making could take place in a domestic context as well as in a more professional setting. The archaeological data reveal that it is not uncommon to find in Iberian towns, such as at Puntal dels Llops (Bonet and Mata 2002, 118) or El Oral (Abad and Sala 2001, 171), elements dedicated to the processing of cereals to produce flour (*e.g.* pounders and grinding stones). Also, in the *oppida* of Alarcos, Calatrava la Vieja and Cerro de las Cabezas we have documented four ovens for bread baking as well as other elements necessary for crop processing, together with storage facilities with a large amount of preserved grains (García Huerta *et al.* 2006). The archaeobotanical analysis revealed the presence of barley and wheat together with some legumes such as vetch and broad bean. This agricultural economy, based on cereals and legumes, is typical not only of the Oretian people but also of other groups such as the *Edetani* (in the present-day provinces of Castelló and València: Guérin 1995).

Referring to the third level of analysis – the social factors – we articulate our discussion based on two parameters: on the one hand, the technological knowledge that the population has for constructing the dwellings and on the other hand the characterization of the domestic unit that inhabited the structure. It is obvious that the conditioning factors, which then limit the typology of the domestic structures, are related to the technology used to build them. From the architectural point of view, the fact that the walls were made of rammed earth already determines the construction system used. The architect Miguel Fisac (1985) in his outstanding study of the *Arquitectura Popular Manchega* (*Popular Architecture from La Mancha*) suggests that the two vertical tables, which are used as a mould to be filled with the clay and soil, and left until the wall is compacted together, determines the fact that the plan of rural building in La Mancha is always square. He also suggests that the rammed earth construction, because of its technology, is prehistoric in character (Fisac 1985, 27). The covering would be made of beams of wood, creating the gable, and to support the clay upon which the tiles are laid. In some cases, straw or reed could be used instead of tiles, so that the building would resemble the protohistorical constructions even more closely. Inside the building two continuous benches (called *poyos* in La Mancha) would have been built all around the walls flanking the fireplace, which has substituted the old central hearth. The floor would be of rammed earth, just like the floors of the Iberian period (for example, in Cerro de las Cabezas). Fisac's work is based on the study of isolated workhouses (*quinterías*) that are normally dispersed in the countryside to give shelter to farm labourers. These are made in a popular architectural type with a pre-industrial technological background, which begins from the early Modern Age and probably took inspiration from the medieval model and technology. A clearly "old" technique is the rammed earth wall construction, a practice well described in specialised accounts about architecture in vernacular language (Prussin 1997, 213–215). This is a technique that is also common during the Middle Ages in other areas such as Valladolid (in Castilla y León; Oliva Herrer 2003, 477). Except for the fireplace which, although morphologically different to the hearth has the same practical and symbolic function, the description of the typical workhouse with its rammed hearth walls, rectangular planning, covering of tiles or straw/reeds, continuous benches and a rammed earth floor is not so different from a medieval domestic space. It was only from the beginning of the the industrial age a substantial change in architectonical characteristics of the households in La Mancha began to appear. Apart from the constructional techniques, prehistoric and medieval households share the same kind of indoor elements, such the continuous benches along the walls and the mostly central hearths (Guerin 1999, 95). The hearth symbolises the household and the domestic group using the building identified itself as a community of co-residents (Guerin 1999, 89).

Knowing the type of household occupying the living space also can give us important information for the current comparative analysis. All human societies have been governed, to varying degrees, by kinship. Kinship organization becomes manifest in the various and different types of families recorded in history and anthropological studies. The family, indeed, corresponds to a quite vague concept. The restricted definition of the word is a group of people having a relationship based on blood, marriage or adoption who normally live together, having both individual and collective sense of self. Despite the fact that family ties can be modified or undone, the relationship endures (Laburthe-Tolra and Warnier 1998, 64). Due to the fact that it is difficult to characterize the exact forms of relationship for the Protohistoric Period, we would rather use the term "domestic unit" to talk about the people living in a household. The domestic unit is a group of people who constitute an economic unit, share a house and bring up and educate their children together. The most common domestic unit is the family; this is the reason why these terms are wrongly used as synonyms (González Echevarría *et al.* 2000, 15). In the case of domestic units in our study, and especially for the Middle Ages, the units would be to the so-called nuclear family: that is the group of relatives formed from the monogamous union of two people and the children of at least one of them, being established in the same dwelling, and without taking into account the existence of wider blood relationships with other relatives (González Echevarría *et al.* 2003, 62). The same kind of domestic unit (nuclear family) is suggested for the Protohisotric Period. Our analysis is based only on part of society: the farmers. This kind of domestic unit was successful among farmers because the parents and children form a sufficient core for carrying out the agricultural work (Meillassoux 1992, 66–70). During the Middle Ages, the people who settled down in the towns and villages did so in a way that the structure of the basic family group relates to the type of housing. Households evolve progressively towards the consolidation of the nuclear family and the space occupied by the household tends to decrease, as seen in the partitioning of the houses and from descriptions in the written sources (Ruiz Gómez 1990, 266).

Further elements show that the structure of domestic units was similar during Protohistory and the Middles Ages: the area of the units and the approximate number of people who occupied these units. The average surface of the Protohistoric and medieval structures is 15–20 m^2. In the case of the Iberian period it has been possible to calculate the number from the study of the *Edetanos* households, similar to those of Ciudad Real discussed here. This space would have been occupied during the Protohistory by an average of five people (Guerin 1999, 97), approximately the same number is also estimated by several authors for the Middle Ages in the region of Castilla-La Mancha (Pastor 1967, 88–118; Ruiz Gómez 1990, 272–274). Therefore, if the same approximate number of people occupied the space related to the domestic structures, the construct of the domestic unit must have been very similar, a further logical similarity to support the similitude of protohistoric and medieval domestic spaces. There is actually the possibility that the Protohistoric and medieval domestic units used the same systems to control the number of members in the nuclear family. In the case of the medieval Castilla, this was carried out through the practice of female infanticide (Ruiz Gómez 1990, 274). In the case of Iberian people (Ortega 1999, 110–111) as well as the Celtiberian people (Cerdeño and García Huerta 1992, 27), young female burials are common in the settlements, however more data is nedeed to clearly understand if this is really also related to female infanticide.

The aim of this work was the analysis of the domestic structures in a range of settlements of the Iberian and medieval period situated in the area of Ciudad Real in La Mancha: Alarcos, Las Cabezas Hill, Peñarroya and Las Nieves Hill. These domestic units show a technological continuum over these periods, put in evidence by the internal organization, size, materials and building techniques that seems to highlight similarities in the social construct of the domestic units of the Iberian and Medieval people of Ciudad Real.

References

Abad, L. and Sala, F. (2001) *Poblamiento Ibérico en el Bajo Segura, El Oral (II) y La Escuera*. Madrid, Real Academia de la Historia.

Benítez de Lugo, L. and Galindo San José, L. (2001) Tres años de trabajos arqueológicos en Villanueva de la Fuente / Mentesa Oretana. In L. Benítez de Lugo (ed.) *Mentesa Oretana*, 21–53. Ciudad Real, Anthropos-Diputación Provincial.

Bonet, H. and Mata, C. (2002) *El Puntal dels Llops, Un Fortín Edetano*. València, Servicio de Investigaciones Prehistóricas.

Caro Baroja, J. (1976) *Los Pueblos de España I*. Madrid, Istmo.

Cerdeño, M. L. and García Huerta, R. (1992) *El Castro de La Coronilla (Chera, Guadalajara) Campañas 1980–1986*. Madrid, Excavaciones Arqueológicas en España.

Estrabón. (2001) *Geografía. Obra completa*. Madrid, Editorial Gredos, 5v.

Fernández Martínez, V. M. (1994) El Poblado Ibérico del Cerro de las Nieves (Pedro Muñoz, Ciudad Real), excavaciones 1984–1991. In *Jornadas de Arqueología de Ciudad Real en la Universidad Autónoma de Madrid*, 111–129. Madrid, Universidad Autónoma de Madrid.

Fernández Martínez, V. M. and Hornero del Castillo, E. (1990) Análisis funcional de los recintos domésticos del poblado Ibérico del Cerro de las Nieves (Pedro Muñoz, Ciudad Real). In J. Adánez, C. Martínez and C. Varela (eds) *Actas del Seminario Espacio y Organización Social*, 163–178. Madrid, Universidad Complutense.

Fernández Ochoa, C. Zarzalejos, M. Hevia, P. and Esteban, G. (1994) *Sisapo I, Excavaciones Arqueológicas en La Bienvenida, Almodóvar del Campo (Ciudad Real)*. Toledo, Junta de Comunidades de Castilla-La Mancha.

Fernández Rodríguez, M. (2000) El poblamiento Ibérico en Alarcos (Ciudad Real). In L. Benítez de Lugo Enrich (ed.) *El Patrimonio Arqueológico de Ciudad Real: Métodos de Trabajo y Actuaciones Recientes*, 123–136. Valdepeñas, UNED.

Fernández Rodríguez, M. and García Huerta, M. R. (1998) El urbanismo del poblado Ibérico de Alarcos (Ciudad Real). In C. Aranegui (ed.) *Actas del Congreso Internacional "Los Íberos, Príncipes de Occidente"*, 47–55. València, Universitat de València.

Fernández Rodríguez, M. and Serrano Anguita, A. (1995) Una necrópolis Iberromana en Laminium (Alhambra, Ciudad Real). *XXII Congreso Nacional de Arqueología*, 191–194. Vigo, Xunta de Galicia, Consellería de Cultura.

Fernández Rodríguez, M. and López Fernández, F. J. (1995) Informe de la excavación arqueológica de El Llano (Viso del Marqués, Ciudad Real). In *Actas del XXIII Congreso Nacional de Arqueología*, 343–350. Elx, Ajuntament d'Elx.

Fernández Rodríguez, M. and García Bueno, C. (1993) La minería Romana de Época Republicana en Sierra Morena: el poblado de Valderrepisa (Fuencaliente, Ciudad Real), *Mélanges de la Casa de Velásquez* 29, 25–50.

Ferreras Chasco, C. and García Rayego, J. L. (1991) La Vegetación. In F. Pillet Capdepón (ed.) *La Provincia de Ciudad Real I, Geografía*, 111–169. Ciudad Real, Biblioteca de Autores Manchegos.

Fisac Serna, M. (1985) Arquitectura popular Manchega. *Cuadernos de Estudios Manchegos* 16, 17–54.

García Huerta, M. R., Morales, J. and Ocaña, A. (1999) El poblado de la Edad del Hierro de Peñarroya, Argamasilla de Alba, Ciudad Real. *I Jornadas de Arqueología Ibérica de Castilla-La Mancha*, 221–258. Toledo, Universidad de Castilla-La Mancha.

García Huerta, R., Morales, J., Vélez, J., Soria, L. and Rodríguez, D. (2006) Hornos de pan en la Oretania Septentrional. *Trabajos de Prehistoria* 63(1), 157–166.

González Echevarría, A., San Román, T. and Grau, J. (2003) *Las Relaciones de Parentesco*. Barcelona, Universitat Autònoma de Barcelona.

González Echevarría, A., San Román, T. and Valdés, R. (2000) *Tres Escritos Introductorios al Estudio del Parentesco y una Bibliografía General*. Barcelona, Universitat Autònoma de Barcelona.

Guérin, P. (1999) Hogares, Molinos, Telares… El Castellet de Bernabé y sus ocupantes. *Arqueología Espacial* 21, 85–99.

Guérin, P. (1995) *El Poblado de Castellet de Bernabé (Llíria) y el Horizonte Ibérico Pleno Edetano*. Unpublished PhD thesis, Universitat de València.

Gutierrez de la Vega, J. (1877) *Libro de la Montería del Rey Alfonso XI*. Madrid, M. Tello.

Laburthe-Tolra, P. and Warnier, J. P. (1998) *Etnología y Antropología*. Madrid, Akal.

López Rozas, J. (1987) El poblamiento Ibérico en la Meseta Sur. *Íberos. Actas de las I Jornadas Sobre el Mundo Ibérico*, 335–347. Jaén, Ayuntamiento de Jaén.

Meillassoux, C. (1992) *Femmes, Greniers et Capitaux*. Paris, L' Harmattan.

Morales, F. J. (2003) *El Poblamiento de Época Ibérica en la Provincia de Ciudad Real*. Unpublished PhD thesis, Universidad de Castilla-La Mancha.

Nájera, T. and Molina, F. (1977) La Edad del Bronce en La Mancha. Excavaciones en las Motillas del Azuer y los Palacios. *Cuadernos de Prehistoria de la Universidad de Granada* 2, 251–300.

Nieto Gallo, G., Sánchez, J. and Poyato, M. C. (1980) Oreto I. *Excavaciones Arqueológicas en España*, 114. Madrid, Ministerio de Cultura.

Oliva Herrer, H. R. (2003) The peasant *Domus* and material culture in northern Castile in the later Middle Ages. In C. Beattie, A. Maslakovic and S. Rees (eds) *The Medieval Household in Christian Europe, c 850–c 1550: Managing Power, Wealth, and the Body*, 469–486. Turnhout, Brepols–Internacional Medieval Research.

Ortega Ortega, J. M. (1999) Microespacio y microhistoria: La arqueología del espacio doméstico. *Arqueología Espacial* 21, 101–115.

Prussin, L. (1997) Materials and building resources, rammed earth: pisé à terre. In P. Oliver (ed.) *Encyclopedia of Vernacular Architecture of the World*, 213–215. Cambridge, Cambridge University Press.

Rappoport, A. (1969) *House Form and Culture*. Englewood Cliffs (N.J.), Prentice Hall.

Pastor, R. (1990) *Relaciones de Poder, de Producción y de Parentesco en la Edad Media y Moderna: Aproximación a su Estudio*. Madrid, CSIC.

Retuerce Velasco, M. (1996) Documentación de una Ciudad Almohade de la Meseta: Calatrava. In R. Izquierdo and F. Ruiz (eds) *Actas del Congreso Internacional Conmemorativo del VII Centenario de la Batalla de Alarcos*, 211–222. Ciudad Real, Universidad de Castilla-La Mancha.

Retuerce Velasco, M. (1994) Calatrava la Vieja. 10 Años de Investigación Arqueológica. In *Jornadas de Arqueología de Ciudad Real en la Universidad Autónoma de Madrid*, 211–241. Madrid, Universidad Autónoma de Madrid.

Rodríguez-Picavea Mantilla, E. (1996) La difusión del molino hidráulico en el Campo de Calatrava (siglos XII-XIV). In R. Izquierdo and F. Ruiz (eds) *Actas del Congreso Internacional Conmemorativo del VII Centenario de la Batalla de Alarcos*, 533–554. Ciudad Real, Universidad de Castilla-La Mancha.

Ruiz Gómez, F. (1990) El parentesco y las relaciones sociales en las aldeas castellanas Medievales. In R. Pastor (ed.) *Relaciones de Poder, de Producción y Parentesco en la Edad Media y Moderna, Aproximación a su estudio*. Biblioteca de Historia, 263–273. Madrid, CSIC.

Vélez Rivas, J. and Pérez Avilés, J. J. (1987) El Yacimiento Protohistórico del Cerro de las Cabezas. *Oretum* III, 168–196.

Villegas Díaz, R. (1993) Edad media. In M. Espadas Burgos (ed.) *Historia de Ciudad Real*, 73–153. Ciudad Real, Caja de Castilla-La Mancha.